AESCHYLUS'
SUPPLICES

AESCHYLUS' SUPPLICES

PLAY AND TRILOGY

A. F. GARVIE

Lecturer in Greek in the
University of Glasgow

CAMBRIDGE
AT THE UNIVERSITY PRESS
1969

Published by the Syndics of the Cambridge University Press
Bentley House, 200 Euston Road, London N.W.1
American Branch: 32 East 57th Street, New York, N.Y.10022

© Cambridge University Press 1969

Library of Congress Catalogue Card Number: 69-10195

Standard Book Number: 521 07182 8

Printed in Great Britain
at the University Printing House, Cambridge
(Brooke Crutchley, University Printer)

CONTENTS

CONCORDIA UNIVERSITY LIBRARY
PORTLAND, OR 97211

PREFACE

The publication in 1952 of *Oxyrhynchus Papyri* 2256 fr. 3 caused a major upheaval in Aeschylean studies. It seemed to place the production of the *Supplices* and its trilogy in the 460's, among the mature works of Aeschylus, thereby vindicating the view of the very few scholars, like Walter Nestle, who opposed the notion that it was an early work, an opinion that had been almost universally held at least since 1908 when G. Müller published his *De Aeschyli Supplicum tempore atque indole*. The reaction of some scholars was in one way or another to deny the authority of the papyrus. Others accepted it, but with certain misgivings, feeling that if the *Supplices* was not after all an early play at least it looked like one, stylistically and structurally, and must represent a reversion to Aeschylus' earlier manner. The papyrus then would provide us with a salutary warning that the style of a poet need not necessarily develop in a straight line. The approach of the present study is rather different. It seeks to use the papyrus as a starting-point for a re-examination of the evidence for the traditional view that the style and structure of the *Supplices* are archaic and immature, and considers whether that view may not to a large extent be based upon the preconceived notion that the play is early. The conclusion is that in fact it fits very well among the surviving works of Aeschylus' maturity, as well as into the political situation of the 460's, and that there is reason neither to reject the authority of the papyrus, even if that were possible or plausible, nor to see in the play an archaic reversion. The importance of the new evidence is that it forces us to revise our ideas of Aeschylus' stylistic and dramatic development. The final chapter deals with the evidence for the lost plays of the trilogy, not in the belief that anything new and positive can be said about their reconstruction, but with the more negative purpose of showing how vague and unsatisfactory is the evidence on which are based so many reconstructions of the lost plays and so many interpretations of the trilogy as a whole.

My thanks are due to many people: first and foremost to Professor D. L. Page who not only suggested the subject of this study, but also read and criticized every chapter, eliminated many errors and misjudgements, and gave me the constant benefit of his knowledge and his wise advice; to Professor H. Lloyd-Jones who read the typescript and made innumerable helpful suggestions; to Mr E. W. Whittle with whom I have had many valuable hours of discussion, who read the typescript, and who very kindly allowed me to read and use a draft of a commentary on the text which he has prepared for a new edition of the *Supplices*; to friends and colleagues in the Universities of Edinburgh and Glasgow: especially to Professor A. J. Beattie for advice on chapter i, and to Miss B. I. Knott for help with chapter ii; and to my wife for her assistance with the Index and the proofs. I am of course solely responsible for the errors that remain. I am grateful also to the University of Glasgow for financing the typing of the final draft, to Mrs R. Pepper for her accurate typing of a difficult manuscript, and to the staff of the Cambridge University Press in Cambridge, London, and New York for their unfailing helpfulness, skill, and care.

A.F.G.

Glasgow
September 1968

Oxyrhynchus Papyri xx (1952) 2256, fr. 3.

Text

ἐπὶ ἀ̣ρ̣[
ἐνίκα [Αἰ]σχύλο[ς
Δαν[αΐ]σι Ἀμυ[μώνηι
δεύτ[ε]ρ[ο]ς Σοφοκλῆ[ς
5 μέσατος [[Ν[
[[Βάκχαις Κωφοῖ[ς
Ποι]μέσιν Κύκ[
σατυ(ρικῶι).

1. ἄρ[χοντος vel Ἀρ[χεδημίδου Lobel: ἐπὶ Ἀρ[χεδημίδου ὀλυμπιάδι ο̄θ ἔτει δ Mette.
2. [Αἰ]σχύλο[ς Lobel: Αἰσχύλο[ς vel Αἰσχύλο[υ Murray. post Αἰσχύλο[ς, Ἱκετίσι? Αἰγυπτίοις? suppl. Snell.
3. post Ἀμυ[μώνηι, σατυρικῆι suppl. Snell.
4. Σοφοκλῆ[ς, τρίτος —· ὁ δὲ Snell: τρίτος Kakridis.
5. Νε[α]ν[ίσκοις Lobel: Ν α̣υ̣π̣[λίωι Snell: Ν[ιόβηι Lesky: Να̣ΐ[σι vel Να̣ΐ[ασι Lasserre.
6. post Κωφοῖ[ς, σατύροις suppl. Snell.
7. Κύκ[λωπι Lobel: Κύκ υ̣[ωι Pieraccioni. cetera suppl. Lobel.

CHAPTER I

THE PAPYRUS

Commentary

Restoration of the fragment is hindered by the impossibility of determining the original length of the lines. Comparison with 2256, fr. 2 indicates that no regularity in these can be expected. But we know the normal form of ὑπόθεσις adopted by Aristophanes of Byzantium,[1] and can compare our fragment in particular with fr. 2, with which several resemblances will be noticed,[2] and whose accuracy is confirmed by the ὑπόθεσις given in the MS M.

Line 1.[3] The choice is almost certainly between ἐπὶ ἄρχοντος and ἐπὶ Ἀρχεδημίδου, archon in 464–3. The only other archon of this decade whose name begins with the letter 'a' is Apsephion, who held office in 469–8, a year already occupied by Sophocles' victory over Aeschylus.[4] Davison argues for the restoration of ἐπὶ Ἀρχεδημίδου on the grounds that ἐπὶ τοῦ δεῖνα, with or without ἄρχοντος, is the normal Aristophanic formula (as well as that of the didascalic inscription).[5] It occurs alone in the ὑποθέσεις to *Septem*, *Persae*, *Philoctetes* (II), *Birds* (I) and (II), and *Frogs* (I); followed by ἄρχοντος in the ὑποθέσεις to *Medea* (II), *Hippolytus* (II), *Alcestis* (II), *Phoenissae* (III), *Acharnians*

[1] The fullest treatment of the ὑποθέσεις of Aristophanes is by Th. O. H. Achelis, *Philol.* 72 (1913) 414 ff. and 518 ff., and 73 (1914) 122 ff. Cf. also F. W. Schneidewin, *De Hypothesibus Trag. Gr. Aristoph. Byz. Vindicandis* (Göttingen 1853); Cohn in *R.-E.* ii A. 998–9; Raddatz in *R.-E.* ix. 1. 414 ff.; D. L. Page, *Euripides. Medea* (reprinted Oxford 1955) liii–lv; G. Zuntz, *The political plays of Euripides* (Manchester 1955) 129 ff.; W. S. Barrett, *Euripides, Hippolytos* (Oxford 1964) 153.

[2] The use of ἐνίκα, if this is the correct restoration in fr. 2, for the more usual πρῶτος is discussed by Achelis, §§ 47–9. It occurs elsewhere only in hyps. *Pers.*, *Knights* II, *Wasps* I, and *Clouds* V. Cf. p. 15 below.

[3] It is not absolutely certain that this line belongs with the rest of fr. 3: cf. Lobel, and W. J. W. Koster, *Welke is de oudste bewaard gebleven Tragedie?* (*Med. d. Ned. Akad. v. Wetenschappen*, N.R. 29 (1966) no. 4). Koster emphasizes also the uncertainty of the restoration of the ρ.

[4] *Marm. Par.* 56: Plut. *Cim.* 8.

[5] *C.R.* n.s. 3 (1953) 144; cf. also Achelis § 41; E. A. Wolff, *Aeschylus' Danaid Trilogy* (Diss. Columbia Univ. 1957) 215 f.

(I), *Knights* (II), *Clouds* (V) (at the end), *Frogs* (III), and *Lysistrata* (I). The order ἐπὶ ἄρχοντος τοῦ δεῖνα is found only in the ὑποθέσεις to *Agamemnon*, *Oedipus Coloneus* (II), *Wasps* (I), *Peace* (I), *Clouds* (V) (at the beginning), and *Plutus* (IV). As the ὑποθέσεις to *Agamemnon* and *Oedipus Coloneus* seem in other respects to have departed from their original form, and as the ὑποθέσεις of Comedy are in their present state generally more varied than those of Tragedy, we are justified in accepting ἐπὶ τοῦ δεῖνα (ἄρχοντος) as the formula generally, if not invariably,[1] employed by Aristophanes of Byzantium. The probability is, then, that ἐπ' Ἀρχεδημίδου is correct. Whether ἄρχοντος is to be added is impossible to tell. Probably it was omitted as in fr. 2.

In many ὑποθέσεις the archon's name is followed by the number of the Olympiad, with or without its year. This practice is much more common for Tragedy than for Comedy, and Achelis suggests that it was introduced by later grammarians for whom this was a more convenient method of dating than by archon-years.[2] Whether Aristophanes originally wrote it or not, it is perhaps to be restored in our fragment, on the parallel of fr. 2. The first line would then run

ἐπὶ Ἀρχεδημίδου ὀλυμπιάδος οθ' (ἔτει α').[3]

Line 2. Murray suggests the restoration Αἰσχύλου instead of the usually accepted Αἰσχύλος, but does not explain how he would interpret this. The continuation of the line is uncertain. Since A. W. Schlegel[4] it has been generally agreed that the Ἱκετίδες, Αἰγύπτιοι, and Δαναΐδες formed a single trilogy, and now we have confirmation that the Ἀμυμώνη was the satyr-play. There is every likelihood then that Snell is right in restoring Ἱκετίσι(ν) Αἰγυπτίοις in the second line.[5] Lesky objects that the line thus constituted is too long for the scheme which he envisages. He suggests that Δαναΐδες may be a single title for the

[1] One cannot assume, as Achelis tends to do, that Aristophanes was rigid in his use of formulae.

[2] § 40.

[3] Or the dative ὀλυμπιάδι, with H. J. Mette (fr. 122), who wrongly gives ἔτει δ̄. In fr. 2 J. Th. Kakridis (*Hellenika* 13 (1954) 171) would restore [οη ἔτει] α'Ϲ, ἐνίκα.

[4] *Vorlesungen über dram. Kunst u. Lit.* (2nd ed. Heidelberg 1817) I. 158. See chap. V for a discussion of the trilogy. Hermann and others thought that the Θαλαμοποιοί was the second play (see pp. 187 ff.).

[5] *Gnomon* 25 (1953) 438 f.

whole trilogy, with which we may compare the Λυκούργεια τετραλογία of fr. 2.[1] But del Corno seems justified in replying that Lesky's line is then too short.[2] Snell's restoration gives a line of 30 letters, of which no fewer than 8 are the letter 'ι', and therefore take up little space. The previous line, as has been suggested, may have had 26 or 31 letters.

Line 3. It is impossible to tell whether 'Αμυμώνηι was followed by σατυρικῆι written in full, or contracted as in line 8.

Lines 4 *and* 5. The existence of the tragic poet Μέσατος can no longer be doubted.[3] The three pieces of evidence are the scholia to Aristophanes' *Wasps* 1501–2, ps.-Euripides *Epistle* 5, and *I.G.* ii^2. 2325. 6. In the first of these the scholiast, commenting on the words υἱὸς Καρκίνου ὁ μέσατος, writes ὁ μέσατος· οὐ τὸν τραγικὸν λέγει Μέσατον. The question is complicated by uncertainty concerning the number of Carcinus' sons.[4] But the natural interpretation of the scholia is, 'He is not speaking of the tragedian Mesatus'. The other explanation, 'It is not the tragedian son of Carcinus whom the poet introduces as μέσατος of the sons',[5] is unlikely in view of the fact that only a few lines later, at 1511,[6] the tragedian is quite clearly designated as the youngest son. This interpretation of course assumes that Μέσατος was sufficiently familiar to the scholiast and his readers to cause a possible misunderstanding of the passage in the *Wasps*. There is no reason why this should not have been so, since he must have been known to them at least from the *Victor-List* (*I.G.* ii^2. 2325),[7] if E. Capps was right when, as early

[1] *Hermes* 82 (1954) 12. The suggestion was made by Wilamowitz in his edition of Aesch. (Berlin 1914) 379. Cf. Schmid–Stählin, *GGL* I. 2. 194 n. 5: see also p. 14 and chap. v p. 187 below.

[2] *Dioniso* 19 (1956) 279: cf. also Wolff 225.

[3] Cf. Lobel; Davison 144; Lesky 10; Kakridis 167; E. C. Yorke, *C.Q.* n.s. 4 (1954) 183 f.

[4] For the disagreement cf. Σ *Wasps* 1502, Σ *Frogs* 86, Σ *Peace* 778, and Σ *Clouds* 1261.

[5] A. Wilhelm, *Urkunden dram. Aufführ. in Athen* (Vienna 1906) 102 f.; Koster 7 n. 14. Koster however accepts Mesatus in our fragment as a proper name (6 ff.).

[6] ὁ σμικρότατος, ὃς τὴν τραγῳδίαν ποιεῖ.

[7] 485–484 Αἰ]σχύ[λος
Εὐ]έτης I
471–470 Πολ]υφράσμ[ων
Νόθ]ιππος |
469–468 Σοφ]οκλῆς ΔΓIII
. . . .τος II [–?
c. 460 'Αριστ]ίας

as 1899, he tentatively suggested the restoration of his name between those of Sophocles and Aristias.[1] The Μέσατος mentioned together with Ἀγάθων in the letter of ps.-Euripides[2] may perhaps have been a younger member of the family.[3] But there is no reason why the Μέσατος of our fragment should not have been writing at the same time as Agathon, who was born *c.* 447 and whose first victory was in 416.[4] In any case we need not expect the author of the Epistle, writing in Imperial times, to have been exact in his chronology. The argument that Μέσατος is an unlikely Greek name[5] is proved false by its appearance in *I.G.* xii. 9. 246 A. 196, a list of δημόται found in the Temple of Apollo at Eretria. Another possible, but doubtful, Mesatus appears on a font of the sixth century A.D. found in a monastery at Karabel in Lycia.[6]

The attempt to take μέσατος = μέσος fails on grounds both of sense and of style. Σοφοκλῆς ὁ μέσατος could mean only the son of Ariston, the grandson of the great Sophocles, whose first play was not produced until 396.[7] Turner mentions the possibility of Σοφοκλῆς ὁ ἐπικαλούμενος μέσατος, but he rejects it in favour of the idea that μέσατος refers to the poet who came third in the contest, for example Phrynichus, son of Melanthus, distinguished as μέσατος from Phrynichus son of Polyphrasmon and the later

[1] *A.J.Ph.* 20 (1899) 401 n. 1. For Μέσατος cf. also Dübner's note at Σ *Wasps* 1502; Meineke, *Fr. Com. Graec.* 1 p. 513 n. 12; K. Kunst, *Studien zur gr.-röm. Komödie* (Vienna and Leipzig 1919) 30 n. 2.

[2] Ἴσθι μέντοι, μηδὲν μᾶλλον ἡμῖν, ὧν νῦν Ἀγάθων, ἢ Μέσατος, λέγει, μέλον, ἢ τῶν Ἀριστοφάνους φληναφημάτων οἶσθά ποτε μέλον.

[3] Cf. Kakridis 167.

[4] Cf. Athen. 217 a; Pl. *Symp.* 175 e. Miss Wolff (217 ff.) accepts Mesatus in the fragment as a proper name, but argues that the *Victor-List* entry is too early to refer to Agathon's contemporary. For her the papyrus is concerned with a posthumous production (cf. pp. 21 ff. below). Cf. also Koster, who argues that if Mesatus had been active since the 460's he would have been better known.

[5] Cf. V. Ehrenberg, *Sophocles and Pericles* (Oxford 1954) 3 n. 3; M. Untersteiner, *Origini della tragedia e del tragico* (1955) n. 3 on 377; and against them Lesky 10.

[6] Published by R. M. Harrison in *Anatolian Studies* 13 (1963) 134. The inscription reads ? ἡ εὐχ]ὴ Νικολάο[υ] ναυκλήρου μεσάτου. Harrison discusses the possible interpretations of μεσάτου as (i) the name of Nicholas' father, (ii) an ethnic adjective, (iii) an adjective equivalent to μέσος, qualifying Nicholas' rank. He himself prefers the last of these. On the other hand he cites C. Wessely, *Studien zur Paläographie und Papyruskunde*, III, VIII (1904–8), 402, 'where μέσατος is more easily taken as a proper-name than as a noun = "arbitrator"' (as LSJ take it).

[7] Koster points out (8) also that the name of the third competitor would be missing.

Phrynichus *comicus*.[1] But this would be an unparalleled way of referring to a man, instead of by his father's name.[2] Equally improbable is Snell's interpretation, Σοφοκλῆς, τρίτος —· ὁ δὲ μέσσατος (i.e. Sophocles).[3] The use of μέσος, let alone μέσσατος, would be an unnatural way of designating the second member of a series of three. The word μέσσατος occurs in Θ 223 and Λ 6 (written μέσσσατος); in Theocritus vii. 10 and xxi. 19; in Menander 233 (K.–T.), Dionysius Periegetes 204 (*c*. A.D. 300), Sulpicius Maximus (*I.G.* xiv. 2012 A. 33—first century A.D.), Nonnus, *Dionysiaca* xxxvii. 46, and xxxix. 304 (fourth/fifth centuries A.D.) and Oppianus Apamensis, *Cyn.* i. 112 (late second century A.D.); and, in the form μεσσάτιος, at Callimachus, *hy*. iii. 78, Nicander, *Ther.* 104 (second century B.C.), Oppianus iv. 442, and Dion. Per. 296. A poetic word of this nature is not one such as Aristophanes would use in a ὑπόθεσις.

Taking all the evidence together we need have no hesitation in restoring:

δεύτερος Σοφοκλῆ]ς· τρίτος
Μέσσατος

Lines 5–8. The remainder of the fragment is hopelessly confused, and it is doubtful whether the truth will ever certainly be obtained. If the word that follows Μέσσατος is the name of a play—and we cannot be sure about this—we have in front of us the titles of five plays, two of which, the Κωφοί and the Ποιμένες, are attested for Sophocles, the former as a satyr-play. The first three titles are enclosed in brackets, the meaning of which is far from clear. Lobel takes them to indicate cancellation, which is *prima facie* the most natural interpretation.[4] The scribe wrote four titles for Sophocles (four if we are to supply one after N-), and then, realizing that they were the wrong plays, cancelled them and proceeded to give another list.

A different explanation[5] is however possible, and seems after all more likely. We are not obliged to take the brackets as an

[1] *C.R.* n.s. 4 (1954) 22. *Contra* Wolff 225 f.

[2] For the normal form cf. hyp. *O.C.* Cf. Lobel 31.

[3] In *Anz. für d. Altertums.* 7 (1954) 135–6 Lesky says he has reason to believe that Snell has changed his mind about Μέσσατος.

[4] Cf. also Koster 10 f.

[5] Kakridis 167 f.; Lesky 11 f.; cf. Yorke 183 f.

indication of cancellation. Parallels are very rare,[1] the normal practice being to draw a line through the words to be deleted, or to mark them by a series of dots underneath or on top.[2] Moreover there are difficulties involved in assigning this Ποιμένες to Sophocles. Hermann remarks that Sophocles' Ποιμένες, like the *Alcestis* of Euripides, 'ex illo genere fuit, quod satyrorum locum tenebat'.[3] If this is so, it is unlikely that we are dealing here with the Ποιμένες of Sophocles, since it is followed in the fragment by the Κυκ—, apparently a satyr-play.

Hermann's view of the Ποιμένες was anticipated in effect by Bothe who remarked of fr. 501 (Pearson), 'Sane haec socco sunt aptiora quam cothurno'.[4] But he goes on, 'sed data opera Sophocles Cycnum finxit rusticum, quo magis Achilli non modo fortiori, verum etiam elegantiori, quippe educato a Chirone, sapientissimo Centaurorum, opponeretur'. Dindorf and Nauck record without comment Hermann's suggestion, while Campbell says that the Ποιμένες is 'a satyric drama'. This it cannot be, if the Chorus is not composed of satyrs.[5] Welcker says of fr. 501, 'Solche Sprache war sonst zureichender Beweis für Satyrspiel'.[6] Pearson, on the other hand, remarks, 'That the play contained comic touches is undeniable, but there is no ground for affirming that its general character was satyric rather than tragic'. Certainly the death of Cycnus, especially when connected with that of Protesilaus, does not suggest itself naturally as matter for a satyr-play. As Pearson says, 'the victory of Achilles over Cycnus was reckoned amongst his most celebrated achievements'.[7] Yet it is hard to believe that fr. 501

[1] Cf. for example *P.S.I.* 1273. 1 and 1160. 13. Koster cites also *Ox. Pap.* x. 1234, fr. 2 (Alcaeus D12–13 L–P), where a line was copied prematurely, then cancelled with brackets, and copied out below in the correct place.

....[.]...

[2] E.g. *Ox. Pap.* 2307, fr. 14, col. ii. 1, ποτουτωνπαλλ[.

[3] *Philol.* 2 (1848) 135. Cf. also N. Wecklein, *Sitz. bay. ak. München* (1890) I. 13; M. Croiset, *Litt. grecque* III (3rd ed. Paris 1913) 416 f.; P. Orgels, *Bull. de l'Acad. de Belgique* 41 (1955) 528. The fragments are 497–521 (Pearson).

[4] *Sophoclis Dramatum Fragmenta* (Leipzig 1846) 129. The fragment is καὶ μή† ὑβρίζων αὐτίκ' ἐκ βάθρων ἕλω | ῥυτῆρι κρούων γλουτὸν ὑπτίου ποδός.

[5] Cf. P. Decharme, *Rev. ét. gr.* 12 (1899) 296 f.

[6] *Die gr. Tragödien* (Bonn 1839) I. 113 ff.

[7] Cf. Pind. *Ol.* ii. 82, *Isth.* v. 39; Arist. *Rhet.* ii. 22, 1396b 16; Ovid *Metam.* xii. 72 ff.

ever occurred in serious Sophoclean tragedy. Admittedly it is not quoted as from the Ποιμένες, but the words are ascribed by Hesychius to Cycnus, while Photius quotes the second line as Sophoclean. There can be no doubt that Welcker's ascription of the fragment is correct.[1] Fr. 507 is similar in character, while the ψό of fr. 521 has hardly a serious ring. Wecklein held that the παρασάγγαι of fr. 520 (= 'couriers') was intentionally comic. Hermann's suggestion seems at least highly probable.

It is just possible, however, that the Ποιμένες was a single title applied to the whole tetralogy, and that the fragments in question are in fact to be attributed to a Κύκνος, dealing with the death of that hero, and following upon a trilogy which portrayed the landing of the Greeks at Troy and the death of Protesilaus at the hands of Hector.[2] We are told by the *Suda* that Sophocles abandoned the practice of writing trilogies, but this need not mean that he never wrote one.[3]

But the problem is more plausibly solved by adopting the alternative explanation, which also has the merit of taking account of the plays of Mesatus. Snell supposes that they were omitted either through ignorance or on purpose,[4] and that such an omission is possible is shown by the absence of Aristias' plays in fr. 2. But it is more satisfactory to assume that there are at least traces of them in our list of five plays. The suggestion of Kakridis and Lesky is that the writer forgot to give the plays of Sophocles in their proper place and realized his error after he had written the name of Μέσατος. He then wrote the names of the Sophoclean plays, enclosing them in brackets (there may have been a note of explanation to the reader in the right-hand margin) and followed on immediately with the plays of Mesatus. This hypothesis gains some support from the position of the bracket directly under the μ of Μέσατος. This does not look like

[1] The boastful side of Cycnus' character is emphasized also in the epigram quoted by Σ Tzetzes, *Antehom.* 257: θυμὸν δὴ Κύκνου καὶ ὑπερφιάλους ἐπινοίας | αἰθὴρ λαμπρὸς ἔχει, σῶμα δὲ τύμβος ὅδε.

[2] Cf. Σ Lycophron 530.

[3] A Τηλέφεια appears in the Aixone Inscription (*I.G.* ii². 3091). Cf. Pickard-Cambridge, *The dramatic festivals of Athens* (Oxford 1953) 52 ff. and bibliography given there; also Lesky, *Die tragische Dichtung der Hellenen* (2nd ed. Göttingen 1964) 138.

[4] Pp. 438–9.

a later addition intended to denote cancellation. It seems to have been written before the words which it encloses.[1]

On this question there can be no certainty at all, and it is quite possible that neither of the explanations given is the correct one. It may be for example that the plays in l. 7 were also enclosed in brackets. But it is at least a probability that N-, the Βάκχαι, and the Κωφοί belong to Sophocles, the Ποιμένες and the Κυκ- to Mesatus. Presumably a title is lost after N-, and it may be that two are missing after Κυκ-. On the other hand, as Lesky suggests, the Ποιμένες of Mesatus may well be a single title applied to a whole trilogy.[2] There is ample evidence for such a designation. Apart from Aeschylus' *Oresteia*[3] we hear of a Λυκούργεια of both Aeschylus[4] and Polyphrasmon,[5] a Πανδιονίς of Philocles,[6] and an Οἰδιπόδεια of Meletus.[7] There is no need to suppose with Turner[8] the addition of a descriptive phrase after Κυκ-.

Various suggestions have been made for the restoration of the title beginning with N-. We might expect it to be one already attested for Sophocles, since we can already identify about 112 of those known to the Alexandrian scholars (perhaps only 113 plays, certainly not more than 123).[9] We know of four Sophoclean plays beginning with the letter N, Ναυσικάα, Ναύπλιος, Νίπτρα, and Νιόβη. The second letter of the title is partly visible in the fragment. Lobel says, 'After ν a curved stroke on the line compatible with the bottom left-hand part of ε'. For what must be the fourth letter Lobel sees 'perhaps the top left-hand angle of μ or ν'. He thus suggests Νεανίσκοις, which is unfortunately attested only for Aeschylus.[10] Palaeographically

[1] Koster (11) argues from the symmetry of the arrangement of the lines that Βάκχαις was originally indented, so that the bracket might well be a later addition. But the indentation seems to come only every second line (cf. p. 10 below).

[2] Cf. also Wolff 224 and 226.

[3] *Frogs* 1124 and Σ.

[4] *Thesm.* 135 and Σ.

[5] Hyp. A. *Sept.*

[6] Σ *Birds* 281.

[7] Σ Plato *Apol.* 18b For connections of subject in Euripidean tragedies cf. Pickard-Cambridge, *Dram. festivals* 82. For a trilogy composed by the philosopher Plato cf. Ael. *Var. Hist.* ii. 30 and D.L. iii. 5.

[8] P. 22: also Wolff 226.

[9] *Vita Soph.* 18; *Suda*: Boeckh, *Gr. Trag. Princ.* 110; v. Blumenthal, *R.-E.* iii A. 1. 1050.

[10] Miss Wolff (221 ff.) finds this the most plausible restoration.

less likely, though not impossible, is the Ναυπλίωι of Snell. The curved stroke on the line seems hardly sharp enough to belong to an α (cf., for example, the α of ἐνίκα; the first α of Δαναΐσι has perhaps, however, a more rounded curve). An ο is possible, but no suitable title presents itself. An ι seems palaeographically out of the question. Lasserre reads Ναΐσι or Ναΐασι,[1] thinking that the diaeresis is identifiable, but the gap after ν is large enough for at least two letters. The choice appears to lie between Νεανίσκοις and Ναυπλίωι,[2] or perhaps Ναυσικάαι. This last is supported by the fact that it seems to have been an early play, since Sophocles himself appeared in the title-role.[3]

Line 6. A *Bacchae* is not otherwise attested for Sophocles, and the ὑπόθεσις to Euripides' *Bacchae*, which records that ἡ μυθοποιία κεῖται παρ' Αἰσχύλῳ ἐν Πενθεῖ, says nothing of a Sophoclean treatment of the story. But no conclusion can be drawn from the silence of so fragmentary a ὑπόθεσις as this, one moreover that is transmitted only in P. For a similar omission we may compare the 2nd ὑπόθεσις to the *Philoctetes*, where L A read κεῖται καὶ (ὡς L) παρ' Αἰσχύλῳ ἡ μυθοποιία, with no mention of the Euripidean play of that title. Sophocles certainly dealt with Dionysiac themes, and it is not impossible that frs. 862 and 959 (Pearson) come from a *Bacchae*.[4] The Βάκχαι may have been an alternative title for the Τυμπανισταί, a title which, according to Pearson, 'undoubtedly describes the chorus, and was applied to devotees of Dionysus or Cybele'.[5]

Line 7. After Κυκ the trace of a letter is just visible, and Lobel, who restores Κύκλ[ωπι, says that 'as a reading ν̣[could not be excluded'. Pieraccioni suggests Κύκνωι,[6] which, as has been noticed, would fit in with the subject-matter of the Ποιμένες of Sophocles. But study of the facsimile does not inspire very great

[1] *Hermes* 83 (1955) 128.

[2] Koster (9) points out that S. wrote two plays entitled Ναύπλιος (καταπλέων and πυρκαεύς), so that the distinguishing epithet would be required; he thinks that there is no room for this in our fragment (cf. p. 10 below).

[3] Frs. 439–41 (Pearson): Eustathius 1553. 63 and 381. 10.

[4] Cf. also frs. 846 and 773.

[5] II. 263. For such double titles, cf. Haigh, *The tragic drama of the Greeks* (Oxford 1896) 395–402. Τυμπανισταί could have been a title coined to distinguish Sophocles' play from those of Aeschylus and Euripides.

[6] *Maia* 5 (1952) 289 n. 1.

confidence in the restoration of either λ or ν. More of their downward stroke should surely be visible, and the κ seems to encroach too far to the right. It is difficult, however, to see what other reading is possible.

Although, as has been said, no conclusions can be drawn from theories concerning the original length of the lines, it is perhaps legitimate at the end of the discussion to see whether any consistent pattern has emerged. A possible restoration, then, is as follows:

	Letters
ἐπὶ Ἀρχεδημίδου ὀλυμπιάδος οθʹ ἔτει αʹ	31
ἐνίκα Αἰσχύλος Ἱκετίσι Αἰγυπτίοις	30
Δαναΐσι Ἀμυμώνηι σατυρικῆι	24
δεύτερος Σοφοκλῆς· τρίτος	22
Μέσατος (Ν....	?
(Βάκχαις Κωφοῖς σατύροις	21
Ποιμέσιν Κύκ....	?
σατυ	4

It will be noticed that the lines gradually become shorter: and that this effect was intended seems a reasonable assumption from the indentation in ll. 3 and 4, and again in 5 and 6. Such a pattern is however no more than a possibility, and it is admittedly difficult to fit into it the position of the π of Ποιμέσιν, unless its leftward extension is to be taken as a resumption of the pattern after the cancellation in the previous line (cf. p. 8 n. 1 above). Other arrangements are possible. The σατυ in the last line, for example, may have been balanced by ἐδιδάχθη[1] in a corresponding position above our first line. At any rate mere carelessness seems unlikely in view of the careful placing of σατυ exactly in the middle of the line.

Discussion

The discovery of the fragment along with eighty-eight other Aeschylean fragments, written apparently in the late second or early third century A.D., shows that we have before us the didascalia of a play of Aeschylus. Whatever we may make of its corrupt last few lines, the information contained in ll. 2–4 is

[1] The omission of ἐδιδάχθη in a ὑπόθεσις is unusual. Cf. Achelis §§ 38–40.

perfectly clear and straightforward. The occasion was one in which Aeschylus defeated Sophocles. The plays of Sophocles cannot be certainly determined, but Aeschylus was victorious with four plays of which the last two were the Δαναΐδες and the Ἀμυμώνη, and the first two presumably the Ἱκετίδες and the Αἰγύπτιοι. The evidence for Sophocles' first production is threefold.[1] The *Parian Marble* (56) tells us that Sophocles won his first[2] tragic victory in the archonship of Apsephion (469–8), without stating that it was also his first contest. This information is contributed by Plutarch (*Cim.* 8). Eusebius (*Chronika* ii. 101–3) states that it was in the 77th Olympiad that Sophocles first produced, and in this Olympiad fell the Dionysia of 468.[3] As 467 is already occupied with Aeschylus' Theban trilogy, this gives us the year 466 as the earliest possible for the production of the *Supplices*. But if the restoration of Ἀρχεδημίδου is correct, 463 is established as the date. Kakridis ignores the evidence of both Plutarch and Eusebius in accepting a date 475–470.[4]

This, then, is the information conveyed by the fragment, and had it not been for the internal evidence of the play itself, and the theory long held by many scholars that the *Supplices* is the earliest extant tragedy and a work of Aeschylus' youth, the information would have been accepted without question or demur. In 1934 W. Nestle argued for a later dating,[5] and Lloyd-Jones writes, 'in the light of the evidence as it now stands, it is perverse to proceed on any other assumption'.[6] Yet there are still scholars for whom the *Supplices* bears so strongly the mark of immaturity and primitiveness, that they are prepared to discount the value of the fragment or seek to interpret it in other than the obvious way. Earp says, 'Scholars have hitherto regarded the *Supplices* as the earliest extant play of Aeschylus; if we now consent to put it late it makes all attempts

[1] Cf. Yorke, *C.R.* n.s. 4 (1954) 10; Wolff 212 ff.: there is no conflict of evidence; cf. Lesky, *Hermes* 82. 4 f.; del Corno, *Dioniso* 19. 277.

[2] It is true, as Yorke points out, that the word πρῶτον is not used, but it is clear from the wording (ἀφ' οὗ Σοφοκλῆς...ἐνίκησε τραγωιδίαι ἐτῶν ὢν ΔΔΓΙΙΙ (28) that the reference is to his first victory.

[3] Despite *GGL* 313 and n. 11; Koster n. 2 on 4. See Jacoby, *F. Gr. Hist.* 239 A 56.

[4] *Hellenika* 13. 170.

[5] *Gnomon* 10 (1934) 413 f.

[6] *Loeb Aesch.* (2nd ed. 1957) II. 596.

to study literature futile'.[1] But a thorough examination of the evidence is required to determine whether another interpretation of the fragment is in fact plausible, or even possible. Attempts to find such an alternative explanation fall roughly into six categories, and we shall deal with them in turn.

1. First, we could dismiss the fragment by saying that it may perhaps have been written by 'an ignorant',[2] that it is not absolutely certain that it belongs with the other fragments grouped under 2256. This would indeed be a desperate remedy. The first five fragments of 2256 all evidently belong to ὑποθέσεις, and the accuracy of fr. 2 is confirmed by the ὑπόθεσις in the MS M. The eighty-nine fragments, which are all apparently in the same hand, and represent, according to Mette,[3] at least sixteen other than extant plays, may well belong to a complete edition of Aeschylus. It is true that Lobel expresses doubts about the ascription of some of the fragments (p. 29), but this cannot affect the authenticity of the large majority. The contents of fr. 3 make it impossible to hold that it does not belong to an Aeschylean play and that it is in the same hand as the other Aeschylean fragments is beyond all reasonable doubt.

2. The Sophocles of the fragment may not be the great tragedian.[4] We know indeed of two other tragic poets of this name: the son of Ariston and grandson of the great Sophocles, who wrote forty plays according to the *Suda* (an alternative tradition of eleven plays is also recorded), and won seven victories.[5] He produced the *Oedipus Coloneus* in 401 and his own first play in 396; and secondly a poet who lived after the Pleiad and produced fifteen plays.[6] The son of Iophon also bore the name of Sophocles,[7] but whether he was a poet is not known. Now if the establishment of Μέσατος as a proper name is correct, it is clear that none of these men can be intended in the

[1] *G. & R.* 22 (1953) 119: cf. also Wolff, *Dissertation* 209, and *Eranos* 56 (1958) 119 f.

[2] Johansen, *Class. et Med.* 15 (1954) 54 ff. But Johansen on the whole reserves judgement.

[3] *Gymnasium* 62 (1955) 393.

[4] Earp 119.

[5] Diod. xiv. 53 gives twelve victories.

[6] *Suda*. He appear as ποιητὴς τραγῳδιῶν in *I.G.* vii. 3197. 28. His father was also called Sophocles. Cf. also E. Bethe, *Prolegomena zur Geschichte des Theaters im Alterthum* (Leipzig 1896) 245.

[7] *I.G.* ii². 1445. 37.

fragment. Mesatus, whose first victory is probably recorded in the *Victor-List* immediately after that of Sophocles (468), is unlikely to have been still producing after 396, when the younger Sophocles made his first appearance. And, even if it were possible, it would not greatly help to take μέσατος as equivalent to μέσος, and understand by Σοφοκλῆς ὁ μέσατος the son of Ariston. For to what kind of a contest would the didascalia now refer? It is true that the plays of Aeschylus could be reproduced after his death,[1] but there is no evidence that this practice was continued into the fourth century. In 386 the custom of presenting an old tragedy before the contest at the Dionysia was instituted, but we have no record of a contest of old tragedies themselves until the middle of the third century.[2] Finally, if μέσατος means 'the middle of the series of three', it is impossible to believe that Σοφοκλῆς, without any further designation, could be other than the great tragedian.[3]

3. The *Supplices* is not certainly a member of the same tetralogy as the *Danaids* and *Amymone*.[4] Schlegel was the first to put the *Supplices*, *Aegyptii*, and *Danaids* together in the one trilogy,[5] and though Bernhardy[6] and Minckwitz[7] denied the very existence of a Danaid trilogy, the theory has been generally accepted ever since. F. Brommer argues from the sudden spate of vase-paintings representing the Amymone story and dating from 440 at the earliest, that a production of a satyr-play *Amymone* about 440 is to be assumed.[8] But he himself admits that the paintings may have been conceived from the play of a later poet. In any case our fragment now proves that the *Danaids* and *Amymone* belong together. The question of the posthumous presentation of the whole trilogy will be dealt with later.[9]

The chief argument against the nineteenth-century view of

[1] Cf. pp. 21 ff. below.

[2] A record of what is possibly a Lenaean festival: cf. B. D. Meritt, *Hesperia* 7 (1938) 116–18; also Pickard-Cambridge, *Dram. festivals* 72 f. and 123 f.

[3] Cf. Wolff, *Dissertation* 216 f. and 223.

[4] Johansen 56 n. 125.

[5] Cf. p. 2 above.

[6] *Berl. Jahr. f. wissenschaftl. Kritik* (1828) I. 247 f.

[7] *Aischylos' Werke* (Stuttgart 1845) II. 697 ff.

[8] *Mitt. Arch. Inst.* 63/4 (1938/9) 171; also *Satyrspiele* (Berlin 1944) 21 f.

[9] Pp. 21 ff. below.

the tetralogy is that its reconstruction has always given rise to difficulty and to controversy. First, the existence of a title Θαλαμοποιοί[1] has proved an embarrassment to some scholars, and Hermann wished to substitute it for the Αἰγύπτιοι as the second play of the trilogy.[2] And secondly, so much material seems available as the subject-matter of the third play, that one might well ask whether Aeschylus could not have written more than one trilogy on the subject of the Danaids. The trial of the Danaids for the murder of their husbands, the trial of Hypermestra for disobedience to her father, the appearance of Lynceus, the foot-race instituted by Danaus with his daughters as the prizes—all this seems too much for inclusion in a single play, and scholars have never managed to agree on what is to be included and what left out. Can we solve this problem and also that of the fragment by suggesting that Aeschylus wrote two trilogies (or, at least, a trilogy and an isolated play) on connected themes? The Προμηθεὺς Πυρκαεύς belongs to a different tetralogy from the other Prometheus plays, while Sophocles treated the Oedipus story on two separate occasions. One piece of evidence however makes this solution improbable. Strabo (v. 221), speaking of the Pelasgians, says Αἰσχύλος ἐκ τοῦ περὶ Μυκήνας Ἄργους φησὶν ἐν Ἱκετίσιν ἢ Δαναΐσι τὸ γένος αὐτῶν. The interpretation of this is not entirely clear, and Hermann emended ἢ to καὶ, which is unnecessary and was rightly rejected by Wilamowitz.[3] We can understand either that Δαναΐδες is a single title given, perhaps by Aeschylus himself, to the whole trilogy, or more probably that Strabo is quoting from memory and cannot remember from which of the two plays he is quoting. What is important for our purpose is that the connection between the *Supplices* and the *Danaids* is definitely established in Strabo's mind. It is indeed not impossible that Strabo is confusing two separate trilogies, each dealing with Pelasgians, but it is much more natural to assume that Aeschylus wrote only one trilogy dealing with such a subject.

4. Lines 5–7 are hopelessly confused. Does this fact entitle us

[1] Pollux vii. 122. [2] See chap. v pp. 187 ff.
[3] Ed. 379. Cf. chap. v pp. 186 f. below.

to distrust the rest of the fragment too, on the grounds that the whole tradition is so damaged as to be unreliable? How far are we from the original ὑπόθεσις as composed by Aristophanes of Byzantium? In a discussion of this question it is important to distinguish between the form and the subject-matter of the ὑπόθεσις. The formulae employed by Aristophanes have been established, perhaps a little too rigidly, by Achelis,[1] and it is clear that the first four fragments of 2256 have all departed somewhat from their original form. Fr. 1 has, apparently, (ὁ) προλογίζων Λάϊος and fr. 4 ὁ προλογίζων for the normal προλογίζει (δὲ).[2] Frs. 2 and 3 have ἐνίκα instead of πρῶτος (ἦν).[3] The word ἐδιδάχθη[4] does not seem to be used in fr. 3. The mention of the Olympiad in fr. 2 is probably a later addition. Yet the style is still basically Aristophanic. Fr. 4 preserves the original formulae ἡ μὲν σκηνὴ τοῦ δράματος ὑπόκειται ἐν[5] and ὁ δὲ χορὸς συνέστηκεν ἐκ.[6] Del Corno is right in saying that we are not here very far from the source.

From the point of view of manuscript tradition, ὑποθέσεις seem at all periods to have been treated as scholia, and therefore with less care than a literary text.[7] A cursory study of the apparatus criticus of, say, the Oxford text of any of the tragedians will demonstrate this. A ὑπόθεσις will appear in some manuscripts and not in others: some will contain only portions of it, while in others the order of the sentences will be varied. To illustrate this point it is worth quoting in full the second ὑπόθεσις to the *Medea* and part of the apparatus criticus as printed by Murray in his Oxford Text:

Μήδεια διὰ τὴν πρὸς Ἰάσονα ἔχθραν τῷ ἐκεῖνον γεγαμηκέναι τὴν Κρέοντος θυγατέρα ἀπέκτεινε μὲν Γλαύκην καὶ Κρέοντα καὶ τοὺς ἰδίους

[1] Cf. p. 1 n. 1 above.

[2] Hyps. S. *O.C.* I, *Ant.* I, *El.* II; E. *Med.* II, *Alc.* II, *I.T.*, *Andr.* II, *Or.* II, *Phoen.* III; Ar. *Knights* II, *Peace* II, *Plut.* II.

[3] Hyps. S. *Phil.* II; E. *Med.* II, *Hipp.* II, (*Phoen.* III); Ar. *Peace* I, *Ach.* I, *Birds* I.

[4] Hyps. A. *Sept.*, *Ag.*; S. *Phil.* II; E. *Med.* II, *Hipp.* II, *Alc.* II; Ar. *Ach.* I, *Knights* II, *Wasps* I, *Lys.* I, *Frogs* I, *Plut.* IV.

[5] Hyps. A. *P.V.*; S. *Ant.* I; E. *Med.* II, *I.T.*, *Andr.*, *Or.* II; without μέν hyps. S. *O.C.* I, *El.* II; E. *Alc.* II, *Ion*, *Hipp.* II.

[6] Hyps. A. *P.V.*; S. *O.C.* I, *Ant.* I, *El.* II; E. *Med.* II, *I.T.*, *Or.* II; Ar. *Peace* II; perhaps E. *Andr.* (only L P have συνέστηκεν).

[7] Cf. Zuntz 139 ff.; also Koster 6 n. 9.

υἱούς, ἐχωρίσθη δὲ Ἰάσονος Αἰγεῖ συνοικήσουσα. παρ' οὐδετέρῳ κεῖται ἡ μυθοποιία [A B P D F]

ἡ μὲν σκηνὴ τοῦ δράματος ὑπόκειται ἐν Κορίνθῳ, ὁ δὲ χορὸς συνέστηκεν ἐκ γυναικῶν πολιτίδων. προλογίζει δὲ τροφὸς Μηδείας. [A B P D].

ἐδιδάχθη ἐπὶ Πυθοδώρου ἄρχοντος ὀλυμπιάδος πζ' ἔτει α'. [A P D F].

πρῶτος Εὐφορίων, δεύτερος Σοφοκλῆς, τρίτος Εὐριπίδης Μηδείᾳ, Φιλοκτήτῃ, Δίκτυι, Θερισταῖς σατύροις. οὐ σῴζεται. [F D P].

Verba ἡ μὲν...Μηδείας hoc loco habent B P, post personarum indicem D, omisit F. in A pars prior (usque ad πολιτίδων) infra post ἔτει, reliqua (usque ad Μηδείας) post personarum indicem leguntur.

Wilamowitz pointed out that the remains of ὑποθέσεις are actually incorporated in the scholia at Sophocles' *Antigone* 1350 (cf. the ὑπόθεσις to the play), *Ajax* 134, and Philoctetes 1; at Euripides' *Hecuba* 1 and *Orestes* 1691.[1] One might compare the modern scholar taking notes from a book he is reading, feeling under no compulsion to copy word for word, but selecting and abbreviating to suit his purpose. But he does not alter the facts. The same seems to have been true of those who transmitted the ὑποθέσεις. They may select and they may omit what seem to us important facts. Why, for example, does fr. 2 not give us the titles of Aristias' plays, while the ὑπόθεσις in M does?[2] It would be misleading to say that the results of Alexandrian research were already corrupt at Oxyrhynchus,[3] if by this were meant that we cannot trust what is in fact transmitted. It is exceedingly rare to find in the ὑποθέσεις any piece of didascalic information that we know to be false, and the ὑπόθεσις of the *Wasps* seems to be the only case where corruption leads to uncertainty of authorship.[4] Admittedly it is also rare to find such confusion as exists in ll. 5–7 of our fragment. But the scribe was certainly aware of his error (if such it was), and defined unmistakably with brackets the limit of his confusion. There are no brackets in

[1] *Einleitung in die griechische Tragödie* (3rd ed. Berlin 1921) 147 n. 39.

[2] Cf. Koster 12.

[3] It is not impossible that the ὑπόθεσις to the *Septem* in M passed through the hands of Didymus, who may well have added the titles of Aristias' plays if they were not already there.

[4] In hyp. *Hipp.* II editors read ἐν Ἀθήναις for the MSS ἐν Θήβαις. In hyps. *Sept.*, *Phoen.* III and *Ach.*, there is confusion of the archon's name: cf. also hyp. *Peace* I.

ll. 2–4, so the scribe felt no uncertainty there. It would be quite unreasonable to suppose that because one or two lines are marked corrupt or confused, the corruption or confusion extends to lines not so marked.

There can be no doubt now that Aristophanes of Byzantium was the original author of the ὑποθέσεις. And it is generally accepted that his information was derived from the *Didascaliae* of Aristotle, either directly or through Callimachus. Aristophanes' work πρὸς τοὺς Καλλιμάχου πίνακας seems to have contained corrections and enlargements of Callimachus' Πίνακες.[1] The exact nature of the latter work is not known, but it seems to have been more than a catalogue, and may have dealt with questions of literary authenticity.[2] Little is known also about Aristotle's *Didascaliae*, and even less about his Νῖκαι Διονυσιακαὶ α′ and περὶ τραγῳδιῶν α′.[3] His principal source was certainly the official records of the archons, but it is disputed to what extent he may have edited those records or introduced material from other sources, such as dedicatory inscriptions or oral tradition.[4] The value of his material is, however, not in doubt, and it is certain that he not only started studies in the field of literary history, but was also the principal source for all ancient scholars in that field.[5] It was from him that Callimachus derived his information concerning dramatic performances, while Aristophanes must have drawn from both.

Is there any evidence of interference in the tradition, either before or after Aristophanes? Many scholars, more or less well known to us, seem to have taken an interest in tragedy. Theophrastus wrote two works περὶ ποιητικῆς,[6] whose nature is quite unknown. Dicaearchus of Messene, another pupil of Aristotle, besides investigating the subject-matter of the plots of

[1] Pearson, *Frags. of Soph.* I. xiii. Cf. Athen. 408 f; *Et. Mag.* 672. 29.

[2] Schneider, *Callimachea* II (1873) 297 ff.; Susemihl, *Griech.-Alex. Litt. Gesch.* I (1891) 339. Callimachus is reported (Harpocr. *s.* Ἴων) as rejecting the ascription of the Τριαγμοί to Ion, in favour of Epigenes.

[3] D.L. v. 26. Hesychius refers to the Νικῶν Διονυσιακῶν ἀστικῶν καὶ Ληναϊκῶν α′.

[4] Cf. Pickard-Cambridge, *Dram. festivals* 105 and bibliography given there.

[5] The evidence is the fragments themselves (618–30 Rose). For Aristotle's pre-eminence in Cicero's day cf. *de Orat.* iii. 33. 132.

[6] D.L. v. 47 and 48.

Sophocles and Euripides, wrote a work called Διονυσιακοὶ ἀγῶνες,[1] dealing apparently with the history of the Attic stage. Alexander of Aetolia (born *c.* 315) classified the tragic poets at Alexandria under Ptolemy Philadelphus,[2] as well as writing tragedies himself. Philochorus (died *c.* 260) wrote a περὶ τραγῳδιῶν,[3] and Hieronymus Rhodius (*c.* 290–230) a περὶ ποιητῶν, one book of which was entitled περὶ τραγῳδοποιῶν.[4] Epigenes seems to have commented on at least the *Agamemnon* of Ion.[5] The influence of Aristarchus on tragedy does not seem to have been great, but he wrote a commentary at least on the *Lycurgus* of Aeschylus,[6] and is sometimes cited by Didymus in his commentary on Sophocles. Eratosthenes seems to have been interested in comedy rather than tragedy, but he is a source for our information about the reproduction of the *Persae* in Sicily. After Aristophanes his pupil Callistratus continued his master's studies in the dramatic sphere, particularly in Euripides and Aristophanes, though he probably wrote commentaries also on Sophocles. Carystius of Pergamum in the second half of the second century wrote περὶ διδασκαλιῶν, which probably did not contain complete lists like the πίνακες but excerpts from them.[7] There is no direct evidence that Didymus, whose work was so important for Sophocles, Euripides, and Aristophanes, also wrote a commentary on Aeschylus. But it is generally accepted that many of our scholia go back to him.

To what extent may such writers as these have affected the tradition? Reisch believed that they may have been responsible for those remarks in our didascaliae which concern the real authorship of a play presented by someone else, information

[1] Σ *Birds* 1403. The book may have formed a section of the work περὶ μουσικῶν ἀγώνων: cf. Martini in *R.-E.* v. 556. The following fragments may be from it: 83 (Wehrli) (the sons of Aristophanes), 76 (introduction of third actor by Sophocles), 80 (defeat of Sophocles with *O.T.*) and 84 (a didascalic notice concerning the *Frogs*).

[2] Cramer, *Anecd. Par.* I. 6.

[3] Σ *Hec.* 3.

[4] Athen. xiv. 635 f; *Suda* s.v. Ἀναγυράσιος. Theophrastus, Hieronymus, and Dicaearchus all appear together with Aristotle in Plut. *mor.* 1096 a as interested in οἱ περὶ χορῶν λόγοι καὶ διδασκαλιῶν καὶ τὰ δι' αὐλῶν προβλήματα.

[5] Athen. xi. 468 c.

[6] Σ Theocr. x. 18.

[7] Athen. vi. 235 e; *F. Gr. Hist.* IV. 359: cf. Jacoby in *R.-E.* x. 2. 2255; Reisch in *R.-E.* v. 400.

which, he says, was not handed down by Aristotle.[1] This however is by no means universally accepted,[2] and, even if it is true, hardly affects our present discussion, unless we are to question the very attribution of the *Supplices* to Aeschylus. In all the activity of Alexandrian scholars it is incredible that the simple statement that Aeschylus defeated Sophocles should have been manufactured or wrongly understood. Such philological investigations are a safeguard rather than a corrupter of the truth. It is interesting that the accuracy of our ὑπόθεσις to the *Agamemnon* is confirmed by the *Fasti*, *I.G.* ii². 2318, col. ii. Finally it is worth noting that Oxyrhynchus seems to have had a tradition of sound classical scholarship, going back to the second century B.C. when Satyrus the biographer of Euripides settled there.[3] A letter of the second century A.D.[4] shows familiarity with the best Alexandrian scholarship.

5. The didascalia may refer to a performance of the *Supplices* after Aeschylus' death.[5] With two exceptions reproductions of old plays at the City Dionysia do not appear to have taken place until the fourth century, though plays could be reproduced at the Rural Dionysia. The story of the banning of Phrynichus' Μιλήτου Ἅλωσις[6] is no obstacle to the truth of this statement. The words used by Herodotus are ἐπέταξαν (οἱ Ἀθηναῖοι) μηκέτι μηδένα χρᾶσθαι τούτῳ τῷ δράματι. It may be that this decree refers to reproductions at the Rural Dionysia.[7] But the use of χρᾶσθαι instead of ἀναδιδάσκειν indicates perhaps that the decree had a much wider application than the mere reproduction of the play; while μηδένα suggests that more than a few people might be likely to 'use' it. The decree may thus have been equivalent to a *damnatio memoriae*,[8] by which the very

[1] *R.-E.* v. 398.
[2] Cf. pp. 24 f. below.
[3] Cf. E. G. Turner, *E.J.A.* 38 (1952) 78 ff., esp. 91 ff.
[4] Roberts 2192.
[5] Cf., for example, Ehrenberg, *Soph. and Pericles* 3 n. 3; Pohlenz, *Die gr. Tragödie* (2nd ed. Göttingen 1954), *Erläuterungen* 23; Wolff, *Dissertation* 210 ff.; M. Bieber, *The history of the Greek and Roman theater* (2nd ed. Princeton 1961) 276 n. 11; V. Citti, *Il linguaggio religioso e liturgico nelle tragedie di Eschilo* (Bologna 1962) 148 n. 58; Koster 13 ff.
[6] Hdt. vi. 21.
[7] A. E. Haigh, *Attic Theatre* (3rd ed. Oxford 1907) 71; *GGL* I. 2. 173.
[8] F. Marx, *Rh. Mus.* 77 (1928) 346; Blumenthal in *R.-E.* xx. I. 914.

reading and circulation of the play were forbidden. The second performance of Aristophanes' *Frogs* was clearly a most unusual case.[1]

The first exception to the general rule concerns plays which were unsuccessful on their first presentation. That it was normal for these to be revised and entered a second time is evident from Athenaeus 374a where it is specially remarked of the comedian Anaxandrides that, ὅτε γὰρ μὴ νικῴη, λαμβάνων ἔδωκεν εἰς τὸν λιβανωτὸν κατατεμεῖν καὶ οὐ μετεσκεύαζεν ὥσπερ οἱ πολλοί. It is clear from *Clouds* 546 that a play was never reproduced by a good poet[2] unless it had first been revised. There were two such versions of the *Clouds* and of the *Thesmophoriazousae*; and possibly of the *Peace*, though ancient critics were uncertain whether they were of the same play or not.[3] There are many examples of such reproductions in Middle and New Comedy. The practice seems to have been less common for tragedy, though it is certainly attested for Euripides' *Hippolytus*.[4] Dindorf held that there were second editions of Sophocles' *Athamas*, *Thyestes*, *Tyro*, *Phineus*, and *Lemniae*.[5] It is more probable that there were two separate plays dealing with Athamas, Thyestes, and Phineus, and possibly with Tyro.[6] But a revision is likely for the *Lemniae*,[7] and to this case may be added the *Autolycus* and *Phrixus* of Euripides.[8] Boeckh indeed wished to go much further, and concluded that there were second editions of Euripides' *Iphigeneia in Aulis*, *Bacchae*, and *Alcmaeon*, but his arguments are no longer acceptable.[9] However there is enough evidence

[1] Hyp. *Frogs*.

[2] Aristophanes of course means himself, but it is reasonable to assume that all the great dramatists shared his standards.

[3] Hyps. *Clouds* and *Peace*; Athen. i. 29a. Cf. Pickard-Cambridge, *Dram. festivals* 102.

[4] Hyp. *Hipp.*

[5] Soph. (3rd ed. Oxford 1860) VIII. 1 f.

[6] Cf. Pearson I. 1 ff., II. 270 ff. and 311 ff.; Pickard-Cambridge, *New chaps. in Gr. lit.* (ed. Powell) 3rd Series (Oxford 1933) 100 f.

[7] Fr. 386 Pearson.

[8] Athen. x. 413c (p. 441 Nauck^2); Meineke, with Nauck's approval, would remove this evidence by deleting πρώτῳ: Σ *Frogs* 1225 and *Etym. Flor.* (fr. 819 Nauck^2).

[9] *Gr. Trag. Princ.* He bases his argument for a second ed. of the *Eum.* on the very doubtful story in the *Vita* 9 and in Pollux iv. 110 of the effect that the Chorus of Furies had upon the audience. For a refutation of his views cf. Hermann, *Opusc.* II. 139 ff. The question raised by l. 1317 of the *Medea* is more difficult: cf. Porson,

already to establish for tragedy as well as comedy the practice of revising and reproducing unsuccessful plays. Is it then possible that our fragment refers to such a reproduction of the *Supplices*? Webster says that 'all the production dates given in our manuscripts refer to first productions'.[1] But the ὑπόθεσις of the *Hippolytus* in fact refers to the second, revised production,[2] while that of the *Clouds* reports both the first and the second. It is not impossible that a lost portion of our fragment mentioned an earlier edition of the Danaid tetralogy.

Yet the improbability is immense. For we may well ask which edition of the play it is that we possess. The first, we are to believe, was performed unsuccessfully in Aeschylus' youth. With the second he defeated Sophocles in his maturity. It is inconceivable that the first and not the second should have survived. But if it is in truth the second edition that we have, this argument against the evidence of the fragment must fall. For it is designed to prove that our *Supplices* is an early play.

The other exception to the general rule that in the fifth century tragedies were not presented twice concerns the posthumous production of Aeschylean plays. The evidence for this has been rightly divided by del Corno into three classes.[3]

(*i*) *Suda* s.v. Εὐφορίων: υἱὸς Αἰσχύλου τοῦ τραγικοῦ, Ἀθηναῖος, τραγικὸς καὶ αὐτός, ὃς καὶ τοῖς Αἰσχύλου τοῦ πατρός, οἷς μήπω ἦν ἐπιδειξάμενος, τετράκις ἐνίκησεν. ἔγραψε δὲ καὶ οἰκεῖα.

(*ii*) Quintilian x. 1. 66: *correctas eius fabulas in certamen deferri posterioribus poetis Athenienses permiserunt, suntque eo modo multi coronati.*

(*iii*) *Acharnians* 10 and scholia: προσδοκῶν τὸν Αἰσχύλον· τιμῆς μεγίστης ἔτυχεν παρὰ Ἀθηναίοις ὁ Αἰσχύλος, καὶ μόνου αὐτοῦ τὰ δράματα ψηφίσματι κοινῷ καὶ μετὰ θάνατον ἐδιδάσκετο.

Σ *Frogs* 868: ἐπεὶ τὰ Αἰσχύλου ἐψηφίσαντο διδάσκειν (Rutherford suggests inserting μετὰ τὸν θάνατον after ἐψηφίσαντο.

Verrall, and Page *ad loc.* It is possible that a variant edition of Aeschylus' *Persae* was produced at Syracuse (Σ *Frogs* 1028; *Vita* 18). H. D. Broadhead, *The Persae of Aeschylus* (Cambridge 1960) xlviii ff. discusses the evidence fully.

[1] *Diogenes* 5 (1954) 86.

[2] For the ὑπόθεσις of the *Hipp.* cf. Barrett 29 f.

[3] P. 283. Cf. also the discussion of Wolff 5 ff. and Koster 13 ff.

Professor Lloyd-Jones suggests to me that one might emend διδάσκειν to ⟨ἀνα⟩διδάσκειν).

Philostr. *Vita Apollon.* vi. 11: ὅθεν Ἀθηναῖοι πατέρα μὲν αὐτὸν τῆς τραγῳδίας ἡγοῦντο, ἐκάλουν δὲ καὶ τεθνεῶτα ἐς Διονύσια, τὰ γὰρ τοῦ Αἰσχύλου ψηφισαμένων ἀνεδιδάσκετο καὶ ἐνίκα ἐκ καινῆς.

Vita Aesch. 12: Ἀθηναῖοι δὲ τοσοῦτον ἠγάπησαν Αἰσχύλον, ὡς ψηφίσασθαι μετὰ ⟨τὸν⟩ θάνατον αὐτοῦ τὸν βουλόμενον διδάσκειν τὰ Αἰσχύλου χορὸν λαμβάνειν.

(*i*) The information of the *Suda* concerns four posthumous premières of plays of Aeschylus, and unfortunately we are not told which plays they were. Could the *Danaid* tetralogy have been among them? As early as 1938 Bonner made this suggestion for the *Amymone*.[1] Two interpretations of the *Suda* notice seem possible. Either it represents a charge of plagiarism against Euphorion, of the kind that was levelled against Iophon,[2] or, much more likely, it records a situation similar to that of the *Oedipus Coloneus* of Sophocles, and the *Bacchae*, *Iphigeneia in Aulis*, and *Alcmaeon* of Euripides, which were brought out posthumously by the younger Sophocles and Euripides as heirs. When this happened it seems that care was taken to record the fact. Capps deduces (190) from the scholia at *Frogs* 67 and from the *Suda* notice on Euripides, our sources for the posthumous Euripides production, that the *Didascaliae* were worded Εὐριπίδης πρεσβύτερος τεθνηκὼς Ἰφιγενείᾳ διὰ Εὐριπίδου, and the *Fasti* probably Εὐριπίδης (τεθνηκώς?) ἐδίδασκεν. It is the ὑπόθεσις of the *Oedipus Coloneus* that records the fact of its presentation by the younger Sophocles, and in 2256 fr. 2 it is again the ὑπόθεσις that informs us of Aristias' production of his

[1] Cf. p. 13 above. For Koster (18 f.) the same evidence from vase-paintings of Amymone points to a posthumous *reproduction* of Aeschylus' Danaid tetralogy. But he has to assume from the absence of such paintings before 440 that the first production of the tetralogy attracted less attention than the second. This is one of several explanations put forward also by Miss Wolff (*Dissertation* 232 ff.). More plausibly she suggests that an earlier group of vase-paintings, showing Poseidon and Amymone but no satyrs, might in fact derive from the first production. But Miss Wolff does not decide between a posthumous first production and a reproduction.

[2] Σ *Frogs* 73 and 78. For this interpretation of the notice cf. E. Capps, *A.J.Ph.* 28 (1907) 191.

father's plays. Now it is true that our fragment says nothing about Euphorion, but no conclusions can be drawn from this, so fragmentary is its state. It would be possible to restore διὰ Εὐφορίωνος either in the first or in the second line. Yet, if the *Supplices* was one of the plays presented by Euphorion, it must surely, like the *Oedipus Coloneus*, the *Bacchae*, *Iphigeneia*, and *Alcmaeon*, have been written at the end of its composer's life. This is the only natural interpretation. The plays were written perhaps in Sicily, and passed to Euphorion at Aeschylus' death. Thus we cannot by this argument preserve an early date for the *Supplices*.[1]

(*ii*) Quintilian is the only source for the information that Aeschylus' plays were presented in a 'corrected' form by later poets. It is difficult to know what to make of this.[2] The third class of evidence concerns the popularity of Aeschylus and the honour paid to him by allowing his plays to be reproduced after his death. The context of Quintilian's remark, that his plays were too primitive in their original form for later taste, is quite different. It looks as if Quintilian preserves a memory of fifth-century reproduction of Aeschylean plays, but confuses it with the fourth-century presentation of παλαιαί.[3] There is perhaps confusion also between the poet and the winning actor.[4] But even if Quintilian's evidence were reliable, it would not help to support an early date for our *Supplices*.[5] For again it would be

[1] But see also p. 27 n. 3 below. [2] Cf. del Corno 284; Wolff, *Dissertation* 6.

[3] Cf. Phryn. soph. *praep. sophist.* p. 69 (de Borries) (Bekker *Anecd.* 39. 19) ἐπικαττύειν και πτερνίζειν· τὰ παλαιὰ ἐπισκευάζειν. ἡ μεταφορὰ ἀπὸ τῶν τοῖς παλαιοῖς ὑποδήμασιν ἕτερα καττύματα καὶ πτέρνας προσραπτόντων. λέγουσι δὲ ἐπὶ τῶν ⟨τὰ⟩ παλαιὰ τῶν δραμάτων μεταποιούντων καὶ μεταρραπτόντων. Cf. D. L. Page, *Actors' interpolations in Greek tragedy* (Oxford 1934) 17 f. Koster suggests (14 f.) that Q. is contaminating the first and third groups of notices: Euphorion might well have had to put the finishing touches to plays left him by his father.

[4] Del Corno quotes D.L. ii. 104, Aelian, *Var. Hist.* xiv. 40, and Arist. *Pol.* vii. 1336b 28 to show that ancient scholars could consider actors as tragic poets.

[5] R. Böhme, *Bühnenbearbeitung Äschyleischer Tragödien* (Basel/Stuttgart 1956 and 1959) takes seriously the evidence of Quintilian and of Phryn. soph., and cites also Ar. *Ach.* 9 ff. (II: 122 f.). He argues that the *Oresteia* as we have it is a substantially rewritten edition prepared by a later poet for performance possibly between 408 and 405 B.C. Cf. also H. Weil, *Rev. ét. gr.* I (1888) 7 ff. (but Weil was much more cautious); J. Vürtheim, *Aischylos' Schutzflehende* (Amsterdam 1928) 242 ff. In his review of Böhme (*Gnomon* 32 (1960) 771) H. J. Rose suggests that

the revised, and not the original archaic edition, that would have survived.

(*iii*) This class of evidence relates to posthumous productions by professional διδάσκαλοι of plays which had already been presented by Aeschylus himself. This is clear from the wording of the *Vita Apollonii*, and is confirmed by the μόνου αὐτοῦ of the scholia at *Acharnians* 10. For we cannot suppose that the source of the scholiast was ignorant of the posthumous first productions of the plays of Sophocles and Euripides. No significance is therefore to be attached to the use of διδάσκειν instead of ἀναδιδάσκειν, which is the normal word for a reproduction.[1] Aeschylus is credited by the *Vita* with thirteen victories, while the *Suda* ascribes to him twenty-eight. Doubtless fifteen of these were posthumous, if indeed the numbers are not corrupt.

How would a didascalia referring to such a production be worded? And how would the original records of the archon run? It has been a matter of prolonged controversy whether the name of poet or producer appeared in the records, when the two were different men.[2] The dispute largely concerns Comedy, and in particular the occasions on which Aristophanes entrusted the production of his plays to Callistratus, Philonides and others. With the general acceptance of Ἀριστοφάνης as the name to be inserted between Ἕρμιππος and Εὔπολις in *I.G.* ii². 2325, col. ii, the controversy has now apparently been settled in favour of the composer of the play.[3] The evidence for Tragedy is scanty but sufficient. In the fourth century Aphareus won two victories διὰ Διονυσίου at the Dionysia (and two δι' ἑτέρων at the Lenaea).[4] In the *Lists of Victors* (*I.G.* ii². 2325, col. iii) he himself is credited with them. Then, for 167 B.C. the *Didascaliae* (*I.G.* ii². 2323, col. iv) record the victory of Παράμονος τεθνηκώς. In any case it is incredible that the records of Aeschylus' post-

the *Supp.* may have been corrected in this manner (cf. earlier Vürtheim 189 f. and 247 f.; Koster 16 ff.). But it is an essential part of Böhme's case that the *Supp.* was not so revised. Cf. chap. III p. 90 n. 1 below.

[1] Cf. hyps. *Frogs* and *Peace*.

[2] Bibliography on 86 n. 6 of Pickard-Cambridge, *Dram. festivals*.

[3] Aristomenes, the other candidate for the position, probably had his first victory late in his career; cf. *I.G.* xiv. 1097 and Capps, *Hesperia* 12 (1943) 1 ff., esp. 3 n. 5.

[4] Plut. *mor.* 839d.

humous productions did not contain his name, since such productions were permitted only as a mark of honour to him. Probably the nearest parallel is that of the παλαιαί, where the names of both poet and producer were recorded.[1] If this is so we should expect both names to appear also in our ὑποθέσεις, as is indeed the case with those of the *Acharnians*, *Wasps*, *Birds*, *Frogs*, and *Lysistrata*. Our fragment says nothing of a ὑποδιδάσκαλος, but his name, or perhaps τεθνηκώς, could have stood after Αἰσχύλος in l. 2. Even if, most improbably, only the producer's name appeared in the archon's entry, the name of Aeschylus might well have been substituted by a later compiler. As Lucas says, the case of Aristias is not strictly comparable, since it involved no special enactment.[2] It is parallel rather with the case of the four victories won by Euphorion, which we have discussed already. It would be wrong to assume in Aristophanes of Byzantium ignorance of an earlier production,[3] but in the fragmentary state of our papyrus, we cannot tell whether the original ὑπόθεσις may not have dealt with both productions.[4] We have only the negative evidence of the ὑπόθεσις of the *Agamemnon*, which says nothing of any reproduction of that play, though it is a fair guess that so fine a trilogy as the *Oresteia* must have been among those reproduced.[5] However, it does seem impossible to prove conclusively that our fragment does not refer to a posthumous reproduction of the *Supplices*.

6. The composition of the play may be separate from the production.[6] The *Supplices* may have been written early, but not performed till late in Aeschylus' life. For examples of such separation del Corno cites the plays written by Euripides in Macedonia. Both he and Aeschylus died far from Athens, so

[1] *I.G.* ii². 2320 Νεοπτόλεμος Ὀρέστηι Εὐριπίδου. Cf. also *I.G.* xiv. 1098, l. 8 where Anaxandrides is victorious (349 B.C.) [διὰ Ἀνα]ξίππου (or possibly Διωξίππου).

[2] *The Greek tragic poets* (2nd ed. London 1959) 65.

[3] Cf. Lesky, *Hermes* 82. 2 f.

[4] Cf. Wolff, *Dissertation* 237 f. She suggests also, but less plausibly, that the second production was recorded as a particularly notable one, since in it Sophocles was defeated by an early tetralogy of Aeschylus.

[5] H.-J. Newiger, *Hermes* 89 (1961) 427–9, argues for a reproduction of the *Oresteia* in the 420's. Cf. also p. 23 n. 5 above.

[6] Pohlenz, *Gr. Trag.* 52 f.; del Corno 285 ff. *Contra* T. B. L. Webster, *Anz. f. Altertums.* 8 (1955) 158; Wolff, *Dissertation* 211 and 227 ff.; Koster 15 f.

that when they wrote their last plays they could have had no immediate production at the Dionysia in sight. Yet these were exceptional cases, and it is natural to suppose that a tragic poet normally wrote for a single performance at a particular Dionysia. At least there is no evidence to the contrary. On the other hand, any statement about the tragedian's method can be only guess-work, and we cannot definitely rule out the possibility that the *Supplices* was written early and produced late. According to Cratinus a chorus was once refused Sophocles by the archon.[1] Perhaps he tried again with the same play later in his life.

Diamantopoulos,[2] who finds in the *Supplices* parallels of the situation at Argos after the defeat at Sepeia in 494, holds that production of the trilogy, intended for 492–1, was postponed when the pro-Spartan party at Athens took over control from Themistocles and his group. But the danger of seeking exact political parallels with a contemporary situation is notorious in tragedy, particularly in the *Supplices*, where supposed allusions have been used to prove a multitude of dates.[3] Few are likely to find convincing Diamantopoulos' suggestion that 'Aeschylus was the man to whom the new Argive rulers had entrusted the re-moulding of the Hypermnestra tradition in conjunction with the institution of the public festival' (that described by Paus. ii. 25. 4), or that Aeschylus wrote his trilogy as a slogan to be used by Themistocles' group against their political opponents. Any argument based on the plot of the Δαναΐδες is exceedingly dangerous, since this is by no means as certain as Diamantopoulos assumes.

Pohlenz suggests two alternative reasons for Aeschylus' postponement of the presentation of his trilogy: the composition of the *Persae* intervening, or the long journey to Sicily with its new impressions. The *Persae* was produced in 472, and the first journey to Sicily may not have taken place until after that (possibly as a consequence of his victory),[4] and certainly not before 476, the year of the founding of Aetna. In his second

[1] Βουκόλοι fr. 15 Kock.
[2] *J.H.S.* 77 (1957) 220 ff.
[3] See chap. IV below.
[4] Cf. Mazon in his ed. I. iv. See further chap. II pp. 49 f. below.

edition indeed Pohlenz abandons the date he formerly favoured in the 490's, and accepts one in the 470's. It is difficult to see why he does not go further and accept the evidence of the papyrus as it stands. For our knowledge of Aeschylus' development is certainly not great enough to enable us, on grounds of structure or style alone, to place a play in one decade and deny that it could have been written in the next.[1]

If the composition is to be separated from the production, it is much more satisfactory to suppose a considerable interval between the two. Yet this too is improbable, since Aeschylus might be expected to have revised a play produced many years after its composition, and to have adapted it to modern taste (and more so if an archon had refused it in its original state).[2] But such revision is excluded by the theory that our *Supplices* is early.[3] It cannot, however, be proved that the play would not be presented in an unrevised form.

Must we then accept the possibility that our didascalia refers either to a posthumous reproduction of the *Supplices*, or to a first but late performance of a play written by a youthful Aeschylus? The impossibility cannot certainly be proved, and yet the improbability seems so great as to amount to virtual proof. It is of the utmost significance that we are told by the fragment that Aeschylus won the victory, and that too before an audience which was used to the plays of his maturity. Miss Wolff says that it is indisputable 'that the style of The Suppliants is, on the whole, *less well suited for drama* than the style of Aeschylus' other extant plays'.[4] Earp talks of its exiguous plot, of its irrelevant ideas and images, of its youthful luxuriance, of the incompetent handling of the second actor.[5] Aeschylus, he says, is learning his art as a dramatist. If all this is true, if the *Supplices* indeed reveals the immaturity of Aeschylus, why was this, of all his

[1] The same objection applies to Koster's dating in the 470's (cf. chap. IV p. 158 n. 4 below.

[2] See p. 26 above.

[3] Cf. Wolff, *Dissertation* 211 and 227 ff. She thinks it possible, however, that Aeschylus wrote the tetralogy between 493 and 482, but was not satisfied with it. He put it aside, and was prevented from revising it by pressure of work or by his service in the Persian Wars, and it was only after his death that it was found and produced for the first time by his son.

[4] *Eranos* 57 (1959) 22.

[5] *Op. cit.*

plays, chosen for revival by a professional διδάσκαλος, and, stranger still, how did it come to win the victory before an audience accustomed to better things?[1] Can it be that what to the twentieth-century reader seems immature was not so to its Athenian audience? Perhaps it is our idea of Aeschylus' development that is due to be revised.

[1] Miss Wolff, *Dissertation* 239 ff., does not really answer this question. Vürtheim suggests (247 f.) that the other two plays of the trilogy might have been more exciting to a later audience than the *Supp.* This does not explain why it is the *Supp.* that survives.

CHAPTER II

STYLE

'Scholars have hitherto regarded the *Supplices* as the earliest extant play of Aeschylus; if we now consent to put it late it makes all attempts to study literature futile.'[1] Earp's statement is based on two kinds of evidence, structure and style. Structure we must leave to the next chapter, the present one will examine the stylistic evidence. Indeed we may well question the validity of the statement before we even proceed to this examination. In the case of perhaps only one classical author, Plato, have stylistic criteria proved satisfactory in the dating of his works, and in that case the conditions are more than usually favourable. For we possess some thirty genuine dialogues, written over a period of fifty years, in fact all the dialogues that Plato wrote. Yet even here stylometry is unable to settle the precise order of composition; it can do no more than arrange the dialogues in groups.[2] Inside each group there remains considerable room for disagreement. When we turn to Aeschylus the conditions are obviously much less favourable. Of the seven extant plays, one, the *Prometheus*, is itself undated, and its authenticity has even been disputed, three belong to the same date 458, while the dated plays together embrace a period of no more than fourteen years. The statement that, 'Freilich fehlen uns mehr als 80 Stücke, aber die sechs erhaltenen erstrecken sich *über einen so großen Zeitraum*, daß wir die Grundzüge der Entwicklung von den Schutzflehenden bis zu den Eumeniden, das Konstante und das Variable, völlig ausreichend zu erkennen vermögen', is

[1] F. R. Earp, *G. & R.* 22 (1953) 119.

[2] The initiative in Platonic studies was provided by L. Campbell in the introduction to his edition of *Sophistes and Politicus* (Oxford 1867) and in Jowett and Campbell, *The Republic of Plato* (Oxford 1894) 46–66. Cf. also W. Dittenberger, *Hermes* 16 (1881) 321 ff.; C. Ritter, *Untersuchungen über Plato* (Stuttgart 1888) and *Neue Untersuch.* (München 1910); Idem, *N.Jbb.* 11 (1903) 241 ff. and 313 ff., and *Bursians Jahresber.* 187 (1921) 1 ff.; W. Lutoslawski, *The origin and growth of Plato's logic* (London 1897); H. von Arnim, *Sitz. Ak. Wiss. Wien* 169. 3 (1912).

plainly untrue.[1] A straight line of development, if such a thing exists, must establish itself over a period of fourteen years, and in that period we have only three points, 472, 467, and 458, from which to work. Let us assume, however, that such a straight line can be established, that certain valid criteria can be found in characteristics which show a consistent increase or decrease from the *Persae* through the *Septem* to the *Oresteia*. This will give us the logical order of Aeschylus' stylistic development. But it still cannot automatically be converted into the chronological one;[2] for that would involve the improbable assumption that an author's style must develop with complete consistency, that he can never return to a technique or a feature of his earlier style, and, in the case of a dramatist most important of all, that the question of style is quite independent of the necessarily varied dramatic requirements of his plays. The 'straight-line' theory would be acceptable for Aeschylus only if we had a large number of his plays, written at all periods of his life, and even then a completely consistent development would be surprising.[3]

This is obvious enough, and there would have been no difficulty if the *Supplices* had appeared close to the *Persae* on the supposed line of development, if the new papyrus fragment had moved the *Supplices* only, say, ten years along that line. The difficulty is caused by the idea that the *Supplices* represents a very much earlier stage of Aeschylus' development, that it is a play of his youth, composed perhaps around 490, while all the other extant plays belong to his maturity. Thus one critic can say that, 'Le style offre un mélange de verdeur naïve et de préciosité sèche, où se révèle un génie jeune, qui n'est pas maître encore de toutes ses ressources';[4] another that, 'eine

[1] W. Schmid, *Untersuchungen zum Gefesselten Prometheus* (Stuttgart 1929) 41. The italics are mine.

[2] A point made, along with other sensible remarks about the method and its pitfalls, by T. B. L. Webster, *Diogenes* 5 (1954) 86 ff.; cf. also H. D. F. Kitto, *Greek Tragedy* (3rd ed. London 1961) 53 n. 1.

[3] Cf. also chap. III pp. 89 f.

[4] P. Mazon, *Eschyle* I (Budé, Paris 1953) 1. Earp does not suggest a precise date for the play, but his judgement agrees with Mazon's. 'We do not know how old Aeschylus was when he wrote the *Supplices*, probably not less than thirty, but the style seems to have a touch of youthful luxuriance' (120); cf. Wilamowitz, *Hermes* 32 (1897) 397 n. 1.

größere Kluft als die zwischen der Danaidentrilogie und der Orestie läßt sich doch kaum denken'.[1] Yet another can speak of the 'epic simplicity' of its language,[2] an interesting judgement in view of the contradictory statement of Schmid that 'Die Entwicklung geht im allgemeinen auf sprachlichem Gebiet bei Aischylos vom Gezwungenen zum Einfacheren, vom Schwerverständlichen zu größerer Durchsichtigkeit'.[3] But such mere statements of opinion are valueless for our present purpose. If one 'knows' that the *Supplices* is the earliest play of Aeschylus, it is easy to find in it the first steps in his stylistic development, and then to use that development to prove that the *Supplices* is an early play.

Despite its inherent improbabilities the present chapter will assume the possibility of a straightforward development, and will seek only to determine whether the *Supplices* is in fact so far removed in style from the other plays. Mere subjective opinions are clearly not enough. Figures and statistics will be required.[4] Nor shall we be content with any argument that rests solely upon the differences between the *Supplices* and the *Agamemnon*. Every play must be taken into account, but it is the difference between *Supplices* and *Persae* that is of crucial importance, since it is here that the major chronological gap is supposed to occur. This means that if the *Supplices* is shown to contain, say, ten examples of any particular feature, it will not be enough to demonstrate that the *Persae* has 12, the *Septem* 14, and each play of the

[1] A. Gross, *Die Stichomythie in der gr. Tragödie und Komödie* (Berlin 1905) 40; quoted with approval by A. Peretti, *Epirrema e tragedia* (Florence 1939) 84 n. 2.

[2] T. G. Tucker, ed. *Supp.* (London and New York 1889) xxiii.

[3] *Loc. cit.*

[4] The dangers inherent in the statistical method, when not practised by an experienced statistician, are well brought out by G. U. Yule, *The statistical study of literary vocabulary* (Cambridge 1944), especially chap. v ('Certain difficulties and sources of fallacy'). A genuine 'random' sample, for example, is something different from the haphazard opening of a book, on the one hand, and on the other hand from the sample which involves a scholar's 'impartial' judgement. Certain ratios, for instance the proportion of Sicilian words in Aeschylus to the number of lines in each play, are liable to be a function of the size of sample, in this case the total number of lines in the play. For the total number of lines may increase without limit, while the Sicilian words can increase only up to the total of Sicilian words at risk (to paraphrase Yule 110). This will affect the *Agamemnon*, which is so much longer than the other plays.

Oresteia trilogy 18. Between *Persae* and *Oresteia* fourteen years elapsed, between 490 and the *Persae* eighteen years. Thus the 'straight-line' theory of development, if it is to be statistically consistent, must show that the difference between *Supplices* and *Persae* is greater than that between *Persae* and *Oresteia*;[1] for room must be left on the line for the many plays that Aeschylus may be assumed to have written between 490 and 472. Furthermore, one might naturally expect his stylistic development to slow down when he reached his maturity, and he was over fifty years of age when he wrote the *Persae*. Finally, any stylistic discrepancy that may be revealed among the three plays of the trilogy, all presumably composed at the same time, will cast grave suspicion upon the very validity of the method.

I

It is reasonable to look for some development in the treatment of the iambic trimeter from the earlier to the later plays, on the analogy of Sophocles and Euripides in whose later work resolutions become increasingly frequent. Table A shows the figures for the plays of Aeschylus.[2]

Since, however, greater licence may be expected with proper names, whose frequency naturally varies with the subject-matter of the plays,[3] more reliance may be placed upon table B, in which proper names are left out of account.

[1] So great, in fact, that it would be surprising that there is no dispute about the authenticity of the *Supplices*.

[2] These figures differ insignificantly from those of J. Descroix, *Le trimètre iambique* (Macon 1931), of E. C. Yorke, *C.Q.* 30 (1936) 116 ff., and of E. B. Ceadel, *C.Q.* 35 (1941) 84. Textual corruption and lines of doubtful authenticity will account for some of these divergencies. For earlier studies cf. J. Rumpel, *Philol.* 25 (1867) 54 ff.; C. F. Müller, *De pedibus solutis in dialog. senariis Aesch., Soph., Eur.* (Berlin 1866). H. Lloyd-Jones, *L'Ant. Class.* 33 (1964) 362, rightly stresses the fact that 'in the case of Euripides, where our material is far ampler than it is for Aeschylus, the order indicated by the incidence of resolution closely corresponds with the order so far as it is known from external evidence'.

[3] No fewer than 17 resolutions in the *Septem* are accounted for by proper names, 8 of these by Πολυνείκης and Ἐτεοκλῆς. The other figures are *Agamemnon* 15 (Ἀγαμέμνων 5 times), *Persae* 12, *P.V.* 9, *Supplices* 4, *Choephori* 7, and *Eumenides* 3. In the *Septem* some form of πόλεμος or πολέμιος causes resolution 8 times. The figures for the *Septem* include the doubtful passage at 803–20, which provides 5 resolutions; cf. A. W. Verrall's commentary, ed. *Septem* (London and New York 1887) 96.

TABLE A

Play	Number of trimeters	Number of resolved feet	Percentage
Persae	429	59	13·8
Septem[1]	543	69	12·7
Supplices	475	44	9·3
Agamemnon[2]	859	56	6·5
Choephori	618	39	6·3
Prometheus	773	46	6·0
Eumenides	640	35	5·5

TABLE B

Play	Number of trimeters	Number of resolved feet	Percentage
Persae	429	47	11·0
Septem	543	52	9·6
Supplices	475	40	8·4
Choephori	618	32	5·2
Eumenides	640	32	5·0
Agamemnon	859	41	4·8
Prometheus	773	37	4·8

The significance of these figures was seen long before the publication of the papyrus fragment.[3] They show a steadily increasing restraint in the use of resolved feet, and in this development the *Supplices* appears after the *Septem* and before the *Oresteia* and *Prometheus*. The fact that the figures for the three plays of the trilogy are practically identical should warn us against attributing this progression to chance. It is noteworthy that in Aeschylus, unlike Sophocles and Euripides, the development is from freedom to restraint. It would be interesting to

[1] The figures are for the whole play, both here and in table B. If lines 1005 to the end are omitted we have 494 trimeters, with 61 resolutions (12·3 %), 46 excluding proper names (9·3 %).

[2] The figures include the chorus's couplets at 1074–1113.

[3] By Yorke, *op. cit.*

TABLE C

	Persae	*Septem*	*Supp.*	*Choe.*	*Ag.*	*Eum.*	*P.V.*
1st foot							
anap.	2	2	1	1	7	3	12
dact.	—	1	—	1	1	—	—
tribr.	1	1	3	7	4	2	1
2nd foot							
tribr.	4	2	1	2	1	—	—
3rd foot							
dact.	20	30	25	13	18	14	14
tribr.	10	6	5	5	5	4	6
4th foot							
tribr.	8	10	3	3	5	6	3
5th foot							
tribr.	2	—	2	—	—	3	1
TOTAL	47	52	40	32	41	32	37

know whether he inherited his earlier laxity from his predecessors in tragedy. For even his latest plays fail to return to the severity of Semonides with his five resolutions in 173 trimeters (2·9 %), while Archilochus with 5 in 58 trimeters (8·6 %)[1] is more restrained than the *Persae* and the *Septem*. Of Sophocles' plays only the *Philoctetes* shows the same freedom as the *Persae*.[2] On the other hand Aeschylus rarely allows more than one resolution in the same trimeter. The *Septem* has four such lines (one of them involving a proper name),[3] while *Supplices*, *Persae* (proper name), *Agamemnon*, *Choephori*, and *Eumenides* all have one. Often trisyllabic feet seem to come in runs (for example *Supp.* 315 ff., and *P.V.* 709–35 where there are no fewer than 9).

Table C shows the composition of the figures in table B, that is to say with proper names excluded.

Table D shows each of these figures expressed as a percentage of the total number of resolutions in the play.

It would be difficult to find in this table any satisfactory evidence for a straightforward development from *Supplices* to *Oresteia*. Clearly a dactyl in the 3rd foot is Aeschylus' favourite form of resolution, and since no play has a greater number propor-

[1] Cf. Descroix. [2] Cf. Yorke, *op. cit.*

[3] Excluding 495, where ὄφεων should probably be scanned as a disyllable.

TABLE D

	Persae	*Septem*	*Supp.*	*Choe.*	*Ag.*	*Eum.*	*P.V.*
1st foot							
anap.	4·3	3·8	2·5	3·1	17·1	9·4	32·4
dact.	—	1·9	—	3·1	2·4	—	—
tribr.	2·1	1·9	7·5	21·9	9·8	6·3	2·7
2nd foot							
tribr.	8·5	3·8	2·5	6·3	2·4	—	—
3rd foot							
dact.	42·6	57·7	62·5	40·6	43·9	43·8	37·8
tribr.	21·3	11·5	12·5	15·6	12·2	12·5	16·2
4th foot							
tribr.	17·0	19·2	7·5	9·4	12·2	18·8	8·1
5th foot							
tribr.	4·3	—	5·0	—	—	9·4	2·7

tionately than the *Supplices* one might argue that lack of variety indicates an early date. But the next highest percentage is displayed by the *Septem* not the *Persae*, while the difference between *Supplices* and *Septem* is not much greater than that between *Choephori* and *Agamemnon*, and much less than that between *Septem* and *Persae*. Why does the *Septem* have so many 4th foot tribrachs, or the *Persae* so many in the 3rd foot? Why do the three plays of the *Oresteia* differ so noticeably in 1st foot tribrachs? Clearly nothing here demands that we place the *Supplices* in a class by itself, as representative of an early stage of Aeschylus' metrical development. The most striking peculiarity in fact concerns not the *Supplices* but the *Prometheus* with its very large number of 1st foot anapaests.

No more revealing are statistics dealing with the proportion of spondaic to pure iambic feet.[1] The *Septem* has the lowest percentage of pure iambic lines (5·1 %), with the *Supplices* next at 5·9 %. Highest is the *Eumenides* with 10·2 %. The principal division is between the three plays of the *Oresteia* on the one hand and the remaining plays on the other.[2] 3rd foot spondees[3] predominate over 1st foot in *Supplices* (13·3/8·7), *Septem* (12·9/

[1] Descroix 46–7; also E. Harrison, *C.Q.* 8 (1914) 206 ff.

[2] *Ag.* 9·1 %, *Choe.* 8·6 %, *Pers.* 6·0 %, *P.V.* 6·9 %.

[3] That is, trimeters with spondees only in the 3rd foot.

10·0), and *Prometheus* (13·4/10·1), while it is the other way round with *Persae* (9·8/11·9), *Agamemnon* (12·4/12·7), *Choephori* (11·2/12·1), and *Eumenides* (10·7/11·7).

There is little sign of evolution in Aeschylus' use of the caesura.[1] Most common throughout is the penthemimeral: *Eumenides* 77·5%, *Septem* 75·8%, *Choephori* 75·4%, *Supplices* 73·3%, *Prometheus* 72·2%, *Persae* 72·1%, and *Agamemnon* 70·8%. It is however interesting that the *Persae* contains no fewer than 9 lines[2] which break in the middle and have no regular caesura, the *Supplices* 5, *Prometheus*, *Agamemnon*, and *Choephori* 2, *Septem* and *Eumenides* only 1. Only the *Persae* moreover offers no line with three strong stops, such as we find in the *Supplices* (907 and 911), and all the other plays.[3] The *Persae* is remarkable also for its strict adherence to Porson's law. It has only two minor[4] infractions (3% of all clausulae | – ∪ –), as opposed to *Septem* with 9 (17·3%), *Supplices* 9 (18·3%), *Agamemnon* 8 (9·7%), *Choephori* 13 (17·5%), *Eumenides* 14 (17·5%), and *Prometheus* 13 (12·8%). On the other hand the manuscripts present a major infraction at *Persae* 321,[5] the only real parallel being at *Prometheus* 821.[6]

[1] Cf. Descroix 267 ff. His full table is on p. 262.

[2] Including line 501, where Porson's word-order would provide a caesura. Cf. H. D. Broadhead, *The Persae of Aeschylus* (Cambridge 1960) 299, who omits this occurrence from his count of 8.

[3] Cf. E. A. Wolff, *Aeschylus' Danaid Trilogy: a Study* (Diss. Columbia Univ. 1957) 157.

[4] By minor infraction is meant one which involves a proclitic monosyllable, e.g. the article or a preposition.

[5] Ἀριόμαρδος Σάρδεσι, retained by Murray. Broadhead follows Bothe in reading ἅρδεσι, but for reasons of sense rather than metre. 'If the sense were wholly suitable, the violation might be excused (i) because of the proper name, (ii) because of the early date of the play (cf. the unusual number of lines without the customary caesura)' (p. 111).

[6] The figures are those of Descroix 320 ff. They diverge slightly from those of G. Dottin, *Rev. de Philol.* 25 (1901) 204. I count 10 in the *Septem* (including 518—4 between 442 and 468: similarly *P.V.* has 4 between 739 and 763), 10 in *Supplices* (11 with the corrupt MS reading at 198), and 14 in *Choephori*. It is doubtful whether *Persae* 762 can really count as a minor infraction. τήνδ' is indeed a monosyllable, and elides into ὤπασεν, but it coheres with τιμήν, not with ὤπασεν. Cf. Broadhead 300 n.1. Pauw's emendation ἐξεκείνωσ' ἐμπεσόν at 761 (accepted by Murray but not by Broadhead) would provide another major breach of the Law. If all three were to be accepted, the *Persae* would be even more distinctive.

TABLE E

Play	Trimeters available for enjambement	Occurrences	Percentage
Prometheus	672	65	9·67
Supplices	399	34	8·52
Persae	429	33	7·69
Agamemnon	780	57	7·31
Choephori	532	35	6·58
Eumenides	573	28	4·89
Septem	457	21	4·60

One might expect Aeschylus to show increasing freedom in his use of enjambement, as he became more experienced in his handling of the trimeter. The question has been studied by W. Ficker,[1] who gives the figures in table E.

The general conclusion from this is that Aeschylus' treatment of the iambic trimeter is largely stichic. The *Prometheus* is at the head of the list, with *Supplices*, *Persae*, and *Agamemnon* not far behind. No chronological conclusions seem possible here. The *Prometheus* (821) shares with the *Supplices* (483) the distinction of having a break after the first syllable of a line following enjambement. The *Persae* is unique with two examples of a break in the fifth foot (457 and 834). The *Septem* alone has no example of two successive enjambements. In no respect does the *Supplices* seem peculiar. The most extreme form of enjambement occurs when a word (especially a word beginning a new clause or phrase) placed at the end of one line looks forward to the next (e.g. a subordinating word like ἵνα or a proclitic or quasi-proclitic). Its effect is obviously to minimize the break between one line and another, and it occurs with great frequency in Sophocles.[2] Yorke finds 18 certain examples in the *Prometheus*, about 7 in the whole of the *Oresteia*, and elsewhere only one

[1] *Vers und Satz im Dialog des Aischylos* (Diss. Leipzig 1935). His table is on p. 7: cf. also J. D. Denniston, *C.Q.* 30 (1936) 73 ff. and 192.

[2] Cf. especially E. Harrison, *Proc. of Camb. Philol. Soc.* 118–20 (1921) 14 f.; D. S. Robertson, *ibid.* 169–71 (1938) 9 f.; E. C. Yorke, *C.Q.* 30 (1936) 153–4.

certain occurrence at *Persae* 486. One might add *Supplices* 769, where a similar effect is produced. Whatever evidence this may provide for the dating of the *Prometheus*, it is obvious that the *Supplices*, from the point of view of iambic trimeter technique, remains very firmly in place with Aeschylus' other plays. On the purely negative side one might notice the absence in the *Supplices* of the trochaic tetrameter as a metre of dialogue, the earliest one in use if we are to believe Aristotle.[1] It is to be found only in *Persae* (114 lines) and *Agamemnon* (a mere 25 lines at the end of the play). If Kranz is right in supposing[2] that Aeschylus had much to do with its replacement by the iambic trimeter, its absence in the *Supplices* would perhaps be surprising if it were really an early play. The *Persae* has a further claim to distinction in the field of quantity.[3] In 543 iambic and trochaic lines it has 18 examples of the lengthening of a vowel before mute and liquid. The *Prometheus* comes next with 18 in 774 lines. In all the other plays put together there are only 29 examples of this.[4]

When we turn to lyric metres statistics are naturally much more difficult to produce, and there is apparently no outstanding characteristic of Aeschylus' lyric technique that shows a significant development from play to play. Schmid[5] says that inexactness in strophic responsion is a criterion of age, and that this is most evident in the *Supplices*. Since however it must always remain uncertain whether apparent freedom of responsion is not a matter of textual corruption, it can hardly be taken as a

[1] *Poetics* 1449a 22; cf. *Rhet.* 1404a 31 f., 1408b 33 f.

[2] W. Kranz, *Stasimon* (Berlin 1933) 9 and 269 f. Cf. also Broadhead 298.

[3] Cf. A. v. Mess, *Rh. Mus.* 58 (1903) 290.

[4] In three plays, *Supp.*, *Pers.*, and *Ag.* the Parodos opens with anapaests. An analysis of the first 25 dimeters of each provides the following figures: Anapaests—*Pers.* 31, *Supp.* 42, *Ag.* 40: spondees—*Pers.* 46, *Supp.* 39, *Ag.* 36: dactyls—*Pers.* 23, *Supp.* 19, *Ag.* 24. For what such meagre statistics are worth (probably not very much; the pattern in the *Persae* is dictated by the large number of Persian proper names) the technique of the *Supplices* seems closer to that of the *Agamemnon* than does the *Persae*. W. Nestle, *Die Struktur des Eingangs in der attischen Tragödie* (Stuttgart 1930) 72, remarks however that the *Persae* and *Agamemnon* have longer anapaestic periods than the *Supplices*. For Aeschylus' anapaests cf. F. Kussmähly, *Beobachtungen zum Prom. des Aesch.* (Berlin 1888) 8 ff.; and more recently Broadhead, Appx. II. 283 ff. Kussmähly remarks that the caesura in the middle of the dimeter is omitted some 17 times in the *Oresteia*, once in *Prometheus* and *Supplices*, never in *Persae* or *Septem*.

[5] *GGL* I. 2 (Munich 1934) 194 n. 1.

reliable indication of age. Responsion of syncopated with complete iambs in lyric iambics will serve as an example. Wilamowitz says[1] that this is avoided from the *Oresteia* onwards. From earlier plays he cites as examples *Septem* 170 = 178 and 330 = 342, and *Prometheus* 163 = 182. Perhaps to be added are *Persae* 280–1 = 286–7 and *Agamemnon* 195 = 208. But in all these places strict responsion has been restored by emendation.[2] It may however be noted that even without emendation the *Supplices* would not disagree with the practice of the *Oresteia*.

Another criterion has been sought in the treatment of the dochmiac, a likely place to look for traces of development if Aeschylus is indeed the creator (or even if he is only the developer) of the lyric dochmiac.[3] G. Müller finds that the dochmiacs of the *Supplices* differ from those of other plays in that they never admit *brevis in longo* or hiatus, but maintain strict synapheia throughout the whole of a system.[4] *Brevis in longo* occurs, however, at *Supplices* 888 and 891, and hiatus at 886 (?) and 891.[5] Both are common enough before a pause (*brevis in longo Sept.* 82, 88, 109, 115; hiatus *Supp.* 886 (?); *Sept.* 88, 97, 891; *Ag.* 1428; *Choe.* 936, 947) or before or after an exclamation (*brevis in longo Supp.* 888 and 891; *Sept.* 83; *P.V.* 575; *Choe.* 157; *Eum.* 837,[6] 840; hiatus *Supp.* 891; *Pers.* 1073; *Sept.* 86; *Ag.* 1125; *Choe.* 159, 869; *Eum.* 145, 781), or before a change of metre. *Choephori* 957 is corrupt. There is nothing odd about the

[1] *Gr. Verskunst* (Berlin 1921) 293–4; cf. J. D. Denniston in *Greek poetry and life* (Essays presented to G. Murray, Oxford 1936) 143; Fraenkel at *Ag.* 403 f. and II p. 351 n. 1. Verrall in his edition of the *Agamemnon*, Appx. II, listed other instances, in all of which emendation is generally accepted.

[2] Cf. P. Maas, *Greek metre* (tr. H. Lloyd-Jones, Oxford 1962) 28–9.

[3] Cf. A. M. Dale, *Lyric metres of Greek drama* (2nd ed. Cambridge 1968) 104; B. Snell, *Gr. Metrik* (2nd ed. Göttingen 1957) 44; Rossbach and Westphal, *Theorie der musischen Künste der Hellenen* (3rd ed. Leipzig 1889) III. 2. 777 ff.; Wilamowitz, *Aischylos. Interpretationen* (Berlin 1914) 248; *GGL* 142; Peretti, *Epirrema e tragedia* 41 and 53. Schmid (*GGL* 194 n. 1) also finds in dochmiacs a criterion of age.

[4] *De Aeschyli Supplicum tempore atque indole* (Halis Saxonum 1908) 61 ff. Cf. Rossbach and Westphal, *loc. cit.*

[5] Müller emphasizes the uncertainty of the text at *Supplices* 886, and argues that 892 is not a dochmiac at all. He ascribes to mere chance the lack of dochmiacs in the *Persae*.

[6] N. C. Conomis, *Hermes* 92 (1964) 35, includes φεῦ in the metre and scans as a dochmiac with irrational anceps (⏑ ⏑ ⏑ – ⏑ ⏑ –). This avoids *brevis in longo* but produces hiatus.

Supplices in all this. The outstanding play is rather the *Eumenides*, with two inexplicable examples of hiatus (157 and 259) and two of *brevis in longo* (149 and 840; perhaps to be emended). Interesting too is the very sparing use of the dochmiac in the *Persae*, where no connected systems occur at all, and the dochmiacs are of the simplest.[1]

Even less reliable than statistics here are general impressions. One may feel, for example, that in the *Septem* a certain monotony of metre indicates an early date. Mainly iambics and dochmiacs are employed, the former often for the 'tragic' element of the play, the ruin of the Labdacidae, the latter for the epic story of the Seven against Thebes.[2] The dochmiac is used here for appeal and reflection, and does not yet seem to have acquired its function as the peculiar metre of violent feeling and excitement.[3] Again one may look upon long rows of dactyls as characteristic of older tragedy,[4] a reminiscence perhaps of the style of Stesichorus.[5] Notable in this respect is *Persae* 852 ff. (cf. also *Supplices* 40 ff.). But *Agamemnon* 104 ff. should prevent us from leaping to any such chronological conclusions. The negative evidence is again as good as any. There is nothing in the metrical technique of the lyrics of the *Supplices* to suggest that this is an early play, earlier that is than the *Persae* or the *Septem*, no sign that here we have a young Aeschylus still learning his craft. Either he developed his skill to maturity at a very early age, or the *Supplices* belongs to the same general period as the *Persae* and the *Septem*. It seems easier to accept the second alternative.

The question of correspondence of thought between strophe and antistrophe has received attention, quite apart from purely metrical considerations. It is claimed[6] that two principles are to

[1] I am grateful to Professor D. L. Page for much of this information about the dochmiac. For dochmiacs in general see esp. the useful study by Conomis 23 ff.

[2] Cf. Wilamowitz, *Gr. Verskunst* 199 f.

[3] Cf. Dale 110.

[4] Cf. E. Fraenkel, *Rh. Mus.* 72 (1917–18) 187; Rossbach and Westphal 779. Professor Lloyd-Jones points out to me that fr. 109 M (74 N²) contains a run of dactyls. Cf. also Ar. *Frogs* 1264 ff., and the parody at 814 ff.

[5] Cf. W. Headlam, *J.H.S.* 22 (1902) 215.

[6] M. Horneffer, *De strophica sententiarum in canticis tragicorum Graecorum responsione* (Jen. Diss. 1914): cf. Kranz 154 ff.; Peretti 142. Cf. also pp. 76 ff. below.

be seen at work in the plays of Aeschylus, the first demanding that a whole lyric composition be treated as a single unity with straightforward development of thought, the other concerning itself with the unity rather of the strophic pair, and requiring that the thought of the antistrophe be closely bound and parallel with that of the strophe: the first of these principles, in which the unity of the whole poem is the important thing, is said to be the product of the developed poetic art, the second to be taken over by Aeschylus from tradition. 'Sententiarum igitur responsus rhythmicam compositionem sequitur. illa autem in genuina poesi lyrica e modis pendet.'[1] Whether this is true or not it is doubtful whether any straightforward development from one principle to the other is to be seen in Aeschylus. At any rate the first principle seems to be exemplified by *Septem* 150–80, *Choephori* 935–8 and 946–9, and *Eumenides* 996–1002 and 1014–20, whereas in the first Stasimon of the *Supplices* the passage from one strophic pair to another is three times eased by transitional lines (537, 571–3, 588–9), thereby showing a greater concern for the unity of the whole.[2] A third kind of progression produces two passages different in rhythm, and presumably music, but united in thought.[3] Thus in the Parodos of the *Supplices* the 3rd strophe, which introduces dactyls, is bound in thought to the 2nd strophic pair, and the 5th strophe is similarly linked with the 4th pair. *Agamemnon* 160 ff. displays the same technique. Very rarely is there no break between a strophe and its antistrophe, or between an antistrophe and the following strophe. Aeschylus has examples at *Supplices* 581–2, perhaps *Septem* 749–50, and *Agamemnon* 237–8, less obviously at *Supplices* 1025–6, *Persae* 870–1 (but the punctuation should probably be a colon rather than a comma), and *Agamemnon* 175–6.[4] If this is a sign of older style, as Kranz suggests,[5] it is clearly not confined to the *Supplices*.

[1] Horneffer 10. [2] Horneffer 22–3. [3] Kranz 156 f.

[4] Cf. Kranz, *Hermes* 54 (1919) 309 f.; W. A. A. van Otterlo, *Beschouwingen over het archaïsche Element in den Stijl van Aeschylus* (Utrecht 1937) 114; E. Fraenkel, *Aeschylus. Agamemnon* (Oxford 1950) II. 135 f.; Denniston and Page, *Aeschylus. Agamemnon* (Oxford 1957) 228.

[5] *Stasimon* 153 f. (cf. 117 f.).

Parallelism of thought between strophe and antistrophe is most obvious when it is emphasized by repetition of words, syllables, or merely vowel sounds, or by the doubling of words in the same position in strophe and antistrophe.[1] The more significant occurrences, those which may be more than mere coincidence, are the following:[2] *Persae* 67, 84, 117, 130, 259, 268, 269, 280, 282, 550 ff., 568 ff., 573, 635, 647, 649–51, 663, 694 ff., 884, 935 (textually corrupt), 937, 940, 954, 955, 957, 960, 985, 1002–4, 1019, 1024, 1038, 1040, 1043, 1045, 1054 to end of play. *Septem* 119, 150, 152, 166, 321†, 327, 350, 351, 420 f., 766, 778, 875, 876, 888, 892 f., 894, 916, 934, 966, 971, 972, 975 ff. *Supplices* 40, 44, 59, 71, 112, 114 f., 156, 395, 524, 527–8 (a subtle, but possibly accidental, instance—the imperative endings are repeated in the antistrophe in the reverse order), 543, 574, 580, 638, 679, 683, 686–7, 703, 750, 752, 776, 778, 799, 812, 815, 866, 889 ff., 1020, 1037, 1042. *Prometheus* 128, 130, 133 (γάρ), 161, 166, 404, 530, 574, 576, 579, 580, 588, 887, 892. *Agamemnon* 121, 160, 221, 369, 407, 683, 692, 693, 698, 763, 983, 1072 ff., 1091†, 1100, 1114, 1136, 1140, 1156, 1158, 1162, 1165, 1483. *Choephori* 25, 27, 28, 42, 46, 47, 315, 320, 327–8, 345, 346, 347, 382, 406, 407, 408, 425, 431–2, 435, 456, 466, 470, 592, 788, 935 ff., 958 f., 961. *Eumenides* 143, 156, 159, 160, 161, 171, 373, 382, 388, 490–2, 497, 512, 516, 553, 555, 778 ff., 837 ff., 996, 999, 1035, 1043. There would be little point in simply counting the number of such repetitions and echoes, since accident could never be ruled out, and there is moreover a considerable difference between the echo of a single vowel sound and the repetition of a whole line or even strophe in the form of a full refrain. It is not so much the number as the nature of the occurrences in the *Persae* that is so striking. Scholars have been led by the character of the Exodos in particular to assume that such repetition is a traditional feature of the pre-literary threnos.[3] Certainly it is to be found in quantity also at *Persae*

[1] On the whole subject cf. A. E. Haigh, *The tragic drama of the Greeks* (Oxford 1896) 378 f.; Horneffer, *op. cit.*; W. Schadewaldt, *Hermes* 67 (1932) 330; Kranz 127 ff.; R. Hölzle, *Zum Aufbau der lyrischen Partien des Aischylos* (Diss. Freiburg i. Br. 1934).

[2] Only the line numbers of the strophe are given.

[3] Cf. chap. III, p. 92 below.

548 ff., in the Exodos of the *Septem*, and in the kommos of the *Choephori* which while not a threnos is similarly related to the dead, and contains a threnos as part of it.[1] But in the absence of other evidence about the pre-literary threnos, it would be rash to judge from the practice of Aeschylus; rash too to look for the origins of the lyrics of tragedy in such ritual forms. One might indeed be tempted to say that the Exodos of the *Persae looks* primitive, yet even if we accept repetition and echo as features of the traditional threnos, the fact that Aeschylus uses them extensively in any play proves nothing either about the date of that play or about the origins of the lyrics of tragedy, but only that he wanted to write something which his audience would recognize as a threnos.[2]

A refrain of a different type, achieved not by word repetition but by the use of rhythm, occurs in Aeschylus only in *Supplices* and *Agamemnon*.[3] The 2nd Stasimon of the *Supplices* (630 ff.) and the 1st of the *Agamemnon* (367 ff.) both display a passage of three strophic pairs each with an identical rhythmical refrain (two pherecrateans followed by a glyconic and pherecratean), an interesting link between the two plays. More difficult is the question of mesodes and ephymnia, since it is often doubtful whether an apparent mesode should be turned into an ephymnium by the restoration of the lines repeated after the antistrophe.[4] Thus Wilamowitz, Verrall, Schroeder, and Mazon follow Burney in repeating ἐφύμνια α′ and γ′ at *Agamemnon*

[1] For a related iambic passage cf. *Choephori* 489–96.

[2] Equally dubious is Hölzle's argument (102 ff.) that Aeschylus' lyrics show a gradual liberation from the restrictions of the prayer form. If all the lyrics of the *Supplices* contain prayers, this does not mean that Aeschylus could not at this stage write any other kind of lyric (he had, after all, the whole of Dorian choral lyric before him), but only that prayer is the natural activity of the Danaid chorus, as the name of the play indicates. For similar views to Hölzle's cf. Schadewaldt, *Monolog und Selbstgespräch* (Berlin 1926) 38 ff., and especially 45; Peretti 83 ff.; V. Citti, *Il linguaggio religioso e liturgico nelle tragedie di Eschilo* (Bologna 1962) 126 ff. (cf. 8, 16, n. 58 on 149; but also 41, 149 n. 59).

[3] Elsewhere only at E. *Her.* 348 ff.

[4] It is convenient to keep the term 'mesode' for something which occurs between strophe and antistrophe, and is not repeated after the antistrophe. The passage at *Ag.* 140 ff. and that at *Pers.* 93 ff. (107 ff.) (if indeed strophic correspondence is not to be restored there) are rather to be classed as epodes, since they occur after the antistrophe.

1448 ff., thereby destroying the sequence of thought.[1] Murray and Denniston–Page treat the passages as mesodes. Similar mesodes are to be found only in the *Choephori* (783 ff. and 935 ff.), and perhaps at *Supplices* 162 ff., which all editors follow Canter in repeating after 175 as an ephymnium. Münscher indeed is inclined to deny this repetition and to treat the passage as a mesode, but yields to his belief that the *Supplices* stands at the beginning of Aeschylus' development, while the mesode belongs only to a later stage. Much less doubtful is the question of the undisputed ephymnia. These too are confined to *Supplices* and *Oresteia* (*Supp.* 117 ff., *Ag.* 1489 ff., and *Eum.* 328 ff.). Once more it is the *Persae* that is peculiar, with its predilection for the triadic structure with epode (93 (107) ff.?, 673 ff., 897 ff., 1066 ff.). Nestle suggests that Aeschylus develops from this triadic form to that with mesode and ephymnium, and one would perhaps be justified in seeing a mark of older style in the triadic structure, with its pedigree going back traditionally to Stesichorus.[2] Aeschylus, however, still employs it in the *Oresteia* (*Ag.* 140 ff. and 475 ff., *Choe.* 75 ff.) and in the *Prometheus* (901 ff.), so there can be no question of a simple chronological development.[3] Nevertheless the structure of the lyrics of the *Supplices* does seem closer on the whole to that of the *Oresteia* than does that of either *Persae* or *Septem*.[4]

It is claimed by Wilamowitz that one can trace a development in the mere size of Aeschylus' strophes,[5] that what in an early play like the *Supplices* would form a complete strophe, is to be found in the later plays as a mere period, a single element in

[1] Cf. Kranz, *Hermes* 54. 312 ff. (and Wilamowitz himself—*Gr. Verskunst* 443 n. 1); W. Porzig, *Aischylos* (Leipzig 1926) 10; Peretti 182; Fraenkel nn. *ad loc.*; M. Pohlenz, *Gr. Tragödie* (2nd ed. Göttingen 1954) *Erl.* 51. On the whole subject cf. especially K. Münscher, *Hermes* 59 (1924) 204 ff.; N. Wecklein, *Philol.* 82 (1927) 467 ff.; Kranz, *Stasimon* 130 ff.; W. Nestle, *Gnomon* 10 (1934) 406; Hölzle 41 n. 88; Peretti 49 ff.

[2] *Suda*, s.v. τρία Στησιχόρου.

[3] In all but three cases the epode occurs after the 3rd strophic pair. Only at *Persae* 93 ff. and *Agamemnon* 140 ff. is it not at the end of a stasimon.

[4] Nothing in *Supplices*, *Persae*, or *Septem* approaches the intricacy of the interlocking strophic patterns that we find in the kommos of the *Choephori*.

[5] *Gr. Verskunst.* 450 f.; cf. also *Interpr.* 248: 'In den Liedern ist zu bemerken, wie die Strophen an Umfang zunehmen, während der Gesang gegenüber dem Dialoge zurücktritt.' Also Kranz, *Stasimon* 144 f.

a much larger composition. And certainly this view would seem to be confirmed by a comparison of the lyrics of the *Supplices* with those of the *Agamemnon*, for example the first strophic pair of the Parodos of each. It is more important however to establish whether any such development is discernible between *Supplices* and *Persae*. In fact it is difficult to see any difference between these two plays. In the latter only lines 548 ff. and 931 ff. are of any considerable extent, and it is just here that we have found some features which, if any, look primitive. *Septem* 109 ff. and 287 ff. are the earliest passages to resemble the extended strophes of the *Agamemnon*. But the latter play itself still displays the 'older' kind, for example at 160 ff., while the strophes of the *Choephori* are on the whole short. The assumption of a simple chronological development would again seem a dangerous one.[1] Fluctuations in the size of Aeschylus' strophes may find a safer explanation in the demands of plot and subject-matter.[2] The long, reflective odes of the *Agamemnon* serve a very different purpose from those of the *Supplices* in which the Chorus is itself the Protagonist, and it is only natural that they should differ also in compass.

II

Since subjective considerations are clearly unreliable in determining the chronological development of an author's style, attempts are made to isolate characteristic words, idioms, or expressions, and to seek in their varying frequency a valid criterion of the age of the play in which they occur. The weakness of this method is apt to appear when the criterion is put to the test. A typical example is the study of epic borrowings in Aeschylus.[3] Aeschylus himself, in well-known but not entirely

[1] It would be unwise to ignore the stage of development that choral lyric had already reached when it began, as it must have done, to influence the lyrics of early tragedy. Cf. Kranz, *Stasimon* 142.

[2] Cf. Wilamowitz himself on the *P.V.* (*Interpr.* 117, 120, 157 f.).

[3] Lists and discussion in M. Lechner, *De Aeschyli studio Homerico* (Erlangen 1862); S. B. Franklin, *Traces of epic influence in the tragedies of Aeschylus* (Baltimore 1895); A. Peretti, *Studi ital.* n.s. 5 (1927) 165 ff.; M. Gigli, *Riv. indo-greca ital.* 12 (1928) i. 43 ff. and ii. 33 ff.; W. Schmid, *Gefess. Prom.* 43 ff.; C. F. Kumaniecki, *De*

unambiguous words,[1] acknowledged his debt to Homer, and it has seemed to some scholars that a development is to be looked for here. Thus Stanford finds in *Supplices*, *Persae*, and *Septem* the largest number of direct, or nearly direct, epic borrowings. But clearly this tells us nothing about any development: it indicates merely that the *Oresteia* is different from the other plays. The only way in which to arrive at accurate conclusions is to draw up complete lists of all epic borrowings for all the plays. But this is hardly possible. How can one ever be certain that a word or phrase, or even a simile, is a genuine epic borrowing, and not one which has been long received into the general Greek poetic vocabulary, transmitted for example by the elegiac, iambic, and melic poets?[2] Thus Peretti's list includes such words as κόμη (*Supp.* 909), κριθή (953), and τρίαινα (218, 755). No significance can be attached to these. Again the simile at *Supplices* 223 ff. (cf. *P.V.* 856 ff.) may conceivably be derived from *Iliad* X 139 ff.,[3] and that at *Persae* 81 f. from X 93 ff.,[4] but equally they may have occurred quite independently to the mind of Aeschylus, possibly as a result of his own observation. Earp includes in his list of epic words 'those only which would probably be felt as definitely archaic and unfamiliar'.[5] But immediately the element of subjectivity has entered in. And, even if we overcome all the difficulties and produce lists that are acceptable to all, lists showing definite variations from play to play in the frequency of borrowings, are we any closer to a reliable indication of date? Is there not here an underlying, and obviously absurd, assumption that the earlier a play is, and therefore the closer to the date of Homer, the more strongly it

elocutionis Aeschyleae natura (=*Archivum Filologiczne* nr. 12, Krakow 1935) 5 ff.; W. B. Stanford, *Aeschylus in his style* (Dublin 1942) 17 ff. and 138; F. R. Earp, *The style of Aeschylus* (Cambridge 1948) 39 ff.; L. Bergson, *L'épithète ornementale dans Eschyle, Sophocle, et Euripide* (Lund 1956) especially 100 ff.; Broadhead 252 f.

[1] Athen. viii. 347e: ὅς τὰς αὑτοῦ τραγῳδίας τεμάχη εἶναι ἔλεγεν τῶν Ὁμήρου μεγάλων δείπνων.

[2] Cf. Franklin 30 and 81: also B. Gerth in Curtius, *Studien zur gr. und lat. Grammatik* I. 2 (1868) 268 f.; G. Björck, *Das Alpha impurum und die tragische Kunstsprache. Attische Wort- und Stilstudien* (Uppsala 1950) 217; Broadhead 251. For a different view see Bergson 100.

[3] Cf. Lechner 20: also O 237–8, Φ 493–4, ο 525–7.

[4] Cf. Gigli ii. 44.

[5] P. 40.

must show his influence? If any play is more indebted than the rest to Homer, this may mean only that its subject-matter lends itself to epic treatment, or that Aeschylus has recently been reading Homer.[1]

In fact no significant conclusions have been reached. Stanford finds that, while the largest number of epic borrowings are to be found in *Supplices*, *Persae*, and *Septem*, of these three plays the *Persae* is in the lead.[2] Earp's figures (for single words) are *Supplices* 27, *Persae* 21, *Septem* 15, *Prometheus* 24, *Agamemnon* 21, *Choephori* 20, and *Eumenides* 18.[3] It will be noticed that the *Prometheus* is closest to the *Supplices*, and that the *Septem* unaccountably has the fewest borrowings, while inside the trilogy the *Agamemnon*, with its greater length, is at variance with the other two plays. Miss Franklin is duly cautious: 'It is impossible to make definite statements here in regard to the number of epic words in each of the tragedies, but even a slight study of the latest trilogy, the *Oresteia*, shows that the Homericisms are by no means confined to the earlier plays.'[4] The same indeterminate results are provided by a study of one particular epic idiom in Aeschylus, namely the ἶς Τηλεμάχοιο type of expression, which occurs, with various modifications and elaborations, some 45 times in the plays and fragments.[5] Rose finds 7 in the *Supplices*, 9 in *Persae*, 8 in *Septem*, 7 or 8 in *Agamemnon*, 4 in *Choephori*, 3 in *Eumenides*, and 2 or 3 in *Prometheus*. From this he concludes that Aeschylus grew less fond of the idiom in his later years. But

[1] Earp's suggestion is that 'Aeschylus at first turned, as was natural, to Homer and to Choral Lyric, and later, finding them unsuitable, used them less and less' (170).

[2] P. 138. Stanford attributes this to the subject-matter of the play (cf. also E. A. Wolff, *Eranos* 57 (1959) 15). But the subject-matter of the *Septem* would seem closer to the epic.

[3] In the *Supplices* list (p. 49) ἄγα is a mere conjecture, so that it is doubtful if it should be considered at all. In the *Agamemnon* list (51) it appears wrongly under 'Rare Words' instead of 'Epic'. In the *Persae* list ἱππιοχάρμης appears twice, which is inconsistent with Earp's method elsewhere.

[4] P. 36 n. 11.

[5] Cf. H. J. Rose, *Eranos* 45 (1947) 88 ff. and 46 (1948) 72: also L. J. D. Richardson, *Eranos* 55 (1957) 1 ff. Richardson makes a stronger distinction between those which follow simple Homeric usage, and the more elaborate phrases which are purely Aeschylean. The *Septem* provides 6 out of the 10 examples of the former (448, 569, 571, 577, 620, 641: Richardson adds 488 and perhaps 428–9), all of which occur in the Messenger's description of the enemy forces, a passage which naturally lends itself to Homeric imitation.

all that one may safely say is that the *Oresteia* and *Prometheus* have slightly fewer occurrences than the other plays.[1] W. Headlam claimed that the *Persae* is particularly rich in Ionic expressions and forms,[2] but many of these are more correctly seen as epicisms;[3] for example the word ἠδέ which occurs more frequently in the *Persae* than in any other play, mainly in catalogues of names.[4] Line 782 however is, if sound, unique in Aeschylus for its combination of two Ionicisms—the lengthening of the final syllable of νέα before φρονεῖ (but cf. E. *El.* 1058 and *Alc.* 542)[5] and the form ἐών, which is found nowhere else in tragedy.

Rather more positive conclusions are provided by Earp's lists of rare words, words which 'would probably be felt by a Greek as unfamiliar or exotic'.[6] Thus he excludes new compounds of or new formations from familiar stems. His figures are *Supplices* 30, *Persae* 21, *Septem* 16, *Prometheus* 14, *Agamemnon* 18, *Choephori* 10, and *Eumenides* 13[7]—which seems to indicate a straightforward development from *Supplices* to *Oresteia*. But a different explanation suggests itself, and indeed is suggested by Earp himself, to account for the large number of such words in the *Supplices*. Many of them are dialect or foreign words, and would qualify as γλῶτται in the Aristotelian sense.[8] And underlying the whole

[1] For Aeschylus' use of Homeric 'ornamental epithets' cf. pp. 60 f. below.

[2] *C.R.* 12 (1898) 189 f.; cf. Stanford 52; *GGL* 194 n. 1.

[3] Cf. Broadhead 250 f. Björck (158 ff.) discusses with scepticism the question of Ionic borrowings in tragedy in general.

[4] Cf. J. D. Denniston, *The Greek particles* (2nd ed. Oxford 1954) 287 f.; Verrall on *Eum.* 188. The *Persae* has 13 occurrences, *Septem* 1 (862), *Agamemnon* 1 (42), *Choephori* 2 (232 and 1025, both doubtful), and *Eumenides* 2 (188 and 414, one doubtful).

[5] Cf. D. L. Page, *A new chapter in the history of Greek tragedy*, 23 f. and 43 n. 22.

[6] P. 39: cf. also W. J. W. Koster, *Welke is de oudste bewaard gebleven Tragedie?* 25. The word 'probably' begs the question. The discovery of some of the lost plays might well reduce considerably the number of words that could be called 'rare'.

[7] If those words which occur in other plays too are omitted, the gap between *Supplices* and *Persae* is considerably narrowed—*Supplices* 19 or 20, *Persae* 17. θρέομαι, which appears in Earp's list at *Supp.* 112 and *Sept.* 78, is omitted at *Ag.* 1165 and *Choe.* 970; πρόπαρ is recorded for *Supp.* 792 but not for *Ag.* 1019 (προπάροιθ' Tri.), εὖνις for *Pers.* 289 but not for *Choe.* 247 (an emendation) and 794, θελεμός for *Supp.* 1027 but not for *Sept.* 707 (an emendation). ἀρή at *Ag.* 374 is doubtful and is omitted by Earp. But he includes ἐξονοτάζομαι (*Supp.* 10), ἀλυκτός (784), and χάμψα (878) which are emendations, none of them printed by Murray.

[8] *Poetics* 1457b, *Rhet.* 1404b and 1406a.

of the *Supplices* is the contrast between Egypt and Greece, between the outlandish appearance of the Danaids (279 ff.), the barbarity of their cousins and of the Egyptian herald on the one hand, and on the other hand the Hellenic civilization of Argos, and the Hellenic origin of the Danaids.[1] The *Persae*, it is true, takes place in a barbarian land, and all the characters are barbarians, but they are treated with honour and dignity, as worthy opponents of the Greeks themselves. Their foreignness is played down. The ethos of the two plays is thus quite different. It is the *Prometheus* that comes next to the *Supplices* in the number of such γλῶτται, a consideration that should cast doubt on any chronological conclusions.[2]

Many words of foreign origin have been detected in the plays,[3] the most interesting of which for our present purpose are those which may be Sicilian, since it is possible to connect these with the events of Aeschylus' life. Some of these words are allegedly to be found in the *Supplices*, and, if definite proof can be brought, their importance for the dating of the play is obvious.[4] They would suggest that it was written some time after Aeschylus' first visit to Sicily. Unfortunately the number and the years of his visits can never certainly be known.[5] He may have gone for

[1] Thus 6 of the 30 'rare words' in the *Supp.* occur in the herald-scene (825–902). Cf. Lloyd-Jones 361.

[2] Most of these words appear in the lyrics, rather than the dialogue, though the balance is more even in *Oresteia* and *Prometheus*. Clearly much depends on the character of the dialogue and lyric passages, and the relationship between them, in the different plays. Cf. Earp 43 ff.

[3] Cf. Stanford 50 ff.; Kranz 81 f.; E. Harrison, *C.R.* 50 (1936) 11; P. T. Stevens, *C.Q.* 39 (1945) 96; Wolff, *Columbia Diss.* 154.

[4] The possible connection between Sicilian expressions in the *Supplices* and Aeschylus' visits to Sicily was first noticed by A. Boeckh, *Graecae tragoediae principum* (Heidelberg 1808) 50 ff.

[5] For discussion of dates and effect on style etc. cf. esp. von Christ, *Sitz. bay. ak. München* (1888) 371 ff.; J. van Leeuwen, *Mnem.* n.s. 18 (1890) 68 ff.; Haigh 50; Wilamowitz, *Hermes* 32. 394 ff. (he later changed his mind in *Interpr.* 42 n. 1; cf. also 242); Dieterich in *R.-E.* iA. 1067; M. Croiset, *Hist. de la litt. grecque* III (3rd ed. Paris 1913) 178 n. 1; F. Focke, *Hermes* 65 (1930) 259 ff., esp. 288; *GGL* 194 n. 2; J. A. Davison, *TAPhA* 80 (1949) 87 f.; Mazon iv. n. 1; M. Pohlenz, *Die griechische Tragödie* (2nd ed. Göttingen 1954) 84; M. Bock, *Gymnasium* 65 (1958) 402 ff.; Wolff, *Eranos* 57. 15 f.; G. Méautis, *L'authenticité et la date du Prométhée Enchaîné d'Eschyle* (Neuchâtel 1960); Q. Cataudella, *Dioniso* 37 (1963) 5 ff.; A. J. Podlecki, *The political background of Aeschylean tragedy* (Ann Arbor 1966) 5 ff. The eruption of Aetna is generally held to be responsible for *P.V.* 366 ff.

the first time as early as 476 or soon afterwards, 476/5 being the date of the foundation of the city of Aetna, in honour of which Aeschylus wrote his play Αἰτναῖαι.[1] But it is possible that this play was not written until after 472, during the same stay that apparently saw the reproduction at Syracuse of the *Persae*.[2] In any case it is clear that if the *Supplices* displays the effects of Aeschylus' visit to Syracuse it cannot have been written before, at the earliest, 475. The hypothesis indeed is no more than a hypothesis. It cannot be proved that Aeschylus did not use Sicilian expressions before he went to Sicily, as a result perhaps of familiarity with Sicilian literature, for example the work of Epicharmus.[3] But this seems in itself the less likely alternative, and it should not be overlooked that little Sicilian influence has been detected in the *Persae*, and that the majority of Sicilian words are claimed for the *Prometheus* and *Agamemnon*.

Proof of Sicilian origin, however, is difficult to establish. Athenaeus, stating that the word ἀσχέδωρος is Sicilian, reports that Aeschylus used many Sicilian words.[4] W. Aly, in a detailed study, considers seriously no more than 9 examples, and concludes that Athenaeus' statement is untrue.[5] W. B. Stanford disagrees with Aly, and claims to detect between 30 and 40 likely Sicelisms.[6] For most the evidence is very slight. They may for convenience be divided into five rough categories: (1) Those words which are common to Aeschylus and Sicilian writers in the fifth century, but occur also in earlier writers: θῶσθαι,

[1] *Vita* 9. The various ancient explanations of the reason for Aeschylus' visits may be safely discounted.

[2] Σ Ar. *Frogs* 1028; *Vita* 18: cf. chap. 1 p. 20 n. 9 above.

[3] Σ *Eum.* 626 shows that Epicharmus was familiar with the work of Aeschylus.

[4] ix. 402c: ὅτι δὲ Αἰσχύλος διατρίψας ἐν Σικελίᾳ πολλαῖς κέχρηται φωναῖς Σικελικαῖς οὐδὲν θαυμαστόν. Cf. also Σ Ar. *Peace* 73, Macrobius, *Sat.* v. 19. 17, Cic. *Tusc. Disp.* ii. 23. The value of these sources is discussed by Aly and Stanford. For ἀσχέδωρος cf. also Hesych. s.v. ἀσχέδωρος; Eust. 774. 25 and 1872. 3 ff.; Bekker's *Anecd.* 457. 21.

[5] *De Aeschyli copia verborum* (Berlin 1906) 99 f. His 9 examples are κυδάζω, θοάζω (=sit), τί μήν; (=*quidne?*), θῶσθαι, βοῦνις, βαθυχαῖος, ὀβρίκαλα, λέπας, πορπάω.

[6] *Op. cit.* 53 and *Proc. of Royal Irish Acad.* 44 Sec. C (1937–8) 229 ff.; cf. also A. Meillet, *Aperçu d'une histoire de la langue grècque* (Paris 1913) 230; Cataudella 9 f.: *contra* Fraenkel III 712 f.

χλούνης, and μῶμαι.[1] There seems no reason why Aeschylus should have derived these words from Sicily rather than from earlier writers. (2) Words which are common to Aeschylus and Sicilian writers in the fifth century, and which do not occur again: ἀσαλής, ἔμπαιος, θεμερῶπις, πολυνεικής.[2] The possibility of coincidence, strong enough here, is stronger still with words which may be assigned to category (3), words which occur in one particular sense in only Aeschylus and Sicilian writers: ἄμεικτος (=what will not blend or mix), ἁλώσιμον (=of or belonging to capture), ταριχεύω (=wither, waste).[3] The words are common enough with other meanings or shades of meaning, and they are very unlikely to be Sicelisms. (4) Words which occur for the first time, or in one particular sense for the first time, in Aeschylus and Sicilian writers, but appear again later, either in the fifth or in the fourth century, or later: ἄπειρος, κυδάζω, λάμπουρις, λέπαργος, πίστωμα, ποίφυγμα, μακραίων.[4]

[1] θῶσθαι (Alcman fr. 1. 81, Page θωστήρια); Epicharmus fr. 139K; Aesch. Δικτυουλκοί fr. 474. 818 Mette; very doubtfully traced by Aly at *Supp.* 1002. It is a Dorian word according to *Et. Mag.* 461. 1 (cf. Orion 73. 5). χλούνης Hom. *Il.* I. 539; Hes. *Sc.* 168 and 177; Hippon. fr. 64D³; Aesch. fr. 74M; χλοῦνις at *Eum.* 188; Xenoph. fr. 43D (very doubtful); μῶμαι Theognis 771; A. *Choe.* 44 and 441; Soph. *O.C.* 836 and *Trach.* 1136; Pl. *Crat.* 406a; Epich. fr. 117 and perhaps 288; also later writers. The *Suda* says the word is Laconian.

[2] ἀσαλής Aesch. fr. 634 and Sophron fr. 113 (ἀσαλία). ἔμπαιος *Ag.* 187 and doubtful in Emped. fr. 2. 2. θεμερῶπις *P.V.* 134 and Emped. fr. 122. 2. πολυνεικής Stesich. fr. 10A Diehl (included by Page in the Adespota 1014) and *Sept.* 830? (cf. ἀμφινεικῆ *Ag.* 686–7 and S. *Trach.* 104). In Aeschylus the sense is active, in Stesichorus clearly passive.

[3] ἄμεικτος *Ag.* 321 and Emped. fr. 35. 8. Also ἀμεικτότατα (Pl. *Phil.* 59c) seems to have this sense. ἁλώσιμον *Sept.* 635 and *Ag.* 10, and Ibycus fr. 282 (a) 14P. ταριχεύω *Choe.* 296 and Sophron fr. 54K. But it is used by Theophrastus of wood (iv. 2. 2 and v. 4. 3 and 8), and metaphorically in the passive by Dem. xxv. 61 (=stale).

[4] ἄπειρος occurs in both Sophocles (fr. 526) and Euripides (*Or.* 25) in this sense (*Ag.* 1382 and Ibycus fr. 287. 3P). It is very common in other senses, and thus it is exceedingly improbable that one of its meanings can be isolated as Sicilian. κυδάζω Aesch. fr. 141 and Epich. frs. 6 and 35. 6 (also S. *Aj.* 722 and Ap. Rhod. i. 1337). λάμπουρις Aesch. fr. 763 and Lycophron 344, 1393 (λάμπουρος Theocr. viii. 65 and *Epic. Alex. Adesp.* 2. 13 Powell). λέπαργος Aesch. fr. 609 and Theocr. iv. 45 (also Nicander and Eustathius). πίστωμα *Pers.* 171, *Choe.* 977, *Eum.* 214, and Emped. fr. 4 (also Arist. *Rhet.* 1376a 17 and later writers). ποίφυγμα *Sept.* 281 and Sophron apud Σ Nicander, *Ther.* 179 (παιδικὰ ποιφυξεῖς) (cf. Athen. vii. 324f). ποιφύσσω (ποιφύζω) and ποιφυγδήν occur in Hellenistic writers. μακραίων Aesch. fr. 284(a) and Emped. fr. 115. 5. LSJ say the word is doubtful in Aeschylus, but it is now confirmed by *Ox. Pap.* 2257 fr. 4: later at S. *O.T.* 518, 1099; *Aj.* 193, *O.C.* 152, *Ant.* 987.

So far the evidence amounts to nothing like positive proof, and those words which recur soon after Aeschylus in the fifth and fourth centuries are particularly dubious. The three words in category (5) are little more than guesses: αἰανής (=perpetual, long-lasting), λέπας and πορπάω.[1]

There remain some dozen words for which more positive evidence has been brought in proof of Sicilian origin, of which six occur in the *Supplices*: ἀσχέδωρος, Εἰδώ and Ὕψω, ἁρμοῖ, βαλλήν, κρωσσός, ὀβρίκαλα, θοάζω, βοῦνις, βαθυχαῖος, γάϊος, μᾶ, and τί μήν; ἀσχέδωρος has already been noted as Sicilian according to Athenaeus. The forms Εἰδώ and Ὑψώ for Εἰδοθέα and Ὑψιπύλη are at Aesch. frs. 5 and 42, and Stanford argues that they are Sicilian on the analogy of Συρακοῦς for Συρακούσας in Epich. fr. 185, κινώ for κίνησις in Emped. fr. 123. 2, and μορφώ in Archytas (Stob. *Ecl.* i. 41. 2). He admits however that Hesychius classes κινώ as generally Dorian, and notes ἀνθρωπώ as Laconian for γυνή.[2] ἁρμοῖ (*P.V.* 615) is stated to be Syracusan by Herodian Technicus.[3] On the other hand the grammarian at Cramer, *Anecd. Ox.* I. 163. 15 states that it is not Dorian. The word occurs in the -οῖ form also at Theocr. iv. 51, Callim. frs. 274 and 383. 4 Pf. (=*Ox. Pap.* 2173. 4), Lycophron

[1] αἰανής (*Eum.* 572 and 672) Kaibel on S. *El.* 506. In the form αἰηνής it is found at Archil. fr. 38. The word is common in Pindar and Sophocles. Cf. esp. J. A. Schuursma, *De poetica vocabulorum abusione apud Aeschylum* (Amsterdam 1932) 25–6, on the relationship between the two meanings of the word. It is often difficult to determine which is the one intended. Cf. also Aly 7 n. 2. Why Aeschylus should have derived it in the sense διηνεκής from Stesichorus, as Kaibel suggests, it is difficult to understand. The word certainly='long-lasting' at S. *Aj.* 672, Lyc. 928, and *I.G.* ix (1) 886. 2 (later Roman period).

λέπας (*Ag.* 283 and 298; also E. *Phoen.* 24 etc.) Wilamowitz, *Herakles* II. 34–5 (on line 121), arguing that it is used in the proper sense of 'kahle felskuppe' only in Sicily (Ἀκραῖον λέπας near Syracuse—Th. vii. 78) and at Simonides fr. 80. 1 D, and may thus be taken as obsolete in fifth-century Athens. But if Aeschylus borrowed it from Sicily at all, he might be expected to borrow it in the sense in which it was current there. Wilamowitz does not go so far as to say that he did borrow it from Sicily. This is apparently a guess rather of Stanford himself.

πορπάω Wilamowitz 212 (on 959) (*P.V.* 61 and προσπορπατός 142). πόρπη is common in Euripides, and Wilamowitz gives no reason for his guess that πορπάω is Sicilian. πόρπαι occurs in Hom. *Il.* Σ 401 and *hy. Ven.* 163.

[2] Cf. also κερδώ in Pind. *Pyth.* ii. 78, Ar. *Knights* 1068.

[3] *Et. Mag.* 144. 50; Her. Tech. i. 502. 10 (Lentz) and ii. 478. 23; Cramer, *Anecd. Ox.* III. 397. Cf. Meineke *Frag. Poet. Com. Ant.* II. 1. 306–9, and H. van Herwerden, *Lex. gr. Suppl. et Dial.* (Lugduni Batavorum 1910) *s.v.* ἁρμοῖ.

106, and Σ Ap. Rhod. i. 972. It is spelt -ῷ at Pindar fr. 10 Schr. (where Schneidewin reads ἁρμοῖ) and Pherecr. fr. 111 Edmonds. The Hippocratic writings vary between the two spellings. βαλλήν is said to be Thurian by the scholiasts at *Persae* 657 and 658 on the authority of Euphorion. But there is equal authority for its being Phrygian.[1] κρωσσός (Aesch. fr. 44, Erinna 5. 1 Bergk) is claimed to be of Celtic origin, and to have entered Sicily *via* Liguria.[2] ὀβρίκαλα (*Ag.* 143) preserves a diminutive suffix not found elsewhere in Greek except in Sophron's Ἡρύκαλος (fr. 142 K).[3] A trace of the α is perhaps to be seen in the Latin stem *Her-cul-*. The suffix may then be a western one.

Of the *Supplices* examples θοάζω (595; also S. *O.T.* 2, Emped. fr. 3. 8) is thought by Aly to be a Tarentine form; it is a characteristic of that dialect that present stems in -κ- and -τ- + ι̯ω terminate in -ζω, instead of the normal -ττ- or -σσ-.[4] But other dialects too show an interchange of ζ/δδ with σσ/ττ,[5] and some of the ancient authorities are content to call it generally Doric.[6] Epicharmus and Sophron use the form θωκεῖν. The word survives in modern Greek. βοῦνις (117 = 128; cf. 776) is said by Phrynichus, in discussing its use by Philemon of Syracuse, to be a Syracusan word.[7] Herodotus on the other hand says that βουνός was used in Cyrene.[8] Traces of it are to be found in proper names in the Peloponnese,[9] so the word may be generally

[1] Sextus Empiricus 672. 26 (Bekker) (II. 123 Fabricius) and Hesychius. Cf. Aly 18.

[2] J. Vendryes, *Rev. ét. gr.* 32 (1919) 495 ff.

[3] For occasional examples of *-lo-* with diminutive force in Greek cf. C. D. Buck, *Comparative grammar of Greek and Latin* (reprinted Chicago 1962) § 472.

[4] Cf. πλάζω, ἀνάζω, νίζω, μέζω, δοάζω. Cf. G. Kaibel, *Glossarum italioticum* in *Comicorum graecorum fragmenta* I. 1 (Berlin 1899) gloss 145; Eust. 824. 29 and 1654. 26; *Et. Mag.* 605. 43; *Anecd. Ox.* I. 274. 24 and I. 62. 16. θοάσσω is found in M at Hom. *hy. Herm.* 468.

[5] Cf. H. L. Ahrens, *De graecae linguae dialectis* II (Göttingen 1843) 101; Buck, *The Greek dialects* (Chicago 1955) § 84. The reverse process also apparently takes place in Tarentine: φράσσω for φράζω, λακτίσσω for λακτίζω, σαλπίσσω for σαλπίζω. Cf. *Anecd. Ox.* I. 62. 16, Eust. 824. 26 and 1654. 24; A. Thumb, *Handbuch der gr. Dialekte* (Heidelberg 1909) 96.

[6] *Et. Mag.* 104. 13 and 573. 25; cf. 124. 22.

[7] Phryn. ed. Lobeck 355 (and Lobeck's note), Rutherford 459 ff.; Philemon frs. 49 and 142 Edmonds.

[8] iv. 199.

[9] Ἥρα Βουναία at Corinth (Paus. ii. 4. 7); Hesych. Τοξίου βουνός· τοῦ Ἀπόλλωνος τοῦ ἐν Σικυῶνι: cf. Hesych. *s.v.* βουνός· στιβάς. Κύπριοι. For βουνός at Rhodes cf. Collitz and Bechtel, *Sammlung der gr. Dialekt-Inschriften* III. 1 (Göttingen 1899) 3758. 168–9 (early second century B.C.). Cf. Preller–Robert, *Gr. Mythologie* (4th ed.

Dorian. Kaibel suggests that it may have been attributed to the Syracusan dialect solely on the strength of its appearance in Aeschylus and Philemon.[1] γάϊος (*Supp.* 156, 826, and 835, *Sept.* 736, Epich. fr. 42. 9, and perhaps *I.G.* xiv. 1432; cf. Hom. *Il.* N 824) is included by Stanford in his list. *Supp.* 156 and *Sept.* 736 are almost certain emendations, but the passage at *Supp.* 826 ff. is corrupt. Eustathius 188. 30 (cf. Hesych. and *Et. Mag.* 223. 24) says γάϊος παρὰ 'Ιταλιώταις καὶ Ταραντίνοις ὁ μίσθιος. But the word does not appear to have this meaning in Aeschylus. Aly argues that the only parallel for the form βαθυχαῖος (*Supp.* 859) is in the name of the fictitious island of Παγχαία placed by Euhemerus of Messana off the coast of Africa.[2] But the word is the same as the Laconian χάϊος, used by Aristophanes in his parody of Laconian dialect at *Lys.* 90 (cf. 1157).[3] In any case the *Supplices* passage is again corrupt, and no reliance can be placed upon the exact spelling of the word, if indeed it is in place at all (it is at least as early as the scholiast in M). μᾶ (890) is said by the scholiast at Theocr. xv. 89 to be Syracusan.[4] At 892 = 902 Stanford favours the emendation ὦ πᾶ γᾶς παῖ Ζεῦ, which produces yet another Syracusan word.[5] Finally we come to elliptical τί μήν;. This combination occurs nowhere in comedy or in the orators, in Aeschylus at *Supp.* 999, *Ag.* 672 (τί μή F Tri.), and *Eum.* 203, in Sophocles at *Ajax* 668 (τί μή *codd.*), and at *Rhesus* 705.[6] A Sicilian origin would seem to be indicated by its occurrence in the fragments of Epicharmus (149 K) and Sophron (55 K).[7] The expression has proved valuable for the dating of

Berlin 1894) I. 162 n. 1 and 170 n. 1; Hitzig–Bluemner, ed. Paus. I. 2 (Leipzig 1896) 509 f. Eust. 880. 30 says it was disputed whether the word was foreign or not.

[1] Gloss 9.

[2] Cf. Callim. fr. 191. 10 Pf.; Clem. Alex. *protrept.* II. 24 p. 102 Klotz; Diod. v. 42–6; Plut. *Is. and Os.* 23. The form χᾳοῦ is restored by Valckenaer to Alexander of Aetolia (fr. 7 Powell, *Collect. Alex.* Oxford 1925).

[3] Cf. *Suda* s.v. χαΐα (Corinthian); Theocr. vii. 5 (χαῶν) and Σ; Hesych. s.v. χαΐα, 'Αχαία, χάσιος.

[4] Cf. Headlam at Herodas (Cambridge 1922) I. 85. LSJ say μᾶ is Aeolian and Doric

[5] Cf. Orion 136. 15; *Et. Mag.* 651. 7; Eust. 565. 2.

[6] Cf. Denniston 333 f. ('practically equivalent to an emphatic affirmative, "of course"').

[7] The equivalent in Megarian conversational Doric is apparently σά μάν; (Ar. *Ach.* 757 and 784). τί μήν;, emphasizing a question, occurs twice in Soph. (*El.* 1280 and *O.C.* 1468) and at *Rhesus* 706 and 955.

the dialogues of Plato, since it appears only in those dialogues that are thought to be written after Plato's first journey to Sicily.[1] But the use of the combination by Sophocles makes it difficult to accept it unhesitatingly as a Sicilian word. Would Sophocles borrow such a foreign expression from Aeschylus? It is by no means the only word in the list we have been considering to be shared by Aeschylus and Sophocles. But it is perhaps easier to suppose that Sophocles would take over a useful noun or adjective than borrow on a single occasion an interrogative expression like τί μήν;

Thus out of all the suggested words not one can definitely be proved to be Sicilian. The occurrence of a word in only Aeschylus and a Sicilian writer is not in itself enough to show that that word is Sicilian; at most it can suggest the possibility. The language of Sicilian writers may not in itself be pure Sicilian.[2] And even when there is some ancient testimony to Sicilian origin, we can never be sure that the word in question is exclusively Sicilian and not, as for example in the case of βοῦνις, common to other Doric dialects. This does not necessarily prove that Athenaeus' statement[3] is false. It is only the supporting evidence, and an adequate number of surviving plays, that is lacking. Nevertheless we are not after all entitled to use these words in the *Supplices* as evidence for the date of the play, unless perhaps some weight may be given to the consideration that very few members of the list occur in *Persae* and *Septem*, and these among the least probable (*Persae* βαλλήν and πίστωμα; *Septem* ἁλώσιμος, γάϊος, πολυνεικής and ποίφυγμα). The cumulative value of six more or less possible Sicilian words in the *Supplices* is perhaps not entirely to be ignored.

The use of particles, which has proved so valuable for the dating of Plato's dialogues, is by no means so helpful when it comes to Aeschylus, largely no doubt because there is in his case so much less material with which to work.[4] Denniston finds that on the whole there is a greater variety of particles in the later

[1] Cf. W. Dittenberger, *Hermes* 16. 323 ff.; C. Ritter, *Untersuch. über Plato* 12.
[2] Cf. F. Bechtel, *Gr. Dialekte* II (Berlin 1923) 213.
[3] Cf. p. 50 above.
[4] Cf. Denniston lxi n. 1 and lxvi ff.

plays than in the earlier. That is, the *Oresteia* and *Prometheus* differ in a number of usages from the other plays, and some of these usages are shared also by the *Septem*.[1] Denniston suggests that these particles and combinations were coming into use towards the end of Aeschylus' life. Conversely δῆτα with an echoed word or thought occurs only in *Supplices*, *Persae*, and *Septem*, while θήν and δῆθεν are confined to the *Prometheus* (unless δῆθεν is to be read at *Septem* 247). As usual the distinction is not between the *Supplices* and the rest, but between the trilogy and *Prometheus* on the one hand, and the remaining plays on the other, with the *Septem* showing one or two signs of development.[2] In one respect the *Supplices* stands almost alone, namely in the rarity of postponed δέ.[3] Denniston gives only one example from the *Supplices*, 5 from the *Persae*, 7 from *Septem*, 8 from *Agamemnon*, 4 from *Choephori*, 8 from *Eumenides*, and none from *Prometheus*.

Various colloquial expressions have been detected, but their frequency seems to bear no relation to the chronology of the plays.[4] Most of them are to be found in *Choephori* and *Prometheus*, and the dramatic purpose is plainly the determining factor, at least in the former play. Wilamowitz thought it possible[5] to see in the herald scene of the *Supplices* a survival of the λέξις γελοία that must have characterized tragedy when it was still in its 'satyric stage', according to the Aristotelian theory.[6] But the text (825 ff). is much too corrupt to permit any such conclusion.[7] Moreover it is difficult to accept that there is any room for burlesque in this the most exciting climax of the play. In fact the

[1] ἦ μήν, μέντοι, ἀλλ' οὖν, δ' οὖν. *Supplices* (347) and *Persae* (386) join in with γε μέντοι.

[2] For ἠδέ in the *Persae* cf. p. 48 above.

[3] Cf. Denniston 187 ff.

[4] Cf. Stevens 95 ff. οὗτος in the vocative (*Supp.* 911) occurs nowhere else in Aeschylus. With 46 occurrences in Aristophanes it clearly belongs to comedy (13 times in Sophocles and Euripides); cf. T. Wendel, *Die Gesprächsanrede im gr. Epos und Drama der Blütezeit* (Stuttgart 1929) 115.

[5] *N. Jbb.* 29 (1912) 469 (=*Kl. Schr.* I. 373 f.), and *Interpr.* 240; cf. also P. Friedländer, *Die Antike* I (1925) 11; J. Lammers, *Die Doppel- und Halbchöre in der antiken Tragödie* (Paderborn 1931) 31; Kranz, *Stasimon* 4; J. T. Kakridis, *Hellenika* 13 (1954) 166.

[6] Cf. chap. III p. 98.

[7] More corrupt, it is true, in the Herald's words than in the Danaids'.

language seems no more 'satyric' than that of the Furies in the *Eumenides*, for example at 117 ff. and 254 ff., passages which Wilamowitz himself quotes. The language is characteristic not of the satyr-play but of the barbarian who utters it. It serves once more to emphasize the contrast between Greece and Egypt.[1]

For ancient and modern critics alike the most outstanding characteristic of Aeschylus' style is undoubtedly its ὄγκος, the luxuriance, boldness, exuberance, and grandiloquence, and often the apparent unintelligibility, that is effected partly by the diction itself—long compound words, many evidently of Aeschylus' own invention—and partly by the use of circumlocution and redundance.[2] At its simplest level, the use of two words where one would apparently suffice (e.g. *Supp.* 951, *Pers.* 5, *Ag.* 315), or the statement of an idea in both its positive and its negative aspects (e.g. *Supp.* 975 f., *Pers.* 392 ff., *Ag.* 663) it would be impossible to measure significant variations from play to play. At any rate no such variations are revealed by B. G. Freymuth in his detailed study of the question.[3] Occasionally, in the use of 'kennings', a circumlocution seems to be of folk-origin (*Supp.* 510, *Pers.* 577 f., 612). It is, however, the compounds that provide the greater part of the Aeschylean ὄγκος,[4] and it is here that the *Supplices* is held to differ from the other plays.

If the *Supplices* were the only extant play of Aeschylus, the popular impression of his style would be almost justified; for in parts of that play the various forms of ὄγκος are not laid on with the brush, but spread with a trowel, and very little of the surface escapes. We find here all the qualities parodied by Aristophanes in the *Frogs*, especially the piling up of mouth-filling words; and, what is more important, the strained language here seems often to be used for its own sake,

[1] Cf. W. Nestle, *Gnomon* 10. 408 ff. and 413 ff.; Peretti, *Epirrema e tragedia* 87 ff.

[2] Cf. Ar. *Frogs* 923 ff.; and, among modern authors, especially Haigh 80 ff.; *GGL* 153 f. and 295; Kumaniecki 39 f.; J. Seewald, *Untersuch. zu Stil und Komposition der Aisch. Tragödie* (Greifswald 1936); Earp, *op. cit.*

[3] *Tautologie und Abundanz bei A.* (Diss. Berlin 1939); cf. also Schmid, *Gefess. Prom.* 55.

[4] That Aeschylus uses proportionately more compound nouns and adjectives than Sophocles and Euripides is shown by D. M. Clay, *A formal analysis of the vocabularies of Aeschylus, Sophocles and Euripides* part 1 (Minneapolis 1960) 50 f. and 103. Cf. also the table of percentages on p. 153.

as a trick of style intended merely to lend ὄγκος, and does not add so much to the meaning as it usually does elsewhere in Aeschylus.[1]

And elsewhere Earp talks of the 'touch of youthful luxuriance' in the style of the *Supplices*.[2] It is easy enough to arrive at a subjective impression of this kind, much more difficult to prove it by a detailed study of the plays. Whether Earp has provided adequate proof of his case is crucial for the present inquiry.

Examination of the compounds in isolation is not very fruitful. Omitting those which he thinks are hardly felt as compounds at all, Earp arrives at the following results:[3] *Supplices* 1 in 7·6 lines (dialogue), 1 in 4·7 (lyric); *Persae* 1 in 9·8 and 1 in 4·6; *Septem* 1 in 5·7 and 1 in 3·8; *Prometheus* 1 in 7·04 and 1 in 6·3; *Agamemnon* 1 in 8·2 and 1 in 4·8; *Choephori* 1 in 10·6 and 1 in 6·5; *Eumenides* 1 in 7·5 and 1 in 6·8. 'It is clear', says Earp, 'that the proportion of such words is no sure clue to the date of a play.' He goes on to analyse the proportion of compounds which are either ἅπαξ λεγόμενα or peculiar in classical Greek to Aeschylus. Of neologisms in general Aeschylus was undoubtedly a prodigious creator. Some 1,100 have been counted in the seven plays and fragments, compared with only 800 from all the plays of Euripides.[4] There is no *a priori* reason why Aeschylus should have been given to coining words at one period of his life rather than at another. And the same is true of words which occur in one play only of the seven. Of these Schmid counts no fewer than 3,509, made up of *Supplices* 461, *Persae* 474, *Septem* 444, *Agamemnon* 782, *Choephori* 387, *Eumenides* 329, and *Prometheus* 632.[5] Whatever conclusions this may suggest about the *Prometheus*, there is

[1] Earp 63. Cited with approval by Koster 25. Schmid is less sweeping (*GGL* 295): 'Denn Schwerverständlichkeit ist ihm, *zumal in den vier älteren Stücken*, Forderung des tragischen Stils, der die Heroenwelt auch auf diese Art von den Gegenwartsmenschen abhebt.' (My italics.) Stanford (*A. in his style* 138) finds the height of the elevated style in the *Septem*.

[2] Cf. p. 30 n. 4 above.

[3] Pp. 6 f. A full analysis of the compounds of the tragedians is given by Miss Clay, *op. cit.* Her classified lists were published separately as part II of her Dissertation (Athens 1958).

[4] Cf. W. Breitenbach, *Untersuch. zur Sprache der Euripideischen Lyrik* (Stuttgart 1934) 117; *GGL* 290 n. 7; Kumaniecki 17 ff. Stanford (61) quotes a figure of 1,100 for the six plays excluding the *P.V.*

[5] *Gefess. Prom.* 43 ff.

clearly nothing abnormal about the *Supplices*.[1] If we had more plays these numbers would doubtless be proportionately reduced.[2] Over 50 words are found only in *Supplices* and *Persae*. Thus the loss of the *Persae* would add these 50 to the list of those which appear only in the *Supplices*.[3] Where chance plays so large a part, it would be foolish to pursue the matter further.

The proportion of ἅπαξ λεγόμενα (and words peculiar in classical Greek to Aeschylus) to the total compounds in Earp's list of compounds does little to strengthen his case. His table is as follows:[4]

	Dialogue (%)	Lyrics (%)
Supplices	40	42
Persae	32	42
Septem	25	49
Prometheus	40	60
Agamemnon	45	63
Choephori	31	64
Eumenides	39	66

The *Supplices* indeed is unique in that the proportion is almost the same in dialogue and lyric. On the other hand *Persae*, *Choephori*, and above all *Septem* fall far below the others in the ratio for dialogue. In general the *Oresteia* and *Prometheus* show a greater boldness than the earlier plays, but among the latter the *Supplices* is no less bold than the others. The figures for Dialogue and Lyric taken together give us: *Supplices* 43 %, *Persae* 44 %, *Septem* 40 %, *Prometheus* 46 %, *Agamemnon* 56 %, *Choephori* 47 %, and *Eumenides* 50 %. Finally Earp examines the nature of the compounds, and finds that the later plays contain a greater

[1] In fact, when reduced to 'characteristic' words, Schmid's figures place the *Supplices* beside *Choephori* and *Eumenides* (*Supp.* 250 in 1,074 lines, i.e. 23·2 %, *Pers.* 29·1 %, *Sept.* 28·9 %, *Ag.* 31·2 %, *Choe.* 23·1 %, *Eum.* 22·1 %, *P.V.* 36·1 %).

[2] Not increased, as *GGL* strangely implies (290 n. 6).

[3] Cf. Peretti, *Studi ital.* 5. 195 f.

[4] P. 9. Some of his calculations are incorrect. *Supplices* (Lyric) should read 45 %, *Persae* (Dialogue) 33 %, *Persae* (Lyric) 50 %, *Prometheus* (Dialogue) 39 %, *Prometheus* (Lyric) 63 %, *Choephori* (Dialogue) 30 %.

number of more striking compounds, the *Septem* being in this respect much closer to the *Agamemnon* than to the *Supplices*. But the theory is weakened by the fact that the *Persae* turns out to have almost as great a proportion of bold and striking words as does the *Agamemnon*, 'though the *Persae* is undoubtedly an early play'.[1] A final distinction between the *Oresteia* and the earlier plays is that in the former many of the compounds 'describe not external qualities, but mental states or emotions, or actions of some kind. They are in fact more active and vital; and in accord with that their formation is much more varied. There are fewer compounds with the familiar φίλο-, πολύ- etc.'[2] This seems true as far as it goes, but it says nothing about the relationship of *Supplices* to *Persae* and *Septem*. In fact if one examines among the total compounds those formed with φιλο-, πᾶς, and πολυ-, the *Septem* has the greatest number with 41 (*Supp.* 35, *Pers.* 34, *P.V.* 15, *Ag.* 28, *Choe.* 24, and *Eum.* 16). Aeschylus seems reluctant at all times to use such simple words as εἷς, δύο, μόνος, ἀγαθός, νέος, preferring compounds formed with μονο-, δι-, εὐ-, νεο-, πάλαι, etc.[3]

There are surprisingly few purely ornamental epithets in Aeschylus. Naturally one does not expect the 'standing' epithets that are the mark of the formulaic style of Homer, yet it is too easy to form the impression that Aeschylus often uses adjectives that add little or nothing to their context. But the numbers in Earp's lists are small.[4] The *Persae* has by far the most with 26 (no fewer than 15 of them typically Homeric),[5] the *Supplices* 15, *Prometheus* 10, *Agamemnon* 8, *Septem* 8, *Choephori* and *Eumenides* 4 each. It is doubtful whether some of these epithets

[1] P. 15. Earp's examination is limited to the first 50 compounds in the lyrics of each play, that is to say it is not a genuine random sample. For some reason only 48 compounds are taken from the *Agamemnon* instead of 50, and πολυάνωρ (line 62) is omitted. It is not true to say with Earp (14) that the words taken from the *Agamemnon* are more polysyllabic than those from the *Supplices*. The latter include 29 with 4 syllables and 17 with 5, the former 27 with 4 syllables and only 9 with 5.

[2] P. 16.

[3] Cf. Seewald 30 f. Peretti, *Studi. ital.* 5. 199 should also be consulted.

[4] Pp. 54 ff.; cf. also Bergson, *op. cit.*; *GGL* 294 f.

[5] Cf. Bergson 152. In general Aeschylus is more daring than either Sophocles or Euripides in giving a non-ornamental value to the epithets he borrows from Homer (Bergson 101 ff.).

are to be considered as ornamental at all. At *Supplices* 301 for instance βουθόρῳ is highly relevant to Zeus's disguise and behaviour as a bull on this occasion, relevant also to the whole motif of Io running through the play. At 432 πολυμίτων serves to point the contrast between the roughness of the male abductor and the soft femininity of the Danaids.[1] Similarly in the *Persae* the many apparently ornamental adjectives that occur in the opening anapaests, while superfluous if taken in isolation with their individual nouns, yet all contribute to a general picture of the luxury and magnificence of the Persian empire.[2] Nevertheless it is interesting that the *Persae* once more stands on its own. The reason cannot be merely that it is an early play. Much must depend on the subject-matter and the dramatic purpose. There is less room for conventional ornament (as Earp points out) where the dramatic tension is strong, where intense emotion is to be aroused. There is thus less room for it in the *Oresteia*. Yet it is perhaps too simple to say with Earp[3] 'that Aeschylus in his later work avoids this form of ornament, or that he has in the *Oresteia* used a dramatic method which renders it superfluous'. The correct question is posed by Bergson:[4] 'le poète peut-il, vers la fin (ou vers le début) de sa carrière littéraire, avoir écrit une tragédie ayant un caractère dramatique tel que l'emploi des epitheta ornantia y soit si fréquent (ou si rare)?' In face of the paucity of the remains of Aeschylus' plays, it is a question that cannot be answered.

The *Persae* contains the greatest number of ornamental adjectives, but it is the language of the *Supplices* that Earp finds most strained, 'a trick of style intended merely to lend ὄγκος'. He tries to demonstrate this thesis in a survey of the first 100 lines of the play.[5] Thus 'In ll. 21–2, ἐγχειριδίοις ἐριοστέπτοισι κλάδοισιν, we have two epithets, one of five and the other of six syllables, of which only the second adds much to the sense'. But the normal meaning of ἐγχειρίδια is 'daggers', and it is by no

[1] Cf. Wolff, *Columbia Diss.* 165.

[2] That is, they fall into Bergson's second category of epithets, those which are in themselves superfluous, but give the principal word a nuance justified by the context (17).

[3] P. 59.

[4] P. 175.

[5] Pp. 63 ff.; cf. also Koster 25.

means irrelevant to provide by a momentary ambiguity this hint of the violent side of the Danaids' character at the beginning of the play.[1] A similar ambiguity is to be found in αὐτογενεῖ φυξανορίᾳ, if the conjecture is correct at line 8. Earp complains, 'In ll. 6–7 οὔτιν' ἐφ' αἵματι δημηλασίαν ψήφῳ πόλεως γνωσθεῖσαν is a strained way of saying "we have not been banished for homicide"; and in the next line αὐτογενεῖ φυξανορίᾳ is a still more strained expression of the thought. Not only are the two compounds unique in classical Greek, but both are ambiguous and their precise meaning can only be gathered from the context.' But might not the ambiguity be deliberate? The surface meaning is clear enough from the previous lines, with φυξανορίᾳ balancing δημηλασίαν, and αὐτογενεῖ balancing ψήφῳ πόλεως γνωσθεῖσαι. But there is also a slight suggestion in φυξανορίᾳ that the Danaids are running away from men,[2] a suggestion that is strengthened by the following lines, γάμον Αἰγύπτου παίδων ἀσεβῆ τ' ὀνοταζόμεναι ⟨διάνοιαν⟩, and we shall see in chapter v that Aeschylus (at least in the first play of the trilogy) never makes it entirely clear whether they are opposed to marriage in general, or merely to the particular marriage with their cousins.[3] Since it would have been so easy for him to avoid it if he had wished, this vagueness seems to be intentional, and here the ambiguity is introduced at the very beginning of the play.[4] Earp objects also to ἀρσενοπληθῆ δ' ἑσμὸν ὑβριστὴν Αἰγυπτογενῆ (29 f.). But every epithet and both parts of both compounds have something to add to the sense. The cousins are male, they are numerous, indeed they are a swarm, they are arrogant, and they are the sons of Aegyptus. Nothing is superfluous. It may be that 'one purpose at least of

[1] Cf. Tucker, n. *ad loc.*; Porzig 152; O. Hiltbrunner, *Wiederholungs- und Motivtechnik bei Aischylos* (Gött. Diss. Berne 1950) 33; Wolff, *Columbia Diss.* 86; R. D. Murray, *The motif of Io in Aeschylus' Suppliants* (Princeton 1958) 79. Cf. also R. P. Winnington-Ingram, *J.H.S.* 61 (1961) 148, who suggests that the Chorus of the Δαναΐδες entered carrying real daggers.

[2] Cf. K. von Fritz, *Philol.* 91 (1936) 123 (= *Antike und moderne Tragödie* (Berlin 1962) 161); Winnington-Ingram 143 n. 15.

[3] Cf. pp. 221 ff. below.

[4] Cf. the ambiguous οἰχομένων in the first line of the *Persae*, described by Stanford (36) as the first example of 'delayed-action' ambiguity in extant Aeschylus.

such things is to give ὄγκος', but it is not the only or even the primary purpose. Earp has the same complaint to make of the first passage of dialogue. At 180 it is no doubt true that κόνιν, ἄναυδον ἄγγελον στρατοῦ is a conceit, but almost the same words recur at *Septem* 81–2, so the phrase can hardly be taken as evidence for the uniqueness of the *Supplices*. Certainly much strained language could be found in the play, but the same is true of all the plays. Whether or not the *Supplices* has more of it than the others could be demonstrated only by a full comparison of all seven plays, and this comparison Earp has not carried out. It is doubtful indeed if it could be, since what strikes one reader as strained might well appear natural or effective to another, and since the 'superfluity' of any epithet can almost always be disputed. But without such a comparison there is no justification for the statement that 'from all this it is clear that the style of the *Supplices* stands alone'. It is pointless to compare with *Supplices* 176 ff. the passage at *Persae* 176 ff. in which Atossa describes her dream. The sententious advice of Danaus to his daughters demands a style as different from the straightforward narrative of Atossa, as a speech of Nestor in the *Iliad* (e.g. the advice to Antilochus at Ψ 306) is different from a passage of epic narrative. There are few occasions for straightforward narrative in the *Supplices*, but the speech of Pelasgus beginning at line 249 is simple and straightforward enough. Conversely the banal sententious remarks of Atossa at *Persae* 598 ff. are clothed in tragic ὄγκος.[1] The truth seems to be that Aeschylus can write in two styles, one simple and direct, the other full of tragic grandiloquence.[2] And whether he employs one or the other is dependent upon the nature of his subject-matter and the character of the person who is speaking. Both styles are to be found in all the plays. Iambic passages lend themselves more readily to the simple style, lyric passages to ὄγκος, but the distinction is by no means clear-cut.

Earp's view is that in the *Supplices* Aeschylus used ὄγκος for its

[1] Cf. also the language which clothes the conventional sentiments at *Eumenides* 526 ff.

[2] Cf. Pohlenz 140. For a useful study of the whole subject see Seewald, *op. cit.*

own sake, that is it little more than a mannerism. It seems more satisfactory to see it as the effect than as the goal of Aeschylus' style. Ὄγκος for its own sake is the same thing as bombast, and one hesitates to charge Aeschylus with descending to that in the *Supplices*. Rather the Aeschylean ὄγκος is the effect of his peculiar method of compression. He sees in many aspects and from many points of view the picture or the idea that he wants to describe, and everything is set down just as it occurs to his imagination. Thus it is misleading to confine one's examination to each epithet in isolation. Each complex of words must be taken as a whole, since into it Aeschylus crowds the sum of the associations which present themselves to his imagination. This is why we have such rows of piled-up adjectives (e.g. *Supp.* 794 ff., *Pers.* 635 f. and 854 f., *Ag.* 193 ff.), such linking of phrase with phrase by apposition and use of participles (e.g. *Ag.* 184 ff., 109 ff., 40 ff.). Syntax withdraws and with it the need for intellectual understanding of the progress of the thought. It is to the imagination and not to the intellect that this style of Aeschylus appeals.[1]

The same point must be borne in mind when we turn to the imagery of Aeschylus. For there we find that simile, with its more consciously worked-out parallelism, its greater explicitness and precision, is very much rarer than metaphor.[2] And such similes as occur are on the whole brief and undeveloped, in contrast with those of Homer. The longest are to be found in *Supplices* (60 ff. and 350 ff.) and *Agamemnon* (49 ff.). With only three similes in all (128, 424 ff., and 745) the *Persae* is easily the poorest of all the plays. Earp's lists provide the figures:[3] *Persae* 3, *Septem* 10, *Supplices* 11, *Prometheus* 6, *Agamemnon* 27, *Choephori* 10, and *Eumenides* 9. The later plays also display rather more variety in the conjunctions which introduce the similes, the earlier plays being content in general with ὡς. δίκην is particularly common in the *Agamemnon*, where it occurs 14 times

[1] Cf. Seewald 13 ff.; also Haigh 83; Pohlenz 138 f.; van Otterlo 115 f., 132 f., 143; Earp, *G. & R.* 22. 121.

[2] Cf. W. Pecz, *N. Jbb.* 29 (1912) 668; Stanford 21; *GGL* 292 n. 5, and 294.

[3] Pp. 121 ff. These are Earp's figures. His lists in fact give 10 similes for *Supp.* and 12 for *Choe.* He omits *Ag.* 724. *Supp.* 60 ff. does not appear in Earp's list, but although there is no conventional formula of introduction surely it is to be taken as a simile (cf. δοξάσει and τὼς καὶ ἐγώ...).

(*Choe.* 4, *Eum.* 4, *Supp.* and *Sept.* 1 each). There are no examples in *Persae* or *Prometheus*.[1]

The favourite figure of Aeschylus is the metaphor.[2] Sometimes he piles them on top of one another, as he does with his epithets, or mixes them in inextricable confusion (e.g. *Supp.* 86 ff. and 466 ff., *Sept.* 599 ff., *Ag.* 896 ff. and 1031 ff.). Again the appeal is to the imagination rather than to the intellect. It is the richness of the effect, and not the logical consistency, that matters. As with its similes the *Persae* is the poorest of all the plays in metaphor, and the *Agamemnon* is the richest. This suggests that Aeschylus used metaphor with greater frequency in his later work. But the other two members of the trilogy do not fit quite so easily into the pattern. One estimate is that the *Persae* has 1 image for every 16·5 lines, *Eumenides* 1 for 15·6, *Septem* 1 for 14·4, *Choephori* 1 for 14·1, *Supplices* and *Prometheus* 1 for 10·9, and *Agamemnon* 1 for 8·4.[3] It is at least interesting to find the *Supplices* so near the *Agamemnon*, with the *Persae* lagging behind. Earp's figures for metaphor are useful in that he treats separately those which are particularly striking. His findings are as follows:[4]

[1] Slightly different are the figures of H. Mielke, *Die Bildersprache des Aischylos* (Diss. Breslau 1934) 150; of H. G. Robertson, *Cl. Phil.* 34 (1939) 219 n. 8; and of Peretti, *Studi ital.* 5. 210.

[2] For Aeschylus' metaphors cf. esp. J. T. Lees, *Studies in honor of B. L. Gildersleeve* (Baltimore 1902) 483 ff.; *GGL* 292 ff.; Mielke, *op. cit.*; J. Dumortier, *Les images dans la poésie d'Eschyle* (Paris 1935); Stanford 86 ff.; Earp 93 ff. Metaphor here includes its related forms, such as metonymy, synecdoche, and personification. All study of metaphor is complicated by uncertainty as to whether any particular word would be felt by a hearer as figurative or allusive. 'Faded' metaphors are an essential part of everyday speech, but they can be given new life by a poet. At the same time one must resist the temptation of assuming that every word has a single literal English equation, and that all other meanings must in consequence be figurative. It is such considerations as these that make imagery less amenable to counting than any other stylistic feature.

A useful study of Greek metaphor is by W. B. Stanford, *Greek metaphor* (Oxford 1936). Much valuable theory is contained in the last chapter of R. F. Goheen's *The imagery of Sophocles' Antigone* (Princeton 1951), a book which refers usefully to modern studies in English style.

[3] Mielke 5.

[4] P. 97. Earp's heading 'Usual' for the left-hand column is misleading. His list in fact gives 90 metaphors for *Supp.* (40 Striking), 73 for *Pers.*, 92 for *Sept.*, and 218 for *Ag.* 83 for the *Sept.* is evidently a misprint for 93 (cf. p. 121). The danger inherent in a subjective judgement is again obvious (cf. p. 48 n. 6 above).

	Total	Striking
Supplices	91	41
Persae	72	26
Septem	93	44
Prometheus	110	47
Agamemnon	222	144
Choephori	105	63
Eumenides	72	40

From the figures the *Oresteia* and the *Prometheus* are evidently bolder than the other plays in their use of metaphor, while the *Persae* is by far the most restrained.

Aeschylus draws his metaphors from a wide variety of sources, from arts and crafts, from the human body and mind, from human pleasures, from the realm of nature, the animal and vegetable worlds and the elements of wind, fire, storm, etc.[1] As one would expect there are variations from play to play, but none of these seems particularly significant. Earp claims to trace a certain chronological development, but the figures in his table[2] are too small for any reliable conclusions. However it is worth observing that as far as they go they do not support an early date for the *Supplices*. 'Naval and Agricultural metaphors', Earp says, 'grow somewhat less common in the later plays, and so even more clearly do metaphors from the sea.' But his figures for sea metaphors are *Supplices* 2, *Persae* 4, *Septem* 6, *Prometheus* 5, *Agamemnon* 1, *Choephori* 1, and *Eumenides* 1, so that the *Supplices* is in this respect closest to the *Oresteia*. The joint totals for naval and agricultural metaphors are *Supplices* 10, *Persae* 5, *Septem* 12, *Prometheus* 5, *Agamemnon* 12, *Choephori* 5, and *Eumenides* 9. Again

[1] Cf. esp. Lees, *op. cit.* The use of legal expressions in Aeschylus is dealt with by H. G. Robertson, *op. cit.*; that of medical vocabulary by J. Dumortier, *Le vocabulaire médical d'Eschyle et les écrits hippocratiques* (Paris 1935); B. H. Fowler, *A.J.Ph.* 78 (1957) 173 ff. Medical metaphors are virtually confined to *P.V.* and *Oresteia* (but cf. *Supp.* 268 and 367) and Dumortier finds at *Supp.* 857 a trace of the outmoded idea of blood as the principle of life (cf. *Sept.* 141–2), whereas, he says, the *Oresteia* is much more in touch with current medical theory: cf. also Stanford 54 ff. For Aeschylus' maritime imagery see D. van Nes, *Die maritime Bildersprache des Aischylos* (Groningen 1963).

[2] P. 104.

Earp says that 'metaphors from Animals are decidedly more frequent in the later plays'. But the *Supplices* stands between the *Septem* and the *Oresteia* (*Supp.* 5, *Pers.* 1, *Sept.* 4, *P.V.* 5, *Ag.* 16, *Choe.* 12, *Eum.* 8). This kind of analysis is not a very profitable one, since here if anywhere variations might be expected to depend not upon the date of the play but upon its subject-matter, and upon the symbols which serve most effectively to present it. If animal metaphors are particularly appropriate to the *Oresteia*, this does not mean that Aeschylus throughout his life gradually became more and more interested in animals, or that his interest in the sea gradually waned. Earp, it is true, tries to find a principle at work in this matter of development. In the earlier plays, he holds, metaphor serves generally to describe external things, while in the later it is employed to describe the effect of an object on the mind, or to describe states of mind. An examination of his lists reveals that there are more of the latter kind in the *Supplices* than in the *Persae* or the *Septem* (e.g. *Supp.* 12, 93, 186 f., 409, 438, 466, 467, 470 f., 563 f., 929). The only safe conclusion is that of Mielke:[1]

Zur Frage der Chronologie der einzelnen Dramen ist die Bildersprache des Aischylos ohne Bedeutung. Eine Entwicklung läßt sich weder hinsichtlich der Zahl der Bilder, noch ihrer Form, noch ihres Gegenstandes erkennen. Alle Unterschiede dieser Art sind, wie schon betont wurde, an den Charakter der einzelnen Werke gebunden. Nicht einmal die H. (*Supplices*), in mancher Hinsicht als Frühwerk erweisbar, zeigen in der Bildersprache den anderen Dramen gegenüber unentwickelte Formen.

Many of the metaphors which recur from play to play are just those which can be applied to very varying situations and contexts, metaphors derived from light and darkness, yokes, storms, etc.[2] But sometimes a metaphor is peculiarly appropriate to the theme of one particular play. Thus the image of weighing in the scales, which occurs five times in the *Supplices* (403, 405, 605, 822 f., 982), while common in the other plays (except the *P.V.*), is obviously appropriate in the context of the decision which the people of Argos must make. Similarly legal expressions naturally

[1] P. 160. [2] *Ibid.* 145 ff.

occur most often in the *Eumenides*, least often in *Persae*, *Septem*, and *Prometheus*.[1] When therefore one finds in the *Septem* a large number of metaphors derived from the sea, from storm and from sailing, the reason is not that in 467 B.C. Aeschylus had suddenly become interested in the sea, but that the subject of the play lends itself to the ship-of-state metaphor, one foreshadowed already in Alcaeus. And this suggests a more fruitful method of study of the metaphors of Aeschylus. Perhaps their most interesting feature is the way in which the same image recurs frequently in the same play, so that it becomes the dominant image of that play.[2] The highest development is to be seen in the *Oresteia*, though there we find not so much a single dominant image as a series of interlocking images and symbols, what has been well termed by Lattimore a 'complex of symbols'—the curb, the yoke, the snare, the snake, light and darkness, etc. 'Cut anywhere into the play, and you will find such a nexus of intercrossing motives and properties. The system gives the play its inner dimension and strength.'[3] What is symbol at one point in the play is the real thing at another, there is no clear-cut division between them. Literal and figurative language are inextricably intertwined. 'Es zeigt sich, daß das Bild für den Dichter nicht ein nur mit der Realität verwandtes Symbol ist, sondern daß für seinen Blick eine letzte Einheit vorhanden ist, die ihren Ausdruck findet in der genannten Vertauschung der Bildsphären.'[4] Thus the net image of the *Agamemnon* becomes the literal cloak in which the king is entangled by his wife. The

[1] Cf. Robertson 217 f.

[2] This characteristic of Aeschylus' style was first pointed out by Headlam, *C.R.* 16 (1902) 434 ff.: cf. esp. Mielke, *op. cit.*; Dumortier, *Images*; Stanford 96 ff.; Hiltbrunner, *op. cit.*; introduction by R. Lattimore to Grene and Lattimore, *The complete Greek tragedies. Oresteia* (Chicago 1953) 15–18; Fowler, *op. cit.*; van Nes, esp. 75 ff.; J. J. Peradotto, *A.J.Ph.* 85 (1964) 378 ff.: also E. Neustadt, *Hermes* 64 (1929) 243 ff.; G. Thomson, ed. *Prometheus* (Cambridge 1932) 16; Kranz 39 and 276. For the *Supplices* in particular see R. D. Murray, *op. cit.*; also J. T. Sheppard, *C.Q.* 5 (1911) 220 ff.; Wolff, *Eranos* 57. 17, and *Columbia Diss.* 85, 155, and 166 ff.; L. Aylen, in *Classical drama and its influence*. Essays presented to H. D. F. Kitto (London 1965) 94 ff. (cf. also *Greek tragedy and the modern world* (London 1964) 35 ff.).

[3] Lattimore, *loc. cit.*

[4] Mielke 152. So one finds a remarkable confusion of image and reality at *Supplices* 530 (τὴν μελανόζυγ' ἄταν).

motif of light takes visible form in the beacon that announces the fall of Troy. Often the same symbol serves to connect two different subjects or situations. The net which first encircled Troy (*Ag.* 357 ff.) is the same as that which destroys Agamemnon. At *Choephori* 249 the snake is Clytaemestra, the murderer of her husband, at 543 ff. and 928 it becomes Orestes, who is about to murder his mother, and at 1050 it is transferred to the Furies. The other plays display the same technique, but in a somewhat less developed form. A single image tends to be the dominant one. In the *Persae* it is the image of the yoke, introduced near the beginning of the play (49–50).[1] In the *Septem* the principal image is that of a ship at sea, introduced, as in the *Persae*, at the beginning of the play (2–3), and finding its fullest development at 758 ff. Along with other, minor, images and ideas this is recapitulated at 792 ff.,[2] just as in the *Agamemnon* the image of the net is resumed at 1611. In the *Prometheus* the image of Prometheus as the proud and wayward horse is developed to its most complete statement at 1009 ff., while another important metaphor is that of Prometheus as a sick man in need of healing.[3]

Where does the *Supplices* stand in all this? The technique of recurring imagery and recurring motifs, so characteristic of Aeschylus' style, might reasonably be seen as the product of his maturity. In an early play we should perhaps expect to find it only in a tentative and undeveloped form. And indeed it has been claimed that in this respect the *Supplices* is patently early. 'Nous ne verrons pas ici la métaphore principale se développer

[1] Other motifs appear at the beginning and again run through the play, the wealth and power of the Persian empire, the contrast between young and old. (Cf. Hiltbrunner 41 ff.) For the technique extends beyond the use of images to that of ideas and themes in general. Nevertheless it seems wise to make a distinction between a mere recurrent theme and a genuine recurrent image or symbol. Only those themes which are not directly related to the plot, but whose recurrence has some symbolic value are relevant to this discussion. Murray (23 n. 6) rightly objects that Hiltbrunner's γάμος and πόλις are too closely connected with the very subject-matter of the *Supplices* to have any significance as recurring themes in the sense we are discussing. The same is true of 'fetters' in the *Prometheus*, which Dumortier apparently takes as an image (63 ff.). Cf. also F. Focke, *NGG* (1922) 165 ff.

[2] ȝυγόν (793) 471, κομπάσματα (794) 436 ff., φερεγγύοις (797) 396 and 449. Cf. Hiltbrunner 55 f.

[3] Cf. Fowler, *op. cit.*

avec ampleur et magnificence comme dans les Sept, une des pièces les plus achevées.'[1] But Dumortier recognizes in the *Supplices* only one principal metaphor, that of the flock of doves pursued by a hawk (223 ff. etc.). R. D. Murray has shown that the imagery of the *Supplices* is very much more complex, that 'the web of imagery woven around Io, the ancestress of the Danaids, conveys much of the meaning of the *Suppliants*, that the story of Io is intended as an "allegory" explaining with remarkable clarity and completeness the character and motives of the Danaids, and is thereby the ultimate vehicle of the basic ideas expressed in the trilogy'.[2] Murray perhaps goes too far in his exposition of his case, finding symbolic significance in the most trivial words and expressions and sounds,[3] and one may quarrel with the details of his interpretation of 'the basic ideas expressed in the trilogy'. But it can hardly be denied that the motif of Io and its attendant imagery is of real importance for the understanding of the play. Murray finds four principal figures, all developed from the wider comparison of Io with the Danaids: (1) bull and cow; (2) contrast of male and female; (3) touch and seizure; (4) breath, wind, and storm.[4] As in the

[1] Dumortier 1.

[2] P. 15. Cf. also Aylen 94 ff. Earp (*G. & R.* 22. 122) completely misses this. 'The Chorus must prove their descent from Io in order to secure the help of Argos and its King, but the many picturesque details that they add are no help to that. A plain statement would in fact be more convincing; but they are dictated by the poet's fancy.'

[3] An example occurs on p. 75 where Murray finds deliberate ambiguity at lines 497–9. But surely any ambiguity is unintentional. Inachus is not represented by Aeschylus in the *Supp.* as the father of Io (cf. Focke 170), so that no relationship to the Io allegory is established here. For further criticism cf. A. Lesky in *Anz. f. d. Altertums.* 14 (1961) 11; A. H. Coxon, *J.H.S.* 81 (1961) 161; D. van Nes, *Mnem.* IV. 14 (1961) 251 ff., and *Die maritime Bildersprache* 18 ff.

[4] Of these the second is a 'theme' rather than an image, and one intimately connected with the subject-matter of the play. Thus it is not strictly relevant here (cf. p. 69 n. 1 above: also Coxon and van Nes, *loc. cit.*). It is the third and fourth which are the most complex. Cf. p. 72 below.

Other themes too may be adduced. Zeus, upon whom everything depends, makes his appearance in the first word of the play (cf. Ἑρμῆ χθόνιε in line 1 of the *Choe.*). The antithesis between male power and female right, supported by the power of Zeus, is brought out by the repeated occurrence of the word κράτος (372, 387, 393, 399, 425, 437, 596, 597, 763, 951, and at the very end of the play 1068); cf. Hiltbrunner 25 f. and 38. A similar motif is the Ζηνὸς (ἱκεσίου) κότος: cf. Kranz 276 n. on 39; A. Lesky, *Die tragische Dichtung der Hellenen* (2nd ed. Göttingen 1964) 91.

Septem and the *Persae* all four principal motifs are introduced at the beginning of the play, three of them together at line 17. It is interesting that one of the two extended similes which occur in the *Supplices*, that of the cow pursued by a wolf, is part of the bull and cow motif (350 ff.). To Murray's figures one may add that rivers occur throughout the play as symbols of fertility, and here in the light of future events the wider symbolism is clear.[1] It becomes almost explicit at 1026 ff., while the meaning has already been hinted at on three previous occasions (281, 497, and 854 ff.). It can hardly then be claimed that the *Supplices* displays a primitive simplicity. It would seem rather to occupy an intermediate position between the more straightforward 'dominant image' of the *Persae*, *Septem*, and *Prometheus*, and the 'complex of symbols' that is the characteristic of the *Oresteia*. Indeed the allegorical use of the myth of Io as the central motif has no real parallel in the other extant plays. Nowhere else does an entire myth serve to illustrate a plot. But it is the *Oresteia* that comes closest to it. For just as the fate of the Danaids is illustrated at every turn by that of their ancestress Io, so we have seen the snake used as a symbol for two different generations of the Atreidae, and so the εἱμάτων βαφάς of *Agamemnon* 960, the prelude to Agamemnon's murder, reminds us of the sacrifice of Iphigeneia with her κρόκου βαφάς (239). One episode in the history of the family serves by its imagery to illustrate another.

The simplest type of recurrent motif is provided by the repetition of a single word. More subtle is the use of words whose sound or form suggests one of the motifs, though its own meaning may be quite different. At *Supplices* 117 βοῦνιν means 'hilly land', but suggests 'land of the cow', while Ἀπίαν recalls Apis, the Egyptian equivalent of Epaphus (cf. 262).[2] This is much more than a play upon words. It springs from the idea

[1] 4, 23, 63, 254 f., *281*, 308, *497*, 553, 561, *854 ff.*, 879 f., 922, 1020, 1024 f., *1026 ff.* Note also the recurrence of βόσκω in the 1st stasimon (μηλοβότου 548, πάμβοτον 558, χιονόβοσκον 559); cf. βόσκημα 620, and the prayer for fertility in the 2nd stasimon: see also Wolff, *Columbia Diss.* 35; E. K. Borthwick, *A.J.Ph.* 84 (1963) 225 ff. (esp. 232 f.).

[2] First pointed out by Sheppard 226. Cf. Hdt. ii. 153.

that a name is not merely a matter of convention, but intimately belongs to the thing it represents, that two words related in sound must be related also in meaning. Hence the interest in etymology, which is revealed so often in the plays of Aeschylus (e.g. *Supp.* 45 ff. and 320 (cf. Vürtheim's note); *Sept.* 405, 536, 658, 670, 829; *Ag.* 681 ff. and 699 f., 1081 f., 1086 f.; *Choe.* 948).[1] The same idea gives all the more force to words which seem to be deliberately chosen for their ambiguous meaning. Stanford says[2] that the use of οἴχομαι in the *Persae* is the first example in Aeschylus of 'delayed-action' ambiguity. In the same play the connection between Πέρσαι and πέρθω is also exploited (65, 1056, and at 178 together with οἴχεται). A possible example in the *Supplices* is the word ἐφάπτωρ with its two ideas of caressing and seizing, the second of which remains latent until it is first hinted at in line 315 by the introduction of the word ῥυσίων (cf. 728).[3] We have seen that the ambiguity in φυξανορίᾳ (line 8) may also be deliberate. Again ἐπίπνοια, which for most of the play is the gentle breathing of Zeus, becomes at the very end (1043) a storm which the Danaids fear, an ominous shift of meaning in the light of future events.[4] Porzig finds even subtler effects than this in patterns of vowel and consonantal sounds.[5] But it is dangerous to let one's imagination roam too far in this field, and only too easy to discover significance in what is either accidental or at most unconscious.[6]

Many evidently purposeless and fortuitous repetitions can be found throughout the seven plays, and are of no importance for

[1] Cf. Pl. *Crat.* 435d (ὃς ἂν τὰ ὀνόματα ἐπίστηται, ἐπίστασθαι καὶ τὰ πράγματα); Porzig 73 ff.; Neustadt, *op. cit.*; Schmid, *Gefess. Prom.* 53; *GGL* 297 f.; Kranz 83 and 287–9; Hiltbrunner 55 f. and 84; Pohlenz 59 and 139, *Erl.* 27 and 29; Wolff, *Columbia Diss.* 158 and 174 ff.; Méautis, *Prométhée* 14.

[2] Cf. p. 62 n. 4 above.

[3] 'Aeschylus skilfully develops the tension in this image, as he varies it from pole to counterpole, and again to an ambiguous neutrality' (Murray 32); cf. also Hiltbrunner 28, 34, and 84.

[4] Cf. Murray 41 (reading ἐπιπνοίας for the ἐπιπνοίαι of M); van Nes, *Die maritime Bildersprache* 22. Cf. p. 70 above.

[5] Pp. 73 ff. Cf. Pohlenz 139, *Erl.* 67.

[6] It would require a perceptive audience to appreciate many of the subtleties that the scholar discovers in his study. This need not mean that they were not intended by the poet. Aeschylus did not write for a reading public, yet no one would deny that the value of his work is more than ephemeral.

our present purpose.[1] It has been claimed that the *Prometheus* has more than its fair share of these.[2] 'No careful reader of Aeschylus needs to be told that when a word or a locution which he had used pleased him and was used again he often (by no means always) repeated it after a short interval, say 100 lines or so of a modern text, or less.'[3] Repetitions in stichomythia, where one speaker picks up what the previous speaker has said, are common enough.[4] Sometimes an iambic passage repeats the theme of a preceding lyric passage, or the ideas contained in a passage of introductory anapaests are resumed in the lyric that follows.[5] More interesting are those phrases and ideas in the *Supplices* which seem to be echoed in other plays. The following list is not necessarily complete: 29–30/*Pers.* 122–3; 100–3/*Ag.* 182–3; 120 (cf. 904)/*Pers.* 125; 122–3/*Sept.* 77 and *Choe.* 483–5; 180/*Sept.* 81–2; 181/*Sept.* 153 and 205; 260/*Ag.* 256–7; 268/*Ag.* 17 and *Choe.* 539; 282–3/*Eum.* 48–9; 431–2/*Sept.* 328–9; 442/*Ag.* 211 and *Choe.* 338; 443 ff./*Ag.* 1007–21 and *Eum.* 645 ff.;[6] 470/*Pers.* 433 and 599–600, *Sept.* 758; 554/*Sept.* 306; 600/*Sept.* 792; 605/*Ag.* 815; 630/*Sept.* 705; 1072–3/*Eum.* 646.[7] And on a larger scale there is the prayer for blessings upon Argos at *Supplices* 625 ff., which can be compared with the similar blessings of the Furies at *Eum.* 916 ff.[8] But it would be dangerous to rely too heavily on this kind of evidence. Few of the echoes

[1] Repetitions of all kinds are discussed by R. Wölfell, *Gleich- und Anklänge bei A.* (Progr. Bamberg 1906). For R. Böhme, *Bühnenbearbeitung Äschyleischer Tragödien* (Basel/Stuttgart 1956 and 1959), repetition is a characteristic of the style of his *Bearbeiter* (cf. esp. I. 52 ff. and II. 66 ff.).

[2] By Schmid, *Gefess. Prom.* 9 ff. and 68 ff.: cf. Hiltbrunner 75 ff.: but see also Focke, *Hermes* 65. 303 n. 2; Méautis, *Prométhée* 20, 28, 42.

[3] H. J. Rose, *Eranos* 45. 96 n. 1. For examples cf. Schmid 11 n. 4.

[4] For the same technique in 'epirrhematic' passages cf. chap. III p. 119 n. 1 and p. 119 n. 3.

[5] Cf. H. Weil, *Rev. ét. gr.* 1 (1888) 16; T. von Wilamowitz, *Die dramatische Technik des Sophokles* (Berlin 1917) 170 ff.; Nestle, *Struktur des Eingangs* 53, 102, 105; Kranz 166 f., and *Hermes* 54. 301 ff.; Schadewaldt 14 n. 1 and 143 f.; Peretti 91 f., 151, 195 and n. 1, 205 f., 216 ff.; W. Helg, *Das Chorlied der griechischen Tragödie in seinem Verhältnis zur Handlung* (Diss. Zürich 1950) 38 ff. and 61.

[6] W. A. A. van Otterlo, *Beschouwingen over het archaïsche Element in den Stijl van Aeschylus* 65 f. (cf. 70 ff. and n. 3 on 105) compares also *Choe.* 61 ff. and 518 ff., and Hom. I 406–9, E. *Supp.* 775 ff.

[7] Cf. *GGL* 298 n. 1.

[8] The differences and resemblances between the two are discussed by Hölzle 6 ff.; cf. also G. Müller 67 ff.

are particularly striking in themselves, and even if they were, they would provide no more than an indication, certainly not proof, that the *Supplices* belonged roughly to the period of the other plays.

A distinctive form of repetition is ring-composition, the technique by which a speaker returns at the end of his speech, or a section of a speech, to his opening words or thoughts. Since 1908 the frequency of this device in the *Supplices* has been used as an argument for an early date.[1] One critic goes so far as to say that it so dominates the iambic trimeter passages in the *Supplices* that it constitutes the fundamental characteristic of the primitive λέξις and the special difference between the *Supplices* and the other plays.[2] As early as 1937 however van Otterlo, after a thorough examination of ring-composition in the dialogue and lyric passages of Aeschylus, concluded that there was no fundamental difference between the *Supplices* and the other plays.[3] The most striking occurrence in the *Supplices* is at 407/417, where μῶν οὐ δοκεῖ δεῖν φροντίδος σωτηρίου; picks up the opening words of the king's speech δεῖ τοι βαθείας φροντίδος σωτηρίου. Very often the repeated words form a framework enclosing a report of some kind, or they form an exhortation with the enclosed passage giving the grounds on which it is made. There are three other passages in the *Supplices* in which close verbal parallelism appears, 277 f./289 f., 605 ff./621 ff., and the more complex speech of Danaus at 710 ff., where σώφρονας in 710 is picked up by σεσωφρονισμένας at 724, and μὴ τρέσητε at 729 answers to μὴ τρέσητε at 711. Less obvious

[1] Cf. G. Müller 56 ff.; also J. Vürtheim, *Aischylos' Schutzflehende* (Amsterdam 1928) 95 f.; Peretti, *Epirrema e tragedia* 238 ff.; Mazon 3; H. F. Johansen, *Class. et Med.* 15 (1954) 31 ff.: cf. also Lesky, *Tr. Dichtung* 92. The fullest treatment is by Peretti, Johansen, and van Otterlo 20 f. and 76 ff.: see also Wilamowitz, *Interpr.* 165 n. 1; Hiltbrunner, *op. cit.*; Fraenkel on *Ag.* 1196; Pohlenz, *Erl.* 47 f.

[2] Peretti 252.

[3] Pp. 102, 104 f., 132, and 143. Van Otterlo rejected particularly the view of Vürtheim that a fundamental difference could be expected between a play composed in 476 (V.'s dating for the *Supp.*) and one composed in 472 or 467. Cf. also his study *Untersuchungen über Begriff, Anwendung und Entstehung der griechischen Ringkomposition* (*Med. ned. Akad.* N.R. 7 (1944) Nr. 3, esp. 1 n. 1; also Johansen 32 n. 78.

is the parallelism at 996/1008, 991 f./1012 f.,[1] 254 f./259, 249/271 f. and 517/522. There is no verbal parallelism at all at 260 f./268–70.[2] If these occurrences were unique among the extant plays, they would constitute a strong argument for setting apart the *Supplices* from the other plays. But in fact ring-composition is to be found to a greater or less extent in all of the surviving plays. The *Persae* has no examples with close verbal correspondence, but parallelism does exist at 609–10/619 ff., 753/7, 603/6 (weak, but φόβου and (ἐκ)φοβεῖ occupy the same position in the line), 179 f./200, and 161/245 (weak). There is repetition of thought at 361–3/372 f., 682/93, 744/749–51 (παῖδ' ἐμόν at 751 also answers the same words at 739 and 744), 759 ff./781 ff. The *Septem* is closer to the *Supplices* than is the *Persae*, since the occurrence at 380 f./391 f. shows as formal a balance as anything in the *Supplices* except 407/417. Slightly less remarkable are 187 f./195, 266/279, 662 f./670 f., 1005/1025, 1013 f./1020, 1028/1037 f. Without schematic form are 487/497, 633/9, perhaps 529 ff./549, and the opening speech of Eteocles.[3] The *Prometheus* is poor in ring-composition. It is only faintly recognizable at 204 ff./214 f., 226 f./237, 298 f./302 f., 309 f./315 f., 645 f./655 f., 663/9, 824–6/842 f., 870/5 (with verbal parallelism), and 1014/30. The *Agamemnon* on the other hand possesses a very striking example with exact verbal responsion at 1/20 and another almost as striking at 1178/83. There is rather less formal balance at 551/581 f., 636/648, 810 ff./821 ff. (cf. 852 f.), 968/972, 1184 f./1196 f., 1412 ff./1419 ff., and 1580/1611 (cf. 1603), 896/903 and 944 ff./956 f. are without verbal repetition. The *Choephori* displays verbal parallelism at 2/19, 10 ff./20 f., 87/91 f., 525/538, 749 f./762, and 1050/1063, and less noticeably at 86/100, 541/550, and 742 f./765.[4] There is no verbal correspondence at 130 f./138 ff., 514/522, and 554 f./

[1] A complex passage, since one occurrence is contained inside another. If Heimsoeth's χρεών is read at 990, this line will balance 980 (cf. Müller 58 f.).

[2] 624 resumes the words of Danaus' last speech (601) and also the τέλος of the Chorus (603).

[3] Van Otterlo (97 f.) however rejects this as an example of genuine ring-composition: at the end of his speech E. gives proof of the sense of responsibility which he has described in the opening lines.

[4] Double ring-composition.

579–82. Finally the *Eumenides* has one example with close balance, 683 f./704 ff. 179 f./196 is less striking, and there is no formal balance at 1/20, 185 ff./193–5,[1] 235 f./241 f., 436/442, 443 f./453, and 681/707 f.[1] Nevertheless it is true that in two respects the *Supplices* stands alone, in the frequency of ring-composition and in the generally more mechanical verbal parallelism with which it is worked out. Nothing else is quite so stark as 407/417, where the effect is strengthened by the fact that the ring-composition frames an entire speech. Yet the difference between the *Supplices* and the other plays is not after all very great, and certainly not great enough to bear the weight of a chronological argument. For both the *Septem* and the *Eumenides* contain examples quite as striking as those at *Supplices* 277 f. and 605 ff. while the nearest approach to the formal balance at *Supplices* 407 ff. is to be found not in the *Persae*, where the chronological argument ought to put it, but in the *Agamemnon* (1/20). In its own way the *Prometheus* is much more isolated than the *Supplices*, and there alone would it be reasonable to talk of a different technique from the other plays. Yet the *Prometheus* must be closer in date to them than an early *Supplices* would be. It may be that the greater frequency of ring-composition in the *Supplices* is to be explained by the character of the iambic passages, which are in general short and thus lend themselves to this kind of framing technique. Very often it occurs in speeches of Danaus, and such repetition may be thought peculiarly fitted to the dramatic function assigned him in this play.[2]

On a wider scale ring-composition has been detected in the *Supplices* and *Persae* between the beginning and the end of the plays.[3] In the *Supplices* 1062 ff. summarizes briefly the themes that were expounded in the opening anapaests of the play, while in the *Persae* the first part of the Exodos resumes the first part of the Parodos with its list of Persian heroes, the second section recalling 65 ff. Still wider is the scale of the *Oresteia*,

[1] Double ring-composition.

[2] Cf. chap. III p. 137 below.

[3] Cf. Seewald 42; Hiltbrunner 81. Méautis (*Prométhée* 41) finds similar parallelism in *P.V.* (8/945, 7/946, 18/944).

where the torch-lit procession at the end of the *Eumenides* may be seen as a resumption of the motif of light and the appearance of the beacon at the beginning of the *Agamemnon*.[1] The technique of ring-composition is to be found also in lyric passages, which is hardly surprising, since a stasimon is by its nature better adapted than dialogue to cyclic composition, less obliged to show a logical progression of thought.[2] Sometimes ring-composition in lyrics is achieved by verbal parallelism. In the *Supplices* only a trace of it may be seen at 40 ff., where the recurrence of the opening theme, Epaphus, at antistrophe θ is underlined by the slight parallelism of καλούμενος (175) and ἐπικεκλομένα (40). At 524 ff. the theme of Zeus forms a framework for the story of Io and Epaphus, and there is faint verbal parallelism (κράτος 526/596 f.). More striking is *Persae* 65 ff. where the resumption of the Hellespont theme is emphasized by the symmetry of ἀμφίζευκτον (130) and ζυγόν (72) and of ἐξαμείψας (130) and ἀμείψας (69).[3] But the most notable example of this kind of ring-composition occurs in the *Septem*, 720 ff., where the last line of the stasimon, μὴ τελέσῃ καμψίπους 'Ερινύς, balances the first strophe with its 'Ερινὺν τελέσαι (723–4) and 788 f. balances 730 f. In the same play at 109 ff. the second strophic pair is enclosed in a framework of appeals to the gods, and ἴδετε παρθένων (110) is balanced by κλύετε παρθένων (171), and θεοὶ πολιάοχοι χθονός (109) by θεοί...γᾶς τᾶσδε πυργοφύλακες (166–8). In the *Agamemnon* at 104 ff. the personal reference of the Chorus in its opening words finds a parallel at the beginning of the last antistrophe (τὰ δ' ἔνθεν οὔτ' εἶδον οὔτ' ἐννέπω).[4] At 367 ff. the idea that the gods take note and punish sinners encloses the theme of Helen, but here there is a subtle

[1] Cf. G. Perrotta, *I tragici greci* (Messina–Florence [1931]) 77; Hiltbrunner 74 and 81. Hiltbrunner also finds ring-composition between the dactyls of the Parodos of the *Agamemnon* and the Exodos of the *Eumenides*.

[2] Cf. pp. 40 f. above. An attempt was once made, by R. Westphal, *Prolegomena zu Aeschylus Tragödien* (Leipzig 1869) 70 f. and 96 ff., to prove that all the non-threnodic lyrics of Aeschylus were composed in accordance with the νόμος of Terpander, with the main theme in the middle as the ὀμφαλός and the other sections arranged symmetrically on either side of it.

[3] Here the final antistrophe remains outside the framework.

[4] See also 177/250 (van Otterlo 79). 975–1034 is similar, where καρδία (1028) picks up καρδίας (977). Cf. also Kranz 157 f.

advance of thought; for at the beginning of the stasimon the reference is to Paris, at the end to Agamemnon himself. The *Choephori* provides an example with faint verbal parallelism, at 22 ff. where the theme of the Chorus' mourning forms the framework, and ὑφ' εἱμάτων (81) perhaps answers to ὑφασμάτων at 27. In the *Eumenides* 388 f. balances 322 f.[1] Clearly this technique is common enough in the plays of Aeschylus, and there is nothing unusual about the *Supplices*. It is the *Septem* this time that displays mechanical verbal parallelism. Indeed in one important respect the *Supplices* is closest to the *Agamemnon*.[2] In the *Supplices* the central theme of the opening anapaests, Epaphus, becomes the first and final subject of the following ode, while the central theme of the latter, Zeus, is taken from the opening and closing themes of the anapaests. This time it is the power of Zeus that is emphasized, and it is this power of Zeus that forms the framework of the next ode (524 ff.). The same interlocking technique appears in the *Agamemnon*, where the central theme of the first stasimon (104 ff.), Zeus, becomes the enclosing subject of the next; while the latter's central theme, Helen, fulfils the same function at 681 ff. To a smaller extent the same thing can be seen in the *Persae*. There the theme of loss and foreboding which appeared at the beginning and end of the opening anapaests is restated in the fourth strophic pair of the following ode. The Persian forces, which form the middle subject of the anapaests, appear again as the framework of the ode.[3] Later in the play, the theme of the blameless Darius at 652 ff., which occupies the middle of its stasimon, is restated as the first subject of the next ode, at 852 ff. But here ring-composition does not occur.

It is commonly said that the style of Aeschylus is paratactic. 'His sentences are arranged in straightforward fashion, more by

[1] Cf. also *Choe.* 22/45 and 48/72 ff. (van Otterlo 79 f.). Van Otterlo discusses also (80 ff.) *Sept.* 875–960, *P.V.* 887–906, the κομμός of the *Choe.*, and *Supp.* 777/806.

[2] Cf. G. Thomson, *Greek lyric metre* (2nd ed. Cambridge 1961) 83 and 101 f.

[3] Cf. also van Otterlo 77–8, comparing 126 ff. and 73–80 with 12–64, 129 with 58 (also 73–86), 133–9 with 61–4 and 122 ff. and perhaps with 13. He points out also an example of ring-composition in the opening anapaests (12 f./59 f.), and suggests that this might support the emendation νυός at 13. Cf. further Wilamowitz, *Interpr.* 34 f. and 166 f.

way of parallel clauses than by the subordination of one clause to another. Rounded periods, with carefully balanced rhythm, polished antithesis, and recurring cadence, are foreign to his style. When he constructs a long sentence, he follows the natural order of the thought, without artifice or studied effect.'[1] And here too Earp sees a development between the *Supplices* and the other plays.[2] 'In this play the structure is usually paratactic, and loose at that. Where the sentences are long they often meander on indefinitely, and seem to have come to an end more than once before they actually stop. They are overloaded with amplifications, explanatory phrases in apposition, and so on.'[3] All this, says Earp, is less true of the *Persae*, and in the *Septem* there is further development. To prove it by means of statistics would obviously be difficult, and Earp contents himself with pointing to a single passage in the dialogue of the *Supplices*, one which 'naturally demands energy and emphasis' but where 'the style is inappropriately long-winded' (938–49). It is an unfortunate example from his point of view, since, with the exception of 946–7, the style of the king's speech is in fact as vigorous and concise as it is possible to imagine.[4] And the same is true of his shorter speech at 911–15. But Earp's criticism is not confined to iambic passages. He compares lines 40–59 of the *Agamemnon* with the first 22 lines of the *Supplices*, and has little difficulty in demonstrating that the structure of the latter is not quite so skilful, that there are too many additions loosely tacked on, and that the sentences might end in any of several places. But this kind of looseness of structure is not confined to the *Supplices*. A study of the Parodos of the *Persae* reveals the same thing. The first sentence could easily end at καλεῖται or at φύλακες; and from line 21 we have simply a list of Persian heroes

[1] Haigh 84; cf. also Kumaniecki 113; van Otterlo 43 ff., 131 f., 142.

[2] *The style of Aeschylus* 84 ff.

[3] P. 84. Cf. also Koster 25.

[4] Cf. Wolff, *Eranos* 57. 20 f. Earp sees a sign of immaturity in 'the opulent lines 996–1009, advice which all we know of the Danaids tells us to be superfluous' (*G. & R.* 22. 121). Aeschylus may be presumed to have noticed this. It is much more likely that the very necessity for the advice tells us something new about the character of the Danaids, something whose significance may become apparent later in the trilogy. It certainly was not superfluous for Amymone.

set down with hardly any attempt at formal sentence-structure. The same catalogue-style recurs in a lyric passage at 865 ff. (cf. the 1st stasimon of the *Supplices*, 540 ff.).[1] But to prove a development in the structure of Aeschylus' sentences requires more than a comparison of individually selected passages. The only satisfactory method is to isolate certain paratactic features and to trace these systematically throughout all the plays.[2] This has been done by Johansen with interesting results.[3]

First he examines the use of καί and δέ with explicative instead of copulative function. He finds three examples of this καί in the *Supplices*, at 443, 399 (retaining the text of M), and 983, and only one certain example elsewhere, at *Septem* 21. *Choephori* 144 is doubtful. To this list should be added *Supplices* 230 and 499,[4] *Persae* 161, and perhaps *Choephori* 129. Here then there is a slight but definite difference between the *Supplices* and the other plays. There is less difference with the use of δέ.[5] Johansen's examples are *Supplices* 190, 496, 994, and 998; *Persae* 706 and 754; *Septem* 599; *Agamemnon* 857; *Choephori* 239; *Eumenides* 62, 197, 579, and 694; *Prometheus* 951. To these should be added *Supplices* 398, 623, probably 774, and 999; *Persae* 473; *Septem* 249 and 662; *Agamemnon* 617 and 1353; *Choephori* 241, 517, 709, perhaps 839, and 1059; *Eumenides* 122 and 750; *Prometheus* 35, 109, 522, 818, and 822. Secondly, Johansen studies the practice of breaking up a parallelism inside a longer period by giving the

[1] Cf. also van Otterlo 46 ff., 52, n. 3 on 105.

[2] A statistical study of the sentence-structure of all the principal Greek authors has been carried out by T. B. L. Webster, *A.J.Ph.* 62 (1941) 385 ff., using a method explained in *Studies presented to M. K. Pope* (Manchester 1939) 381 ff. He does not give comparative figures for the individual plays of Aeschylus, but some of his figures are interesting for our present purpose. Thus in length of sentence the *Supplices* with 14 'terms' is very close to the Aeschylean average of 16. In the number of clauses per 1,000 terms there is an imperceptible difference between Homer and *Supplices, Persae, Septem. Supplices* (86) and *Persae* (84) are alike in the number of sentences with no complications, the Aeschylean average being 73. But what emerges most clearly is the complete isolation of the *Prometheus*, with a sentence-structure far more complicated than that of any other play (cf. esp. 402 n. 63). This kind of test is useful, but not exact, since in the first place the samples are not genuine random samples but continuous passages, and in the second place there is a natural tendency for short sentences to occur together: cf. Yule, *Biometrika* 30 (1938) 371.

[3] *Op. cit.*

[4] Denniston (250) compares Ar. *Birds* 1251.

[5] Cf. also Denniston 169.

latter part of the parallelism syntactical independence, and here he finds no difference between the *Supplices* and the other plays. 'It is not a more extensive use of paratactic structure in general that characterizes *Suppliants* as against the other plays.'[1] Indeed it is the *Persae* that stands alone. Out of eleven instances of gradual change to a paratactical structure after a subordinating word or expression no fewer than five occur in the *Persae*.[2]

A special form of parataxis is 'comparatio paratactica', a comparison in which the two elements are joined by τε. . . τε, καί, or δέ. As with ring-composition the *Supplices* contains one example with detailed parallelism achieved by the repetition of words (226 ff.). *Septem* 584 and *Agamemnon* 322 show rather less formal balance. Other instances are *Supplices* 443 and 998, *Septem* 602, *Agamemnon* 966, *Choephori* 258 and 247. There are no examples in *Persae*, *Prometheus* or *Eumenides*.[3] Aeschylus frequently attaches a new period to a clause or a single word in the preceding period, instead of to the whole of it, thus changing the direction of his thought. Johansen finds eleven instances, three of them in the *Supplices* (176, 710, and 998). The first and third of these are rather different from any of the other examples, in that neither do they involve a γάρ clause, nor does the speaker return to his original line of thought. But two such occurrences are hardly significant. Finally Johansen examines the question of logical connection, and finds (1) that Aeschylus seldom takes up more than one subject in a speech without logically connecting them with each other; (2) that when he does so he mostly uses formulae which show clearly that the speaker is passing to something new.[4] There are no such formulae, he says, in the *Supplices*.[5] Ambiguity there is avoided instead by the framing technique of ring-composition rather than by logical expressness, and this constitutes the principal difference between

[1] P. 52. [2] Pp. 14–17.

[3] Van Otterlo however considers *P.V.* 345–74 in this connection as a 'praeambulum' or 'Priamel' (67 f.). He examines also lyric passages which display the same technique (52 ff.).

[4] *Persae* 200 f., *Agamemnon* 829 f., 844, 912, 950, *Eumenides* 453 f., 707 f. Cf. also van Otterlo 107 f.

[5] Surely there is such a formula of transition at *Supplices* 259.

the *Supplices* and the other plays. The point is a valid one. The change of subject at *Supplices* 991 is more abrupt than anything else in Aeschylus, and 1009 of the same play is not much easier. Again, however, one may question whether two occurrences are enough to prove that the *Supplices* is so clearly detached from all the other plays. The *Septem* provides no transitional formulae because it contains no example of a complete change of subject inside a speech. The *Prometheus* on the other hand has many such formulae where there is hardly any break in thought at all.[1] Indeed Johansen in his summary leaves the *Prometheus* out of account altogether, since it is so isolated from the other plays.[2] But a theory of development which fails so signally with the *Prometheus* cannot fairly be used to establish the date of any other play, particularly when the evidence for such a development is in itself comparatively insignificant. It is perhaps another matter if one is prepared to deny the authenticity of the *Prometheus*.

A few miscellaneous points of grammar and syntax must complete this survey.[3] The resultative perfect tense of the verb, while common in comedy, is comparatively rare in tragedy, occurring 9 times in Sophocles, 11 times in Euripides, and some 9 times in the surviving plays of Aeschylus, 5 of these instances being in the *Prometheus*.[4] There is one occurrence in each of the *Supplices*, *Septem*, *Agamemnon*, and *Eumenides*, none in *Persae* or *Choephori*.[5] It is doubtful, says Wackernagel, if there are any examples before Pindar.[6] At any rate it is rare until the second half of the fifth century, so that its occurrence in an early play of

[1] 221–6, 500, 801 f., 842 ff.; cf. *Eumenides* 480 ff. *Septem* 1012 is similar.

[2] Earp too confesses (87) that the *Prometheus* has features 'that do not fit easily into the general development'.

[3] Koster (24 f.) gives figures for *schema pindaricum* (*Supp.* 1, *Pers.* 1), *nominativus pendens* (*Supp.* 2, *Sept.* 1, *Choe.* 1) and 3rd person plural optatives in -οίατο (*Supp.* 2, *Pers.* 3, *Sept.* 1, *Choe.* 1), but fails to establish any difference between the *Supplices* on the one hand and the remaining plays on the other.

[4] Cf. J. Wackernagel, *Studien zum gr. Perfektum* (Göttingen 1904) 9 ff., esp. 11 (=*Kl. Schr.* II. 1006 ff., esp. 1008); also Peretti, *Studi ital.* 5. 205 ff.; Focke, *Hermes* 65. 298 f.

[5] *Prometheus* 211, 446, 586, 821, 825 (rejected by Peretti as an instance); *Supplices* 246, *Septem* 583, *Agamemnon* 267, *Eumenides* 587.

[6] *Isth.* iv. 41 and *Nem.* ii. 8.

Aeschylus would perhaps be surprising. A major development in the use of the infinitive with article took place in the lifetime of Aeschylus, both in its frequency and in the manner of its use.[1] According to Birklein Homer provides only 1 possible example, Hesiod 2, Pindar 9, and other lyric poets 9. But no fewer than 52 examples are to be found in Aeschylus (Sophocles 97, Euripides 93, Aristophanes 65). Of these 47 belong to the *Oresteia* and the *Prometheus* (*Ag.* 22, *Choe.* 4, *Eum.* 10, *P.V.* 11). Though the *Choephori* is surprisingly poor in occurrences, it can hardly be accidental that the *Oresteia* in general has so many. In the earlier plays the usage is still at an experimental stage. The *Persae* and the *Septem* have only one example each, while the *Supplices* has three.[2] The *Supplices* looks rather less tentative than the other two. Only the *Prometheus* and the *Agamemnon* venture outside the nominative and accusative cases, the *Prometheus* at 381 and 681, the *Agamemnon* at 253 and 1369. The emendation of Schütz at 802 would introduce a dative into the *Supplices*, but the nominative is the commonly accepted reading.

A similar development is to be seen in the form of the final clause. Table F shows the variety employed by Aeschylus. The *Persae* and the *Agamemnon* have remarkably few final sentences at all. Clearly the commonest type employs ὡς with subjunctive or optative. But it is the next most important category that provides the greatest interest, that with ὡς ἄν or ὅπως ἄν + the subjunctive or, once (*Ag.* 364 ff.), the optative. Again the development seems to take place during Aeschylus' lifetime. In Homer the proportion of final clauses without to those with ἄν or κε is 7:1, in Hesiod 8:1, in the Homeric Hymns 4:1, in Pindar 15:1, in the other lyric poets 7:1, and in Aeschylus nearly 2:1.[3] Yet the latter type of final clause does not occur in

[1] Cf. B. L. Gildersleeve, *TAPhA* 9 (1878) 5 ff., esp. 12; F. Birklein, *Entwicklungsgesch. des substant. Infinitivs* (Schanz: *Beitr. zur histor. Syntax d. gr. Sprache* III. 1 Würzburg 1888) esp. 10 ff. and 91; also Müller 65; Goodwin, *Greek moods and tenses* (London 1897) 314 ff. Birklein omits *Eumenides* 301, thus reaching a total of 51. The two examples at *Choëphori* 417 and 958 are textually very dubious and should perhaps be omitted.

[2] *Supplices* 802, 995, and 1013; *Persae* 292; *Septem* 232.

[3] Cf. P. Weber, *Entwicklungsgesch. der Absichtssätze* (Schanz II. 1 Würzburg 1884) 81. His figures do not include paratactic μή clauses. ὅπως ἄν does not occur before

either the *Persae* or the *Septem*, whereas the *Supplices* already has four.

The stylistic evidence for the date of the *Supplices* turns out, as we expected, to be in one sense inconclusive. There is no stylistic feature which is striking enough in itself to be accepted as a valid criterion for the dating of the play, and there is no set of such features which show an equally consistent development from play to play. Yet by its very inconclusiveness it demonstrates that the *Supplices* cannot be far removed in date from the other plays, that it cannot be isolated as a youthful work, in contrast with the plays of Aeschylus' maturity. That is to say, on grounds of style alone we can hardly place it as early as the 490's, and even the 480's would seem unlikely. A date in the 470's on the other hand, a few years before the *Persae*, would be consistent with the evidence, and this is where the *Supplices* is now put by, for example, Pohlenz.[1] On grounds of style alone then this date would be acceptable. But it ignores, or has to explain away, the evidence of the papyrus. And it is impossible now to feel satisfied with the assumption that the stylistic conclusions are precise enough to outweigh this external evidence, or to prove that the *Supplices* must have been written in the 470's, and could not possibly have been composed some ten years later. In fact it is clear from our survey that not only is there no great gulf set between the style of the *Supplices* and that of the *Persae* and the *Septem*, but that in some respects the style of the *Supplices* is closer to the 'mature' style of the *Oresteia* than are the other two plays. Leaving the *Prometheus* out of account for the moment, we may say that the surviving plays of Aeschylus can be divided into two groups, the three early plays on the one hand and the *Oresteia* on the other. And just as with the Platonic Dialogues it is by no means easy to settle the order of composition within each group, so with Aeschylus it is impossible on stylistic

Aeschylus (cf. Goodwin §§ 313 and 328). On the other hand it is the almost exclusive formula of classical inscriptions. Cf. K. Meisterhans, *Grammatik der Attischen Inschriften* (3rd ed. Berlin 1900) 253 ff. The earliest occurrence quoted by Meisterhans is 'not after 447 B.C.' The first ὅπως + subj. appears in an inscription dated 343 B.C. ὡς ἄν does not occur until the Roman imperial period, ἵνα twice in the fifth century.

[1] P. 53 (cf. *Erl.* 24): cf. chap. 1 p. 27.

TABLE F

	ὡς +subj. or opt.	ὡς ἄν +subj.	ὅπως ἄν +subj. or opt.	ὅπως +subj. or opt.	ὅπως +fut. indic.	ἵνα +subj. or opt.	ὡς, ὅπως or ἵνα with past tense of indic.	para-tactic μή	TOTAL
Supplices	3	3	1	—	2	—	—	2	11
Persae	1	—	—	2	—	—	—	1	4
Septem	3	—	—	1	—	1	—	1	6
Agamemnon	1	1	1	1	—	—	—	2	6
Choephori	5	4	1	1	1	—	2	—	14
Eumenides	4	—	2	2	—	1	—	2	11
Prometheus	5	3	1	1	—	1	2	3	16
	22	11	6	8	3	3	4	11	68[1]

[1] Cf. Weber, 80; G. Müller 64 f. Ca[illegible]ter's emendation at *Supplices* 399 is included in table F. The para[illegible]actic μή clauses include those which follow verbs of precaution (φ[illegible]λασσε, πάπταινε, etc.). The ἵνα at *Eumenides* 268 and *Choephori* 3[illegible]9 are restored by conjecture (the latter by Mazon, the former by Abresch after Triclinius)—dangerous restorations perhaps in view of the fact that ἵνα introduces a final clause in only two other places in Aeschylus. *Sept.* 55 f. is included in column 1. Four of the instances of paratactic μή (*Supp.* 498, *Ag.* 148, *P.V.* 334 and 390) are classified as fear (or precaution) constructions by G. Italie in his *Index Aeschyleus*.

grounds alone to settle the order of composition of *Supplices*, *Persae*, and *Septem*, while even within the trilogy itself there are considerable differences of style. In some respects the *Supplices* stands alone, and the other two plays seem to show the beginning of a development towards the *Oresteia*; for example, in the structure of sentences and in the technique of ring-composition. But in other ways the *Supplices* is nearer to the *Oresteia* and it is the *Persae*, as in the frequency of simile and metaphor, or *Persae* and *Septem* together, as in metrical technique, that give the impression of being early. It is between the *Oresteia* and the early plays that the gulf is set, with one or other of these containing the first seeds of development. This difference in style must remain a subject for astonishment, and we can only speculate on the reasons for it. No doubt it is partly a matter of chronology: Aeschylus had reached the fullness of his maturity. Perhaps he spent longer on the composition of the *Oresteia*, or was more deeply satisfied with his theme. Possibly the subject-matter itself required a different treatment. A remark of Yule is perhaps relevant here:[1] 'If all the works of an author could be assigned valid marks for quality the difference between the extreme value observed and the second *tends* to be greater than the difference between the second and the third: the difference between the marks of the first prize man and the marks of the second prize man *tends*, for example, to be greater than the difference between the marks of the second man and the marks of the third.' And again, 'We should always expect an author's best work to exceed his second best by far more than the second best exceeds the third. His *best* work should normally stand out well above the rest.' But the difference between the *Oresteia* and the other plays cannot really be judged in terms of quality at all.

The question of the *Prometheus* is notoriously difficult. In many respects it belongs to the group formed by the *Oresteia*, and often it seems to have carried to much greater lengths the development that is discernible between the early plays and the *Oresteia*; to such lengths, in fact, that any attempt to explain that development on purely chronological grounds is manifestly

[1] *Statistical Study of Literary Vocabulary* 279 f.

absurd. Aeschylus died in 456 B.C., only two years after the production of the trilogy. One solution is to deny the authenticity of the *Prometheus* altogether,[1] or to suppose that it was completed posthumously by Aeschylus' son or nephew.[2] At any rate one could not with logical consistency believe that the *Prometheus* is an authentic late play of Aeschylus, and at the same time demand that the *Supplices on stylistic grounds* be assigned to the beginning of Aeschylus' career.[3]

[1] Schmid, *Gefess. Prom.* and *GGL* I. 3. 281 ff.

[2] D. S. Robertson, *Proc. Camb. Philol. Soc.* 169–71. 9 f.; cf. also Earp 88; A. D. Fitton-Brown, *J.H.S.* 79 (1959) 59 f.; Wolff, *Columbia Diss.* 8 ff.

[3] R. D. Murray argues (pp. 48 ff. and 88 ff.) that the *Supplices* and the *Prometheus*, being 'based on identical theological doctrine', and using similar legendary symbols, were composed in the same period.

CHAPTER III

STRUCTURE

Even more than stylistic considerations it is the structure of the *Supplices* that has led to the conviction that this is an early play. The chorus is virtually the protagonist, more than half of the play consists of lyrics, and, since Aristotle says that it was Aeschylus who τὰ τοῦ χοροῦ ἠλάττωσε, it has generally been assumed that the *Supplices* must stand somewhere near the beginning of this development. Secondly the handling of the second actor seems clumsy, or at least archaic, and many have found in the play a dramatic simplicity that suggests an early date.[1] Quotations from two writers will perhaps serve to illustrate the almost universal view:

[1] The extent of the lyrics is emphasized by for example Th. Bergk, *Gr. Literaturgeschichte* III (Berlin 1884) 307; T. G. Tucker, ed. *Supp.* (London and New York 1889) xxiii; A. E. Haigh, *The tragic drama of the Greeks* (Oxford 1896) 34 ff.; E. Bethe, *Proleg. zur Geschichte des Theaters im Alterthum* (Leipzig 1896) 15 f.; G. Müller, *De Aeschyli Supplicum tempore atque indole* (Halis Saxonum 1908) 52 ff.; W. Ridgeway, *The origin of tragedy* (Cambridge 1910) 128; H. Weir Smyth, *Aeschylean Tragedy* (California 1924) 52; A. Winterstein, *Der Ursprung der Tragödie. Ein Psychoanalytischer Beitrag zur Geschichte des gr. Theaters* (Leipzig/Vienna/Zürich 1925) 178; R. C. Flickinger, *The Greek theater and its drama* (3rd ed. Chicago 1926) 168; J. Geffcken, *Griechische Literaturgeschichte* I. i. 151; A. W. Pickard-Cambridge, *Dithyramb, tragedy, and comedy* (1st ed. Oxford 1927) 87 ff.; M. Croiset, *Eschyle* (Paris 1928) 66 and 99; J. Vürtheim, *Aischylos' Schutzflehende* (Amsterdam 1928) 94; Schmid–Stählin, *GGL* I. 2. 193 and 194 n. 1; A. Peretti, *Epirrema e tragedia* (Florence 1939) 83; B. Snell, *The discovery of the mind* (Eng. tr. Oxford 1953) 99; M. Untersteiner, *Le origini della tragedia e del tragico* (1955) 248; W. J. W. Koster, *Welke is de oudste bewaard gebleven Tragedie?* (*Med. ned. Akad.* N.R. 29 (1966) 18 ff. K. Ziegler, *R.-E.* VI. A. 2. 1956 f., gives the following percentages for choral and solo lyrics: *Supp.* about 60 %, *Pers.* 50 %, *Sept.* 43 %, *Oresteia* average 42 % (*Ag.* 48 %, *Choe.* 42 %, *Eum.* 36 %), *P.V.* less than 30 %.

For the handling of the second actor see also A. Körte, in *Mélanges Nicole* (Geneva 1905) 296 ff.; G. Müller 46 ff.; Weir Smyth 54 and 59 f.; Flickinger 163 f., 169 f., and 173; Pickard-Cambridge 195; Croiset 63 ff.; W. Nestle, *Die Struktur des Eingangs in der attischen Tragödie* (Stuttgart 1930) 17 f.; J. Lammers, *Die Doppel- und Halbchöre in der antiken Tragödie* (Paderborn 1931) 34; *GGL* 69 and 196 ff.; W. Kranz, *Stasimon* (Berlin 1933) 167; Ed. Meyer, *Geschichte des Altertums* IV. 1 (3rd ed. Stuttgart 1939) 430; Peretti 227 f.; Pickard-Cambridge, *The dramatic festivals of Athens* (Oxford 1953) 139 f.; P. Mazon, *Eschyle* (6th ed. Paris 1953) I. 3; M. Pohlenz, *Gr. Tragödie* (2nd ed. Göttingen 1954) 52; Unter-

It would be interesting to know how far a story could be told in dramatic form by means of the appliances accessible to Thespis. The best solution of this question is to be found in the Supplices of Aeschylus, the earliest of extant Greek dramas, and one which, being written before Aeschylus had advanced very far in his dramatic innovations, approximates far more closely in structure to the compositions of Thespis, than to those of Sophocles and Euripides. More than half of it is choral, and the spoken part consists almost entirely of dialogues between the chorus and a single actor. The second actor, though introduced on two occasions, is used in such a sparing fashion, that with the alteration of about seventy lines he might be dispensed with altogether. This play, therefore, with its archaic simplicity of arrangement, will serve in some degree as a substitute for the lost works of Thespis and his contemporaries; and it may be possible, by a detailed analysis of the plot, to form some conception of the methods of composition employed in the primitive drama.[1]

And

The chorus (of the Supplices) is no doubt less dominant than it had been, but it is the most important feature, even to a modern reader. To an ancient spectator it must have appeared of even greater moment. The number of singers was still fifty, and the lyrics, which were accompanied by music and the dance of this great company, occupy more than half of our present text. We have left Phrynichus behind, but he is not out of sight.[2]

If all this is true, only two courses seem open to us. Either we must reject (or explain away) the evidence of the papyrus, on the grounds that Aeschylus could not possibly write such a play as late as the 460's, or we must account for the fact that he did. The latter course is not difficult, since the 'straight-line' theory of development is no more satisfactory for the structure of Aeschylus' plays than it is for the style. There is no reason to suppose that Aeschylus could not in his maturity revert to a method of composition that he had used much earlier.[3] The

steiner 269; E. A. Wolff, *Eranos* 57 (1959) 12; M. Bieber, *The history of the Greek and Roman theater* (2nd ed. Princeton 1961) 21 and 276 n. 11; A. Lesky, *Die tragische Dichtung der Hellenen* (2nd ed. Göttingen 1964) 68; G. F. Else, *The origin and early form of Greek tragedy* (Harvard 1965) 94; Koster 23; G. Thomson, *Aeschylus and Athens* (3rd ed. London 1966) 167.

[1] Haigh 34 f.

[2] G. Norwood, *Greek tragedy* (4th ed. London 1948) 12 (cf. 77 and 85 n. 1).

[3] See J. Th. Kakridis, *Hellenika* 13 (1954) 169; Lesky, *Hermes* 82 (1954) 7; H. J. F. Jones, *On Aristotle and Greek tragedy* (London 1962) 65 ff.; H. Lloyd-Jones

seven extant plays are varied enough to show that Aeschylus was no slave to a rigid pattern of development. Moreover our examination of his style may lead us to consider whether there is not in fact a greater difference between the *Oresteia* and the other plays than there is between the *Supplices* and the rest.[1] There is the further consideration that the very subject-matter of the play demanded a form of tragedy in which the chorus dominated the actors.[2] Thus there is no insuperable difficulty in accepting a late date for a play that is old-fashioned in structure. The present chapter however will follow a different line of inquiry, in seeking to determine whether those criteria may not themselves be false, by which the *Supplices* is judged to be archaic in form. In the sentences quoted above it was clear that Haigh, accepting as proved that the *Supplices* is an early play, attempted to work back from there to the character of pre-Aeschylean tragedy. And yet the argument for an early dating depended on an *a priori* view of the original form of tragedy.

L'Antiq. Class. 33 (1964) 363. Wolff, *Eranos* 56 (1958) 120 f. and Koster (21 and 31) admit the possibility of a divergence from the straight line of A.'s development. Even before the publication of the papyrus salutary warnings were given by Vürtheim (94) and Peretti (15 and 148). Wilamowitz, *Aischylos. Interpretationen* (Berlin 1914) 158, reminded us that the *Bacchae* and *I.A.*, plays very different in structure, were written in the same year. Pohlenz (136) presents the 'straight-line' theory in its most uncompromising form. Cf. also Weir Smyth 33 f. (cf. 153); Croiset 267 f.; Bieber 21.

[1] The difference between the *Oresteia* and the other plays is emphasized by for example E. Petersen, *Die attische Tragödie als Bild- und Bühnenkunst* (Bonn 1915) 373 f.; W. Schadewaldt, *Monolog und Selbstgespräch* (Berlin 1926) 53; G. Murray, *Aeschylus the creator of tragedy* (Oxford 1940) 177; Norwood 126; Pohlenz 97; Lesky, *Tr. Dichtung* 89. For G. Perrotta, *I tragici greci* (Messina–Florence [1931]) 76 (cf. 59 f.), the superiority of the *Oresteia* over the other plays is one of technique, not of poetry. For R. Böhme, *Bühnenbearbeitung Äschyleischer Tragödien* (Basel/Stuttgart 1956 and 1959) there is no problem, since the *Oresteia* as Aeschylus wrote it (cf. chap. I p. 23 n. 5 above) was as archaic as the other extant plays (see esp. I. 10, 122 f., II. 61 n. 3, 63).

[2] Cf. Vürtheim 94; H. D. F. Kitto, *Greek tragedy* (3rd ed. London 1961) 24 f.; Lesky 66; I. Trencsényi-Waldapfel, *Acta Antiqua Hung.* 12 (1964) 261 f.; Lloyd-Jones 363. It must however be admitted that Aeschylus need not have chosen such a theme had it not suited the form of tragedy that he wished to compose. Lesky suggests too (*loc. cit.* and *Hermes* 82. 6) that the first play of a trilogy might require more explanatory lyrics than the other two (cf. the figures for the *Oresteia* quoted on p. 88 n. 1 above); cf. also *GGL* 256. Weir Smyth (53) refused to admit any saving possibility: 'The prominence of the chorus in the *Suppliant Maidens* is not due to an abnormal situation or to the plot. It is the survival of primitive tragedy, in which the group uniformly played the chief part.'

The danger of a circular argument is very great. The discovery of the papyrus fragment must lead us to reconsider the whole question of the relationship between the *Supplices* and pre-Aeschylean tragedy, since it is no longer safe to use the *Supplices* itself as evidence for the latter.[1] The starting-point must be the origins of tragedy and what little we know about the work of Aeschylus' predecessors.

It is no part of our present purpose to cover yet again the whole subject of the origins of tragedy.[2] Only those theories which depend upon, or conclude in, an early dating for the *Supplices* will be treated as relevant.[3] We may ignore all views which are based on ethnological parallels and primitive survivals in modern Greece (Viza, Scyros, etc.), or places far removed from Greece, be it Guatemala or the Hebrides. Nor is there any need to discuss the question of religious δρώμενα, at Eleusis or the Anthesteria in Athens, the duel between Xanthus and Melanthus at Eleutherae, spring-rituals and the Eniautos-Daimon, hero-cults, or primitive intiation rites. Most of such theories require no further refutation today, and where they do

[1] Cf. G. F. Else, *TAPhA* 70 (1939) 147: 'In general, it has become increasingly evident in recent years that generalizing about early tragedy on the basis of the *Suppliants* is a hazardous business.'

[2] A useful recent bibliographical summary of the problem is given by C. del Grande, ΤΡΑΓΩΙΔΙΑ. *Essenza e genesi della tragedia* (2nd ed. Milan–Naples 1962) 293 ff.: for a much briefer summary see Peretti 3 n. 1. The most valuable work in general remains Pickard-Cambridge's *Dithyramb, tragedy, and comedy* (1st ed. 1927, 2nd ed. substantially revised by T. B. L. Webster, Oxford 1962).

[3] The theories of Usener, Ridgeway, Jane Harrison, Murray, Farnell, Dieterich, Cook, Thomson, etc., are less accepted today, though they still find their adherents (for example Th. H. Gaster in *Thespis. Ritual, myth and drama in the Ancient Near East* (New York 1950) esp. 54 and 100 ff.; J. Lindsay, *The clashing rocks* (London 1965) esp. 257, 293 ff.). For objections to them see M. P. Nilsson, *N. Jbb.* 27 (1911) 613 ff. (=*Opusc. Selecta* I. (Lund 1951) 68 ff.); Wilamowitz, *N. Jbb.* 29 (1912) 471 ff. (=*Kl. Schr.* I. 377 ff.); Flickinger, *Cl. Phil.* 8 (1913) 263 and 282 f., *Gr. theater* 4 ff. and 33 ff.; Ziegler 1946 ff.; Pickard-Cambridge (most fully in the 1st ed.); E. Howald, *Die gr. Tragödie* (Munich and Berlin 1930) 30; Peretti 285 f.; G. Björck, *Das Alpha impurum und die tragische Kunstsprache. Attische Wort- und Stilstudien* (Uppsala 1950) 374 ff.; H. Koller, *Die Mimesis in der Antike* (Diss. Bernenses I. 5 1954) 39; Pohlenz 24 and *Erläuterungen* 10 f.; H. Patzer, *Die Anfänge der gr. Tragödie* (Wiesbaden 1962) 39 ff.; Lesky 11 f.; Else, *Origin and early form* 26 ff. The Freudian psycho-analytic methods of Winterstein have not found acceptance. Untersteiner's problematical attempt to carry back the origins of tragedy to a pre-Hellenic nature-goddess and her male partner, is no more relevant for our present purpose than the earlier theories (for criticism of it cf. del Grande 324 ff.; Lesky 14).

contain elements that are still valid in themselves,[1] they in no way concern the structure of the *Supplices*. Indeed it was in Euripides rather than in Aeschylus (or Sophocles) that Murray claimed to find most clearly the forms of his *Sacer Ludus* of Dionysus, the daimon of the Year-Cycle of death and rebirth.[2]

The most fruitful investigation of cult origins has lain in the field of the ritual threnos or lament.[3] Though we have little evidence for the form of the threnos in the post-Homeric period there is no reason to deny that the many threnoi of tragedy exhibit stylistic peculiarities which may well derive from such a traditional ritual lament.[4] It is not difficult to see Xerxes at the end of the *Persae* as the exarchon of a threnos.[5] But the existence of threnodic forms in extant tragedy proves nothing about the origins of tragedy.[6] The subject-matter of the plays requires that they should abound in laments, and consequently in threnodic

[1] Thus it is by no means impossible that the δρώμενα at Eleusis, whether or not they contained a dramatic element, influenced the origins of tragedy, but that does not mean that they were the only or even an important influence: cf. Lesky 15: Peretti, *loc. cit.*; Untersteiner 201 ff.; Ziegler 1950 f.

[2] A criticism made by Pickard-Cambridge (1st ed.) 190 f.; cf. 199 f. Webster (2nd ed.) 128 f. (cf. also *Univ. Lond. Inst. Class. Stud. Bull.* no. 5 (1958) 43 ff.) is more inclined to favour Murray's theory. Murray (in J. Harrison's *Themis* 348 and 357) claimed that the epiphany of Aphrodite in the *Danaids*, the Agon in the *Supplices* (826–910), the Peripeteia, the Messenger (Danaus 980–1013), and finally 'not exactly a Threnos, but a song of prayer (1018–end)' are features of his *Sacer Ludus*. Cf. also Gaster 100 ff.

[3] Not in the extreme form of the theory presented by Ridgeway, *The origins of tragedy*, but in, for instance, the modified form put forward by Nilsson, *Opusc. sel.* I. 61 ff. (=*N. Jbb.* 27 (1911) 609 ff. and 673 ff.). He held that tragedy comes from a union of the ritual threnos (or rather two forms of threnos—an epic and a lyric) with the cult of Dionysus, which latter provides the mimetic element: cf. Winterstein 113 ff. and 167 f. A similar line is taken by Peretti, for whom pre-Aeschylean tragedy is born from the union of a severe Dorian mimetic canto in honour of Dionysus with a ritual Ionian threnody. The threnos formed part of Dieterich's theory concerning the δρώμενα at Eleusis (*Arch. f. Rel.-Wiss.* 11 (1908) 163 ff.=*Kl. Schr.* 414 ff.). Lesky (35) also lays stress on the importance of the threnos. For bibliography see Patzer 41 n. 3.

[4] Cf. Wilamowitz, *Gr. Verskunst* (Berlin 1921) 208 and 467 (see also *Kl. Schr.* I. 378 ff.); W. Porzig, *Aischylos* (Leipzig 1926) 40 and 90 ff.; Nestle 17 ff., 62 ff., 128; Kranz 127 ff.; R. Hölzle, *Zum Aufbau der lyrischen Partien des Aischylos* (Diss. Freiburg i. Br. 1934) 12 ff.; Peretti, *Riv. di Fil. e di Istr. Class.* n.s. 15 (1937) 56 ff.; Pohlenz 114 f., and *Erl.* 176; Else, *Origin and early form* 71: *contra* F. M. Cornford, *C.R.* 27 (1913) 41 ff. See further chap. II p. 42, and below p. 115.

[5] Cf. Wilamowitz, *Hermes* 32 (1897) 389; Nilsson 85 f.; Peretti 31 ff. (cf. 132 f.).

[6] Despite the modern and other parallels that are produced for mimetic mourning by Dieterich 435 ff.

forms of expression.[1] And the same is true of cult in general.[2] The *Supplices* is full of prayers and the traditional forms of prayers not because it is an archaic play, but because the theme demands it.

The starting-point of our inquiry must be rather the *Poetics* of Aristotle; for it is here and only here that we seem to find irrefutable proof that the structure of the *Supplices* is archaic. In chapter 4 of the *Poetics* Aristotle makes two statements about the origin of Tragedy:

(1) γενομένη δ' οὖν ἀπ' ἀρχῆς αὐτοσχεδιαστικῆς – καὶ αὐτὴ καὶ ἡ κωμῳδία, καὶ ἡ μὲν ἀπὸ τῶν ἐξαρχόντων τὸν διθύραμβον, ἡ δὲ ἀπὸ τῶν τὰ φαλλικὰ ἃ ἔτι καὶ νῦν ἐν πολλαῖς τῶν πόλεων διαμένει νομιζόμενα – κατὰ μικρὸν ηὐξήθη προαγόντων ὅσον ἐγίγνετο φανερὸν αὐτῆς· καὶ πολλὰς μεταβολὰς μεταβαλοῦσα ἡ τραγῳδία ἐπαύσατο, ἐπεὶ ἔσχε τὴν αὑτῆς φύσιν (1449a 9–15).

(2) ἔτι δὲ τὸ μέγεθος· ἐκ μικρῶν μύθων καὶ λέξεως γελοίας διὰ τὸ ἐκ σατυρικοῦ μεταβαλεῖν ὀψὲ ἀπεσεμνύνθη, τό τε μέτρον ἐκ τετραμέτρου ἰαμβεῖον ἐγένετο. τὸ μὲν γὰρ πρῶτον τετραμέτρῳ ἐχρῶντο διὰ τὸ σατυρικὴν καὶ ὀρχηστικωτέραν εἶναι τὴν ποίησιν, λέξεως δὲ γενομένης αὐτὴ ἡ φύσις τὸ οἰκεῖον μέτρον εὗρε (1449a 19–24).[3]

For Aristotle then tragedy was derived (*a*) ἀπὸ τῶν ἐξαρχόντων τὸν διθύραμβον, and (*b*) ἐκ σατυρικοῦ. How far is he to be

[1] Cf. Ziegler 1946 ff. (but also 1914 f.); *GGL* 29 n. 4; Pickard-Cambridge (1st ed.) 178 ff. (cf. 197); H. D. Broadhead, *The Persae of Aeschylus* (Cambridge 1960) 310; Else, *Origin and early form* 74 f.

[2] For ritual and cult forms in general in the extant plays see esp. F. Leo, *Abh. Ges. Wiss. Gött.*, Phil.-hist. Kl. 10 (1908) 7; Schadewaldt, *Monolog*, and *Hermes* 67 (1932) 348 f.; Ed. Fraenkel, *Philol.* 86 (1931) 1 ff.; Kranz, *Stasimon* 127 ff.; Hölzle; Peretti, *loc. cit.*, and *Epirrema e tragedia* esp. 83 ff., 101 f., 201 ff., 257 ff., Patzer 124; V. Citti, *Il linguaggio religioso e liturgico nelle tragedie di Eschilo* (Bologna 1962). For dramatic elements in the sacred songs of modern primitive peoples cf. C. M. Bowra, *Primitive song* (1962) 55 f.

[3] See Else, *Aristotle's Poetics: the argument* (Harvard 1957) 170 f. for the various ways of relating τὸ μέγεθος to the sentence. There is as little agreement about its meaning and that of μικρῶν in the phrase ἐκ μικρῶν μύθων. Is Aristotle referring to the *length* or to the gravity of the first tragedies? Or is a combination of the two a possibility? Else's discussion of the difficulties of the passage deserves the closest attention. It is difficult however to see why the sentence beginning ἔτι δὲ τὸ μέγεθος must necessarily refer to the period of Sophocles or later (p. 169), merely because S. is the last name to be mentioned. A. has brought the increase in actors to its completion with S., and now returns to the beginning to trace the course of a different development. Else's earlier treatment in *TAPhA* 70 (1939) 139 ff. should also be consulted. For the possibility of a lacuna in the text cf. also Patzer 68 f. and Kassel's apparatus (OCT).

believed? As usual scholars are divided into two camps. The first[1] considers that we have no right to reject Aristotle's authority, since he lived much nearer to the origins of tragedy than we do, since he had a vastly greater corpus of tragedies on which to base his statements, and since he very likely had before him documentary evidence in the form of official archives. He could draw too upon the considerable output of sophistic literary studies that were carried on in the fifth century, still closer to the early days of tragedy than he was himself.[2] Moreover he remarks explicitly at 5. 1449a 37 ff. that αἱ μὲν οὖν τῆς τραγῳδίας μεταβάσεις καὶ δι' ὧν ἐγένοντο οὐ λελήθασιν, ἡ δὲ κωμῳδία διὰ τὸ μὴ σπουδάζεσθαι ἐξ ἀρχῆς ἔλαθεν. His statement (1449b 4–5) that it is not known who gave comedy its masks and prologues, or increased the number of its actors, seems to imply that he was aware of no such gap in his knowledge of early tragedy. Confidence then in Aristotle's authority, together with the various notices that refer to the activity of Arion in Corinth[3] and to τραγικοὶ χοροί at Sicyon[4] has led to the widespread adoption of a theory that, with various minor differences of opinion, runs more or less as follows:[5] At the end of the seventh century in Corinth Arion

[1] For example Crusius, *R.-E.* v. A. 1212; I. Bywater, *Aristotle's Poetics* (Oxford 1909) 134 f.; Wilamowitz, *Kl. Schr.* I. 371 ff.; *Einleitung in die gr. Tragödie* (reprinted Berlin 1921) 49 ff. (with reservations); Flickinger, *Cl. Phil.* 8. 261 ff., and *Gr. theater* 5 f. and 21; Pohlenz, *NGG* (1920) ii. 143, *NGG* (1926) ii. 298 f. and 302, *Erl.* 7; Kranz, *N. Jbb.* 43 (1919) 145 ff.; *Stasimon* 3 ff.; Weir Smyth 3 f.; Geffcken I. ii. 139 n. 7; A. Gudeman, *Aristoteles* Περὶ Ποιητικῆς (Berlin and Leipzig 1934) 132; Ziegler 1905 ff.; Norwood 42 f.; Lesky, *Tr. Dichtung* 16 ff. (cf. 227); Thomson 165 (cf. 220 ff., 349 f.): cf. also Lindsay 331 ff.

[2] Cf. esp. Kranz, *Stasimon* 4 ff., and Gudeman 9 ff.

[3] *Suda* s.v. 'Αρίων (λέγεται καὶ τραγικοῦ τρόπου εὑρετὴς γενέσθαι, καὶ πρῶτος χορὸν στῆσαι, καὶ διθύραμβον ᾆσαι καὶ ὀνομάσαι τὸ ᾀδόμενον ὑπὸ τοῦ χοροῦ καὶ Σατύρους εἰσενεγκεῖν ἔμμετρα λέγοντας); Ioannes Diaconus, *Comm. in Hermogenem* (Rabe, *Rh. Mus.* 63 (1908) 150); Proclus, *Chrest.* 12; Hdt. i. 23. The ancient sources are assembled by Pickard-Cambridge.

[4] Hdt. v. 67: cf. also Them. *Or.* 27 p. 406.

[5] See for example Haigh 16 ff.; Dieterich, *Kl. Schr.* 419; Wilamowitz, *Kl. Schr.* I. 374 ff.; *Einleitung* 82 ff.; *apud* T. v. Wilamowitz, *Die dramatische Technik des Sophokles* (Berlin 1917) 314 n. 1; Petersen 56 ff.; Flickinger, *Gr. theater* 8 ff.; E. Kalinka, *Die Urform der gr. Tragödie* (Comment. Aenipontanae X Innsbruck 1924) 37 ff.; Pohlenz, *NGG* (1926) ii. 321, and *Gr. Tragödie* 19 ff.; Howald 23 ff.; E. Tièche, *Thespis* (Leipzig and Berlin 1933); Gudeman 140; Ziegler 1909 ff.; F. Brommer, *Satyrspiele* (Berlin 1944) 5 f.; Lesky 30: cf. also A. Frickenhaus, *Jahrb. Arch. Inst.* 32 (1917) 1 ff.; Geffcken I. i. 142.

invented a new literary genre (with a heroic content?) by introducing goat-like satyrs into the dithyramb, a previously improvised hymn to Dionysus, and the name τραγῳδία (ᾠδὴ τῶν τράγων) was given to it. This new satyr-dithyramb shortly afterwards spread to Sicyon, at the time when the tyrant Cleisthenes took away from Adrastus the τραγικοὶ χοροί that were held in his honour, and gave them to Dionysus. Later still they came to Athens, when Peisistratus was organizing the Great Dionysia and instituting dramatic contests as its chief ingredient. In Attica the form was adapted to the native horse-type Sileni, which alone appear on early vase-paintings,[1] but the name τραγῳδία was retained. The first actor was the invention of Thespis in the year 534 or 533. Opinions vary as to who first substituted human choruses for the animal-type ones, but it is generally agreed that a strong grotesque or burlesque element must have been in evidence for a considerable time, and that the plots must have been μικροί.[2] As 'tragedy' became serious and began to depart from Dionysiac themes a reaction set in, as the proverb οὐδὲν πρὸς τὸν Διόνυσον indicates.[3] Pratinas, who came to Attica from Phleius, catered for this feeling by re-introducing the chorus of satyrs, which failed nevertheless to oust tragedy from the festival. A compromise was arranged with the performance of a satyr-play following upon that of three

[1] But see now Webster in Pickard-Cambridge (2nd ed.) 113 ff.

[2] Else, *TAPhA* 70. 147 n. 27, shows how vague scholars have been in assigning a date to the change from μικροὶ μῦθοι (whether in the sense of 'short' or 'undignified'). Gudeman, for example, makes Thespis responsible (141) (also Geffcken I. i. 142 f.), Peretti (74 ff.) says that the development must have occurred at least by the time of Phrynichus and Aeschylus, while for Bywater (138) 'the time meant is presumably the age of Phrynichus'. The major achievement is usually given to Aeschylus: cf. Wilamowitz, *Interpr.* 252; *Einleitung* 94 and 106 f.; Dieterich 416 f.; Kranz, *N.Jbb.* (1919) 152, *Stasimon* 9 f. and 270; Murray, esp. 13 ff., 19 ff., 160 ff. For Howald (36) Aeschylus restored tragedy to a σεμνότης which it had already possessed before it became satyric. There is still greater reluctance to propose a date for the change from a satyric to a human chorus.

[3] Variously referred by the ancient sources to Epigenes, Thespis, Phrynichus, and Aeschylus. Cf. Pickard-Cambridge (2nd ed. 124 ff.). If the view is correct that Pratinas' work represents a reaction to the change in the character of tragedy, then obviously that change (or at least its beginnings) must pre-date Pratinas. Cf. Peretti 67 ff. The titles of Phrynichus' plays are serious enough, and so are those of Thespis. Cf. Pickard-Cambridge (2nd ed.) 85 and 124.

serious tragedies. By a similar process to that of tragedy the dithyramb also became serious, with the result that we can see in the remains of Simonides, Bacchylides, and Pindar. The original satyr-dithyramb of Arion was thus the ancestor of fifth-century developed tragedy, satyr-drama, and dithyramb.

The opposite view, that Aristotle's statements about the origins of tragedy are not to be trusted, has found a considerable number of supporters.[1] It is doubted whether he can have had much more documentary evidence for the early period than we have ourselves.[2] He is attempting a theoretical reconstruction that is no more valuable than the reconstructions of modern scholars, one that is based upon the existence in his own day of a semi-dramatic dithyramb and a satyr-drama that looked more primitive than tragedy, and might reasonably be supposed to pre-date it. And it is a reconstruction that is moulded into an *a priori* form determined by his view of nature advancing to a τέλος that is already potentially contained within itself (cf. the language at 1449a 14–15 καὶ πολλὰς μεταβολὰς μεταβαλοῦσα ἡ τραγῳδία ἐπαύσατο, ἐπεὶ ἔσχε τὴν αὑτῆς φύσιν: and at 22–4 τὸ μὲν γὰρ πρῶτον τετραμέτρῳ ἐχρῶντο διὰ τὸ σατυρικὴν καὶ ὀρχηστικωτέραν εἶναι τὴν ποίησιν, λέξεως δὲ γενομένης αὐτὴ ἡ φύσις τὸ οἰκεῖον μέτρον εὗρε. The statement that tragedy was originally satyric contradicts, it is argued, Aristotle's own division of poetry into two streams according to whether its

[1] Most notably Pickard-Cambridge (1st ed.) 121 ff. (Webster in the 2nd ed. 95 ff. is more inclined to accept the authority of Aristotle). See also L. R. Farnell, *Cults of the Greek states* v (Oxford 1909) 230; Ridgeway 8 and 57; Nilsson, *Opusc. sel.* I. 61 ff. and 90 f.; Howald 28 ff. (but for H. Aristotle's theorizing is correct); *GGL* 38 ff., 42 f., 49; Peretti 57 ff. and 66 f.; Björck 372 ff.; E. Roos, *Die tragische Orchestik im Zerrbild der altattischen Komödie* (Lund 1951) 117 f. (with further literature); H. D. F. Kitto, *Form and meaning in drama* (London 1956) 220; Patzer 70 ff. and 123 f. Else goes so far as to bracket the words τρεῖς δὲ... ἀπεσεμνύνθη as an anti-Athenian Peripatetic interpolation (or two interpolations), believing that Aristotle cannot have contradicted himself so seriously, and that the language of the passage betrays a later authorship.

[2] There is no reason to believe that Aristotle knew any plays older than the age of Phrynichus and Aeschylus. Those attributed to Thespis in the fourth century were acknowledged to be forgeries (cf. p. 113 below). The didascalic material, on which A. must have drawn for his Διδασκαλίαι and Νῖκαι Διονυσιακαί, does not seem to go back before 509/8.

subject-matter was τὰ σπουδαῖα or τὰ φαῦλα. In terms of this pattern tragedy is the direct descendant of epic, and there is no room anywhere for the grotesque or the burlesque. Furthermore it is hardly credible that a satyric form of drama can ever have developed into the essentially solemn performance that is fifth-century tragedy, or that even in the sixth century the πάθεα of Adrastus, the hero of the War against Thebes, can have been celebrated by a chorus of satyrs.[1] Aristotle's statement contradicts the evidence of the *Suda* that Pratinas was the inventor of satyr-drama (πρῶτος ἔγραψε Σατύρους).[2] His defenders reply that ἐκ σατυρικοῦ need not mean satyr-drama as we know it from the fifth century, but merely something *satyrhaft* or 'satyr-like'.[3] Yet is is difficult to understand anything other than δράματος with the adjective σατυρικοῦ.

For our present purpose it does not matter greatly whether on this point Aristotle's authority is to be accepted or not. We need not re-examine the vexed question of the relation between satyrs, sileni, fat men, and Pans in Attica or the Peloponnese.[4] For

[1] Some have attempted to explain the new serious character of tragedy in terms of a difference in *Zeitgeist* between the fifth and sixth centuries: see, for example, Ziegler 1940; Geffcken I. i. 143; Pohlenz, *Gr. Trag.* 31 ff. For Wilamowitz's horticultural similes cf. *Kl. Schr.* I. 382 f. For various other explanations cf. Bethe 40 ff.; Murray 169 f.; Peretti 102 f.; Untersteiner 256 ff.; Lesky 37; del Grande 49, 143, 147 f., 375; Thomson 222 f.

[2] It has been plausibly argued however by Pohlenz (*NGG* (1926) ii. 298 ff.) that the ascription of the invention of satyr-drama to Pratinas represents an anti-Peripatetic attempt of local Attic patriotism to establish tragedy as an Attic and not a Peloponnesian invention.

[3] See E. Reisch, *Festschr. Theodor Gomperz* (Vienna 1902) 472; Dieterich 416 f.; Flickinger, *Cl. Phil.* 8. 263 f., and *Gr. theater* 22 f.; D. S. Margoliouth, *The Poetics of Aristotle* (London, N. York, Toronto 1911) 149 (satyric='with the dance predominating'); Pohlenz, *NGG* (1926) ii. 298 n. 1, and *Gr. Trag.* 28; Kranz, *Stasimon* 9 ff.; Untersteiner 256 ff. (the satyrikon represents above all 'dismisura', that which goes beyond the ideal measure); Patzer 53 and 84 ff.; Brommer 5; Thomson 220 ff. *Contra* Ziegler 1903 n. 7; Peretti 67 f.; Pickard-Cambridge (2nd ed.) 91; Else, *TAPhA* 70. 140, *Poetics* 172 f., *Origin and early form* 111 n. 21.

[4] Those who reject a satyric (i.e. with goat-chorus) origin for tragedy have to explain τραγῳδία and τραγῳδοί in some other way. The theory of a goat-sacrifice or goat-prize, which may be a Hellenistic invention (cf. Pohlenz, *NGG* (1926) ii. 303 ff.; Tièche 21 ff.), has had its modern adherents. The one does not necessarily exclude the other: cf. Reisch 466 ff.; Flickinger, *Cl. Phil.* 8. 269 ff., and *Gr. theater* 13 ff.; Murray 1; Else, *Hermes* 85 (1957) 18 f. and 42; *Origin and early form* 69 f. Cf. Pickard-Cambridge and Webster, *loc. cit.* From time to time attempts are

there is nothing satyric about the *Supplices* and it is clearly in the interests of Aristotle's defenders that that play should be placed as late as possible in the development of tragedy, particularly if it was Aeschylus himself who was responsible for making tragedy serious. It is true that Wilamowitz and Kranz have found traces of λέξις γελοία in the herald-scene (see chap. II p. 56), but this is little more than a half-hearted attempt to reconcile the supposed early date of the play with the satyric origin of tragedy. Much more important is the statement that tragedy was derived from the dithyramb, and there is nothing to prevent this view from being considered apart from the question of a satyric origin; for even if we find it difficult to accept Else's deletion of the latter from the text of Aristotle, it remains true that Aristotle himself nowhere combines his two statements, or tries to relate one to the other in a historical context. The hybrid 'satyr-dithyramb' is the invention of modern scholars.[1] That tragedy came from the dithyramb is in itself a more credible view than that it was originally satyric, and it has the virtue of accounting for many of the facts. Not least it explains why tragedy was inseparably connected with Dionysus, and why, through this connection with the god of ecstatic experience, impersonation and the wearing of masks was natural for it.[2] It is easy too to see how the later dithyramb could itself be influenced by tragedy and become mimetic, if the two genres were con-

made to dissociate τραγῳδία altogether from goats. Cf. most recently del Grande 356 ff. Flickinger, *Cl. Phil.* 8. 269 ff. gives a useful summary of earlier views. It is disputed whether Hdt. at v. 67. 5 means by τραγικοῖσι χοροῖσι *goat-choruses* or choruses that were somehow akin to the choruses of tragedy in his own day. Cf. Pickard-Cambridge (1st ed.) 136 ff. (cf. 81 n. 1), *contra* Webster 103 f., 129; and for bibliographies of the subject Lesky 36 n. 1, del Grande 348.

[1] Despite Crusius 1212, according to whom Aristotle says that the dithyramb and σατυρικόν were originally identical. O. Hoffmann, *Rh. Mus.* 69 (1914) 250, also states that the only thing certain for A. is that tragedy came from a dithyramb presented by a satyr-chorus. Proper attention to what A. does say is paid by Patzer 52: cf. esp. Else, *Hermes* 85. 18 n. 2, *Poetics* 172, *Origin and early form* 16; Webster 96.

[2] Cf. Farnell 102 and 150 f.; Nilsson 111 ff.; Peterson 61; Kranz, *N. Jbb.* (1919) 161; Peretti 275, 284, 287; Bieber 8 f.; Patzer 45 and 122; Lesky 12 f. and 33. Some have thought that Dionysus himself is to be seen in the first actor: for example Bethe 42 ff., and *N. Jbb.* 19 (1907) 85; Nilsson 142; Flickinger 163; Geffcken I. i. 145; Untersteiner 197 ff.; Thomson 160 and 172. But see also Howald 44; Ziegler 1932 and 1952; del Grande 151 f. and 375; Lesky 32.

nected from the beginning.[1] Confirmation may be sought in the *Suda*'s statement that Arion was said to be τραγικοῦ τρόπου εὑρετής, and in John the Deacon (τῆς δὲ τραγῳδίας πρῶτον δρᾶμα Ἀρίων ὁ Μηθυμναῖος εἰσήγαγεν, ὥσπερ Σόλων ἐν ταῖς ἐπιγραφομέναις Ἐλεγείαις ἐδίδαξε). Even here however there are difficulties. The circular dithyrambic chorus of fifty is different from the square tragic chorus of twelve.[2] There is no proof that the three innovations ascribed by the *Suda* to Arion (cf. p. 94 n. 3) do not refer to three separate poetic genres.[3] If tragedy was originally a dithyramb sung in honour of Dionysus it is hard to explain why its subject-matter should so rarely be Dionysiac, so firmly fixed in the world of heroic myth.[4] And even what seems at first sight to be strong evidence in support of Aristotle, fragment 77 of Archilochus,[5] turns out on closer examination to

[1] For the new dithyramb see Pickard-Cambridge (2nd ed.) 38 ff.; also Wilamowitz, *GGA* (1898) 142; *Einleitung* 80; Crusius 1222 ff.; R. C. Jebb, *Bacchylides* (Cambridge 1905) 45 ff.; A. Severyns, *Bacchylide* (Liége and Paris 1933) 59 ff.; Koller 46 f. For the semi-dramatic Θησεύς of Bacchylides see below pp. 115 f.

[2] Cf. Pickard-Cambridge (2nd ed.) 32 and 94. For the original size of the tragic chorus see chap. V p. 207 n. 9.

[3] Cf. Reisch 471; Pickard-Cambridge (1st ed.) 21 and 132 ff.; Patzer 54 f. and 66; Else, *Origin and early form* 16 f. *Contra* Crusius, *R.-E.* ii. A. 840 f. and V. A. 1211; Flickinger, *Cl. Phil.* 8. 268 n. 2, and *Gr. theater* 10 n. 2; Ziegler 1910 ff.; Lesky 30; Webster 100. For the metrical objection to accepting τῆς τραγῳδίας δρᾶμα as a quotation from Solon cf. Wilamowitz, *Kl. Schr.* I. 375 f.; J. M. Stahl, *Rh. Mus.* 69 (1914) 587; Flickinger, *Cl. Phil.* 266, and *Gr. theater* 8; *GGL* I. I. 407 n. 8; Ziegler 1911; Pohlenz, *Erl.* 10; Pickard-Cambridge (2nd ed.) 99 f. (cf. Webster 103); G. A. Privitera, *Maia* 9 (1957) 107 n. 1; Else, *Origin and early form* 17: *contra* Kalinka 38, Untersteiner 231 f.

[4] That tragedy was originally Dionysiac in subject-matter and dealt with the life and passion of the god has been held by many scholars: for example, Bethe 46; Haigh 14 ff. and 33; Flickinger, *Cl. Phil.* 8. 274 ff., and *Gr. theater* 20 f., 23, 125 f., 135 f., 162; Petersen 56 ff. and 114; Gudeman 134 f.; Peretti 276 ff.; Murray 145 ff., and *C.Q.* 37 (1943) 52; Lindsay 341; Thomson 169 ff. Opinions differ as to whether Epigenes, Thespis, Phrynichus, or Aeschylus was responsible for the change to hero-saga. In fact there is nothing in the titles of Aeschylus' predecessors to suggest that Dionysus ever played a greater role than he does in extant tragedy, and that is small. Cf. Wilamowitz, *Einleitung* 60 ff.; Nilsson 91 ff.; *GGL* 42 and 87 ff.; Ziegler 1952; Pohlenz, *Gr. Trag.* 27 and 130 f.; Lesky 33 f.; Patzer 11 and 44; Else, *Origin and early form* 31, 63. Del Grande (esp. 26 ff. and 55 f.) and Untersteiner (esp. 191 ff.) attempt to reconcile the contradiction. Wilamowitz pointed out (*Einleitung* 108 ff.) that the importance of hero-saga is the most serious omission in Aristotle's account of the origins of tragedy (cf. Patzer 76 and 124). The importance was seen by A.'s successors, for example Theophrastus (τραγῳδία ἐστὶν ἡρωικῆς τύχης περίστασις: Diomed. p. 487 12 K); cf. *GGL* 36 f.

[5] ὡς Διωνύσοι' ἄνακτος καλὸν ἐξάρξαι μέλος
οἶδα διθύραμβον οἴνῳ συγκεραυνωθεὶς φρένας.

raise serious doubts about the validity of his statement. The fragment shows us Archilochus as the ἐξάρχων of a dithyramb, performing some kind of solo improvisation to which others respond with a refrain. There can hardly remain any doubt that this is what is meant by ἐξάρχειν, both here and in the *Poetics*,[1] though some have seen in the ἐξάρχοντες a chorus that is set over against a responding second chorus or a congregation.[2] It is the same function as we see the ἔξαρχος performing in sundry θρῆνοι in the *Iliad* (ω 720 ff., Σ 50 ff. and 316).[3] The plural need not mean that there was more than one ἐξάρχων per dithyramb. Here then, it may be thought, we have the rudiments of an actor confronted by a chorus. Yet if the *Suda*'s evidence about Arion means anything at all it is surely that Arion turned the dithyramb into a literary composition, with a set text performed by the chorus itself.[4] With this change the ἐξάρχων must have lost his independent position, and, if he survived at all, can have done so only as leader of the chorus.[5] Whether or not Aristotle thought of Thespis as an ἐξάρχων in the same sense as Archilochus, his view that tragedy was derived from the ἐξάρχοντες of the dithyramb ignores Arion's reform. Again it has been suggested that Aristotle is theorizing,[6] on the basis perhaps of the same Archilochus fragment that is

[1] Cf. Reisch 470; Crusius, *R.-E.* v. A. 1208; Nilsson 76 ff.; Stahl 588; Petersen 56; Kalinka 34 f.; Pickard-Cambridge (2nd ed.) 9 f.; Tièche 29; Ziegler 1907 f. and 1944 n. 25; Thomson 158 and 174; Pohlenz 19; Lesky 17; Else, *Poetics* 157 f.; H. Koller, *Glotta* 40 (1962) 187; Patzer 90 ff. For some modern primitive parallels cf. Bowra 49 ff. Del Grande accepts the view that the ἐξάρχων is a soloist, but explains the term as referring to the giving of the tone to the chorus, and to the production of the performance (2 ff. and 31 ff.); cf. also Bywater 134; Privitera 96 ff.

[2] Kranz, *N. Jbb.* (1919) 153, and *Stasimon* 17 and 272; Howald 28; Untersteiner 243 ff. and 235 n. 54. For F. Bradač, *Philol. Wochenschr.* 50 (1930) 284 f., Gudeman 133 f., and G. Rudberg, *Eranos* 45 (1947) 15, the ἐξάρχοντες are simply the singers of the dithyramb.

[3] See however Privitera 101.

[4] Del Grande (30 f.) concludes from a misinterpretation of Hdt. i. 23 that Arion's innovation pre-dated Archilochus' boast. Privitera (95 ff.) argues that in no real sense can Arion be considered as the inventor of the dithyramb.

[5] Cf. Patzer 81 ff. (P. accepts the derivation of tragedy from the dithyramb, but rejects that of the actor from the ἐξάρχοντες); Pickard-Cambridge (2nd ed.) 91 ('the cyclic dithyramb, as we know it in the fifth century, had a coryphaeus but no *exarchon*'; cf. Webster 129).

[6] Cf. Pickard-Cambridge (2nd ed.) 94.

used by modern scholars to confirm his theory. It is true that the ritual threnos may have had an ἐξάρχων (cf. p. 92 above), but Aristotle says nothing about that.

Nevertheless, whatever we may make of the details of Aristotle's statement about the dithyramb, it is difficult to deny that tragedy had its origin in some form of choral lyric. If it was not the dithyramb it must have been some other.[1] 'Wir müßten dies auch ohne die Angabe des Aristoteles postulieren, denn die Form der historischen Tragödie läßt sich nur als ein Zweig der Chorlyrik erklären, und daß das Chorlied im Dionysosdienst Dithyrambos heißt, weil es an Stelle des kultischen Dithyrambus trat, ist selbstverständlich.'[2] This indeed was one of the principal answers to those who tried to derive tragedy from some kind of ritual duel, the difficulty of separating its origins from a performance that was entirely choral, and only gradually gave way to a drama sustained by individual actors, with the chorus occupying a position of ever decreasing importance.[3] Αἰσχύλος... τὰ τοῦ χοροῦ ἠλάττωσε, says Aristotle, and in this at least it seems that we must believe him. G. F. Else indeed has recently denied[4] that tragedy is basically in origin a choral performance. For him the origin of both the genre and the name is to be seen in the activity of the τραγῳδός, a term coined on the analogy of ῥαψωδός. He argues that 'tragedy was an exclusively Athenian affair in origin' (*Origin and early form* 71), and that Thespis created both the actor and the tragic chorus, which was to be 'a sounding board for the heroic passion' (65). It is only *after* the creation of this new genre that heroic dithy-

[1] Cf. Patzer 124. Else remarks (*Hermes* 85. 46) that the choral odes of tragedy show affinities 'with almost every known variety of choral lyric *except* the dityramb'. Pickard-Cambridge stressed the influence on the work of Thespis of Peloponnesian choral lyric in general (1st ed. 148, 162 f., 174, 219).

[2] Howald 26 (cf. 1 ff.): see also Dieterich 414 ff.; Meyer, *Geschichte des Altertums* IV. 1. 424.

[3] Cf. Flickinger, *Cl. Phil.* 8. 283, and *Gr. theater* 4 f. and 133; Pickard-Cambridge (1st ed.) 162 f. and 194 f.; Ziegler 1948 ff. and 1954; Thomson 169 f.

[4] *Hermes* 85. 17 ff., and more fully in *Origin and early form*. Else accepts (53, 119 n. 12) the truth of the statement attributed by Themistius to Aristotle that τὸ μὲν πρῶτον ὁ χορὸς εἰσιὼν ᾖδεν εἰς τοὺς θεούς, Θέσπις δὲ πρόλογόν τε καὶ ῥῆσιν ἐξεῦρεν (Them. *or.* 316d: cf. p. 103 below). Yet that statement implies a pre-existing choral performance.

ramb exerted a stylistic influence upon tragedy in Athens 'during the last quarter of the sixth century and the beginning of the fifth' (74). Else does not explain however what the tragic chorus can have been like before it came under this influence. He can hardly mean that Thespis invented a tragic chorus without any knowledge of or reference to existing Dorian choral lyric. It seems easier to suppose that Thespis' new creation (and that it was new Else rightly stresses) resulted from the amalgamation of something new (the actor) with a traditional form of choral lyric, whose function was thereby transformed into that of the tragic chorus. In deriving tragedy directly from the recitations of the epic rhapsodes at the Panathenaea Else fails to take enough account of the importance of choral lyric for the development of hero myth. The subjects of tragedy are in fact as little tied to the *Iliad* and *Odyssey*, the subject-matter of the recitations at the Panathenaea, as they are to the story of the passion of Dionysus.[1] The myth had long been an essential feature of choral lyric in general, as well as of the dithyramb.[2] It can be seen in its most highly developed form in the epinikia of Pindar, it appears also as early as the *Partheneion* of Alcman. The poems of Stesichorus seem to have been largely narrative in content, and it is mainly his choice of metre that separates him from the epic poets. The myth might be used as a paradigm from the heroic world, a 'divino esempio',[3] or it might be merely an excuse to tell a good story. The borderline between plain

[1] Cf. Lycurg. 102. It was for this reason that Schmid suggested (*GGL* 26 n. 6) that tragedy was to be seen as *supplementing* in its subject-matter the recitations at the Panathenaea. Else shows on pp. 13–15 that he is aware of the hymn to the gods as 'a possible route from Homer to tragedy'.

[2] Cf. Crusius, *R.-E.* v. A. 1209f.; Wilamowitz, *Timotheos. Die Perser* (Leipzig 1903) 102 ff., and *Einleitung* 73 and 104f.; Dieterich 416; Tièche 29; Kranz, *Stasimon* 252 f.; Croiset 2 f.; Ziegler 1933; Meyer *loc. cit.*; Snell, *Discovery of the mind* 93; Untersteiner 235 f.; Else, *Poetics* 162 (with further references); del Grande 26 ff.; Patzer 94 ff. There is uncertainty about the criteria used by the Alexandrian editors to distinguish the dithyramb from other lyric poetry, and the genre to which poems xiv–xix of Bacchylides belong has been disputed. That one such criterion was narrative content is indicated by Pl. *Rep.* iii. 394c (cf. [Plut.] *de Mus.* 10). See D. Comparetti in *Mélanges H. Weil* (Paris 1898) 25 ff.; Wilamowitz, *Sappho und Simonides* (Berlin 1913) 133 f., *Einleitung* 80, and *apud* T. v. Wil. *Dram. Technik des Soph.* 314 n. 1; Pickard-Cambridge (2nd ed.) 10 f., 25 ff., 93; A. E. Harvey, *C.Q.* n.s. 5 (1955) 160 and 173 f.

[3] Del Grande (esp. 80 ff.).

narrative and direct representation might be easily obscured. Aristotle notes it as one of the virtues of Homer that he lets his characters speak for themselves: αὐτὸν γὰρ δεῖ τὸν ποιητὴν ἐλάχιστα λέγειν· οὐ γάρ ἐστι κατὰ ταῦτα μιμητής. οἱ μὲν οὖν ἄλλοι αὐτοὶ μὲν δι' ὅλου ἀγωνίζονται, μιμοῦνται δὲ ὀλίγα καὶ ὀλιγάκις· ὁ δὲ ὀλίγα φροιμιασάμενος εὐθὺς εἰσάγει ἄνδρα ἢ γυναῖκα ἢ ἄλλο τι ἦθος, καὶ οὐδέν' ἀήθη ἀλλ' ἔχοντα ἦθος (*Poet.* 1460a 7 ff.).[1] The same possibility lay open to the lyric poet.[2] Greater vividness and life could be given to a narrative by letting the characters speak *in propria persona*. It has been remarked that '*all* Greek genres craved to be dramatic and partly succeeded'.[3] It was then only a matter of time[4] before someone took the step of putting the direct speech into the mouth of an individual chosen to represent the character, and either taken out of the chorus itself or added to it as an entirely new element, and with recitation rather than singing as his natural vehicle of expression. And so the myth received dramatic form.[5] There seems no good reason to deny that it was Thespis who first took this step. It is true that his name does not occur in the *Poetics*, but the statement of Themistius that his master Aristotle ascribed to Thespis the invention of the rhesis and the

[1] Similarly, at 1448a 21–2, Homer is assigned to the intermediate class between pure narrative and pure dramatic representation. Cf. also Pl. *Rep.* 392d ff. The rhapsode's delivery of such passages of direct speech would no doubt be mimetic (cf. *GGL* 27; Else, *Hermes* 85. 34 ff.).

[2] Cf. Wilamowitz, *Timotheos* 104 f.; Howald 34 f.; *GGL* 27; Ziegler 1944 f.; Pohlenz, *Gr. Trag.* 20 f.

[3] Else, *Poetics* 100 f.: cf. Howald 5 f., *GGL* 27 n. 2. Aristotle himself in the *Poetics* sees drama as the culmination of the development of literary form: cf. Else 152. Pickard-Cambridge (2nd ed.) 30 remarked upon the extensive use of direct speech in the dithyrambs of Bacchylides.

[4] And a suitable environment. For it was only in Athens that the step seems to have been taken. Else devotes chap. II of his *Origin and early form* to a discussion of that environment (cf. also 68), but he exaggerates the closeness of the connection between Solon and early tragedy, and in particular the importance of the occasion on which Solon delivered his poem on Salamis while pretending to be mad. This is a long way from the dramatic impersonation of a mythical hero. It is Solon's use of the iambic metre that is most important for tragedy (cf. pp. 105 f. below: Else, 62, 64, 68).

[5] For this as the crucial step towards genuine drama see Bethe, *Prolegomena* 27 ff., and *N. Jbb.* (1907) 85; Reisch 470 f.; *GGL* 27; Peretti 276; Norwood 4 f.; Patzer 127 f.; Webster 112; and, in general, Bowra 57. But see also H. J. F. Jones 18.

prologue, is explicit enough, and most probably derives from the lost Περὶ ποιητῶν.[1] Some have thought that the step must have already been taken in the Peloponnese, that in Dorian choral lyric a soloist may already have been allowed to speak in iambic or trochaic verses,[2] but the evidence from Doric forms in the dialogue passages of tragedy is hardly strong or clear enough, and the *Suda*'s statement that Arion introduced satyrs ἔμμετρα λέγοντας is not much help.[3] The tradition is overwhelmingly in favour of Thespis.[4] The claims of people like Epigenes may be ascribed to Peloponnesian polemic,[5] or to a

[1] See Wilamowitz, *Kl. Schr.* I. 371; Lesky, *Wien. Stud.* 47 (1929) 8 ff., in *Studi in onore U. E. Paoli* (Florence 1955) 470, and *Tr. Dichtung* 40 f.; Nestle 13; Gudeman 114; Tièche 5 ff.; E. Bickel, *Rh. Mus.* 91 (1942) 141; Rudberg 15; Pickard-Cambridge (2nd ed.) 78, and *Dram. festivals* 131 f.; Ziegler 1930 f. (with further references); Untersteiner 283 n. 2 (with references); Else, *Hermes* 85. 20 n. 4; *Origin and early form* 53; Pohlenz, *Erl.* 15; del Grande 372. *Contra* E. Hiller, *Rh. Mus.* 39 (1884) 330 ff.; Kranz, *N. Jbb.* (1919) 154 n. 1, and *Stasimon* 10 f. and 270; Patzer 25 ff. The *Marmor Parium* gives 534/3 as the date of Thespis' first victory. But the fact that a contest was then established indicates that his innovation must itself have come earlier. For the various problems connected with the traditional account of Thespis cf. esp. Tièche; also Ridgeway 57 ff.; Kalinka 33; Lammers, *Doppel- und Halbchöre* 167; Pickard-Cambridge (2nd ed.) 69 ff.; A. von Blumenthal, *R.-E.* vi. A. I. 62 ff.; *GGL* 44 and 48 n. 2; Ziegler 1929 ff.; Peretti 276 ff.; Untersteiner 242 n. 28 and 271 ff.; Patzer 25 ff., 46 ff., 127; del Grande 131 ff.; Lesky, *Tr. Dichtung* 39 ff.; Else, *Origin and early form* 51 ff.

[2] For example J. D. Rogers, *A.J.Ph.* 25 (1904) 285 ff.; Hoffmann 244 ff.; K. Münscher, *Hermes* 54 (1919) 27 f.; Ziegler 1916 and 1930 f.; Bickel 123 ff. *Contra* Kranz, *Stasimon* 18 and 272; *GGL* 148 n. 6; Pickard-Cambridge (1st ed.) 146 ff., esp. 147 n. 1; Lesky, *Wien. Stud.* 47. 4 n. 8, and *Tr. Dichtung* 37 f.; Björck esp. 212 ff.; Pohlenz, *Erl.* 13. Those who accept the derivation of the actor from the ἐξάρχων naturally assume some kind of confrontation of individual and chorus at the pre-Thespian stage. Pickard-Cambridge himself (2nd ed. 86 f.) inclines to this possibility. Lammers finds in the Doric α a survival of his original purely lyric dialogue (cf. p. 111 below).

[3] Indeed it is difficult to find any meaning in it at all (though it has been accepted at face value by Haigh 19 f. and 23 f.; Flickinger, *Cl. Phil.* 8. 268, *Gr. theater* 10; Kalinka 36 and 39; Norwood 1 and 4; Ziegler 1912): cf. Lesky, *Tr. Dichtung* 31; also Pohlenz 21 and *Erl.* 9; Else, *Hermes* 85. 20 n. 2, *Origin and early form* 16 and 112 n. 26; Webster 99. The satyrs can only be the chorus, and it is improbable that a chorus was allowed to recite iambics or trochaics instead of sing. Attempts to get round this difficulty have not been successful (e.g. del Grande 47 f.; Untersteiner 229 f.; cf. 234 n. 26).

[4] For the ancient sources see Pickard-Cambridge (1st ed.) 97 ff.

[5] Cf. Gudeman 113; Ziegler 1915; Pohlenz, *NGG* (1926) ii. 299 f.; Untersteiner 213; Else, *Origin and early form* 21 f. Similarly the statement of the ps.-Platonic *Minos* (321 a) that tragedy is much older than Thespis belongs to Attic anti-Peloponnesian literary polemic; cf. Pohlenz 307; *GGL* 44 n. 1; Ziegler 1928; del Grande 52; Patzer 30; Else, *Origin and early form* 114 n. 54.

difference of opinion about what stage in the development was to be described as the first 'tragedy'.[1]

It is impossible to determine whether the actor emerged from the chorus itself or was imposed upon the chorus from without.[2] Those who accept Aristotle's statement about the ἐξάρχοντες of the dithyramb naturally uphold the former alternative. It is no real argument against it that it does not provide the possibility of a genuinely *dramatic* development, that there can be no conflict or tension between a chorus and an individual who has emerged from its own ranks. For dramatic conflict may come in only at a later stage, perhaps not even with the first appearance of the second actor. It is conceivable that the earliest drama was little more than a messenger-speech with lyric comment.[3] On the other hand without the view that the actor is superimposed from outside it is very difficult to understand the different forms taken by the choral and dialogue passages, the Doric colouring of the former, the Ionic/Attic of the dialogue.[4] The latter looks back to Ionian elegy and iambic verse, and

[1] Flickinger, *Cl. Phil.* 8. 265. There seems no reason to doubt the existence of Epigenes altogether. Cf. Dieterich, *R.-E.* vi. A. 64; Kalinka 43; Lesky, *Tr. Dichtung* 35.

[2] See for example, for the former view, Haigh 19 f.; Petersen 56; Flickinger, *Gr. theater* 16 and 162 f.; Kalinka 35; Winterstein 177 f.; Nestle 26 and 69; Kranz, *Stasimon* 17, 20, 272; Ziegler 1908, 1944 f.; Peretti 78 f.; Webster, *Greek theatre production* (London 1956) 35; Untersteiner 268 ff.; Jones 60 n. 3 and 67. For the latter view see Bethe, *Proleg.* 27 and 37 ff.; Nilsson 65; Howald 33 ff.; *GGL* 39; Gudeman 133; Lesky, *Tr. Dichtung* 17 and 40 ff.; Patzer 82 and 123. See also below p. 120.

[3] Despite Kranz, *Stasimon* 55; Kitto, *Greek tragedy* 27. But Kitto is inconsistent (cf. 31 f.).

[4] The difference between the two spheres of expression is dealt with most fully by Peretti; cf. also Schadewaldt, *Monolog* 39 f.; *GGL* 135; and, from a different point of view, Björck, esp. 191 ff. See further Bethe, *Proleg.* 36 f., and *N. Jbb.* (1907) 85; Crusius, *R.-E.* v. A. 1218; Nilsson 65 and 88 f.; Wilamowitz, *Kl. Schr.* I. 155 and 374; *Interpr.* 247 f.; *Gr. Verskunst* 41 and 204 ff.; *Einleitung* 88; Winterstein 114 f.; Pickard-Cambridge (2nd ed.) 111 f. (cf. Webster 130); *GGL* 28 f. and 139; Pohlenz 21 f., *Erl.* 13; Untersteiner 270; Patzer 122 f., 127. *Contra* Hoffmann; Kranz, *Stasimon* 17 and 138; Ziegler 1960. For Ionicisms in the Μιλήτου ἅλωσις of Phrynichus cf. Diels, *Rh. Mus.* 56 (1901) 29 ff.; F. Marx, *Rh. Mus.* 77 (1928) 358 f.; von Blumenthal, *R.-E.* xx. I. 912 and 916; *GGL* 147 n. 9; Lesky 47: cf. Ar. *Thesm.* 160 ff. *Contra* Björck 163 and 218. Björck in general minimizes both the dependence of tragic dialogue on the Ionian iambic (cf. chap. II p. 48 n. 3), and also the extent of the Doric forms in the lyrics of tragedy (esp. 29, 171, 221 ff.); cf. also Else, *Origin and early form* 71 ff.

particularly to Solon, who may be presumed to have been largely responsible for making them at home in Athens. In any case the question does not affect the main argument. From now on begins the process by which the actor's part grows at the expense of the lyrics.

Where so much is uncertain it may seem hazardous to make any statement at all about the structure of the *Supplices* in the light of pre-Aeschylean tragedy. Yet if any fact seems to be reasonably established, it is that tragedy derives from what was originally a purely choral performance, and that the actors only gradually prevailed over the chorus. When therefore we find that in the *Supplices* the Chorus plays a more important part and that the lyrics are far more extensive than in any other extant play, while the choral passages of the *Persae* are only a little less extensive,[1] it may seem natural to conclude that the *Supplices* represents the earliest extant stage of the development. Nevertheless such a conclusion is totally unjustifiable without further examination. The counting or measuring of lyrics is in itself a hopelessly unreliable criterion.[2] For while the *Supplices* and the *Persae* may be alike in the extent of their choral passages, their choruses are quite different in function and in composition. This is a difference not of quantity but of kind. The Chorus of the *Supplices* is the protagonist of the drama, a group of people who are properly at home in myth, with an existence independent of their place in Aeschylus' play. 'These people are no band of singers and dancers, but the Danaids, and they could never for a moment be confused with the Chorus of another play.'[3] The Chorus of the *Persae* is protagonist only in the sense that it represents the people of Persia,[4] which is involved in the more specific tragedy of its king Xerxes. They remain themselves anonymous and colourless. No one could imagine that any single member of this Chorus could become a character in his own right in a later play of a trilogy. It is absurd then to class

[1] See p. 88 n. 1 above for Ziegler's figures.

[2] Schmid points out (*GGL* 256) that the extent of the lyrics varies greatly among the three plays of the *Oresteia* trilogy.

[3] Kitto 23 (cf. 29).

[4] Cf. Croiset 79 f.; Perrotta, *I tragici greci* 65 f.; Kranz, *Stasimon* 167 f.; Ziegler 1957; Peretti 131.

the two plays together as evidence for an earlier stage of tragedy.[1] One or other may be the more archaic: it is not immediately self-evident that the development is from *Supplices* to *Persae*.

Aristotle says (*Poet.* 1449a 15 ff.): καὶ τό τε τῶν ὑποκριτῶν πλῆθος ἐξ ἑνὸς εἰς δύο πρῶτος Αἰσχύλος ἤγαγε καὶ τὰ τοῦ χοροῦ ἠλάττωσε καὶ τὸν λόγον πρωταγωνιστὴν[2] παρεσκεύασεν. He does not say, although this is how his statement is often interpreted, τὸν ὑποκριτὴν (or τοὺς ὑποκριτὰς) πρωταγωνιστὴν (or -εῖν) παρεσκεύασεν. Aristotle is concerned here not with the relationship between actor and chorus as actor, but with the relative extent of the dialogue and lyrics. The previous protagonist was not ὁ χορός but τὰ τοῦ χοροῦ. He is using the word 'protagonist' in a metaphorical sense. This is the only natural interpretation of his words.[3] As the dialogue expanded, so the relative extent of the lyrics decreased; and we have no reason to dispute it. Never for a moment does Aristotle suggest that the chorus was normally the protagonist of early tragedy in the sense that it was the principal character in the plot. It is the failure to distinguish between the function of the chorus and the extent of its choral utterances that has led to so much confusion, in interpreting both Aristotle and the *Supplices*.[4] The *Supplices*, we are told, is an early (or an old-fashioned) play because the chorus is still the protagonist.[5] The statement may be true, but

[1] As is done, for example, by Bethe, *Proleg.* 15 f.; Gudeman 137; Kranz, *Stasimon* 171.

[2] R. Kassel, *Rh. Mus.* 105 (1962) 117 ff., gives good reasons for preferring the emendation of Sophianus πρωταγωνιστεῖν.

[3] Yet Wilamowitz can say (*Einleitung* 51; cf. 94) that according to A. Aeschylus 'hat...*den chor* von der protagonistenstelle zurückgedrängt' (my italics): cf. also Croiset (12): 'Nous savons par le témoignage d'Aristote que le chœur, avant Eschyle, jouait le premier rôle.' Cf. also Perrotta 14 (cf. 107 f.). Kitto (24 n. 2) draws attention to the exact meaning of A.'s words: cf. also A. M. Dale in *Classical drama and its influence,* Essays presented to H. D. F. Kitto (ed. M. J. Anderson) (London 1965) 17 f.; Else, *Origin and early form* 13.

[4] The confusion is very marked in the passage quoted from Norwood on p. 89.

[5] Cf. Ridgeway 128 ('the prominence given to the chorus over the actor points to a period when as yet the drama had advanced but little from the stage in which Aeschylus took it over from Thespis, Pratinas and Phrynichus...Moreover, the whole plot centres not on one of the actors, but upon the fate of the chorus of the fifty Danaids'); Tucker xxiii; Petersen 117 and 370; Wilamowitz, *Interpr.* 240; Weir Smyth 52 ff.; Croiset 43 f., 50 (cf. 143), 276; Kranz, *Stasimon* 10 and 167 ff.;

we must recognize that Aristotle gives it no support. If it is based on any evidence at all, other than the preconception that the *Supplices* is an early play, then that evidence must be sought elsewhere. In the whole extant corpus of Greek tragedy the *Supplices* is almost unique[1] in that the Chorus is the principal character of the play. Is its age the only or even the likeliest reason for this uniqueness?[2] Or would it remain unique even if we had before us the entire body of pre-Aeschylean and early Aeschylean tragedy? Since proof either way is clearly impossible, once more we must be content with probabilities.

The question may be phrased in another way: is the chorus of choral lyric itself inherently dramatic, or is the possibility of genuine drama created only with the invention of the first actor? Is he invented merely to increase the dramatic potentialities of the situation of the chorus, or is it his own situation that is to be the subject of the drama? If what we have said above (pp. 102 f.) is true there can be no doubt about the answer. It is the actor and not the chorus that is dramatic. The chorus of choral lyric narrates a myth and comments on it lyrically. Thespis (or someone else) conceives the idea of bringing on an individual to represent one or more of the characters of that myth. He now tells his own and/or someone else's story, and the chorus's function is to ask him questions and to comment. The earliest tragedy is a messenger's speech, and tragedy indeed retains the messenger-speech as one of its most constant elements.[3] 'Die Erzählung eines Mythos durch Lied und Rede in mimetischer Form ist die Keimzelle der Tragödie, und ihre Formgeschichte hätte zu zeigen, wie die Erzählung durch das

Ziegler 1956 f.; Peretti 77 f.; W. Jaeger, *Paideia* I (Eng. tr. Oxford 1939) 248, 259, 263; Meyer 430; Pohlenz, *Gr. Trag.* 52; Mazon, *Eschyle* I. 3; Bieber 21. Pohlenz (136) finds a clear straight-line development from *Supp.* to *Oresteia*: cf. Norwood 76.

[1] In the *Eumenides* the Chorus is again the principal character, yet the *Eum.* is not an early play. E. *Supp.* is the next closest parallel.

[2] Before the discovery of the papyrus few even asked whether there might not be other reasons. But see A. Körte, *Philol. Wochenschr.* (1928) 1300; *GGL* 39, 70, 117, and 200.

[3] For the pains taken by Aeschylus to make his messenger-speeches as dramatic as possible see, for example, Weir Smyth 79; Croiset 87 ff., 187, and 271; R. D. Dawe, *Proc. Camb. Philol. Soc.* n.s. 9 (1963) 31.

der Mimesis entwachsende, völlig neue dramatische Element überwunden wurde (ganz geschah das nie) und welche Kräfte dies bewirkten.'[1] The chorus remains what it has always been, or rather it is given some sort of dramatic character by being made to represent an anonymous body of citizens or soldiers, etc. It is on the individual that all the genuine drama is concentrated. The dramatization of the chorus remains rudimentary.[2] It is difficult to imagine anything less like the situation of the *Supplices*, with its plot centring upon the fortunes of a chorus. But with this exception the position of the chorus remains basically unaltered throughout the whole history of Greek tragedy. The least important of its functions is to be a character in the drama.[3] When the Chorus of the *Choephori*

[1] Nestle, review of Kranz's *Stasimon*, *Gnomon* 10 (1934) 413. Cf. also Else, *Wien. Stud.* 72 (1959) 102 ff.; Thomson 168 f. This is why for Wilamowitz (*Einleitung* 109; cf. 88 and 93) Aristotle's phrase δρώντων καὶ οὐ δι' ἀπαγγελίας (*Poet.* 1449b 26) is misleading: for Attic tragedy the dramatic is only secondary. Cf. Nilsson 87 f.; Stahl 592; Wilamowitz, *Interpr.* 2 f.; Howald 1 ff.; Peretti 25 and 89 f.; Pohlenz, *Gr. Trag.* 22 f., 40 f., 58, 136, and 140; del Grande 137 f., 148, and 150; Patzer 136 f. See also below pp. 125 f. This does not mean that the Attic dramatists did not make of the myth 'precisely what they wanted' (Kitto 102). Else (*Hermes* 85. 39) (cf. also *Origin and early form* 63 f., 68 ff.) sees Thespis as substituting an epic hero speaking verses for a rhapsode reciting them at the Panathenaea. Schmid is led into inconsistency by his belief that the *Supp.* is early. In *GGL* 194 n. 1 the 'stärkeres Hervortreten der lyrischen und epischen Partien' appears as a criterion of age. But at 69 (cf. 197 n. 10) the small narrative content of the *Supp.* is said to indicate that this epic element was even less developed in pre-Aeschylean tragedy. Two fragments of Phrynichus, fr. 5 N and *Ox. Pap.* 2 no. 221 (p. 59) come respectively from messenger-speeches in iambics and trochaics: cf. also Webster (64) on fr. 6 N.

[2] Cf. [Arist.] *Probl.* 19. 15. 918b 28: ὁ μὲν γὰρ ὑποκριτὴς ἀγωνιστὴς καὶ μιμητής, ὁ δὲ χορὸς ἧττον μιμεῖται (cf. 48. 922b 26). For the general anonymity and lack of dramatic potential of the chorus see esp. Petersen 115 ff.; Weir Smyth 53; Nestle 16; *GGL* 38 n. 5, 57 ff., 70; Pohlenz 24; Kitto 29; del Grande 137 ff.; Patzer 80 f. and 136 f.; Else, *TAPhA* 70. 152 f., and *Origin and early form* 58, 65 ff., 74, 95; Dale 17. Flickinger (136 ff.) (cf. also Kranz, *Stasimon* 167 ff.; Schadewaldt 48; Kitto 29) wrongly supposes a development *towards* this anonymity. But he betrays his confusion (137): 'Thus it appears that from the standpoint of choral technique, Aeschylus' earliest play, the *Suppliants*, and his last play, the *Eumenides*, are the most successful.'

[3] Kranz (*loc. cit.*) divides the functions of the tragic chorus into three. It is (*a*) a character in the play, (*b*) an accompanying instrument for deepening the drama, (*c*) a tool of the poet's own personality as teacher of his people. The relative importance of these three functions naturally varies from playwright to playwright and from play to play: it varies even inside a single play. The Chorus of the *Septem* changes from a band of frightened girls into solemn representatives of the people of Thebes; cf. Wilamowitz, *Interpr.* 68 f. (cf. 124); Kranz 172; F. Solmsen,

takes the initiative in changing the orders of the Nurse (770 ff.) this is a quite abnormal step. A Greek tragedy deals with the fortunes not of a chorus but of an actor,[1] and there is as yet no reason to believe that it was ever otherwise. As Patzer says (137), a chorus that itself takes part in the action must be morphologically younger, not the oldest dramatic choral-form.

If the *Supplices* really is archaic, in the sense that it looks back to a pre-tragic chorus that was itself *qua* chorus (that is, without reference to a solo exarchon) inherently mimetic, then one might reasonably expect to find traces of such a chorus. But the search is in vain.[2] Few would now believe in the attempt of Welcker and Boeckh to find traces of 'lyric tragedy' in the ancient notices about the δράματα τραγικά of Pindar, Simonides, and Empedocles.[3] Indeed it is difficult to understand what scholars mean when they talk about a 'mimetic chorus' performing, for example, in honour of Adrastus at Sicyon. Snell says (90), 'We know, through some remarkable pieces of evidence, that even the early choral odes often contained some dramatic elements'. But what are these 'dramatic elements'?[4]

TAPhA 68 (1937) 200 f.; Kitto 47 n. 3; Dawe 31 ff.; Else, *Origin and early form* 90 (but see also K. von Fritz, *Antike und moderne Tragödie* (Berlin 1962) 214 f.). The Chorus changes roles with Eteocles (cf. p. 131 below). A similar change occurs in the *Choephori* after the ode at 585 ff. See in general Wilamowitz, *Interpr.* 240 f., *Einleitung* 79; Petersen 142 ff.; Ed. Fraenkel, *Philol.* 86. 15 ff.; Hölzle; *GGL* 41, 70 ff., 257; Pohlenz, *Gr. Trag.* 24 and 221 f.

[1] The chorus concerns itself in its songs 'mit den πάθη eines andern, hier aber (in the *Supp.*) mit seinen eigenen (wie später noch einmal in den Eum.' (Nestle 16): cf. also Haigh 28. Else too lays proper stress on the hero's *pathos* as the root from which the development of tragedy flowered (*Origin and early form*, esp. 65 f., 76, 83).

[2] Cf. Nilsson 69 f. and 101 ff.; Pickard-Cambridge (1st ed.) 135, 139 f., 148; *GGL* 39; Untersteiner 232. For the belief that older choral poetry contained dramatic or mimetic elements see Bethe, *Proleg.* 27 ff.; R. W. Macan, ed. *Herodotus IV–VI* (London 1895) I. 209; Ridgeway 28 f., 67, 185; Winterstein 101 and 113; Ziegler 1944; Jones 68.

[3] The reference to δράματα τραγικά in the *Suda* s.v. Pindaros was ascribed to a late grammarian by E. Hiller, *Hermes* 21 (1886) 357 ff.: cf. Pickard-Cambridge (2nd ed.) 107 f. See also below p. 115 n. 4.

[4] Cf. K. J. Dover, *C.R.* n.s. 15 (1965) 165: 'What is meant by "elements of drama" in dithyramb? If people sing as if they were the daughters of Danaus that is drama; if they sing *about* the daughters of Danaus, that is not.' Cf. also Else, *Origin and early form* 5, for a discussion of the different connotations of the term 'dramatic'.

It is easy enough to envisage a band of people dressing themselves up to represent animals or daemons or satyrs.[1] But a chorus of twelve (or fifty) characters from myth is quite a different matter. Not a single extant choral lyric poem might lead us to suppose that such a performance ever existed, and it is more than improbable in itself.[2] A chorus may indeed perform mimetically in that it accompanies its story of some hero with appropriate gestures and dance-steps and uses direct speech,[3] but its story remains the story of someone else's fortunes, not its own. Perhaps it is this difficulty that has lent some support to the theory of Lammers that tragedy was born from a performance by a double chorus.[4] With two choruses in opposition genuine drama might seem to be possible even before the invention of an individual actor. But the evidence on which Lammers based his theory is very slight indeed. Subsidiary choruses in extant drama have a very subordinate part to play. Our knowledge of the lost plays of Aeschylus and Phrynichus is far too frail to support any such far-reaching conclusions. And whatever one may make of Pratinas fr. 1 D as evidence for a satyr-

[1] Cf. Pollux iv. 103 (ὁ δὲ μορφασμὸς παντοδαπῶν ζῴων ἦν μίμησις). See Flickinger, *Gr. theater* 43 f.; Reisch 469 f.; Winterstein 119 ff.; Pickard-Cambridge (2nd ed.) 151 ff.; Patzer 57.

[2] Jebb (*Bacchylides* 365) suggested that B.'s dithyramb xiv may have been performed by a chorus representing the fifty sons of Theano and Antenor. But there is nothing in the text to support the suggestion. Cf. Pickard-Cambridge (1st ed.) 42; J. D. Beazley, *Proc. Brit. Acad.* 43 (1957) 240 n. 1. Snell argues (91 f.) that at the end of Bacchyl. xvi 'the Cean chorus takes on the personality of the youths and maidens accompanying Theseus'. But even if this were so, the poem is *about* Theseus, not the fortunes of the chorus.

[3] Cf. for instance Pollux iv. 101 on the γέρανος-dance at Delos; also Athen. i. 15. See Haigh 14 ff.; Hoffmann 251 n. 1; Pickard-Cambridge (1st ed.) 139 f.; *Dram. festivals* 251 ff. Flickinger (16) denies the use of gesture, etc., in early dithyramb. For mimesis in general see esp. H. Koller, *Die Mimesis in der Antike* (Berne 1954). For K. the primary meaning of μιμεῖσθαι is 'durch Tanz zur Darstellung bringen', and it involves rhythm, musical accompaniment, and the narrative word.

[4] J. Lammers, *Die Doppel- und Halbchöre in der antiken Tragödie* (Paderborn 1931): cf. Kranz, *Stasimon* 16 ff. (he is more cautious at p. 273) (cf. p. 100 above); Untersteiner 79 ff., 214 f., 243 ff., 266 (U.'s theory that one chorus was formed of satyrs and performed a σατυρικόν, while the other was of τράγοι who sang a song with heroic content is pure fantasy); Patzer 126; also F. Stoessl, *A.J.Ph.* 73 (1952) 126. The weakness of their position is shown by *GGL* 39; Ziegler 1944 n. 25; Peretti 63 ff., 91 ff.; Pohlenz 21, *Erl.* 13; Lesky 42 f.; del Grande 316 f., 325 f., 332 f., 343 ff. See also chap. v pp. 192 ff.

chorus confronting or attacking a chorus of tragedy[1] or comedy,[2] this chorus has nothing in common with that of the *Supplices*. The main foundation of the theory indeed is the *Supplices* itself, and this is no longer available to Lammers as a proven early play. What sort of a plot such a play might have is not easy to imagine. There are few enough situations in myth to provide even one group of clearly defined and related characters, without having to look for two in opposition. And if we are to think rather of two choruses singing to each other of the fortunes of some hero, we are still no nearer to the situation of the *Supplices*. It does not help at all to adduce the doubtful possibility of amoebaic singing or contesting choruses in Homer, Sappho, or early popular poetry: or again Alcman's *Partheneion*, whether we accept in that poem the unlikely division among the choreutae once proposed by Bowra and others, or the more plausible theory of a contest between Alcman's chorus and a chorus of Peleiades.[3] Such things are fundamentally different from the mimetic performance of a myth. Alcman's girls never claim to be anyone other than themselves, and we even know their names. It is, so far as we can tell, only when the narrative of the myth is over that the rival charms of Agido and Hagesichora come into question. And if there is a competition with

[1] Tièche 25 ff.; Ziegler 1936 ff.; Pohlenz, *NGG* (1926) ii. 311 ff.; *Gr. Trag.* 36 f., *Erl.* 16; *GGL* 83 and 178 ff.; Koller 172; Lesky 21.

[2] Howald 43 f.; Koller, *Glotta* 40. 189 ff. Wilamowitz believed the fragment to be a dithyramb (*Sappho und Simonides* 133); cf. also Crusius, *R.-E.* v. A. 1223; Geffcken I. ii. 144 n. 4; A. M. Dale, *Eranos* 48 (1950) 19 f.; Webster 20; Lindsay 328. Roos 230 ff. (with bibliography) argues that it is a parody of a dithyramb of the school of Lasos. Lammers himself (65 ff.) declined to use the fragment as evidence for his theory. H. W. Garrod, *C.R.* 34 (1920) 129 ff., esp. 133 ff. assigned it to a satyr-play, but not one with a double chorus. In any case, if Garrod is right (132), the fragment may belong to a date as late as the 460's.

[3] For the search for amoebaic or contesting choruses see Bethe 27 ff.; Ziegler 1944; Peretti 16 ff. Untersteiner (50 ff.) relentlessly pursues double-choruses that are quite irrelevant to the origins of tragedy (e.g. the γέρανος-dance at Delos). For Alcman cf. esp. Bowra, *Greek lyric poetry* (1st ed. Oxford 1936) 35 ff. In the 2nd edition (Oxford 1961) (38 ff.) he changed his view: also D. L. Page, *Alcman. The Partheneion* (Oxford 1951) 52 ff.; J. A. Davison, *Hermes* 73 (1938) 449; A. Garzya, *Alcmane. I Frammenti* (Naples 1954) 52 ff.; del Grande 33 ff. Del Grande (32 ff.) shows how uncertain is the early evidence for musical and poetic contests and for opposed choruses. He also rightly points out (37) that it is illegitimate to pass from the idea of a musical contest to that of two choruses carrying on a dialogue in competition.

another chorus it is a contest of singing and beauty (and running?), not a conflict between the characters of the myth.

Choral lyric poetry may be mimetic in the sense that its narrative of a myth can be accompanied by gesture and the use of direct speech. But when the first actor appears this dramatic or mimetic function is transferred to him, and the chorus is left with the sole task of question and comment. Nothing in our scanty knowledge of the lost plays of Aeschylus or his predecessors contradicts this view. The few fragments and the four titles of Thespis' plays are almost certainly spurious,[1] but they at least indicate what kind of plays the fourth century imagined him to have written.[2] The Ἆθλα Πελίου ἢ Φόρβας and Πενθεύς can hardly concern the fortunes of a chorus, while the Ἠίθεοι may possibly deal with the Theseus story of Bacchylides (xvi).[3] Of the plays of Phrynichus the Ἀκταίων, Ἄλκηστις, Ἀνταῖος ἢ Λίβυες, Τάνταλος, Τρωίλος? must have treated the stories of these individual heroes;[4] the Πλευρώνιαι evidently concerned the fortunes of Althaea and/or Meleager;[5] the Μιλήτου ἅλωσις and Φοίνισσαι, possibly the same play as the Δίκαιοι ἢ Πέρσαι ἢ Σύνθωκοι,[6] were historical plays comparable with the *Persae* of Aeschylus, in which the chorus can have been protagonist only in the same limited sense.[7] Only the Αἰγύπτιοι and the Δαναΐδες might be taken as comparable with the *Supplices* of Aeschylus.[8]

[1] Heracleides Ponticus (a pupil of Plato) was said by Aristoxenus to have forged plays of Thespis (D.L. v. 92). Cf. Gudeman 134; Pickard-Cambridge (1st ed.) 117 f.; Else, *Origin and early form* 119 n. 2. Wilamowitz (*Kl. Schr.* I. 373 n. 3) was inclined to distrust Aristoxenus.

[2] Cf. Ridgeway 69; Tièche 18; Pickard-Cambridge (2nd ed.) 85; Peretti 276 f. and 280.

[3] Cf. *GGL* 49 n. 6. The Ἱερεῖς is quite uncertain.

[4] Pickard-Cambridge (1st ed.) 91 thought that the *Alcestis* was probably a satyr-play; cf. Wilamowitz, *Einleitung* 93. But see also L. Weber, *Rh. Mus.* 79 (1930) 35 ff.; Webster 64. For the plays of Phryn. in general see A. von Blumenthal, *R.-E.* xx. I. 911 ff. and literature there.

[5] F. Marx, *Rh. Mus.* 77. 340 restored ⟨Ἀλθαία ἢ⟩ Πλευρώνιαι: but cf. Lesky 46; v. Blumenthal 915 (cf. 912 f.). The latter suggests ⟨Ἀγκαῖος ἢ⟩ Πλευρώνιαι.

[6] Cf. Lammers 59; Marx 348 and 350; F. Stoessl, *Mus. Helv.* 2 (1945) 159. *Contra* Howald 45; v. Blumenthal 915. Lesky (48) remains undecided. Cf. also *GGL* 171 n. 10.

[7] For a possible double-chorus in the *Phoen.* cf. Lammers 55 ff.; *GGL* 171 n. 10 and 176; Stoessl 159; Pohlenz, *Erl.* 25; Lesky 48; Webster 65.

[8] See below pp. 138 f.

Only one title of Choerilus survives, the Ἀλώπη, and that refers to an individual.[1] Of the lost plays of Aeschylus himself it is reasonable to assume that those titles which consist of an individual's name or a combination of such a name with that of a group, belong to plays which dealt with the fortunes of that individual. Most of the rest indicate an anonymous chorus of attendants or companions of a hero or a god,[2] or citizens of the land in which the play is set.[3] In only a few plays does there seem to be any real possibility that the chorus may have been the protagonist—Ἀργεῖαι (wives of the Seven against Thebes?),[4] Ἐπίγονοι, Ἡλιάδες,[5] Ἡρακλεῖδαι, Κάβειροι,[6] Ὀστολόγοι,[7] Λήμνιοι (dealing with the Argonaut saga), Φορκίδες,[8] and Ξάντριαι[9] (dealing with Pentheus or the daughters of Minyas). But one can only guess. Had the *Septem* been lost one might have been tempted to deduce from the title that the chorus was

[1] Cf. *GGL* 170. For Pratinas see Pickard-Cambridge (2nd ed.) 67 f.

[2] Μυρμιδόνες (Achilles), Νηρεΐδες (Thetis), Θρῇσσαι (Ajax), Ἱέρειαι (Artemis), Τοξότιδες (Artemis), Βασσάραι (Dionysus).

[3] Ἐλευσίνιοι (Theseus), Μυσοί (Telephus), Σαλαμίνιαι (Teucer), Ἠδωνοί (Lycurgus), Αἰτναῖαι, Κρῆσσαι (Polyidus and Glaucus, sons of Minos), Περραιβίδες (Ixion and Eïoneus).

[4] There is doubt about the title. The Medicean Catalogue (cf. *E.M.* 341. 5) gives Ἀργεῖοι. Ἀργεῖαι is the reading of Harpocr. *Lex. rhet.* p. 184. 21 Bekker, Hesych. A 6627 L. Cf. H. J. Mette, *Fragm. der Trag. d. Aisch.* (Berlin 1959) 93 f.; also *Der Verlorene Aischylos* (Berlin 1963) 39 f. M. Schmidt, *Philol.* 16 (1860) 161 suggested Ἀργεία. Cf. Weir Smyth, Loeb *Aeschylus* II. 383 f.

[5] But the chorus of Heliades is probably subordinate in importance to their brother Phaethon. Hermann (*Opusc.* III. 135 f.) argues for a chorus of Nymphs or Oceanids. If individual members of the chorus were named (Mette, *Verlor. Aisch.* 181) this play would be highly exceptional. Lammers (43 ff.) finds a double-chorus.

[6] The chorus may be composed of Argonauts; cf. Hermann, *Opusc.* II. 125. But the play is possibly a satyr-play; cf. Wecklein, *Sitz. bay. ak. München* (1891) 381 f. See also Weir Smyth 412, Mette 131 f. Lammers again argues for a double-chorus (48 ff.).

[7] The chorus is perhaps formed by the relations of Penelope's suitors. But this too may be a satyr-play: cf. Nauck 58; J. C. Schmidt in *Comment. Ribbeck* (Leipzig 1888) 108 ff.; *contra* Wilamowitz, *Interpr.* 247 n.; Wecklein 382. See also Weir Smyth 440, Mette 128 f.

[8] Some have taken the Φορκίδες as a satyr-play; Nauck 83; Wecklein 383; but cf. also Brommer 70. In any case the play must have been about Perseus. If the chorus were the three Graiai, sisters of the Gorgons, we should have an interesting parallel for the *Eum.* (and E. *Supp.*) in which a mythological group is expanded to form a tragic chorus. The same may be true of the *Heliades* and *Kabeiroi*: cf. Hermann, *Opusc.* II. 124 ff. and III. 136.

[9] Lloyd-Jones (Loeb *Aesch.* II. 566) lists some recent discussions of this play.

protagonist in that play. The titles of lost plays, even if we knew their dates, cannot be used to prove anything. But at least they provide no support for the view that in the 'normal' early tragedy the chorus was the protagonist.[1]

On the contrary they suggest that the *Persae* is closer to the early norm, a play in which a messenger brings a report to a chorus of anonymous citizens, and in which the subject of that report (Xerxes in the *Persae*) himself appears later in the play. The chorus's task is to comment. The possibilities of genuine drama remain strictly limited. Early tragedy, like the *Persae*, may well have been reminiscent rather of a cantata or an oratorio, and the Μιλήτου ἅλωσις and the Φοίνισσαι of Phrynichus (in which the Persian defeat was reported at the beginning of the play) can have been little more than a prolonged threnos.[2] In this context the *Theseus* dithyramb of Bacchylides (xvii) deserves attention. Here we see a lyric dialogue between an individual (King Aegeus of Athens) and a chorus in which the former brings news of the approach of a stranger (Theseus). The chorus is anonymous. It is disputed whether this dithyramb is a survival of a pre-tragic form of dithyramb with exarchon,[3] or, as is more likely, it shows the influence of developed tragedy and is the forerunner of the new mimetic dithyramb.[4] It does not

[1] Howald (52) admits that very few mythical situations are suitable for what is supposed to be the normal early tragedy.

[2] Cf. Wilamowitz, *Hermes* 32. 389, and *Einleitung* 92 f.; Flickinger 16; Croiset 77; Ziegler 1935; Peretti 25; Mazon I. 56; Snell 102; Kitto 34; Broadhead, ed. *Persae* xxxiii; Pohlenz 22 f., 40 f., 54, 140; Lesky 47 f.; Else, *Origin and early form* 74, 87. *Contra* Lammers 63 f.; Stoessl 161. The *Supp.* (despite Ziegler) is altogether different. Kitto (28 f.) is strangely inconsistent in that, while accepting a late date for the *Supp.*, he insists on using it as evidence for the form of early tragedy. 'The cantata theory', he says, 'does not explain the *Supplices*.' If it is a late play there is no reason why it should.

[3] See, for example, Comparetti 34; Crusius, *Philol.* 57 (1898) 174; Reisch 470; C. Robert, *Hermes* 33 (1898) 148; Cornford, *C.R.* 27. 45; Geffcken, I. i. 143; Ziegler 1909 n. 15 and 1961 f.; Untersteiner 270 f. For Peretti (94) the role of Aegeus is that of Thespis' ὑποκριτής.

[4] Cf. Wilamowitz, *GGA* (1898) 142; Flickinger, *Cl. Phil.* 8. 268, and *Gr. theater* 10; Dieterich 415; Kranz, *Stasimon* 32; Pickard-Cambridge (1st ed.) 44; Gudeman 134; Severyns, *Bacchylide* 62. But how the poem can have been performed remains a mystery (cf. Webster 29). The idea of a soloist confronting a chorus is doubted by many: Wilamowitz (141) envisaged a dialogue between two soloists (Aegeus and an anonymous person); F. G. Kenyon, *The Poems of Bacchylides* (London 1897) xli f. a dialogue between Aegeus and Medea, each represented by a semi-

matter for our present purpose. If the former view is correct we have valuable confirmation of the anonymous and undramatic nature of the pre-tragic chorus, since this chorus exists only for the sake of someone else's story. And if the poem does reflect the form of contemporary tragedy, that tragedy must have been very different from the *Supplices*. Severyns argues[1] that the date of the poem is after 485 and not later than 470 (he prefers the latter part of this period). It is very like what, in a longer and more complex form, we should expect to find in tragedy of the earliest period. We find it in the *Persae*. It is absurd to suppose that the *Supplices* is more primitive by up to twenty years.

The *Theseus* dithyramb is suggestive also of the relationship between the single actor and the chorus in early tragedy.[2] There is no dramatic opposition, no conflict between the two parties. The individual's part is to narrate and answer the chorus's questions.[3] Whether ὑποκριτής means 'answerer' or 'interpreter' (either of the poet's text to the audience,[4] or of the myth, the subject of the chorus's songs) is a question that is as far as ever from solution.[5] But the former interpretation has always

chorus. But cf. Crusius 174; Robert 148; Comparetti 34. Untersteiner (270 f.) assumes two semi-choruses each with ἔξαρχος (cf. also Comparetti 34 f.), but it does not become apparent what part would be played by Aegeus' semi-chorus on the one hand, and the ἔξαρχος of the Athenian citizens on the other. Cf. also del Grande 11 ff. and 321. It is difficult to say whether this dithyramb might throw light on the δράματα τραγικά ascribed to Pindar (see p. 110 above). Cf. Kenyon 175; Comparetti 35; Crusius, *R.-E.* v. A. 1215: but cf. also Dieterich 415. See further Haigh 24; Stahl 590 n. 2; Untersteiner 242 n. 25; Lesky 18.

1 Pp. 56 ff. Comparetti (35–6) suggested 469 B.C., the year in which Cimon brought back to Athens the remains of Theseus.

2 Cf. Ziegler 1909; Pohlenz 22.

3 Cf. Howald 34 ff.; Kranz, *N. Jbb.* (1919) 155, 158. See above p. 105 and p. 109 n. 1.

4 In this case the term can have been applied to the actor only after he ceased to be the poet himself (cf. Else, *Wien. Stud.* 72 (1959) 77). For Thomson (170 ff.) the ὑποκριτής is the interpreter of a mimetic rite to an uninitiated audience.

5 For the interpretation 'answerer' see esp. Else, *Wien. Stud.* 72. 75 ff., *TAPhA* 76 (1945) 1 ff.; cf. also *Origin and early form* 58 f. and 86 (for E. the ὑποκριτής was the *second* member of the tragic company, with the task of 'answering' the questions of the τραγῳδός; cf. p. 126 n. 4 below. But see Pickard-Cambridge, *Dram. festivals* 131 ff.). See too Haigh 27 n. 5; J. B. O'Connor, *Chapters in the history of actors and acting in ancient Greece* (Chicago 1908) 3 f.; Wilamowitz, *Gr. Verskunst* 467; Flickinger, *Cl. Phil.* 8. 268, and *Gr. theater* 16 and 339; Geffcken I. i. 143; Lammers 164; Kranz, *Stasimon* 14 and 272; Howald 33 ff.; Gudeman 136; Ziegler 1909;

been the more popular and seems to fit the situation. The chorus questions the actor either about himself or about some other person, then comments lyrically on what it has been told. There are three possible ways in which this may be done.[1] First, the actor may deliver a report in the form of a ῥῆσις, and this ῥῆσις will then be followed by a choral stasimon. Secondly the chorus and actor may carry on an 'epirrhematic' dialogue, either in pure lyric form[2] or with the chorus singing and the actor reciting iambic or trochaic verses. Thirdly the chorus may be represented by its κορυφαῖος, speaking in dialogue metre like the actor. There seems little point in trying to isolate any one of these three methods as *the* original form of tragedy.[3] The possibility of using all three existed from the beginning. Kranz, for instance, in *Stasimon*, argued that the second method is the oldest, and that it derives from a lyric dialogue between two choruses in the pre-tragic satyrikon, in which one chorus comes to be replaced by an individual singer (the exarchon) whose

Peretti 228 and 283; Norwood 1; Pohlenz 22; Patzer 127 n. 4. The principal exponent of the meaning 'interpreter' is Lesky, in *Studi in onore U. E. Paoli* (Florence 1955) 469 ff. (but cf. D. L. Page, *C.R.* n.s. 6 (1956) 191 f.), and *Tr. Dichtung* 43 f.: see also Bywater 136, Lindsay 334 ff., and Thomson *loc. cit.* Koller, *Glotta* 40. 183 ff., argued that the poet-exarchon of a citharodic dithyramb became a ὑποκριτής when, with the change from Dionysiac to non-Dionysiac themes, the audience required the performance to be expounded in advance (cf. also *Mus. Helv.* 14 (1957) 100 ff.). *GGL* (58 n. 3) and Pickard-Cambridge (2nd ed.) 79 reserve judgement, but in *Dram. festivals* 132 the latter seems to favour 'answerer'. Lesky's statement (*Wien. Stud.* 47. 13 n. 33) that in the *Vorstufe* of tragedy the chorus answers the ἐξάρχων and not *vice versa* has little to commend it; cf. Ziegler 1909 n. 14; also Lammers 164; Peretti 33 f., 210, 228.

[1] Cf. Haigh 31; Stahl 592; del Grande 135, 150.

[2] That a *singing* actor is a secondary development was maintained by Bethe, *Proleg.* 35 (cf. *N. Jbb.* (1907) 87); cf. Kalinka 35; Lammers 32, 162 f., 167 ff. L. rejects a singing herald at *Supp.* 825 ff.; cf. chap. v pp. 193 f.). According to Wilamowitz (*Einleitung* 94) it was Aesch. himself who made the actor into a singer. The earliest extant monodies occur in the *P.V.* (88 ff. and 561 ff.). Not until *Ag.* 1072 ff. does a chorus-leader respond in iambics to the lyrics of an actor; cf. Kranz, *Stasimon* 20; also Lammers 169 f. This scene develops into purely lyric dialogue, the opposite of what happens at *Supp.* 825 ff.

[3] Howald, for instance, argued (34 f.) that the first method must be secondary; but there is no reason to distrust Themistius' attribution of the rhesis to Thespis (cf. p. 103 above). Nor must one assume with Else (*Origin and early form* 59) that *this* was the only original method. Aeschylus' epirrhematic scenes are usually introduced by a rhesis; cf. Peretti 203 f.; also Wilamowitz, *Herakles* (2nd ed. Berlin 1895) II. 59 f. Rhesis and epirrhema are combined most notably at *Sept.* 375 ff.

lyrics then give way to recited verses.[1] All the other elements of the dramatic form would be derived from this original exchange. The omission of the actor's part of the epirrhema would lead to the choral stasimon (as at *Supp.* 418 ff.: cf. Kranz 21 and 115), while the omission of the choral part would lead to the actor's rhesis. But that the stasimon of tragedy is only a secondary element not only contradicts what Aristotle says: it is highly improbable in itself.[2] The whole process of development is said to be reflected at *Supp.* 825 ff., where short lyric exchanges give way to lyrics and trimeters in responsion, and these in turn to a regular trimeter dialogue.[3] But Lesky shows how the epirrhematic scenes grow naturally out of the action itself, when excitement bursts out into lyric expression.[4] Kranz's theory relies too heavily on the hypothetical origin of tragedy in a performance by a double chorus, and on the three epirrhematic scenes of the *Supplices*, which alone, he says, contain dramatic life.[5] Now that the early date of the play is no longer available as a starting-point, the argument is seen to be circular: the *Supplices* is early because it still displays the original form of the 'satyrikon': this is the original form of the satyrikon because it is still displayed in the *Supplices*. Moreover, Peretti points out that it is hardly true to say that these scenes of the *Supplices* are the only dramatically effective ones or that they contain the decisive moments of the play.[6] They are rather waiting scenes, since it is only when they are finished that the culminating

[1] Kranz's theory is accepted by Untersteiner, esp. 263 ff., and Ziegler 1957 ff. A similar process of development (but without the singing actor) is presented by Lammers (161 ff.). For criticism see Nestle, *Gnomon* 10. 404 ff. (esp. 408 ff.); *GGL* 39 and 145 n. 2; Peretti 63 ff., 99 ff.; Pohlenz, *Erl.* 13; Lesky, *Wien. Stud.* 47. 4 ff., and *Tr. Dichtung* 42 f.; Else, *Poetics* 157 n. 108; del Grande 316 f. and 324 ff. *Stasimon* develops a slightly different theory from that argued in *N. Jbb.* 43 (1919) 145 ff. where the earliest stage is said to be a lyric dialogue between individual and chorus. Cf. also Thomson 168, 175 f.

[2] For K. (21, 24, and 162) the stasimon's original function is to fill a pause in the action or to allow the actor to change his costume. But it is only in the last days of tragedy that the stasimon is reduced to this. The development is the opposite of what K. says. Cf. Peretti 99 ff.; Lesky, *loc. cit.*

[3] Kranz 16; cf. Ziegler 1958 f.; Untersteiner 268.

[4] See also Nestle 411, Pohlenz, *loc. cit.*

[5] Kranz 15. The passages are 348 ff., 734 ff., and 825 ff.

[6] Peretti 108 ff., 206 f., 222 f.; cf. also Lesky, *Wien. Stud.* 47. 6 f. By line 437 the action has not advanced at all. Pelasgus is still faced with his dilemma.

point in the action arrives. Peretti himself finds a progression from the liturgical and threnodic parallelism and static quality of the epirrhematic scenes of the *Supplices* and *Persae* to the freer and more dramatic scenes of the other plays.[1] Those of the *Oresteia*, he says, contain within themselves the tragic acme and ethical significance of the whole action. One may question whether the *Supplices* is really as static as the *Persae* in this respect. The scene at *Persae* 249 ff. consists merely of a series of lyric comments on the messenger's report; that at 694 ff. is brief and rigidly symmetrical;[2] while the scene at 908 ff. is merely an extended threnos. The epirrhematic scenes in the *Supplices* contain an agon and are full of genuine dramatic life.[3]

At any rate the mere occurrence of epirrhematic scenes in the *Supplices* proves nothing about its date. Every time a chorus and an actor converse the dramatist is obliged to use one of the three methods. If any chronological development is discernible it is perhaps from the second to the third. An epirrehmatic dialogue is not the most rapid or dramatic of forms.[4] It was an obvious convenience to replace it with an individual appointed to speak for the chorus as another actor. So the κορυφαῖος emerges from the chorus. He never however becomes an individual in his own right. The coryphaeus remains anonymous. He may address his

[1] For parallelism and word-repetition in epirrhematic scenes cf. Peretti 47 n. 8, 114, 123, 128 f., 136 ff., 152 ff., 155, 159 ff., 163 f., 168, 176, 180, 193, 220. Cf. also Kranz, *Stasimon* 23 and 127 ff.; Hölzle 17 and 22 ff.; Untersteiner 279. See also chap. II p. 73. For the view that epirrhematic sections originated in ritual cult see also Nestle, *Gnomon* 10. 413; Untersteiner 294 n. 3; Else, *Origin and early form* 98 f.

[2] Indeed it is the only epirrhematikon formed of a single syzygy in the extant plays. Wilamowitz (*Kl. Schr.* I. 364) compared the opening of S. *Ichn.*

[3] Cf. Nestle (412): 'Der Reichtum und die dramatische Bedeutung der epirrhematischen Formen, der Umfang der sie umrahmenden Reden und Stichomythien weisen also die Hiketiden in die Zeit zwischen Sieben und Orestie.' Peretti says (130 and 153 f.) that at *Supp.* 876 ff. the thought of the Chorus develops without any close connection with that of the herald. But this is certainly not true of the scene beginning at 348, where ἄνατον (356) is picked up by 359, ἐγώ (368) by σύ τοι (370), κραίνοιμ' (368) by ἐπικραίνεις (375), κρατοῦσι (387) by κράτεσιν (393), and φροντίδος (417) by φρόντισον (418). Cf. O. Hiltbrunner, *Wiederholungs- und Motivtechnik bei Aischylos* (Berne 1950) 21.

[4] 'Und doch hat er auch in dieser scheinbar undramatischen Einkleidung mit der großen Hauptszene der Choephoren (306–478) ein Non plus ultra dramatischer Belebung und Steigerung geschaffen' (*GGL* 288).

chorus, but he never truly separates himself from it.[1] He is for instance only gradually give a separate role in epirrhematic passages (not in *Persae* or *Septem*, first at *Supplices* 736 ff.: cf. the κομμοί of *Agamemnon* (1072 ff.) and *Choephori* (306 ff.),[2] and rarely is he allowed to deliver a long rhesis.[3] If an actor seeks information from a chorus-leader, stichomythia is the medium used.[4] This anonymity of the chorus-leader is one of the strongest arguments against those who derive the first actor from the exarchon (in the sense *Vorsänger*) or the coryphaeus of the dithyramb. Moreover the assumption that these scholars often make,[5] either explicitly or implicitly, that the exarchon is the same man as the coryphaeus, necessitates the further assumption that after Thespis had changed the exarchon/coryphaeus into the first actor a new coryphaeus had to be appointed to represent the chorus in its dealings with him.[6] It is altogether easier to believe that the first appearance of the coryphaeus, in any other sense than that of leader of the chorus, postdates and is made necessary by the introduction of the actor from outside.[7]

According to Themistius Aristotle said that Thespis was the inventor of the prologue, and this must mean a monologue

[1] The *Suda*'s description *s.v.* κορυφαῖος· ὁ πρῶτος τῶν ὑποκριτῶν is thus not at all accurate. See esp. Wilamowitz, *Einleitung* 88; Howald 33 f.; Kranz, *Stasimon* 19; *GGL* 38 n. 5 and 74 f.; del Grande 8 ff. Cf. also Peretti (268 f.) on the function of the exarchon of his liturgical canto. Nestle says (*Struktur des Eingangs* 17) that as the coryphaeus is assimilated to the actor only the individuality determined by a name (and, one might add, by a dramatic function) is lacking. But that 'only' is fundamental.

[2] Cf. Kranz 20; Nestle 115 f.; Peretti 122 f. and 175; del Grande 150.

[3] 5 lines at *Supp.* 328; 11 at *Pers.* 215; 6 at *Sept.* 369 and 677; 5 at *Ag.* 615 and 1612, 6 at 258 and 1643, 14 at 489 (but Denniston–Page follow the MSS in giving 489–500 to Clytaemestra: cf. also Dale, in *Classical drama and its influence* 18 and 21 f.); 5 at *Choe.* 264 and 535; 10 at *Eum.* 244, 8 at 299, and 5 at 652. For the frequency of quatrains delivered by the chorus-leader in the *P.V.* see C. J. Herington, *C.R.* n.s. 13 (1963) 5 ff. Gross, *Die Stichomythie in der gr. Tragödie und Komödie* (Berlin 1905) 42, sees these ῥήσεις as primitive survivals.

[4] Cf. Peretti 210 and 228; Dale 18 ff.

[5] But not Murray 50; cf. also Pickard-Cambridge (1st ed.) 123 (his view is stated more strongly by Webster 90); Koller, *Glotta* 40. 187.

[6] See Flickinger 168; Nestle 102; Ziegler 1909; Pohlenz, *Erl.* 13.

[7] For the coryphaeus as the descendant rather than the ancestor of the first actor see Bethe, *N. Jbb.* (1907) 87; Wilamowitz, *Interpr.* 2 f., *Einleitung* 88; Nestle 115 f.; *GGL* 39 (cf. 128); Untersteiner 282; del Grande 137. It is wrong then to use the large part played by a coryphaeus as evidence for early date (Flickinger 168; K. Münscher, *Rh. Mus.* 69 (1914) 189 f. on S. *Ichn*).

spoken by the actor before the entry of the chorus. It can hardly mean a speech by the actor *after* the parodos,[1] or the introductory anapaests of the chorus itself.[2] Many have been inclined to see in the *Supplices* the earliest form of opening, and point out that the earliest attested prologue belongs to the *Phoenissae* of Phrynichus (476?).[3] In 472, they say, Aeschylus can still begin a play with the parodos. But in the *Persae* we see Aeschylus consciously preferring this type of opening to the monologue which Phrynichus had used.[4] There is no reason why one method should necessarily be chronologically earlier than the other. Thespis may very well have employed both.[5] The natural function of prologue or parodos would be to explain to the audience the situation and the setting of the play.[6] Some have seen in Euripides' expository and undramatic prologues an archaizing reversion to the manner of Thespis,[7] who may even have delivered his prologues at first in his own person and not

[1] Cf. Flickinger 298 f. *Contra* Untersteiner 285 n. 25.

[2] See Pohlenz, *Erl.* 15. For the distinction between the technical (Peripatetic) and non-technical uses of the word πρόλογος see Nestle, whose work is of fundamental importance for the whole subject: also F. Leo, *Plautinische Forschungen* (2nd ed. Berlin 1912) 188 ff.; F. Stoessl, in *R.-E.* xxiii. 1. 632 ff.

[3] For the view that the prologue is a late invention cf. for example Petersen 370; Wilamowitz, *Einleitung* 88 and 92 (but also *Interpr.* 56); Flickinger 55 f., 192, 209 f., 298 f.; Weir Smyth 38 f., 76, 130 f.; Geffcken 1. i. 149; Croiset 107, 139, 269; Marx 349 f.; Howald 56; Lammers 164 n. 3; *GGL* 70 and 194 n. 1 (but cf. also 56, 117; 49 n. 6 is not clear); Pohlenz 35 f., 53, 136, *Erl.* 15. For papyrus evidence for prologues in the lost plays see Lesky 86.

[4] Cf. Nestle 25 (cf. 13); Lesky, *Wien. Stud.* 47. 9 ff., and *Tr. Dichtung* 42; Else, *Hermes* 85. 40 f., and *Origin and early form* 59; Webster 61; Koster 21 f.; also Haigh 31 n. 1. The usual dating of the *Phoen.* to 476 depends on Plut. *Them.* 5, but it is by no means certain; cf. W. G. Forrest, *C.Q.* n.s. 10 (1960) 235 ff. The argument of Marx (348 ff.) that Phrynichus' play must be later than the *Pers.*, since its opening is more modern and artistic, has been generally rejected. There is no reason to doubt the statement of Glaucus of Rhegium as reported in hyp. *Pers.* See esp. v. Blumenthal 915; Lammers 61 f.; Pohlenz, *Erl.* 25; *GGL* 174 ff.; Peretti 148; Lesky, *Wien. Stud.* 47. 10 f. (cf. *Tr. Dichtung* 42 n. 1 and 47): also Wilamowitz, *Interpr.* 49 f.

[5] See del Grande 136 and 148; cf. also Stoessl, *R.-E.* xxiii. 2. 2315 and 2319.

[6] That prologue and parodos may both have this function is recognized in hyp. *Pers.* (ἐνταῦθα δὲ προλογίζει χορὸς πρεσβυτῶν): cf. hyp. E. *Rhes.* For the expository task of the chorus in *Supp.* and *Pers.* cf. Weir Smyth 38 f.; Croiset 52; Howald 56; Nestle 15; Hölzle 72; *GGL* 117. See in general E. Spring, *Harv. Stud.* 28 (1917) 168 ff.

[7] See Stahl 591 n. 3; Flickinger 299 f.; Körte, *Philol. Wochenschr.* (1928) 1299 f.; Nestle 124 f.; *GGL* 116; Else, *Hermes* 85. 41 f.; Lesky, *Wien. Stud.* 47. 12, and *Tr. Dichtung* 42 (with further references). *Contra* Pohlenz, *Erl.* 174.

in the mask and costume of a character in the play.[1] The situation revealed in the prologue would provide the theme for the entrance song of the chorus, and in this respect it is not very different from the rhesis of the actor inside the play itself.[2] It would be interesting to know whether, in the two surviving plays of Aeschylus which begin with the Parodos, the *Supplices* and *Persae*, it is the whole chorus or merely its leader that delivers the opening anapaests and announces the theme that is to be developed thereafter in lyric form.[3] If the latter view is correct, it is possible that this function of the coryphaeus is older than his task of answering the single actor. Some have seen in it a survival of the ritual προκήρυγμα of the exarchon, calling upon the chorus to sing or pray, and similar relics are said to be visible also within the plays.[4] But even if this is true it is the actor rather than the chorus-leader who naturally takes over the function of the exarchon, and only secondarily is it given to the coryphaeus.[5] The *Supplices* and the *Persae* are only superficially similar in their manner of opening. In the former play we are introduced immediately to the principal characters and their situation, just as in the *Septem* we meet Eteocles and in the *Choephori* Orestes.[6] And if there is any justification for the criticism that in the *Persae* Aeschylus fails to motivate the entrance of the Chorus,[7]

[1] Cf. Else, *loc. cit.*; *Origin and early form* 59 f.

[2] Lesky sees *Supp.* 600 ff. as such a 'prologue': cf. also Wilamowitz, *Interpr.* 7 and (*Eum.* 235 ff.) 180; Untersteiner 285 n. 25. The *Choe.* too has a 'prologue' within the play (554 ff.); cf. Petersen 382; Weir Smyth 187.

[3] On this question see Broadhead 37 n. 1 (and references there). The Parodos of the *Ag.* too has an anapaestic introduction.

[4] *Supp.* 625–9, *Pers.* 532–47 and 623–32, *Sept.* 822–31, *Ag.* 355–66, *Choe.* 719–29, *Eum.* 307–20. Cf. Nestle, esp. 25 f., 69, 101 f.; Peretti, esp. 203 ff. and 268 ff.; Fraenkel, *Ag.* II. 184; Pohlenz, *Erl.* 94; also Kranz 135; Schadewaldt 45 ff.; Citti 32.

[5] The 'ritual προκήρυγμα' is found as frequently in an iambic rhesis (*Supp.* 520 f., 724 ff. and 772 f., *Pers.* 619 ff., *Sept.* 265 ff., *Choe.* 150 f.) as in anapaests, and not until the *Oresteia* is such a rhesis given to the coryphaeus (*Ag.* 351 ff., *Choe.* 931 ff., *Eum.* 306). See Nestle 25 f.; Peretti 269 ff. See further p. 137 below.

[6] Cf. Nestle (19 ff., 84, 102), for whom the prologue delivered by the principal character is a later development than that spoken by a πρόσωπον προτατικόν; cf. *GGL* 115 f.

[7] Cf. Wilamowitz, *Interpr.* 42 f. and 49; also *Kl. Schr.* I. 158 n. 1; Spring 173; Flickinger 150 f.; Stoessl, *Mus. Helv.* 2. 148 ff.; Kitto 35; Lesky 62. But cf. also Pohlenz, *Erl.* 26. In *Ag.* and *Eum.* the prologues arise naturally out of an everyday situation (cf. Leo, *Abh. Ges. Wiss. Gött.* 10. 8 and 115; Nestle 23 and 104 f.). *Supp.*, *Sept.*, and *Choe.* begin with a unique but self-explanatory situation.

that is certainly not true of the *Supplices*. Aeschylus, unlike Euripides, seems to have tried in various ways to integrate his prologues in the dramatic structure of his plays, and to overcome the necessity for mere straightforward exposition directed towards the audience.[1] Thus in the *Septem* the germ of dialogue is present, but not yet developed as it is in the *Prometheus*. The *Eumenides* with its elaborate three-part prologue is the most successful in this respect. The *Supplices* and *Choephori* are very similar in technique, with their prayers uttered by the principal characters arising naturally out of their own dramatic situation (cf. also *Septem* 69 ff.). Lloyd-Jones remarks[2] that 'the force and passion of the opening anapaests [of the *Supplices*] make them almost the finest beginning to any play of Aeschylus'. The *Persae* has an archaic air in that it is more content with mere exposition, though even here the forebodings of the Chorus set the mood for the rest of the play.[3]

One may suspect that stichomythia was the regular form of dialogue between the single actor and the chorus-leader, but whether it was the obligatory form[4] and whether it possessed from the beginning its later qualities as a medium of lively and

[1] See esp. Leo, *loc. cit.*; Körte 1300; Nestle 15 f., 22 f., 25, 70, 84, 87, 102 ff., 117 f.; Croiset 269; *GGL* 116 f. and 242 f.; Pohlenz 87 and 136 f. Spring finds the *Supp.* and *Pers.* less skilful than the other plays in this respect.

[2] *L'Antiq. Class.* 33. 374.

[3] The narrative style is seen in the opening τάδε, borrowed from the first line of Phrynichus' *Phoenissae*: cf. Nestle 23. For the setting of mood in Aeschylus' prologues see esp. Lesky, *Wien. Stud.* 47. 10 f.; *Hermes* 66 (1931) 208 f.; *Tr. Dichtung* 42 and 73: G. Méautis, *Eschyle et la trilogie* (Paris 1936) 47 ff., 70 f., 103, 122 f., 212 f., 247 ff., and *L'authenticité et la date du Prométhée Enchaîné d'Eschyle* (Neuchâtel 1960) 8 f.; and in the *Pers.* in particular Spring 173; Croiset 79 ff.; Nestle 15; Stoessl, *Mus. Helv.* 2. 148 ff.; Wolff, *Aeschylus' Danaid trilogy: a study* (Diss. Columbia Univ. 1957) 174 ff.; Broadhead xl.

[4] That stichomythia is the oldest form of dialogue is stated by Gaerte, *R.-E.* iii. A. 2. 2489; Gross 72, 93, 102 f.; Lammers 159 and 163. Some have derived it from a lyric stichomythia: Gross 95 ff.; Wilamowitz, *Interpr.* 240; *Gr. Verskunst* 467; *Kl. Schr.* I. 380; Lammers 22, 34, 159, 163; Untersteiner 278 ff.; Koster 21: cf. *GGL* 288: *contra* Pohlenz, *Erl.* 176. Others see in epirrhematic composition the intermediate stage; Howald 35, 37, 39; Kranz 20 and 23; Untersteiner *loc. cit.*: *contra* Peretti 143. Thomson sees in stichomythia a survival of the ritual catechism of a novice in the secrets of initiation (177 ff.); cf. also J. Myres, *Proc. Brit. Acad.* 36 (1948) 199 ff. (M.'s search for symmetry led him to extreme conclusions in his study of stichomythia). Lindsay (280) sees its origins in a mantic riddle-contest. Porzig found (43) at *Supp.* 207 ff. a ritual response between priest and congregation (cf. *Choe.* 479 ff.).

excited conversation it is impossible to say. It can hardly be an earlier development than the rhesis of the actor,[1] which in the earlier plays of Aeschylus normally contains the important dramatic moment, with stichomythia being used only to expand and analyse further the ideas of that rhesis, so that the regular pattern is rhesis–stichomythia–rhesis.[2] Wilamowitz found in the extent of the stichomythia in the *Supplices* a sign of its early date.[3] As far as its frequency is concerned, however, one can see Aeschylus using it more and more in his later plays. The *Persae* and *Septem* have 3 occurrences each (*Septem* 4 if the Exodos is included), *Supplices* 6, *Agamemnon* 10, *Choephori* 8, *Eumenides* 7, and *Prometheus* 8.[4] W. Jens has shown conclusively that it is not only in quantity that the *Supplices* represents a clear advance beyond the technique of the earlier plays and already looks forward to the *Oresteia*.[5] In the *Persae* stichomythia is used only for question and answer, in the *Septem* for persuasion of one party by another. The *Supplices* uses both of these but adds the excited and passionate quarrel type of stichomythia.[6] Except in detail the *Oresteia* shows no further advance. Jens demonstrates also how the *Supplices* shares with the *Oresteia* the practice of using one stichomythia to pick up and continue with increasing force a discussion begun between the same two parties in an earlier stichomythia and to drive one of them to a decision. At *Choephori* 164 ff. for the first time a decisive dramatic event (the discovery of the hair) takes place in the stichomythia itself.[7] But the development is foreshadowed in the *Supplices*, where at 337 there is a change of direction inside the dialogue.[8] The Chorus

[1] According to Diog. Laert. Thespis invented the first actor ὑπὲρ τοῦ διαναπαύεσθαι τὸν χορόν (D.L. iii. 56).

[2] Cf. esp. Peretti 229; Nestle 32 n. 2; Lesky, *Hermes* 66. 200; W. Jens, *Die Stichomythie in der frühen griechischen Tragödie* (Munich 1955) esp. 11 ff., 22, 33, 103. Jens points out (12 and 22) the similarity in form between *Supp.* 176–233 and *Choe.* 84–151.

[3] *Interpr.* 240; Koster 21.

[4] Passages of stichomythia in Aesch. are conveniently tabulated by Gross 47 ff.

[5] Jens, esp. 10 ff., 19, 102 f.

[6] Cf. also Gross 77 ff., and Peretti 222 f. See further p. 133 below.

[7] Cf. *Eum.* 415 ff., where the decision is handed over to Athena inside the stichomythia.

[8] Cf. also Myres 206. Lesky (*J.H.S.* 86 (1966) 79 f.) notes that it is only in the stichomythia at 455 ff., with its threat of suicide, that the deadlock between equally strong forces is broken and Pelasgus' decision made.

asks the question for Pelasgus to answer; and the stichomythia turns suddenly from question and answer to persuasion, from the antecedents of the Danaids to their request for asylum. It is this request that allows the action proper to begin and provides the theme of the next stichomythia (455 ff.).

Die erhöhte Bedeutung und die Vervollkommnung der Stichomythie im Vergleich zu den Persern und den Sieben ist offenkundig. Die Stichomythie ist ihrer Funktion nach Trägerin der für die Handlung wesentlichen Stellen und hat Anteil an den entscheidenden Punkten des Dramas, wenn auch das Entscheidende (die Annahme in der Volksversammlung, das Eintreten des Pelasgos für den Chor selbst gegenüber der Kriegsandrohung des Boten) in der ῥῆσις ausgedrückt wird. Inhaltlich umfaßt die Stichomythie Gebet, Streit, Überredung: also alle wesentlichen γένη.[1]

That the introduction of the second actor by Aeschylus was a vitally important step in the development of drama is obvious, but it is not easy to define precisely what the original significance of that step was. It must certainly have increased the possibilities of genuine drama, in that the situation of the first actor might now change in the course of the play. No longer is the playwright restricted to a narrative with lyric comment by the chorus. The development of a plot becomes a possibility.[2] There seems however no reason to believe that the second actor was intended in the first place to provide a dramatic ἀγών with the protagonist.[3] His function is a humbler, but nonetheless important, one. He 'can come in with fresh news—as Darius does, or the Spy in the *Septem*—or can present different facets of the situation to the hero—as do Oceanus and Io in the *Prometheus*.[4]

[1] Jens 18.

[2] See esp. Haigh 36 and 39; Bethe, *N. Jbb.* (1907) 85; Flickinger 169; Howald 41; *GGL* 58 f.; Pohlenz 24 and 37 f. (cf. 140); Else, *TAPhA* 70. 153; *TAPhA* 76. 5; *Wien. Stud.* 72. 102 ff.

[3] As Weir Smyth (19 f.) for example implies.

[4] Kitto 32 (cf. 44 and 51): see also Peretti 89 f.; Untersteiner 332; Else, *Wien. Stud.* 72. 106 ('In two-actor tragedy, then, the second actor is not another hero; he is, in type and characteristic function, the Messenger'); also *Origin and early form* 86 f., 94. This need not mean that Kranz is wrong (*Stasimon* 64) to say 'Alle Tragödie ist aus dem Zwiespalt geboren, ist Verkörperung des Zwiespalts'. But in early tragedy this *Zwiespalt* does not take the form of a conflict presented between two characters before the eyes of the audience. Kranz himself had earlier suggested (*N. Jbb.* 1919. 163 f.) that the agon of tragedy was an importation

In the *Persae* the chorus remains the focal point and is the first to be addressed by the Messenger and by Darius when they arrive on the scene.[1] The excuse made by Atossa for her silence (290 ff.), and the device employed to transfer attention from the Chorus to Atossa at 703 perhaps indicate that Aeschylus was aware of the natural improbability inherent in this convention.[2] Gradually the possibility of using the second actor as an antagonist of the first must have become apparent, so that for the first time a genuine conflict is presented before the eyes of the audience.[3] Yet even in the extant plays the use of dialogue between two actors develops only slowly, and in Aeschylus' three-actor period a conversation among all three is hardly to be found at all.[4]

It has long been maintained that the *Supplices* must have been composed soon after the introduction by Aeschylus of the second actor, since in this play he is so sparingly used.[5] Aeschylus has not yet learnt how to make the most of his invention. There are only two scenes of dialogue between the two actors (490 ff. and 903 ff.). Danaus, we are told, is a mere 'Annex

from comedy. Pickard-Cambridge (1st ed.) 195 remarked that '(the agon of tragedy) is never so formal or persistent in shape as the agon of the Old Comedy, which was really primitive'.

[1] Cf. Flickinger 165 f.; Peretti 228; Pickard-Cambridge, *Dram. festivals* 140; Dawe 51 n. 2 (on the *Ag.*) (cf. 62).

[2] This is not to say that he does not turn the convention to excellent dramatic effect: cf. Broadhead xxvii f. and xl ff. (B. however lays too much stress on the character of Atossa, as if it had an independent existence outside the play). For a similar excuse for silence cf. *P.V.* 436 ff. Technical considerations, as well as dramatic, preclude the use of two actors in an epirrhematic scene of this kind (cf. p. 130 below).

[3] The second actor's characteristic and original function may be that of the Messenger. But that does not mean that he is '*irrevocably* cast as Messenger, Herald, and the like' (Else, *Origin and early form* 96: my italics). Cf. p. 133 below. For Else confrontation of protagonist with chorus comes before that of actor with actor.

[4] For example at *Eum.* 744 ff. Cf. Flickinger 169 ff.; Croiset 275; *GGL* 59 n. 1 and 121; Pohlenz 136, cf. 222 f.; Dale 26 f. That Aesch. himself, not Soph., was responsible for the introduction of the third actor is maintained by Else (*TAPhA* 76. 1 ff.; cf. *TAPhA* 70. 141 f.) on the evidence of *Vita Aesch.* 15, etc.; cf. *Origin and early form* 96, 86 (cf. p. 116 n. 5 above): cf. also Pohlenz 41, *Erl.* 36. For Else this means that A. used 2 ὑποκριταί + the τραγῳδός (himself); Soph., when he gave up acting, substituted a 3rd ὑποκριτής. But cf. Lesky, *Studi U. E. Paoli* 471 f. Most scholars believe that the *Vita* was mistaken.

[5] See p. 88 n. 1 above and p. 135 below.

seiner Töchter'.[1] His function is to give advice of the most platitudinous and irrelevant kind. He remains silent throughout the long scene in which the Chorus supplicate Pelasgus (234–489) and is not even mentioned by the king. When at last he does address Pelasgus (490–9) his words serve only to motivate his own exit from the scene. He abandons his daughters at the very moment when they need him most (775), and for no other reason than that he is required to play the part of the Egyptian herald. An excuse has to be manufactured (968 ff.) to allow him to return, and even this return is artificially delayed to allow the herald time to change.[2] The criticism that Danaus leaves his daughters at a critical moment may be dismissed immediately, is so far as it is based on a misplaced feeling for natural probability rather than dramatic considerations.[3] Yet even from the naturalistic point of view the argument fails if, as many believe, the herald is accompanied by a singing 'Nebenchor' or even a silent retinue of soldiers. What could the single Danaus do against so many? His obvious duty is to go for help. But such considerations are irrelevant. The position of Danaus in the *Supplices* must be judged in terms purely of the poet's dramatic purpose. Does he do what Aeschylus wants him to do, or does his handling prove the poet's youthful incompetence? Can we really believe that Aeschylus introduced to tragedy a second actor for whom as yet he had no use?[4]

A curious inconsistency is apparent in the arguments of certain scholars, those who uphold the theory that the first actor is the descendent of the exarchon of the dithyramb. The position of the first actor is illustrated, they say, by the position of Danaus in the *Supplices*. In his relationship of father he

[1] Wilamowitz, *Interpr.* 13; cf. also Bergk 310; Körte, in *Mélanges Nicole* 298 (Danaus is more like the old servant of the Danaids than a king and their κύριος: this is 'nur aus der Unbeholfenheit einer noch kindlichen dramatischen Technik zu erklären'); G. Müller 47 (D. 'non tam persona quam umbra'); Ed. Meyer, *Forschungen zur alten Geschichte* I. (Halle a. S. 1892) 83 and 88; Koster 19.

[2] A. C. Schlesinger, *Cl. Phil.* 28 (1933) 176, remarks that he 'must have had to step lively'.

[3] See esp. Lloyd-Jones' attack on the use of naturalistic arguments in the interpretation of Aeschylean tragedy (*L'Ant. Class.* 33, esp. 365, 367 f., 369 f., 374); cf. also Kitto 9, 27 f., 30, 52, 106 f.

[4] Kitto (94 n. 1) points out the weakness of this position.

coheres closely with the chorus, as one would expect an exarchon to do. Precisely analogous, it is argued, is the position of Papposilenus in the satyr-plays.[1] The argument could hardly be clearer: Danaus represents the first actor, invented long ago by Thespis. Yet we are told also that in Danaus we see Aeschylus' awkward and archaic handling of the *second* actor. No one suggests that Aeschylus does not know what to do with Pelasgus. To be consistent the argument must at least be reformulated: Aeschylus has already learnt how to handle his second actor effectively, but in so doing he has forgotten what to do with the first. Put in these terms it is less immediately attractive. It may perhaps be saved if we are prepared to reject the exarchon-theory and look to Pelasgus for the offspring of Thespis' first actor. But exarchon-theory or no, Danaus still behaves as we should expect the first actor to behave, in that he brings news to the Chorus and thus provides the themes of its songs. It seems then that other than simple chronological reasons must be sought for the treatment of Danaus in this play. Is it not possible that that treatment is determined by the unusual position of the Chorus? The Chorus here is the protagonist, and we have seen no reason to believe that this was a normal state of affairs in archaic tragedy. It is only natural therefore that the position of the actors too should be unusual. In a sense it would be more reasonable to call Danaus the tritagonist, with the Chorus as protagonist, and Pelasgus as deuteragonist. This Chorus is no mere interested spectator of what the two actors do and say. Indeed if there is any awkwardness in the exit of Danaus to fetch help and his failure to return with Pelasgus it

[1] The same relationship is said to be found between Oceanus and the Chorus of the *P.V.* See esp. Wilamowitz, *Interpr.* 2, 120, 240; cf. also *Kl. Schr.* I. 366 f. and 371; Frickenhaus, *Jahrb. Arch. Inst.* 32. I ff.; Kranz, *N. Jbb.* (1919) 158, and *Stasimon* 19 (cf. 24); Geffcken I. i. 143 and 151; O. Regenbogen, *Hermes* 68 (1933) 68; Ziegler 1908; Pohlenz, *Erl.* 19. For Silenus as the first actor cf. also A. Hartmann, *R.-E.* iii. A. I. 51; Kalinka 42. *Contra* Bethe, *Proleg.* 39 f.; Howald 34; *GGL* 42 n. 5; Bieber 12 ff. Nestle saw the relationship between Danaus and the Chorus as having its prototype in that between Dionysus and his θίασος and that between the exarchon and chorus of the ritual θρῆνος (17 ff., 25 f., 69, 108): cf. also Peretti 77 f., 204 f., etc. For Porzig (151) Danaus stands over against the Chorus like a priest before a congregation (cf. p. 166 on Atossa and 173 on Xerxes). Murray thought that Danaus, Pelasgus, and the Egyptian herald were all exarchontes of their respective 'choruses'. Cf. chap. v p. 193.

shows rather that the need for a third actor is already beginning to be felt.[1] Rather different is the *Persae*, where at 851 Atossa leaves the stage because she is dramatically superfluous, not because an additional actor is required.[2] Stoessl indeed argues[3] that Aeschylus is merely taking over from Phrynichus' *Phoenissae* a motif which in that play was forced upon the playwright by his use of only a single actor. If it could be proved that Phrynichus was still writing single-actor tragedy in the 470's, this would be valuable evidence for the late date of the *Supplices*.[4] But Stoessl's whole reconstruction of the *Phoenissae* from Aeschylus' *Persae* is too uncertain to provide such evidence. It is unlikely that Aeschylus blindly and unnecessarily repeated in his play a motif for which he had no use.

The part of Danaus in the *Supplices* is small because Aeschylus wants the Chorus to be the protagonist. All our interest is to be concentrated on it and its relations with Pelasgus. Danaus is indeed the πατὴρ καὶ βούλαρχος καὶ στασίαρχος (11–12)[5] of his daughters, but Aeschylus has chosen to give to the girls the task of negotiating with the Argive king. So too they must face alone the Egyptian herald. The agon is to be between a band of weak and helpless girls and the strong and menacing Egyptian male (or males). In this basic conflict there is no place for

[1] Cf. *GGL* 69 n. 4 and 198; Wecklein, ed. *Supp.* 13; Croiset 67; Lesky 68; Koster 23. Mr E. W. Whittle suggests to me that the confrontation between Danaus and his enemies is perhaps made all the more effective by its postponement till later in the trilogy.

[2] See Wilamowitz, *Interpr.* 46 f.; Schlesinger, *Cl. Phil.* 25 (1930) 230; Broadhead xxxix n. 1; *GGL* 69 n. 4 and 205; Pohlenz, *Erl.* 28 f.; Kitto 106. Much less convincing are Flickinger 175; Croiset 13 and 98 n. 1; Norwood 87 n. 1; Pickard-Cambridge, *Dram. festivals* 140. Miss Bieber finds (21 f.) that the use of two actors in the *Persae* is merely 'awkward and unskilful', in that Xerxes and Atossa never meet. In fact A. does not want them to meet, and takes pains to ensure that they will not. Once more naturalism is the least important consideration.

[3] Stoessl 154 and 158 ff. Verrall too (*Proc. Camb. Philol. Soc.* 79–81 (1908) 13 ff., and *The Bacchants of Euripides* (Cambridge 1910) 283 ff.) believed that the *Persae* was closely modelled on Phrynichus' play, and actually incorporated sections of it unaltered: see also Weir Smyth 75 f.

[4] Stoessl (160), writing in 1945 and still accepting an early date for the *Supp.*, had to ascribe to natural conservatism Phrynichus' use of only one actor. In *A.J.Ph.* 73 (1952) 125 f. he assigns the *Supp.* to a date *c.* 476, to bring it as close as possible to Phrynichus' play.

[5] Lloyd-Jones (369) stresses the fact that 'throughout the play identity of purpose between father and daughters is complete, and when they speak together, Danaus is always in command'. Cf. also chap. V pp. 202 f. below.

Danaus.[1] On technical grounds alone a second actor is in early tragedy excluded from an epirrhema between actor and chorus. 'Aeschylus' practice seems to be that when an epirrhematic episode verges into one containing long speeches, an actor takes over from the chorus; but so long as not more than three trimeters at a time are being spoken on the side the chorus represents, these are given to the coryphaeus.'[2] And now in this supplication scene between Chorus and Pelasgus and in this contest between the Chorus and the Egyptian something quite new is to be seen. For the first time in the extant plays of Aeschylus we see a genuine conflict presented before our eyes. Or rather we see two different kinds of conflict, an inner conflict in the mind of Pelasgus and a direct confrontation of two utterly opposed and hostile characters.[3] If in the dramatic sense the Chorus is the protagonist of this play, in the purely technical sense it must be Pelasgus.[4] Whether it is Danaus or Pelasgus who more truly reflects the position of Thespis' first actor it is Pelasgus who has the more significant and dramatically rewarding part. Many scholars have seen in Eteocles the first truly tragic character and individualized hero in tragedy. 'He is,' says Murray,[5] 'if I am not mistaken, the first clearly studied individual character in dramatic literature.' And 'Eteocle è il primo uomo veramente tragico che appare nella tragedia greca'.[6] Much attention has

[1] See Howald 54; Nestle 16; Weir Smyth 55; *GGL* 196 f.; Pohlenz 44; Kitto 14 and 25. Aeschylus seems rarely to be embarrassed by the presence of a silent actor (but see p. 126). Indeed in the case of Pylades he uses him with notable effect. Ar. *Frogs* 911 ff. makes fun of the device. Other effective silent characters are Cassandra in the *Ag.*, Prometheus, Achilles in the *Phrygians*, and Niobe in the play named after her. Cf. Wecklein, *Sitz. bay. ak. München* (1891) 343 ff.; Wilamowitz, *Interpr.* 176; Pohlenz, *NGG* (1920) ii. 162; Flickinger 170 and 229 f.; Nestle 118; Méautis, *Eschyle et la trilogie* 87 f., and *Prométhée* 14 (cf. 28); W. B. Stanford, *Aeschylus in his style* (Dublin 1942) 138; Fraenkel, *Ag.* III. 485; Stoessl, *R.-E.* xxiii. 2. 2315; Denniston–Page 116 f.; Broadhead 103; Kitto 73 f., 108, 111 f., and *Form and meaning* 27 ff., 53; Jones 100 f.; Thomson 166.

[2] Lloyd-Jones 364 f. See also above pp. 119 f.

[3] Else's discussion (*Origin and early form* 85 ff.; cf. 57) of this development in Aeschylean tragedy is good.

[4] Cf. Croiset 13; Else 94. Norwood (84 n. 1) and Vürtheim (128) make Danaus the protagonist.

[5] Murray 143.

[6] Peretti 147 (cf. 157 ff.); but cf. also 115; see also Wilamowitz, *Interpr.* 64 ff. and 243; Weir Smyth 131 (cf. 147 ff.); Croiset 101, 105 ff., 109, 126 f.; Perrotta 66 ff.; *GGL* 193 and 218 ff.; Regenbogen 69; Nestle 26 f. and 91; Kitto 44 ff. (esp. 52) and 101. The view is carried to its limits by von Fritz, *Antike und moderne*

been paid in recent years to the question of the relationship between Eteocles' own conscious decision and the family-curse. How far he is aware from the beginning of the full implications of that curse, and to what extent his character changes at line 653, are matters which are still keenly debated.[1] It is enough for our present purpose to note that we do not see him in the play reaching his decision. The mind of Eteocles, for all the entreaties of the Chorus (677 ff.), is already made up:[2] ἐπεὶ τὸ πρᾶγμα κάρτ' ἐπισπέρχει θεός... (689) and θεῶν διδόντων οὐκ ἂν ἐκφύγοις κακά (719). Nothing in the *Septem* approaches the mental turmoil of Pelasgus which culminates in his speeches at 407 ff., 438 ff., and 468 ff. His dilemma is insoluble.[3] Either he will refuse the Danaids' supplication and bring upon himself and Argos the wrath of the god of suppliants, or he will grant their request and involve his city in a war waged for the sake of women (410 ff. and 472 ff.). The nearest parallel is the situation of Agamemnon in the Parodos of that play.[4] There is nothing

Tragödie 193 ff. and 226 (esp. 218 f.: 'Aber die Individualisierung der Gestalt geht, wie mir scheint, weit darüber hinaus (i.e. beyond the view of Wilamowitz), und eben damit auch hinaus über die Individualisierung der Gestalten der gesamten *Orestie*, nicht nur von Orest, der verhältnismäßig unindividualisiert bleibt, sondern auch Agamemnon, Klytaimnestra, Kassandra, Aigisth und Elektra.' Cf. also Mazon I. 106 ff. ('...cette figure d'homme, la plus belle à coup sûr de tout le théâtre grec') quoted with approval by Méautis 103): *contra* Howald 68 and 73; Kranz 57 f. and 281; Jones 18; F. L. Lucas, *Greek drama for Everyman* (London 1954) 29 ('But one wonders if such critics know one end of a human being from another'); Dawe 41 n. 1.

[1] See esp. Regenbogen 63 ff.; F. Solmsen, *TAPhA* 68 (1937) 197 ff.; K. Reinhardt, *Aischylos als Regisseur und Theologe* (Berne 1949) 123 ff.; L. A. Post, *Class. Weekly* 44 (1950–1) 44 ff. (also *From Homer to Menander* (California 1951) 71 ff.); Lloyd-Jones, *C.Q.* n.s. 9 (1959) 80 ff. (esp. 84 ff.); *C.Q.* 12 (1962) 197; *Gnomon* 34 (1962) 740 ff.; E. Wolff, *Harv. Stud.* 63 (1958) 89 ff.; H. Patzer, *ibid.* 97 ff.; F. Egermann, *Gymnasium* 68 (1961) 502 ff.; Lesky, *Wien. Stud.* 74 (1961) 5 ff., and *J.H.S.* 86. 83 f.; von Fritz, *loc. cit.*; Pohlenz 92 ff.; Dawe 31 ff.; A. J. Podlecki, *TAPhA* 95 (1964) 283 ff.; R. P. Winnington-Ingram, in *Classical drama and its influence* (London 1965) 38; Else, *Origin and early form* 90 ff.; L. Golden, *In praise of Prometheus* (North Carolina [1966]) 42 ff.

[2] Cf. Solmsen 203 n. 22; Pohlenz 94; Lesky, *Wien. Stud.* 74. 6.

[3] For the dilemma of Pelasgus see esp. Schadewaldt 38 f. and 204 ff.; B. Snell, *Aischylos und das Handeln im Drama* (*Philol.* Suppl. 20 (1928)) 59 ff.; Porzig 156 ff.; Croiset 57 ff.; Kranz 55 f.; Pohlenz 47, *Erl.* 20; Mazon I. 7; Kitto 8 ff., 26, 29; Else, *Origin and early form* 95; Lesky, *J.H.S.* 86. 79 ff. Marx (340) saw the first introduction of conflict into tragedy by Phrynichus in the choice forced upon Hypermestra between obedience to Danaus and her love for her husband.

[4] Compare *Supp.* 442 with *Ag.* 211: see also *Eum.* 470 ff. Lesky, *loc. cit.*, brings out well the parallels between *Supp.* and *Ag.* For L. both Pelasgus and Agamemnon

like it in either *Persae* or *Septem*. It is sometimes stated that the later plays of Aeschylus show an increasing skill in characterization.[1] Here as elsewhere it is rash to look for development in a straight line. It has become increasingly recognized that Aeschylus is not concerned with character for its own sake.[2] He gives us enough only to explain and motivate the actions of his people. The determining factor is not the date of the play but the dramatic necessity. This is why Orestes in the *Eumenides* seems to us a less fully portrayed character than he does in the *Choephori*.[3] It is not that Aeschylus' powers of characterization had suddenly failed. So in the *Supplices* we are interested not in the character of Pelasgus but in his dilemma. And Aeschylus' presentation of that dilemma finds no parallel in either *Persae* or *Septem*.[4]

face 'situations in which necessity and man's personal decision to act are indissolubly united'. For the problem of the kommos of the *Choe.* cf. esp. Schadewaldt, *Hermes* 67 (1932) 312 ff. (also Weir Smyth 197 ff. (cf. 194 f.); Pohlenz 114, *Erl.* 58 ff.; Kitto 81, and *Form and meaning* 43 ff.; Egermann 510 ff.); Lesky, *Sitz. Wien. Akad.*, Phil.-hist. Kl. 221. 3 (1943) (also *J.H.S.* 86. 84 f.).

[1] Thus for Ridgeway (128) the faintness of the character-painting (he exempts the Chorus from the criticism) in the *Supp.* is a sign of its early date: cf. Tucker xx and xxiii; Weir Smyth 59; Wilamowitz, *Interpr.* 11; Croiset 60 and 67 (cf. 99 f.); Norwood 86 (cf. 103). Murray (121) finds the *Pers.* deficient in character-study. For Stanford (*A. in his style* 112 f.) the three earliest plays (*Supp.*, *Pers.*, *Sept.*) are the weakest in stylistic characterization (but the *Pers.* is the weakest of all; cf. 138). For Miss Wolff (*Columbia Diss.* 79 f.) the development comes between *Pers.* and *Sept.* Nestle contrasts the scout in the *Sept.* with the watchman of the *Ag.* and the Pythia of the *Eum.*; cf. Wilamowitz, *Interpr.* 62 and 85; Weir Smyth 161 f.; Croiset 185 and 275; *GGL* 118 f.; Kitto 64 f. and 71. See in general Weir Smyth 153; Croiset 201 ff.; Kranz 56 ff.; *GGL* 193, 201, 206, 243; Regenbogen 68 f.; Pohlenz 141.

[2] See, for example, *GGL* 122 ff. and 285; Norwood 109 and 113; Pohlenz 104 f., 141; Kitto 9 (cf. 23 f.), 26 f., 52, 101 f. and *Form and meaning* 46, 48 ff., 201 ff.; Weir Smyth 160 f. (cf. 174 ff.); Lloyd-Jones 373 f., 370 f. For Aristotle (*Poet.* 1450a 20 ff., etc.) character in tragedy is included for the sake of the action. This is the starting-point for H. J. F. Jones' important attempt to eliminate the tragic hero from the interpretation of the *Poetics* and to study tragedy from the point of view of the action of the plays rather than the character or individual consciousness of the stage-figures (but cf. also Lloyd-Jones, *Rev. of English Studies* n.s. 15 (1964) 221 f.). The problems raised by T. von Wilamowitz concerning deliberate neglect of consistency in plot and character in Soph. have been recently studied in the light of Aeschylus' technique (R. D. Dawe, *Proc. Camb. Philol. Soc.* n.s. 9 (1963) 21 ff.).

[3] Cf. Petersen 385; Weir Smyth 206; Croiset 263 f.; *GGL* 255 f.; Pohlenz 141.

[4] Petersen (164 ff.) found a big advance in the characterization of minor characters between *Pers.* and *Sept.* on the one hand and *Supp.*, *Oresteia*, *P.V.* on the other.

In the second place we see for the first time in the *Supplices* a direct confrontation, an agon, between two hostile parties.[1] In the *Persae* there is no agon of any kind at all. The *Septem* contains lively scenes in which first Eteocles tries to calm the terrified Chorus and secondly the Chorus seeks to dissuade Eteocles from going out to meet his brother in single combat. What we do not see is an agon between Eteocles and Polyneices. Only one side appears before the audience. The real conflict is reported. The *Supplices* is very different, and this difference is reflected in the new use that Aeschylus finds here for stichomythia.[2] The Danaids come face to face with their enemy in an epirrhema, Pelasgus and the herald quarrel violently in stichomythia. In the absence of evidence for pre-Aeschylean tragedy we can never be certain that conflict was not already inherent in the single-actor stage of development. But it is at least as reasonable to suppose that it came in only gradually, with the invention of the second actor. If that is true, we may well believe that before he presented a chorus in conflict with an actor Aeschylus had already had experience in portraying an agon between two actors. This may be pure speculation, and with so few plays from which to judge there is no place for dogmatic assertions. If Eteocles and Polyneices do not confront each other in the *Septem* we need not agree with Weir Smyth (78) that this was 'an opportunity missed', because Aeschylus did not realize its possibilities.[3] What does seem certain is that in this respect at least the *Supplices* is closer to the technique of the *Oresteia* than are either the *Persae* or the *Septem*.[4] The herald-scene in the

[1] Cf. Bergk III. 306; Kitto 20 f.; Norwood 86 (N. also notes (91) that in the *Sept.* there is no dramatic conflict of personalities; cf. Weir Smyth 142). Kranz recognizes (55) that struggle in the *Pers.* is no more than a background and an echo. For Untersteiner, on the other hand (264 ff.; cf. 251), the tragic discords of the *Supp.* are a sign of antiquity. Weir Smyth says (169) 'In Aeschylus' earlier plays conflict is shown in its effects. The conflict in the *Agamemnon*, as in the other members of the trilogy, takes audible and visible form'. But so it does in the *Supp.* For the effectiveness of the Herald/Pelasgus scene see also Kitto 14 and 25; Peretti 108 f.; Lloyd-Jones 363 f. and 374.

[2] Cf. p. 124 above.

[3] Kitto (45 f.) is right to warn us that the concentration on one side of the quarrel is not necessarily a sign of technical immaturity.

[4] Cf. esp. Nestle, *Gnomon* 10. 413 f. Schmid (*GGL* 201) judged the *Supp.* to be the best of the three earliest plays from the point of view of dramatic design. Many

Supplices was not written by a novice. It is difficult to understand the arguments of those who say that the lack of dramatic action in the *Supplices* proves it to be an early play.[1] It contains, says Kranz, only three scenes of dramatic life.[2] How many such scenes, Nestle pertinently asks,[3] are to be found in the *Persae*? Kitto says (51) that the situation of the *Supplices* is 'static' compared with that of the *Septem*. But what could be less static than the arrival of the herald?[4] It is sometimes said that the dramatic movement of Aeschylus' plays, unlike those of Sophocles, proceeds in a straight line to its inevitable conclusion,

have drawn attention to the lack of genuine action in the *Pers.*: for example Wilamowitz, *Einleitung* 109; *GGL* 205; Murray 115, 121, 177; Peretti 136 ff.; Pohlenz 58; Broadhead xxxii ff.; Dawe 30 f.; Else, *Origin and early form* 64, 87 f. For similar judgements on the *Sept.* see Wilamowitz, *loc. cit.*; Murray 141; Norwood 91; Else 64; and on the *P.V.* Wilamowitz, *Interpr.* 150; Petersen 373 (not very different from the *Supp.*); Weir Smyth 99 ff.; Norwood 96; Kitto 53 ff. The seven pairs of speeches at *Sept.* 375 ff. have a non-dramatic and unmistakably archaic ring: cf. esp. Petersen 371; *GGL* 213 (cf. 119 n. 10); Lesky 89. See also pp. 115 f. above.

[1] For criticism of such a view cf. Kitto 3. In general it is stated that Aeschylus' later plays are richer in dramatic action than are his earlier ones. Cf. Murray 177 ff. (esp. 185: 'in the *Oresteia* for the first time Aeschylus creates the drama of plot and action'); *GGL* 252 (on the *Eum.*) (cf. 119 n. 10); Peretti 114. Petersen (370) found in the *Sept.* a great advance to normal tragedy. Even inside the *Oresteia* trilogy, however, the pace of the action varies considerably. Contrast the first part of the *Eum.* with that of the *Ag.* See Wilamowitz, *Interpr.* 186; Bethe, *N. Jbb.* (1907) 92 and 95; Perrotta 77 and 93; Murray 179 ff.; *GGL* 233 and 242 f.; Peretti 197; Lesky 73 and 89; Kitto 86, and *Form and meaning* 49 f.

[2] Kranz 15 (cf. p. 118 above). Cf. also Bergk 307 and 309; Tucker xvi ('There is no thrilling action in the piece, and, despite its admirable poetry, it would have fallen flat as a drama if only twelve or fifteen Danaids had provided the spectacle') (cf. xxiii); Geffcken I. i. 151 f.; Porzig 150; Weir Smyth 52 and 59; Croiset 269 f. (contradicted by 271); Norwood 85 f.; Koster 18 ff. For Croiset (99; cf. 269 ff.) the *Pers.* compared with the *Supp.* represents a remarkable progress towards the full realization of the dramatic potentiality of tragedy. Wilamowitz found signs of immaturity in the *Supp.* (*Interpr.* 187). But he found such signs in most of Aeschylus' plays. He criticized the *Pers.* for its lack of dramatic unity (*Interpr.* 42 ff.; cf. also Weir Smyth 72; Kitto 42; Broadhead xxxv ff.: *contra GGL* 205 n. 3; Perrotta 62 ff.; K. Deichgräber, *NGG* Phil.-hist. Kl. N.F. I. 4 (1941) 155 ff.; Lesky, *Tr. Dichtung* 61 f.). For Wilamowitz on the *Sept.* cf. *Sitz. Akad. Wiss. Berlin* (1903. 1) 438 ff. and 447); *Interpr.* 67 ff. and 187 (cf. Howald 67; Pohlenz 95 f.; Else, *Origin and early form* 89 ff.: but also *GGL* 211 n. 8; Perrotta 68 ff.; and literature on p. 131 n. 1 above). On the *P.V.* see *Interpr.* 125, 150, 187, and on the *Ag. Interpr.* 167 ff.

[3] *Gnomon* 10. 410 ff. Welcker (*Kl. Schr.* IV. 126 f.) was one of the few early scholars to reject the view that the *Supp.* lacked dramatic action. Cf. also Wecklein, ed. *Supp.*, 21. See now W. Jens, *Studium Generale* 8 (1955) 249 ff.

[4] Kitto (28) recognizes that 'the middle part of the *Supplices* and the whole of the *Septem* are much more specifically dramatic in form' (than the *Pers.*).

without any περιπέτεια.[1] A περιπέτεια of a kind however may be detected in the *Agamemnon*, when the victorious king comes home only to be murdered.[2] It is foreshadowed in the *Supplices* when the victorious prayer of blessing on behalf of Argos is followed immediately by the arrival of the Egyptian ships.[3] And, so far as one can tell, an even more striking περιπέτεια is in store for the sons of Aegyptus later in the trilogy.

The advanced dramatic technique that Aeschylus displays in the *Supplices* and its similarity to that of the *Oresteia* must cast grave suspicion on the view that because Danaus is so sparingly used we can deduce from the *Supplices* what single-actor tragedy must have been like.[4] For Kitto 'the play is in all essentials single-actor drama up to the point where Danaus is able to do something useful by going into Argos'.[5] On the contrary the relationship between Pelasgus and the Chorus in the first part of the play presupposes a reasonably long period of two-actor drama,[6] which the agon between the king and the herald merely serves to confirm. Why then is Danaus there at all, when for most of the play he appears to be dramatically superfluous? It is not very difficult to imagine the *Supplices* without his

[1] See, for example, *GGL* 133 f., 285 f., 288; Croiset 273 f.; Kitto 53 (on the *Sept.*).

[2] Cf. *GGL* 133 f. and 285; Petersen 378. Petersen finds a περιπέτεια also in the *Choe.* (p. 383) and the *Sept.* (p. 372) (cf. also Thomson 331). It is strange that (like Tucker xxiii; Croiset 269) he did not notice the very much more obvious one in the *Supp.* What Aristotle meant by περιπέτεια is of course disputed. If it means 'reversal of intention' rather than 'reversal of situation', a further περιπέτεια may be seen in the *Choe.*, where Clytaemestra's sending of libations to Agamemnon's tomb to appease his wrath results in the meeting of Electra and Orestes, and thus sets in train the events leading to her own destruction.

[3] Cf. Howald 64; Croiset 63 and 66 (contradicting 269); Peretti 266.

[4] 'Its (the *Supp.*'s) principal value for us lies in the fact that it could readily be revamped for presentation by one actor and in the light which it thus sheds upon the character of one-actor drama' (Flickinger 164): cf. also Haigh 34 ff.; Weir Smyth 52; Peretti 227 f. (cf. 100); Schmid (*GGL* 59 n. 1) is more cautious.

[5] Kitto 23 (cf. 8 f. and 27 ff.). But K. recognizes (25) that 'the difficulty that Aeschylus has in using him is *not simply* a sign of primitive technique and inexperience, but a special consequence of this legend'. (My italics.)

[6] The scene is itself unusual in that it is the actor who seeks information from the Chorus, and not *vice versa*. This is why (Peretti 210) the epirrhema is introduced by a stichomythia, and not, as everywhere else, by a rhesis. Mr Whittle points out to me that the attribution of lines adopted by Murray and others at 291 ff. gives a particularly sophisticated kind of stichomythia, one in which (until 313 or 314) questions are *formally* asked by the chorus-leader, but it is Pelasgus who is really seeking and eliciting the information: cf. E. *I.T.* 810 ff. Cf. further p. 124 above.

presence, with Pelasgus appearing unannounced before the Chorus, and later himself reporting the decision of the Argive assembly.[1] Various reasons may be suggested, some more cogent than others. It is possible that the second actor was already so much an accepted stage convention that Aeschylus could not dispense with his presence for this play. Danaus moreover was provided by the myth, and could hardly be omitted from any treatment of the story. Indeed his presence may have been essential to clarify the legal position of the Danaids.[2] If he were dead their cousins would have a stronger legal claim to marry them. It may be also that he played a much larger part in the later plays of the trilogy,[3] in inciting his daughters to the murder of their husbands. From the immediate dramatic point of view Danaus is useful when it comes to fetching Pelasgus to rescue the Chorus from the herald. But perhaps the most important reason for his presence is that the scenes with Danaus provide a contrast of mood, a contrast that so often in Greek tragedy is provided by the stasima of the chorus.[4] The Chorus here is itself an actor in the drama, and we inevitably miss the odes of quiet, lyrical contemplation that serve to set the immediate situation of the dramatic characters against a wider and a deeper background. Only in the prayer for the blessing of Argos does the Chorus of the *Supplices* strike this note.[5] Danaus, with his wise advice (176 ff., 490 ff., 724 ff., and especially 991 ff.), strikes it instead.

[1] Cf. Thomson 167.

[2] See chap. v pp. 219 f.

[3] Cf. Croiset 69; Kitto 15 and 25; Thomson 167. Cf. the emphasis laid on Danaus' importance at 11–12.

[4] See Wilamowitz, *Interpr.* 118 and 158 on the contrast between Io's wild utterances in the *P.V.* and the quiet stasima of the Chorus (see however also 174). On the subject of contrast of mood in Aeschylus cf. also Petersen 369 ff. (*Pers.*, *Sept.*); Croiset 149 f. (*P.V.*); *GGL* 161 n. 4 and 285 f.; Kranz 169 (*Choe.*); Méautis 59 ff. (*Supp.*), 73, 89, 92 f. (*P.V.*), 114 (*Sept.*); Broadhead xxxix; Kitto 57 ff. (*P.V.*); Dawe 28 n. 1 (*Pers.*) and 43 ff. (*Ag.*); L. Aylen, in *Classical drama and its influence* 91 f. In the first half of the *Sept.* the contrast is between the excited terror of the female chorus and the manly calm of Eteocles; cf. *GGL* 77, 135, 212, and 218; Weir Smyth 134 ff.; Pohlenz 88 (cf. 140 on the *P.V.*); Mazon I. 108; Kitto 47; Citti 46 ff. Kranz points out (162) that at *Supp.* 966 ff., *Ag.* 1331 ff., *Choe.* 719 ff. and 855 ff., where the excitement does not permit a full stasimon, a short anapaestic passage by chorus or chorus-leader is substituted: cf. Fraenkel at *Ag.* 1341 f.

[5] For this break in the tension cf. Hölzle 11.

It is in these scenes that the tension is relaxed. And the ring-composition that is a feature of Danaus's speeches contributes to the effect, by slowing down the dramatic pace.[1] Peretti saw[2] in the rheseis of Danaus strong traces of the ritual προκήρυγμα or κατακελευσμός of the actor-exarchon. This original προκήρυγμα has been transformed into a narrative that motivates the exarchon's command. The typical form, he says, of the archaic rhesis is tripartite: (1) the basis, which consists usually of the exhortation, (2) a description or a reflection that provides the motive for the exhortation, (3) the conclusion, which in the *Supplices* often repeats the thought of the basis of the speech. Peretti finds too in the impersonal, objective character of the speeches of the *Supplices* a sign of their epic-Ionic origin.[3] But the character of these speeches is entirely explicable in terms of their place in the overall economy of the play. If they appear stylized and archaic it is not because Aeschylus could do no better, but because they suit their function in the play. Danaus' proverbs and γνῶμαι (e.g. 190, 203, 499, 760 f.) are not unlike the platitudes that spring so readily to the mouths of the normal tragic chorus.[4] Danaus utters the kind of lines that the chorus-leader so frequently inserts between the two speeches of an agon.[5] It is Danaus too who announces new characters to the Chorus (180 ff., 710 ff.), instead of *vice versa* as is the usual early practice.[6] If the subsidiary chorus of handmaids is to be

[1] See chap. II pp. 74–6.

[2] Peretti, esp. 203 ff., 227 ff. He finds in the *Supp.* that of 15 rheseis addressed to the Chorus 11 begin with an exhortation or resolution (176 ff., 222, 249, 407, 438, 517, 600, 710, 954, 980, 991 (that speech being in two parts). The same προκήρυγμα is said (220 f.) to be visible in the epirrhematic scenes. For the form of the Aeschylean speech of advice cf. also Porzig 34 ff.; Else, *Origin and early form* 60 f.

[3] Peretti 247 ff. and 271. Note, for example, the use of impersonal verbs (176, 203, 407/417, 724, 980). For the objective character of speeches in Aesch. cf. also Schadewaldt 39; Lesky 92; Else, *Origin and early form* 60. This character begins to disappear from the rhesis, says Peretti (208, 245 ff., 273 ff.) after the *Supp.*, and esp. in the *Sept.*: the rhesis becomes dramatic. Lesky however says that it is only with Eur. that the archaic rhesis really loses it.

[4] For proverbs and γνῶμαι in Aesch. cf. *GGL* 287. Schmid finds that of 15 γνῶμαι in the *Supp.* 4 belong to Pelasgus, 6 to Danaus: in the *Ag.* 16 out of 25 are put in the mouth of the Chorus. For Danaus cf. also Stanford 112.

[5] According to Wilamowitz (ed. *Herakles* II. 59 f.) this practice was first established in the period 460–440 B.C. Its beginnings are to be seen for example at *Pers.* 843 f.

[6] Cf. Flickinger 208 ff.; *GGL* 288 n. 3.

accepted at the end of the play, we may see it as another consequence of the unusual position of the main Chorus of the *Supplices*. The Danaids cannot comment lyrically on their situation from any point of view except their own. To set that situation against a wider background another voice is required.[1] In making the Chorus the protagonist of the *Supplices* Aeschylus has had to curtail the actor's part. But at the same time he has compensated him by giving him some of the functions of the normal tragic chorus.[2] From the point of view of the plot Danaus may be superfluous, and his words may not be profound. But nowhere is he irrelevant or incompetently handled. Aeschylus has given him an unusual function to perform, and he performs it well. If he is not in his own right dramatically interesting it is because he was never intended to be so.

The general conclusion is clear enough. While the evidence for the origins of tragedy and its development before 472 B.C. remains fragmentary and at every point obscure, nothing in it compels us to accept that the *Supplices* belongs to an early stage of that development. On the contrary there is reason to believe that it does not. Those features in the structure of the play which seem at first sight to be archaic are due entirely to the position of the Chorus as protagonist.[3] And that position itself is not archaic. Rather it represents a deliberate attempt to integrate the chorus in the action of a tragedy, to give it a dramatic life and character of its own.[4] Whether it was the first such attempt we cannot tell. It may be that Phrynichus had already tried it

[1] Cf. Peretti 97 ff.; del Grande 161.

[2] This view has occurred independently to one of my students, Miss K. J. V. Bell. Schadewaldt remarks (43) that in the *Choe.* (84 ff.) Electra asks the Chorus how she is to pray. In the *Supp.* it is Danaus who advises the Chorus. Professor Lloyd-Jones points out to me that to some extent the position of Athena at the end of the *Eum.* is analogous to that of Danaus here. It is all the more interesting then that in the *Eum.* too Aesch. employs a second chorus.

[3] Cf. esp. Lesky 68.

[4] Cf. Else, *Wien. Stud.* 72. 105 ('a sophisticated experiment in making the chorus a chief actor in the play'); cf. also *Origin and early form* 58. Cf. also *GGL* 70 and 128 for the striving by the tragedians to integrate the undramatic element, the chorus, in the structure of the play; cf. also Nestle 16; Kitto 53, and *Form and Meaning* 33. Körte, *Philol. Wochenschr.* (1928) 1300, suggested that the giving of the expository prologue to the κορυφαῖος instead of an actor might be an attempt of a similar kind.

in his own Αἰγύπτιοι and Δαναΐδες.[1] Aeschylus may have copied him as later he was apparently to borrow the third actor from Sophocles. Certainly he used Phrynichus' *Phoenissae* in his *Persae*.[2] Elsewhere in Aeschylus there are traces of a similar desire to make the chorus an 'actor' in the drama. The Chorus of the *Choephori* by its interference (766 ff.) plays a vital part in the plot.[3] The Choruses of *Septem* and *P.V.* are given a life and character of their own.[4] But the experiment was tried again to anything like the same extent only in the *Eumenides*, and by Euripides in his *Supplices*.[5] Perhaps it was the appearance of the third actor who checked the development of the chorus in this direction. The use of three actors in one play provided the tragedian with all the dramatic possibilities that he required. Aeschylus may have made his experiment at any date, but it would come most naturally in a period in which the third dramatic force or character was already felt to be needed, that is to say shortly before the introduction of the third actor. And this not only agrees with the date of the papyrus. It makes sense of those scenes of conflict, both inner and external, which the *Supplices* so markedly presents.

In terms then of what we may conjecture about the development of Aeschylus' dramatic technique the *Supplices* fits very well into the period between the *Septem* and the *Oresteia*. But it would be wrong to suppose that we are in any better position to dogmatize about that development than were those who before

[1] The date of Phrynichus' plays is quite unknown. Wilamowitz (*Interpr.* 243) put them before Aeschylus': cf. also *GGL* 172 n. 2. Hyp. *Sept.* suggests that he was dead by 467 (cf. v. Blumenthal, *R.-E.* xx. 1. 911).

[2] See pp. 121 and 129 above.

[3] The first example of interrupted stichomythia in Aesch. (cf. Jens 24). For this interference Dawe (56) compares Euripides' *Ion*.

[4] Lloyd-Jones remarks (373) that the Aeschylean chorus 'is as a rule deeply involved, at least emotionally, in the action': cf. also Croiset 276. Aristotle (*Poet.* 18. 1456a 25–6) says καὶ τὸν χορὸν δὲ ἕνα δεῖ ὑπολαβεῖν τῶν ὑποκριτῶν, καὶ μόριον εἶναι τοῦ ὅλου καὶ συναγωνίζεσθαι μὴ ὥσπερ Εὐριπίδῃ ἀλλ' ὥσπερ Σοφοκλεῖ. In fact it is Aesch. (despite Else, *TAPhA* 70. 153 n. 48) who goes furthest in this direction. Warnecke, *R.-E.* xi. 2. 1461, thought that A. had in mind scenes where the coryphaeus took part in the dialogue.

[5] Cf. Pohlenz 24. C. J. Herington, *TAPhA* 94 (1963) 113 ff. (esp. 116 f.), describes the Chorus of the *Eum.* as 'unique among extant tragic choruses in its spiritual nature, its physical appearance, and its functions'.

the discovery of the papyrus fragment believed the *Supplices* to be an early play.[1] We, like them, have only seven plays from which to judge. On that basis no clear pattern of development can be established. If the papyrus fragment makes us turn from the vain pursuit of such a development to the study of each play for its own sake, if it allows us to see the earlier plays not just as steps towards the perfection of the *Oresteia*, and Aeschylus himself not just a stage in the direction of Sophocles, its services to Aeschylean scholarship will be out of all proportion to its size.[2]

[1] Else is, if anything, too confident (*Origin and early form* 6): 'we can see the play as an important link in a close-knit sequence which leads from *Persians* to *Oresteia*'.

[2] Cf. the remarks of Lloyd-Jones 372 f. (cf. also *Gnomon* 34. 738): 'That way of looking at the growth of tragedy as a kind of linear progression has been taken for granted as the only way by the great majority of modern scholars.' Lloyd-Jones sees its origins in Aristotle's *Poetics*. See also Kitto 31 and 96 f., and *Form and meaning* 207 f.; Jones 67 ff.; von Fritz 193 (cf. 223 f.); Trencsényi-Waldapfel, *Acta Antiqua Hung*. 12. 262; Dale 26; Else, *Origin and early form* esp. 7.

CHAPTER IV

BACKGROUND

Attempts to establish the date of the *Supplices* on the basis of its supposed allusions to contemporary events may be treated more briefly. As early as 1808 Boeckh argued from the similar praises of Argos in the *Supplices* and the *Eumenides* that the two plays must belong to the same period.[1] Since Boeckh's day this has indeed been one of the principal arguments against the early dating of the play, and now that the evidence from style and structure is no longer seen to contradict it, it is hardly necessary to say much more on the subject. The search for political allusions in tragedy is notoriously fraught with danger. Zuntz, in his study of Euripides' political plays, has shown that at most one can show that a play conveys 'a definite, if general, teaching growing out of a definite situation and addressed to a definite public'. What one must not do is to treat some details in a play 'as charades on contemporary events'.[2] It is undeniable that Aeschylus was interested in politics, and was prepared to incorporate in his plays references to contemporary events. The *Eumenides* is proof enough of that.[3] But the *Eumenides*, with its

[1] A. Boeckh, *Graecae tragoediae principum* (Heidelberg 1808) 54. It must be added that Boeckh combined with this argument others that were far less acceptable.

[2] G. Zuntz, *The political plays of Euripides* (Manchester 1955) 79 f. (cf. also 5, 55, 91, and *passim*). See also K. J. Dover, *J.H.S.* (1957) 230 ('The ransacking of Tragedy for indications of the political views of tragic poets is seldom profitable and may be disastrous'); W. G. Forrest, *C.Q.* n.s. 10 (1960) 239 n. 7. It is curious that in Euripides' *Supplices* too there is a supposed allusion to an alliance between Athens and Argos (Zuntz 63 ff.).

[3] For politics in the *Eumenides* see esp. Wilamowitz, *Aristoteles und Athen* II (Berlin 1893) 329 ff., esp. 338 ff.; R. W. Livingstone, *J.H.S.* 45 (1925) 120 ff.; C. M. Smertenko, *J.H.S.* 52 (1932) 233 ff.; W. Kolbe, *Hermes* 72 (1937) 262 f.; F. Jacoby, *F. Gr. Hist.* III b Suppl. i. 25 and ii. 26 f. and 528; F. Stoessl, *A.J.Ph.* 73 (1952) 136 ff.; E. R. Dodds, *C.Q.* n.s. 3 (1953) 19 f., and *Proc. Camb. Philol. Soc.* n.s. 6 (1960) 19 ff.; Dover 230 ff.; C. D. N. Costa, *G. & R.* 2nd ser. 9 (1962) 22 ff.; J. H. Quincey, *C.Q.* n.s. 14 (1964) 190 ff.; A. Lesky, *Die tragische Dichtung der Hellenen* (2nd ed. Göttingen 1964) 76, and *Greek tragedy* (Eng. tr. 1965) 84 ff.; A. J. Podlecki, *The political background of Aeschylean tragedy* (Ann Arbor 1966) 80 ff. That Aristophanes thought of Aeschylus as a political teacher is clear from *Frogs* 1419 ff.

quite specific treatment of the Areopagus, is clearly an exception.[1] No other extant play of Aeschylus, or of Sophocles and Euripides, is so inextricably linked with the events of the period in which it was composed. It has been said that both *Persae* and *Eumenides* were first and foremost topical dramas.[2] But in reality there is little in common between the two plays. The theme of the *Persae* is taken from recent history, but it is not treated from the standpoint of Athenian politics. It is not even primarily a patriotic celebration. Persia is the setting, and the subject is Persia's ὕβρις and tragedy.[3] The play was certainly not written primarily 'ad maiorem Themistoclis gloriam'.[4]

It may be true that 'the more fully we know the actual conditions of political and social life contemporary with the Greek drama, the more explicit seems the applicability of many plays

[1] Cf. C. J. Herington, *TAPhA* 94 (1963) 117 f.; Dover 230 and 235. Yet even 'the *Oresteia* is certainly not a play written for a political purpose' (Jacoby IIIb Suppl. ii. 27). From time to time attempts are made to find political significance or even allegory in the *Septem* and *P.V.* L. A. Post, *Class. Weekly* 44 (1950–1) 49 ff. (also *From Homer to Menander* (California 1951) 73 f.), argued unconvincingly that the *Septem* is a manifesto for Pericles, with Polyneices representing Themistocles, and Eteocles Pericles. For J. A. Davison, *TAPhA* 80 (1949) 66f., the *P.V.* is based on the situation at Athens between 463 and 457, and Prometheus is to be identified with Protagoras, Zeus with Pericles. For G. Méautis too, *L'authenticité et la date du Prométhée Enchaîné d'Eschyle* (Neuchâtel 1960) 59 ff., the *P.V.* has a political background, that of Sicilian tyranny, of which it is an indictment. Podlecki gives a useful discussion of such views (*Sept.* pp. 27 ff., *P.V.* pp. 101 ff.). For Stoessl Aeschylus' tragedies 'were all political in their very essence' (121). His attempt to prove this is refuted by G. Freymuth, *Philol.* 99 (1955) 64 ff.

[2] Livingstone 131.

[3] See esp. H. D. Broadhead, *The Persae of Aeschylus* (Cambridge 1960) xv ff.; also G. Perrotta, *I tragici greci* (Messina–Florence [1931]) 62 ff.; W. Jaeger, *Paideia* I (Eng. tr. Oxford 1939) 254 ff.; V. Ehrenberg, *Sophocles and Pericles* (Oxford 1954) 16 f.; H. D. F. Kitto, *Poiesis*; *structure and thought* (California 1966) 74 ff.

[4] M. Cary, *C.R.* 36 (1922) 162; cf. also Forrest 236. It has often been remarked that not a single Greek is named in the *Persae*. That A. sympathized with Themistocles and that the *Pers.* partly reflects that sympathy, there is however no reason to deny. Cf. esp. Podlecki 8 ff.; also G. Busolt, *Gr. Geschichte* III. I (Gotha 1897) 113; E. Cavaignac, *Rev. de Philol.* 45 (1921) 104 f.; A. W. Gomme, *A historical commentary on Thucydides* I (Oxford 1945) 401; Forrest 235 ff. See also pp. 146 ff. below. What Phrynichus made of his *Phoen.* and Μιλήτου ἅλωσις we cannot tell. But we must beware of the view that it was probably Themistocles who 'hit upon the idea of employing the tragic stage for purposes of political propaganda' (E. M. Walker, *C.A.H.* IV. 172): cf. also Schmid–Stählin, *GGL* I. 2. 173 f.; Ed. Meyer, *Geschichte des Altertums* (3rd ed. Stuttgart 1939) IV. I. 294; Post, *Class. Weekly* 44. 50; Stoessl 117; G. Thomson, *Aeschylus and Athens* (3rd ed. London 1966) 218; Podlecki 14 and 20. *Contra* Freymuth 51 ff.

to specific situations then existing'.[1] And indeed it is partly our imperfect knowledge of such conditions that is liable to lead to false interpretations of the dramatist's intention.[2] But the problem goes deeper than that. The playwright is first and foremost a dramatist, not a political propagandist, and it is the critic's first duty to interpret supposed contemporary allusions in the light of their dramatic context. It is the poet's initial choice of the subject of his play or trilogy that determines the details of its treatment. When Aeschylus decided that the story of the Danaids made a suitable theme for a trilogy, he was bound to set that trilogy in Argos.[3] And there is no compelling reason to believe that it was political rather than dramatic considerations that influenced that initial choice.[4] In the case of the *Supplices* we are hampered too by the loss of the rest of the trilogy. It is all too easy to find in it details which appear dramatically irrelevant or over-emphasized, such as the insistence on Argos' democratic constitution.[5] Equally inexplicable in the context of the *Supplices* alone is the insistence on the lodgings of the Danaids (957 ff. and 1009 ff.),[6] and no one has suggested that there is any political significance in that. It must then be accepted at the outset that we cannot identify with certainty any specific contemporary allusion in the *Supplices*. The *Eumenides* is several times explicit in referring to an alliance between Athens and Argos (289 ff., 669 ff., 762 ff.), the *Supplices* does not mention Athens at all.[7]

[1] Smertenko 234.

[2] Cf. Dover 230, Forrest n. 7 on 240; Podlecki vii, 124.

[3] Cf. T. G. Tucker, ed. *Supp.* (London and New York 1889) xxii f. H. D. F. Kitto, *Greek tragedy* (3rd ed. London 1961) 7 f., argues from Pelasgus' speech at 249 ff. that A.'s 'mythical Argos, with its anachronistic democracy, stands for Greece in general, *any* Greek city'.

[4] Despite Podlecki (174 n. 48) who finds it necessary 'to speak out against the insidious tendency to explain away "political" features of the story on the grounds that these were "demanded by the myth". As if Aeschylus had to write about Argive acceptance of the Danaids in 464/3!'

[5] F. Focke, *NGG* (1922) 183, finds the praise of Argos not adequately grounded in the drama itself. He cites esp. 980 ff., but that passage is obviously in place in its dramatic context. Cf. also A. Diamantopoulos, *J.H.S.* 77 (1957) 224 ('the theme in itself has no dramatic interest'; i.e. the theme of democracy); Forrest 240.

[6] See chap. v p. 182.

[7] Cf. also G. Müller, *De Aeschyli Supplicum tempore atque indole* (Halis Saxonum 1908) 5 f.; Kitto 7 f.

At the most then we may say that the general spirit of the *Supplices*, its portrayal of the god-fearing king of Argos and the democratic constitution of the city, its generally favourable attitude, suggest that the play was written in a period when Athens was on friendly terms with Argos;[1] or rather, since no one sees in the *Septem* proof of any special friendship between Athens and Thebes in 467, it suggests one in which she was not on hostile terms. Even of this we cannot be certain. Argos may have appeared in a different light in the remaining plays of the trilogy.[2] But at least it is a reasonable assumption. Furthermore it is rightly pointed out that friendship with Argos involved at the same time hostility towards Sparta.[3] Only two periods have to be considered, the 460's where the papyrus fragment puts the play, and the 490's where it was formerly placed by the general consensus of opinion. Argos' medism before Salamis was in any case unlikely to recommend her to a patriotic Athenian at any time in the 470's.[4] Boeckh held that the sympathy shown towards Argos in the *Supplices* was to be referred to the period in which Athens and Argos made an alliance towards the end of the 460's, the same alliance that was clearly referred to in the *Eumenides*.[5] The latter play makes it clear that Aeschylus was in favour of the alliance. Is there then any real objection to Boeckh's view?

[1] Cf. W. J. W. Koster, *Welke is de oudste bewaard gebleven Tragedie?* (*Med. ned. Akad.* N.R. 29 (1966)) 28 f.

[2] Cf. Costa 31 f.

[3] Cf. Focke 183 f.; Jacoby IIIb Suppl. ii. 27; Diamantopoulos 220.

[4] Hdt. vii. 148 ff. Cf. Cavaignac 105; Focke 183; Diamantopoulos 220; Koster 29. For Argos' medism see esp. Busolt II (2nd ed. Gotha 1895) 657 f.; J. A. R. Munro, *J.H.S.* 22 (1902) 300 ff., and *C.A.H.* IV. 278 ff.; Meyer 334, 343, 347, 576; A. R. Burn, *Persia and the Greeks* (London 1962) 349 f. Thucydides (i. 92 and 95.7) emphasizes the friendly relations that existed between Athens and Sparta in the early 470's. Cf. K. J. Beloch, *Gr. Geschichte* II. 2 (2nd ed. Strassburg 1916) 153 f. and 186 f.

[5] Th. i. 102. 4. The same view was held by C. O. Müller, *Dissertations on the Eumenides of Aeschylus* (Eng. tr. Cambridge 1835) 116 ff.; F. Bücheler, *Rh. Mus.* 40 (1885) 629; O.Könnecke, *Woch. f. Klass. Philol.* (1916) 387; Forrest 240; Podlecki 61 f., 126, 167 n. 39: cf. also Costa 31 ff. It was rejected by Welcker, *Kl. Schr.* IV. 126; Th. Bergk, *Gr. Literaturgeschichte* III (Berlin 1884) 306 f.; Tucker xxi; A. E. Haigh, *Tragic drama of the Greeks* (Oxford 1896) 101 n. 2; G. Müller 5 ff.; Cavaignac 103; K. Kunst, *Die Frauengestalten im attischen Drama* (Vienna and Leipzig 1922) 2 n. 1; J. Vürtheim, *Aischylos' Schutzflehende* (Amsterdam 1928) 90 f.; Diamantopoulos 226 f.

The dating of the events of the 460's is a notoriously difficult problem, involving as it does the question of the duration of the third Messenian war, Sparta's conflict with Arcadia, Argos' subjugation of Mycenae and Tiryns, the revolt of Thasos from Athens, and the career of Cimon which led up to his ostracism in 461. But it seems reasonably certain that Cimon's expedition to assist Sparta against the Helots in Ithome took place in 462,[1] and that it was in consequence of his dismissal by the Spartans that the breach between Athens and Sparta occurred and the alliance was made with Argos and Thessaly. As Thucydides expressly says (i. 102. 3): καὶ διαφορὰ ἐκ ταύτης τῆς στρατείας πρῶτον Λακεδαιμονίοις καὶ Ἀθηναίοις φανερὰ ἐγένετο.[2] If then the *Supplices* was produced at the City Dionysia of 463 it was before the breach took place. There is however ample evidence that not all the Athenians were in favour of Cimon's pro-Spartan policy.[3] His expedition was opposed by Ephialtes (Plut. *Cim.* 16), his Thasian campaign had been attacked at the εὔθυναι of 464/3 (Plut. *Cim.* 14; Ἀθ. πολ. 27). The beginning of the recovery of the anti-Spartan democrats may well be dated to the disaster of Drabeskos in 465 or 464.[4] Thasos in revolt from Athens had appealed to Sparta to help her by invading Attica, and Sparta, having promised secretly to do so, was prevented only by the earthquake of 464 and the outbreak

[1] The Atthis apparently put the expedition in 468/7 (cf. Σ Ar. *Lys.* 1141 and 1144), Diodorus in 469/8 (xi. 63–4); cf. Gomme 403 ff.; D. M. Lewis, *Historia* 2 (1953–4) 414; Plut. *Cim.* 17 seems to envisage two expeditions, and this is accepted by G. A. Papantoniou, *A.J.Ph.* 72 (1951) 176 ff.; N. G. L. Hammond, *Historia* 4 (1955) 378 and 404 (autumn 464 and autumn 462) (cf. further *Historia* 8 (1959) 400); R. Sealey, *Historia* 6 (1957) 370 (468/7 and 462). But see Wilamowitz 291 n. 3; Busolt III. 1. 260 n. 3; J. Wells, *Studies in Herodotus* (Oxford 1923) 144; A. Weizsäcker, *Untersuchungen über Plutarchs biographische Technik* (Berlin 1931) 63 f.; Meyer 535 n. 4; Gomme 411 n. 1. See further n. 1 p. 146 below.

[2] Cf. also i. 103. 3: κατ' ἔχθος ἤδη τὸ Λακεδαιμονίων ('in accord with their new hostility to Sparta'—Gomme); Meritt, Wade-Gery, and McGregor, *ATL* III (Princeton 1950) 164; C. A. van Rooy, *Historia* 3 (1954–5) 410 f. Cf. Diod. xi. 64. 3.

[3] For the democratic opposition cf. C. O. Müller 119; Busolt III. 1. 256 f., 260, 294 f.; Beloch II. 2. 198; Wells 141 n. 2; Meyer 535; Jacoby, *J.H.S.* 64 (1944) 51; Gomme 300; Hammond 377; Forrest 240.

[4] Cf. Forrest, *loc. cit.*; Wells 139; Beloch II. 1 (2nd ed. Strassburg 1914) 151. For the dating of Drabeskos cf. Wilamowitz 291; Busolt III. 1. n. 5 on 201 f.; Beloch II. 2. 194 f.; Meyer 502 n. 1; Gomme 390 f.; G. Klaffenbach, *Historia* 1 (1950) 231 f.; *ATL* III. 176; J. Scharf, *Historia* 3 (1954–5) 158.

of the Helot revolt.[1] Sparta's promise was a secret one[2] but at least it indicates that hostility between Athens and Sparta was already being prepared.[3] There is therefore every reason to believe that by 463 there was in Athens considerable democratic opposition to Cimon's conservative policy of friendship towards Sparta, and Forrest may be right in suggesting that an alliance with Argos was already being put forward as an alternative policy. Whether or not Aeschylus belonged to the party of Ephialtes and the democrats it is impossible to say.[4] It is enough for our purpose that the *Eumenides* makes it certain that he favoured the democratic foreign policy of friendship with Argos.

When the *Supplices* fits so easily into the political situation of the 460's it is strange that the attempt has recently been made to put it back in the 490's.[5] Diamantopoulos indeed tries to show not only that it fits but that it was immediately inspired by the political situation of that early period, that the Danaid trilogy 'furnishes a slogan' which 'could be used (by Themistocles'

[1] For the dating of the Atthis and Diodorus see n. 1 p. 145 above. For the whole problem of the dating of the third Messenian War see esp. Wilamowitz 295 f.; Busolt III. 1. n. 5 on 200 ff. and n. 2 on 298 ff.; Beloch II. 2. 194 ff.; T. Lenschau in *Bursian's Jahresbericht* 180 (1919) 143 f.; Kolbe 241 ff.; Meyer 237, 502 n. 2, 556 n. 1; *ATL* III. 162 ff.; Gomme 401 ff.; Klaffenbach 231 ff.; D. W. Reece, *J.H.S.* 70 (1950) 76; S. Accame, *Riv. di Fil. e di Istr. Class.* n.s. 30 (1952) 114 f.; Lewis 412 ff.; Scharf 153 ff.; van Rooy 407 ff.; Hammond 371 ff.; Sealey 368 ff.

[2] For scepticism about the Spartan promise cf. Beloch II. 1. 149 n. 2; Walker, *C.A.H.* V. 72; Sealey 369 f.

[3] Cf. Beloch II. 1. 152 and 164; Meyer 501, 526, 534. G. Dickins, *J.H.S.* 32 (1912) 34 ff. (cf. also *C.Q.* 5 (1911) 238 ff. and *J.H.S.* 33 (1913) 111 f.), argued that from the accession of a philo-Athenian Archidamus in 468 an anti-Athenian party in Sparta, led by the ephors, was already preparing for war. His view of a conflict between kings and ephors was rejected by G. B. Grundy, *J.H.S.* 32 (1912) 261 ff.

[4] The old view of Aeschylus as a political reactionary has yielded to the view that he was a moderate or even a wholehearted democrat (but see still Méautis, *Prométhée* 59 ff.). Cf. for example Livingstone and Smertenko *op. cit.*; Jacoby IIIb Suppl. ii. 27 and 528; Stoessl 138 f.; Dodds, *C.Q.* 3. 19 f., and *Proc. Camb. Philol. Soc.* 6, esp. 21 ff.; Dover *op. cit.*; Costa *op. cit.*; Podlecki 80 ff.: also W. Kranz, *Stasimon* (Berlin 1933) 172 f. Dover rightly points out that A.'s praise of the mean at *Eum.* 526 ff. does not necessarily prove that he did not unreservedly accept the democratic revolution: cf. also Podlecki 94 ff.

[5] Diamantopoulos 220 ff. He argues that production was postponed until the 460's, as a result of a change in the political situation in Athens in 492. Cf. also J. Lindsay, *The Clashing Rocks* (London 1965) 91.

group) to frustrate the adhesion of Athens to the Spartan league'. One may accept that Aeschylus in the 490's sympathized with the aims of Themistocles, as he seems to have done at the time when he wrote the *Persae*, and as he sympathized with the democratic foreign policy when he composed the *Oresteia*. But very strong evidence will be required to prove that the Danaid trilogy is merely or even primarily a political slogan.[1] Diamantopoulos finds in the *Supplices* various topics which seem to him to suit the early date—the seniority of Argos over Sparta in the Peloponnese, the consequences of the battle of Sepeia, pre-Dorian Argos, the democratic Argive constitution, the supplication theme, and Athenian friendship for Argos. Little need be added to Forrest's demonstration that most of these topics were more relevant or as relevant in 463. The strongest argument against Diamantopoulos' theory is that, as he himself admits (226), there is no evidence at all for an Athenian/Argive *rapprochement* at the end of the 490's. And such a *rapprochement* is very improbable in itself. It is true that little is known about the state of political parties in Athens in the first decade of the century.[2] The somewhat niggardly force of twenty ships sent by the Athenians to help the Ionians when they revolted from Persia, and the sudden recall of even that small fleet, suggest an equal division of opinion in Athens, while the election of Hipparchus to the archonship of 496/5 shows perhaps that the faction of the tyrants still had a formidable following in the city.[3] On the other hand the interference of Cleomenes in

[1] The *Persae* is not a political slogan. Cf. p. 142 above.

[2] On the whole subject see, for example, Busolt II. 565 ff.; Beloch II. 1. 13 and II. 2. 130 ff.; Munro, *J.H.S.* 19 (1899) 190 ff., and *C.A.H.* IV. 230 ff.; Walker, *ibid.* 138 f., and 167 ff.; How and Wells, *A commentary on Herodotus V–IX* (2nd ed. Oxford 1928) 359 f.; H. Berve, *Hermes* Einzelschr. 2 (1937) 66 ff.; Meyer 284, 291 ff.; C. A. Robinson, *A.J.Ph.* 60 (1939) 232 ff.; M. F. McGregor, *Harv. Stud.* Suppl. vol. 1 (1940) 71 ff.; Gomme, *A.J.Ph.* 65 (1944) 321 ff.; H. T. Wade-Gery, *Essays in Greek history* (Oxford 1958) 177 f. (=*BSA* 37 (1936–7) 269); Diamantopoulos 227 ff.; Forrest 234 f.; Burn 201, 223 ff., 238 f., 260 ff. The Alcmaeonidae had the most to fear from Spartan intervention in Athenian affairs.

[3] McGregor however argues (80 ff.) that for this period twenty ships were by no means a negligible force. He contends also that there was no significant pro-tyrant party at Athens after the expulsion of Hippias. Cf. also Gomme, for whom differences of opinion may have been a matter of individuals rather than of parties.

Athenian affairs in the last decade of the sixth century had doubtless not yet been forgotten, so that there is no great difficulty in accepting that in 493 a play could be written with a tone that was hostile to Sparta. But it is very difficult to believe with Diamantopoulos that in that year Themistocles, the archon for 493/2, could himself have commissioned such a play with the express purpose of acquiring in Argos an ally for Athens in the Peloponnese. If Themistocles and the democrats were serious in a policy of non-appeasement of Persia they must have recognized that the only practicable Peloponnesian ally was Sparta herself. The military power of Argos had been crippled in the battle of Sepeia in 494,[1] and it can hardly have seemed likely that the Persian menace would wait until a new generation of Argives had grown up. In 491 it was to Sparta that Athens turned when she wished to punish and forestall the medism of Aegina (Hdt. vi. 49), it was to Sparta that she sent when the Persians arrived in Greece.[2] It would be hard to find a time less

[1] Hdt. vi. 76–81, Paus. ii. 20. 8–10 and iii. 4. 1, Plut. *mor.* 245d ff. That this is at least the approximate date of Sepeia is now generally accepted. Cf. for example R. W. Macan, *Herodotus IV–VI* (London 1895) II. 85 f., 96 f., and note on Hdt. vi. 76; Busolt II. 561 n. 1; Beloch II. 1. 14 n. 1; J. B. Bury, *Beitr. zur alten Gesch.* (*Klio*) 2 (1902) 14 ff.; G. Müller 66; How and Wells 352; Walker 164 f.; J. L. Myres, *Herodotus father of history* (Oxford 1953) 187; Parke–Wormell, *The Delphic oracle* (Oxford 1956) I. 158; Forrest 221 f. Pausanias (iii. 4) puts it near the beginning of Cleomenes' reign, and this was accepted by Wells, *J.H.S.* 25 (1905) 193 ff., and *Studies* 74 ff. Herodotus (vii. 148. 2) says 6,000 Argives fell at Sepeia, Pausanias (iii. 4. 1) about 5,000. As a result of the battle Tiryns and Mycenae were able to assert their independence. For the decisive nature of the defeat and its consequences cf. esp. G. Gilbert, *Handbuch der gr. Staatsalterthümer* II (Leipzig 1885) 75 f.; Grundy, *J.H.S.* 28 (1908) 91 f.; Beloch II. 1. 14; Walker 166 and 262; Meyer 300 ff.; R. F. Willetts, *Hermes* 87 (1959) 495 f. Cf. also pp. 151 f. below.

[2] Cf. Walker 166 and 259 f. ('We may be certain that but for the victory of Sepeia the appeal would never have been made'). For the *rapprochement* of Athens and Sparta before Marathon cf. esp. Cavaignac 102; also Macan 97 ff.; Busolt II. 571 f.; Munro, *J.H.S.* 19. 191, and *C.A.H.* IV. 231; How and Wells 352 f.; Grundy, *J.H.S.* 32. 268; Berve 68 ff.; Meyer 303; Myres 176 and 187 f.; Burn 226 f. The change of feeling at Sparta, which is shown by Leotychidas' demand at Athens that the Aeginetan hostages be returned (Hdt. vi. 85–6) is later than Marathon. For the dating of the resulting war between Athens and Aegina cf. U. Köhler, *Rh. Mus.* 46 (1891) 6 ff.; Wilamowitz 89 f. (cf. 284); Macan 112 ff.; Busolt II. 575 and 644 n. 3; Beloch II. i. 25 n. 3 and II. 2. 57 and 141; How and Wells on vi. 93; Walker 254 ff.; A. Andrewes, *BSA* 37 (1936–7) 4; Meyer 331 n. 1; Burn 267 ff. Of recent writers only Hammond 408 ff. accepts Herodotus' dating before Marathon.

suitable for the production of a play advocating an alliance with Argos.[1]

Diamantopoulos, believing that the main theme of the tetralogy is that of forced marriage, finds the examples of Hypermestra and Amymone particularly appropriate at a time when the Argive state had been newly bereaved of 6,000 men. Indeed we are told by Plutarch that Argive women were given in marriage to the best of the newly enfranchized περίοικοι.[2] In the absence however of the other members of the tetralogy it is dangerous to base any conclusions on hypothetical views of its theme.[3] It is in the Chorus's prayer of blessings on behalf of Argos at 625 ff. that Aeschylus is supposed to show us most clearly the consequences of Sepeia. In this prayer 'Eschyle développe donc uniquement le premier élément de la formule, la dépopulation (659–690), et réduit les deux autres (prayers for crops and herds) à deux phrases brèves (690–692)'.[4] If there is any significance in this supposed lack of symmetry it would be as easy to argue that it rules out the years that followed the depopulation of Argos after Sepeia. For it does not seem probable that only a year after Argos suffered the horrors of war Aeschylus should have put into the mouth of a chorus a prayer that she should never suffer such horrors. At the very least one would be justified in criticizing him on the grounds of bad taste. What

[1] Meyer (299) includes Argos among the Greek states which in 492 might be expected to welcome the approach of the Persians. 1,000 Argive volunteers took part on the Aeginetan side in the Nicodromus episode of the war with Athens (Hdt. vi. 92). Andrewes assigns this episode to a war fought *c.* 493, and suggests that the volunteers were Argive aristocrats, escaping from the slave domination in Argos (cf. p. 151 below); cf. also Burn 274 and 275 n. 43. Even however if he is right, we cannot use the Argive assistance as evidence for hostility between Athens and the Argive state (cf. Focke 183; Quincey 198), since Argos officially refused the Aeginetan appeal for help. The incident would show only that Aegina thought it reasonable to make the request. But the episode probably belongs to the war which broke out after Marathon (cf. n. 2 p. 148 above).

[2] Plut. *mor.* 245 f. Cf. p. 152 below.

[3] Cf. chap. v pp. 211 f. for the different views that have been held about the main theme of the tetralogy.

[4] P. Mazon, *Eschyle* (6th ed. Budé Paris 1953) I. 36 f.; cf. also 3, and *Hésiode* (Budé 5th ed. Paris 1960) 95 n. 1; Tucker xxii; M. Croiset, *Eschyle* (Paris 1928) 44; B. Lavagnini, *Riv. di Fil. e di Istr. Class.* n.s. 10 (1932) 370; Diamantopoulos 222 f. Bergk (III. 308 f.) also found political significance in the prayer for Argos, but he put the play after the Persian wars. For A. Lesky too (*J.H.S.* 86 (1966) 79) A. was interested in it 'mainly for political reasons'.

too is the contemporary relevance of the allusions to music (694 ff.) and to international agreements (701–3)? If the prayer in the *Supplices* dwells at length on the health, safety, and fertility of the human population the reason is more likely to be that this theme becomes important in the second play of the trilogy. The emphasis is purely dramatic. But there is no reason to believe that it is anything other than a conventional prayer, fully explicable in its immediate dramatic context, as conventional as or more conventional than that of the Furies at *Eumenides* 916 ff.[1] Diamantopoulos seems to be denying the very possibility of interpreting a play in the light of such dramatic considerations, or in terms of the basic requirements of the myth, when he argues that the *Supplices* cannot have been written in the same period as the *Agamemnon*; for, he says, in the former we are shown a city under threat of war, afraid of reprisals coming from the sea, while in the *Agamemnon* we see a city itself undertaking a war of reprisals and 'the sea is celebrated as the source of wealth' (quoting *Ag.* 958!). 'The spirit of the Danaid trilogy,' he says, 'unlike that of the *Oresteia*, is anything but encouraging to an expansive and commercial foreign policy.'[2] If we could be sure that Aeschylus is writing a political tract and not a play the argument might have some weight.

The position of Pelasgus as a constitutional monarch has for long been of interest to those who look in the *Supplices* for contemporary allusions. It is clearly emphasized in the play that the king cannot by himself accept or reject the Danaids' plea for asylum. Only the sovereign people can decide (cf. 365 ff.,

[1] 'In *Supplices* the order and relative importance of the prayers are dictated by the dramatic context; hence the aversion of war, μάχλος Ἄρης, takes first place (633–9; cf. 663–6), while the aversion of stasis receives the briefest mention (661–2). In *Eumenides* the words of both Athena and the Chorus are determined not by the dramatic context but by the political circumstances of 458 B.C.; hence war is welcomed (θυραῖος ἔστω πόλεμος, 864–5), Ares is linked with Zeus as honouring φρούριον θεῶν, the champion of the Greek gods against the barbarian (918–20), but stasis and faction are the danger most to be feared (858–66 and especially 976–87)' (Dover 235). G. Müller, despite his advocacy of an early date for the Danaid trilogy, rejected the argument from the supposed external allusions in the Danaids' prayer (67 ff.). He gives a useful list of formulas of blessing in other writers. Cf. also Focke 184; Koster 28.

[2] Cf. also G. Müller 5 f.

397 ff., 517 f., 601, 605 ff., 739, 942 ff., 963 ff.). It is generally agreed that this situation is anachronistic, and many believe that the emphasis laid on it by Aeschylus must reflect in some way the political situation in Argos at the time of the play's composition.[1] In short it is argued that Argos at that time must have been a democracy. Diamantopoulos goes further. Not content with accepting that the *Supplices* fits such a political situation he goes on to argue that it was directly inspired by that situation; that Aeschylus wrote his tetralogy by arrangement with the new democratic rulers of Argos after the battle of Sepeia, when, as he believes, they were trying to remould the legends and traditions of their city in the light of their democratic standards.[2] The tetralogy, he suggests, was meant to be produced in Argos as well as in Athens. It is not clear how this view is to be reconciled with the opinion that the tetralogy was composed in agreement with Themistocles. Nor is any evidence produced that the Attic tragedians ever wrote plays for production in other cities of the Greek mainland.[3] More important is the question of democracy in general in Argos. If it could be proved that Argos had a democratic constitution for only a short time after Sepeia, and not again during Aeschylus' life, the argument would have to be considered seriously. But the situation is by no means as clear as that. It is not even clear what constitutional changes were made at Argos after the battle of Sepeia. Herodotus' account (vi. 83. 1) runs as follows: Ἄργος δὲ ἀνδρῶν ἐχηρώθη οὕτω ὥστε οἱ δοῦλοι αὐτῶν ἔσχον πάντα τὰ πρήγματα ἄρχοντές τε καὶ διέποντες, ἐς ὃ ἐπήβησαν οἱ τῶν ἀπολομένων παῖδες. ἔπειτέ σφεας οὗτοι ἀνακτώμενοι ὀπίσω ἐς ἑωυτοὺς τὸ Ἄργος ἐξέβαλον. ἐξωθεύμενοι δὲ οἱ δοῦλοι μάχῃ ἔσχον Τίρυνθα. It is disputed whether δοῦλοι are to be taken as

[1] Cf. Bergk 307 ff.; Beloch II. 1. 139 n. 1; A. Körte, in *Mélanges Nicole* (Geneva 1905) 295 f.; Meyer 302 n. 1; Wilamowitz, *Aischylos. Interpretationen* (Berlin 1914) 11.

[2] Cf. also Lindsay 91 ff.

[3] The production of the *Persae* and Αἰτναῖαι in Sicily, and Euripides' productions in Macedonia are another matter. Professor D. L. Page points out to me that the Scholiast at E. *Andr.* 445 says that play was not produced at Athens, and it may therefore have been written for production elsewhere. Bergk (307 ff.) also argued that the *Supp.* was composed for performance in Argos.

slaves or serfs in the literal or in a metaphorical sense, or whether Plutarch is more correct in explaining the reform as the partial enfranchisement of the περίοικοι.[1] Still there is no reason to deny that whatever the precise nature of the constitutional change involved it was in the direction of democratic government. It is not so easy to judge how long this period of democratic government lasted. Herodotus says it was until the sons of those killed in the battle grew up. Busolt held that this must have been by 487, since only a Dorian Argos could demand punishment from Aegina and Sicyon for their assistance to Cleomenes (Hdt. vi. 92).[2] Others argue that the expulsion of the δοῦλοι from Argos cannot have taken place before 478, since troops from Tiryns and Mycenae fought at Plataea, and the contingent from Tiryns can hardly have consisted of the expelled slaves.[3] Forrest connects the expulsion with the driving out of Themistocles from Argos, which he places in 469 or 468.[4] He argues further that the aristocratic interlude was short and that the Epigoni may have been ejected and the democrats restored to power as early as the winter of 464.[5] Where so much is uncertain it would be hazardous indeed to assert that a play in which Argos appears with a democratic constitution can have been written only in the years immediately after Sepeia.

It is in any case an unproven hypothesis that the situation in

[1] *Mor.* 245 f. Aristotle too refers to the enfranchisement of the perioikoi at *Pol.* v. 1303a 6–8. W. L. Newman, *The politics of Aristotle* IV (Oxford 1902) 304, equates these with Herodotus' δοῦλοι, on the grounds that the word is always used of serfs by Aristotle: Forrest (222 ff.) discusses fully the various possible interpretations of the Herodotus passage. Cf. also Gilbert II. 74 f.; Macan on Hdt. vi. 83; Busolt II. 564 and III. I. 113 f.; Beloch II. I. 14 n. 3 and 139; G. Müller 8 f.; How and Wells 97; P. A. Seymour, *J.H.S.* 42 (1922) 24 ff.; Wells, *Studies* 29; Meyer 302 n. 2; Willetts 495 ff.; Burn 231.

[2] II. n. 2 on 565 (cf. III. I. 114). In 481 Spartan envoys in Argos deal with the βουλή, and there is no mention of the δῆμος (Hdt. vii. 148–9); cf. Gilbert 76 f.; G. Müller 7 ff.; Vürtheim 78. But that is no proof that Argos had ceased to be a democracy: cf. Forrest 225 f.; also Seymour 25; Meyer 302; Willetts 500.

[3] Seymour, *loc. cit.*; Willetts 499 f.

[4] For Forrest the collapse of democracy at Argos is responsible for Themistocles' flight. Podlecki on the other hand argues (58 ff.) that the flight was a cause of the collapse.

[5] For Argive democracy in the Peloponnesian War cf. Thuc. v. 27–9, 31. 6, 41, 44, 81–2; cf. also Arist. *Pol.* 1302b 18; Σ Ar. *Knights* 855. See in general Gilbert 77 ff.; Busolt III. I. 114; Beloch II. I. 139 n. I.

the *Supplices* does reflect the contemporary situation in Argos.[1] It is pointed out that the position of Pelasgus is not very different from that of the Homeric king.[2] Pausanias tells us that the Argives had long been proud of their democratic traditions, and that it was their democratic spirit that had caused the collapse of the Temenid dynasty.[3] It is not only Aeschylus who involved the Argive demos in the story of the Danaids. It seems to have been connected with it independently in the tradition.[4] Moreover it is possible that Aeschylus makes Pelasgus a constitutional monarch partly at least because he is writing for an audience with democratic sympathies at a time when democratic reform was in the air at Athens.[5] But the main reason is probably dramatic: the emphasis becomes dramatically important in the following plays. If the view is correct that Pelasgus is killed in battle during the period between the *Supplices* and the Αἰγύπτιοι the constitutional position of the δῆμος may well be crucial in the latter play.[6] Certainly the fate of Argos is an important

[1] Cf. G. Müller 7 ff.; Vürtheim 78. H. Lloyd-Jones, *L'Ant. Class.* 33 (1964) 357 ff., remains cautious.

[2] Lloyd-Jones 358 f. (also *C.Q.* n.s. 9 (1959) 94). A king appears in Argos as late as 480 (Hdt. vii. 149), but he seems, from an inscription of *c.* 450 B.C., to have been no more than an annual magistrate (Tod, *Greek historical inscriptions* I (2nd ed. Oxford 1946) 33 line 43 (cf. p. 62)). Meyer and Körte thought his position equivalent to that of Pelasgus, but clearly the latter is more than an annual magistrate; cf. G. Müller 11; also M. Pohlenz, *Gr. Tragödie* (2nd ed. Göttingen 1954) 46 f.

[3] Paus. ii. 19. 2. For the treatment of this theme by Ephorus cf. A. Andrewes, *C.Q.* n.s. I (1951) 39 ff.

[4] E. *Or.* 872 f. and Σ; Paus. ii. 19. 3. Cf. G. Müller 10 f.

[5] Cf. Dover 234. Dover remarks that 'Euripidean tragedy freely attributed contemporary democratic principles to the Athens of the heroic age': cf. Paus. i. 3. 3. G. Müller suggested (12 f.) that A.'s picture of Pelasgus was drawn from Athenian ideas of Theseus as the good king. Costa (33) compares him with Theseus in E. *Supp.* For Stoessl (122 f.) 'Pelasgus seems to be the poetic incarnation of the ideal of the democratic ruler of the state'. V. Ehrenberg, *Historia* I (1950) 517 ff. (cf. also *Sophocles and Pericles* 3 n. 3), argued that 'the picture of democracy is strongly influenced by the democracy of contemporary Athens'. By 'contemporary' he meant the 490's, but the influence would be much more natural in the 460's: cf. Costa 33; Podlecki 57 and 62.

[6] See chap. v pp. 197 ff. If the theory of Winnington-Ingram were correct (see chap. v p. 211) it would become even more important in the Δαναΐδες, when the demos repudiates the action of its king (Danaus). In the *Supp.* Pelasgus and the people are one. Ed. Meyer had earlier supposed (*Forschungen zur alten Geschichte* (Halle 1892) 84) that the position of the demos in the *Supp.* prepares for the trial of Hypermestra before the people at the end of the trilogy: cf. also Diamantopoulos 225 f.

theme in the trilogy.[1] Podlecki indeed finds (52) that 'the poet's desire to reserve for the Argive *demos* the glory of making the final decision and so breaking the deadlock seriously debilitates Pelasgus as a tragic agent'. For Lesky (79) on the other hand the decision is made with the words of Pelasgus (478 f.), with the result that 'the theme of a final decision by the people of Argos has lost much of its weight'. The truth seems to be that Aeschylus is concerned to show us that the decision is a joint one, that both Argos and its king are responsible for granting asylum to the Danaids. Or rather Pelasgus is the representative of Argos. His dilemma is really the dilemma of the city itself. If, as Diamantopoulos objects, Argos in the *Oresteia* is not a democracy, the reason is that such a situation was ruled out by the dramatic theme.[2]

A connection has sometimes been sought between a contemporary situation and the basic subject of the *Supplices*, the Danaids' appeal for asylum at Argos. In 499 B.C. Aristagoras came to Greece soliciting help for the Ionian revolt, and, having been rebuffed at Sparta, he came to Athens, where he pleaded the ties of kinship between Athens and Ionia.[3] Some have seen an echo of this in the *Supplices* where the Danaids base their appeal on similar grounds of kinship (274 ff.).[4] But it could hardly be maintained that there is any close equivalence

[1] See chap. v pp. 181 and 198.

[2] Dodds however (*Proc. Camb. Philol. Soc.* 6. 19 f.) draws attention to the not infrequent appearance in *Ag.* and *Choe.* of terms drawn from contemporary politics. As he remarks, 'references to the δῆμος (of Argos) are more frequent than we expect in a Mycenaean monarchy' (*Ag.* 456 f., 640, 938, 1409, 1616). On the δήμου προβούλοις at *Sept.* 1006 cf. Lloyd-Jones, *C.Q.* 9. 94 f.; also C. Robert, *Oidipus* (Berlin 1915) 376 f.; Ehrenberg, *Soph. and Pericles* 101 and 114 n. 1; R. D. Dawe, *C.Q.* n.s. 17 (1967) 21 f.

[3] Hdt. v. 49 ff. and 97.

[4] G. Müller 66 f.; Focke 185; *GGL* I. 2. 194 n. 2 (but with reservations); Pohlenz (1st ed. 1930) 39, *Erläuterungen* 11: *contra* Vürtheim 77 f. Diamantopoulos too favours the idea. But if J. B. Bury's suggestion (*Beitr. zur alten Gesch.* 2. 17 f.) is right that Aristagoras was rebuffed also at Argos in 499 (cf. also M. Cary, *C.A.H.* IV. 220; Myres 197; Burn 227 f.), such a reminder in 493/2 would turn the trilogy into a deliberate insult to Argos, the very opposite of Diamantopoulos' main thesis. M. Croiset, *Eschyle* (Paris 1928) 51, supposed that A. had in mind the supplication of the Plataeans at Athens in 510 B.C. (Hdt. vi. 108). Andrewes, *C.Q.* n.s. 1 (1951) 44 n. 2, very tentatively suggests a possible allusion in the situation of Pelasgus to the downfall of Meltas, the grandson of Pheidon of Argos (Diod. vii. 13. 2).

between the Danaids seeking protection from their unwelcome suitors at Argos, and Aristagoras at Athens seeking help in a revolt against Persia. If any such parallel is to be found at all between a contemporary situation and that of the trilogy, more probable is the view that Aeschylus had in mind the reception at Argos of the ostracized Themistocles.[1] This would mean that the *Supplices* looked back to an event of a few years earlier, just as the *Eumenides* was composed some years after the Areopagus reforms, and the *Persae* after the battle of Salamis. But here again the parallel is not immediately obvious between the situation of Themistocles and that of fifty foreign-looking girls running away from a forced marriage with their cousins.[2] Moreover the reception of the Danaids at Argos almost certainly involved that city in war and in defeat. Themistocles fled before there could be any war.[3] Would it really be a compliment to Argos to recall that she had failed to go to the same lengths as her mythical ancestors in the protection of a suppliant? It is not easy to see why the suppliant theme must have a parallel in fifth-century politics at all. No one is likely to argue that the subject of the *Septem* must have been suggested to Aeschylus by a real duel in which two brothers had recently killed each other. Since there is no means of telling why he selected the

[1] The suggestion was first made by Cavaignac, who dated the trilogy in consequence to 470 (cf. further *Nouvelle Clio* 7–9 (1955–7) 123 ff.). His theory has found favour with Forrest ('In the *Supplices* he writes of refugees in Argos at a time when the most important political figure of Athens had himself been a refugee in Argos' (236); and 'In 470 Argos had been faced with just this dilemma and had answered it, as she does in the play, by accepting the suppliant and by risking war...' (239)), and with Podlecki 52 ff. Cf. also I. Trencsényi-Waldapfel, *Acta Ant. Hung.* 12 (1964) 270 ff., who finds further parallels between Themistocles and the Danaid myth in T.'s connection with the water-supply of Athens (Plut. *Them.* 31) and with the cult of Artemis (Plut. *Them.* 22), and in his policy of building ships (cf. Danaus as the inventor of the pentekonter). Stoessl argued (121 ff.) that in the *Supp.* A. 'supported the policy of Themistocles' alliance with Argos against Sparta', but he dated this to about 476.

[2] Forrest indeed acknowledges that Danaus and his daughters 'do not, in any real sense, represent Themistokles' (239 n. 7): cf. also Podlecki 56.

[3] The chronology of Themistocles' ostracism, expulsion, and flight is far from clear. Diodorus (xi. 54–9) narrates the whole under the year 471/0. See, for example, Wilamowitz, *Aristoteles und Athen* I. 138 ff.; Busolt III. I. 112 n. 2 and 130 n. 4; Beloch II. 2. 188 and 192 f.; Lenschau 143; Cavaignac 103 f.; Cary, *C.R.* 36. 161 f.; U. Kahrstedt, *R.-E.* V. A. 2. 1693 ff.; Meyer 486 n. 2; Gomme I. 397 ff.; Forrest, esp. 221 n. 2 and 226 f.

Danaid myth as a fitting subject for a tetralogy, speculation is fruitless.

The only other possible reference to contemporary politics in the *Supplices* concerns the relations of Athens with Egypt. Some have thought that the important part played by Egypt in the play reflects the Athenian interest in that country which must have been awakened by the Egyptian revolt from Persia and the help sent by Athens to the Egyptians.[1] Others replied that the Egyptians are presented in the play in a highly unfavourable light, citing lines 741 f., 760 f., 953, and the general behaviour of the Egyptian herald.[2] All that this means however is that the play can hardly be as late as 462, the earliest possible year for the Athenian expedition.[3] It is no argument against a production in 463. The part played by the large Egyptian contingent in Xerxes' fleet in 480 is quite enough to explain Athenian hostility to Egypt in the succeeding years.[4] It is in any case by no means certain that Aeschylus is thinking of the Egyptian nation in these uncomplimentary references. Αἰγύπτου γένος (741) clearly means the family of Aegyptus, not the Egyptian people.[5] Nor can we be sure that the sons of Aegyptus were not presented in a different light in the second play of the trilogy.[6]

Occasional attempts have been made to find other internal evidence for the dating of the play. F. Bücheler once adduced

[1] C. O. Müller 119; F. Bücheler, *Rh. Mus.* 40 (1885) 629 (arguing for the date 460 or 459); Könnecke, *Woch. f. Klass. Philol.* (1916) 387 (as close as possible to 458): cf. now R. D. Murray, *The motif of Io in Aeschylus' Suppliants* (Princeton 1958) 90; Trencsényi-Waldapfel 273 f.

[2] Tucker xxi; G. Müller 15 f.; P. Roussel, *Rev. de Philol.* 44 (1920) 241 ff.; Cavaignac 103; Vürtheim 91. Tucker saw a parallel with the situation of 492 or 491 when Attica was threatened by the Persian attack, the Egyptians of the play representing orientals in general: cf. also Haigh 101 n. 2. For Méautis (*Prométhée* 60) Aeschylus could not have approved of Athens' Egyptian expedition; cf. also Trencsényi-Waldapfel.

[3] But this is probably too early. For the chronology cf. Wilamowitz, *Arist. u. Athen* II. 297; Busolt III. 1. 304 n. 1; Beloch II. 1. 151 f. and 166, II. 2. 200 ff.; Lenschau 144 f.; Meyer 552; Gomme 410 and 306 f.; J. Barns, *Historia* 2 (1953–4) 163 ff., esp. 174; Scharf 308 ff.

[4] Cf. Roussel, *loc. cit.*, quoting *Pers.* 33 ff., Hdt. vii. 89, viii. 17, ix. 32. R. dated the trilogy to 478–3; cf. also Tucker xxi f. For the Egyptian contingent in Xerxes' fleet see esp. W. W. Tarn, *J.H.S.* 28 (1908) esp. 221; also Munro, *J.H.S.* 22 (1902) 329 f.; Myres 267 ff.; Burn 453 (cf. 10). See Diod. xi. 17. 2.

[5] See chap. v p. 231 n. 3.

[6] See chap. v p. 196.

lines 145–7 (ἁγνά μ' ἐπιδέτω Διὸς κόρα, ἔχουσα σέμν' ἐνώπι' ἀσφαλές) in support of the year 460 or 459.[1] He argued that the goddess referred to was Athena, and that the σέμν' ἐνώπια was an allusion to the still uncompleted Parthenon, visible to the audience in the Theatre of Dionysus below. With the discovery that the building of the Parthenon was not begun till some years after Aeschylus' death, this argument collapsed. But others followed Bücheler in the belief that Aeschylus must be referring to some building that the audience could see. Dörpfeld and Loeschcke maintained that it was the south wall of the Acropolis, rebuilt by Cimon after the victory of Eurymedon, and until the time of Pericles the only imposing part of the Acropolis visible to the audience in the theatre.[2] Körte held that it was the pre-Persian Propylaea, built between Marathon and Salamis.[3] G. Müller accepted Körte's argument about the Propylaea, but showed that the goddess referred to is almost certainly not Athena but Artemis.[4] Aeschylus, he supposed, was thinking of Artemis-Hecate Propylaea (cf. Paus. i. 38. 6; i. 23. 7). Vürtheim however demonstrated that the word ἐνώπια could not possibly be used of the Propylaea, and that in any case that building would not in fact be visible from the theatre.[5] Others took the phrase to mean something represented in the theatre itself, for example an altar of Artemis-Hecate in front of the wall that enclosed the κοινοβωμία of the gods (cf. p. 160 below).[6] Vürtheim showed that there was no evidence in the play for any such altar or wall.[7] Rather more plausible was the

[1] *Rh. Mus.* 40 (1885) 627 ff.

[2] W. Dörpfeld, *Mitt. Arch. Inst.* 27 (1902) 389; G. Loeschcke, *Jahrb. Arch. Inst.* 19 (1904) 22.

[3] In *Mélanges Nicole* 292 ff. But he later retracted this opinion (*Philol. Wochenschr.* 49 (1929) 372 f.).

[4] Pp. 14 ff. M. showed that Διὸς κόρη is used by Greek writers, the dramatists included, more frequently of Artemis than of Athena, that the epithet ἁγνή is never applied to Athena in drama, and that she is never given the title ἀδμήτα (149) in the sense of 'virgin'. Artemis is described as ἁγνά at 1030 (and *Ag.* 135). Cf. also Wilamowitz, *Hermes* 21 (1886) 608 n. 1 (= *Kl. Schr.* I. 159 n. 1). For other references to Artemis as ἁγνά and Διὸς κόρα cf. V. Citti, *Il linguaggio religioso e liturgico nelle tragedie di Eschilo* (Bologna 1962) 21.

[5] Pp. 83 ff.

[6] Wilamowitz, *Interpr.* 5 ff.

[7] Cf. also A. W. Pickard-Cambridge, *The theatre of Dionysus in Athens* (Oxford 1946) 34 n. 1.

suggestion that Aeschylus meant an Argive temple of Artemis. Pausanias mentions one such on Mount Lycone.[1] But there is no reason to believe that Aeschylus had any specific temple in mind at all. The words are chosen to emphasize the defenceless status of the homeless Chorus by contrasting it with the secure position of the virgin Artemis in her stately home.[2]

A little more helpful is the idea that when Aeschylus at 559 describes the Nile valley as χιονόβοσκον, he is reproducing the theory of the Nile flooding which was evidently held by Anaxagoras. Herodotus attacks it without naming its author, but the name is supplied by Diodorus and Athenaeus.[3] Diels argued that Anaxagoras put his view forward in a work published after 468/7, so that the *Supplices* must have been composed after that date.[4] Unfortunately Diels's theory cannot be proved. The date of the publication of Anaxagoras' view is uncertain, and his chronology in general disputed.[5] Most scholars accept

[1] N. Wecklein, *Äschylos. Die Schutzflehenden* (Leipzig 1902) 39, quoting Curtius, *Pelop.* II (Gotha 1852) 364; cf. Paus. ii. 24. 5. Pausanias mentions also a sanctuary of Artemis dedicated by Hypermestra (ii. 21. 1). In *Attische Studien* I (Göttingen 1862) 39 ff. Curtius tried to locate the κοινοβωμία at Mt Pontinus (cf. Paus. ii. 36. 8 ff.): *contra* Wilamowitz, *Interpr.* 8 f.

[2] Cf. Vürtheim 89 f.; Pickard-Cambridge 34. R. D. Murray 29 finds sexual symbolism in the phrase. Whatever the answer to the problem may be, the choice of the word ἐνώπια is odd. ἑδώλια (suggested, but not adopted in his text, by Tucker) would give good sense in this context of virginity (cf. *Sept.* 454 f. πωλικῶν ἑδωλίων, *Choe.* 71 νυμφικῶν ἑδωλίων), but it is not easy to see how the corruption could have arisen.

[3] Hdt. ii. 22; Diod. i. 38. 4; Athen. ii. 87. Cf. also Σ Ap. Rhod. iv. 269–71; Seneca, *nat. quaest.* iv. 2. 17: Diels–Kranz, *Fragm. d. Vorsokratiker* 2 A 91; Aesch. fr. 193 M (300 N² 2–5).

[4] H. Diels, *Abh. Berl. Akad.* (1885) ii. 8 n. 1; cf. also *Hermes* 22 (1887) 434 f. The view was accepted by W. Nestle, *N. Jbb.* 19 (1907) 327 f.; Wecklein, *Philol. Wochenschr.* 30 (1910) 738 f.; and, in principle, by Vürtheim 79 ff. But V. argued, on the strength of some uncertain parallels in Pindar, for a date *c.* 476. In this he is tentatively followed by Koster 29 ff. K. tries to reconcile this dating with his view of the archaic character of the play by arguing that A.'s art may not have developed in a straight line: see however chap. I p. 27 n. 1. Anaxagoras mentioned a fall of meteorites that took place at Aegospotami in 467 (Diels–Kranz 2 A 1. 11, A 11 and 12), but the Nile-flooding theory may have been propounded in a different work; cf. Vürtheim.

[5] The principal uncertainty is about the date of his arrival in Athens. Most put this about 460: e.g. Busolt III. 1. 9 n. 1; Th. Gomperz, *Greek thinkers* I (London 1901) 209; A. Döring, *Gesch. d. gr. Phil.* I (Leipzig 1903) 216 f.; Zeller–Nestle, *Die Philosophie der Griechen* I. 2 (Leipzig 1920) 1196 ff.; Jacoby, *F. Gr. Hist.* 228 F 2 and 244 F 31; Vürtheim 81; Körte, *Philol. Wochenschr.* 49 (1929) 373; J. S. Morrison, *C.Q.* 35 (1941) 5 n. 2; cf. also H. T. Wade-Gery, *J.H.S.* 52 (1932) 220;

that he was born about 500 B.C., and this would be enough to show that the *Supplices* could not be as early as the 490's, if we could be sure that Aeschylus is in fact borrowing from the philosopher. But the possibility of a common souce cannot be ruled out.[1]

In some respects the *Supplices* and the *Prometheus* differ in their treatment of the Io story, and these differences have been used to demonstrate the priority of the one play or the other. Most notably in the *Supplices* Io is turned completely into a cow (cf. Bacchyl. 19), whereas in the *Prometheus* she is depicted as a maiden with horns (cf. especially 588). At about 470 B.C. a similar change in the representation of Io is to be found in vase-paintings. It is not implausibly suggested that the dramatists may have been the first to represent Io as a βούκερως παρθένος, since it was obviously impracticable for them to bring on Io in the form of a cow.[2] If then the new type was copied by the vase-painters from the dramatists as early as 470, it would follow that the *Supplices*, with its older form of representation, must have been composed before that date.[3] Even however if the premise is correct, there is no reason to believe that the change was abrupt or irrevocable. Since Io does not appear in the *Supplices*, the difficulty of stage-representation did not arise.[4] And in any case at *Supplices* 568 Io is described as βοτὸν μειξόμβροτον,

A. R. Burn, *Pericles and Athens* (London 1948) 22 n. 1. A. E. Taylor, *C.Q.* 11 (1917) 81 ff., argued for 480 B.C.: cf. also J. Burnet, *Early Greek philosophy* (4th ed. London 1930) 251 f.; Kirk and Raven, *The Presocratic philosophers* (Cambridge 1957) 362 ff. J. A. Davison, *C.Q.* n.s. 3 (1953) 39 ff., suggests 475 or 4 as the date of A.'s first settlement in Athens. Others again put his stay much earlier; e.g. G. F. Unger, *Philol.* Suppl. 4 (1884) 534 ff. (*c.* 494–*c.* 465 B.C.).

[1] Cf. Wilamowitz, *Kl. Schr.* I. 159 n. 1; G. Müller 28 ff. M. argued that the knowledge of Egypt displayed in the *Persae* is derived from the same source, and that this must therefore be older than Anaxagoras. But cf. Nestle and Vürtheim. Thales and Hecataeus held different theories about the Nile floods, and these too were attacked by Herodotus (ii. 20–1). Diels's view was rejected also by Körte, *Philol. Wochenschr.* 49 (1929) 373 f.; H. F. Johansen, *Class. et Med.* 15 (1954) 55: cf. also W. Capelle, *N. Jbb.* 33 (1914) 340.

[2] Cf. R. Engelmann in Roscher's *Lexicon* II. A *s.v.* Io 270 ff., and *Jahrb. Arch. Inst.* 18 (1903) 37 ff.; J. C. Hoppin, *Harv. Stud.* 12 (1901) 342 ff.; Eitrem, *R.-E.* ix. 2. 1739; L. Deubner, *Philol.* 64 (1905) 488; Wecklein, ed. *Supp.* 21; M. Bock, *Gymnasium* 65 (1958) 432 f.: *contra* Meyer, *Forschungen* 78 n. 2; G. Müller 34 ff.

[3] Cf. Hoppin, *loc. cit.*; also Körte, *Mélanges Nicole* 290 f.

[4] Cf. R. D. Murray 91 ff.

which suggests that she could already be thought of as a girl with cow's horns.[1] In the *Supplices* (540 ff.) Io's wanderings are described much more simply and briefly, and are altogether less fabulous, than in the *Prometheus*. It has been argued that this proves the chronological priority of the *Supplices*, that in the *Prometheus* we see Aeschylus trying to make attractive a well-worn story.[2] It would be as easy to argue that the *Supplices* describes the wanderings in brief because they have already been dealt with at length in the *Prometheus*.[3] But to attempt to date one undated play on the basis of differences between it and another play that is itself undated is a hopeless task.

The staging of the *Supplices* is too uncertain to be of much use for the dating of the play.[4] The usual view is that it was performed in a theatre without a background-building, but with a raised section, or mound of earth or wood, at a tangent to (or less probably in the middle of) the orchestra (cf. 189). This formed the κοινοβωμία of the gods, and on this the Chorus take up their position at 222 ff. (cf. 423 and 508).[5] The *Supplices* then,

[1] Engelmann concluded from this that either the *P.V.* was earlier than the *Supp.* (cf. also Wecklein 21), or the new type of representation of Io was to be ascribed to a forerunner of Aeschylus. He modified his view in *Jahrb. Arch. Inst.* 18, arguing that the βοτὸν μειξόμβροτον of the *Supp.* was to be understood rather as a cow with human face, a representation which he thought came chronologically between that of Io as a cow and as a woman with cow's horns, and was derived from vase paintings. Mr E. W. Whittle points out to me that the Sphinx is described as μειξοπάρθενος at E. *Phoen.* 1023. For the different representations of Io see also A. B. Cook, *Zeus* III. 1 (Cambridge 1940) 630 ff. For the view that the Greeks early equated the horned Io with the Egyptian Isis see chap. V p. 173 n. 2 below.

[2] Cf. Körte, *Mélanges Nicole* 291 f.; also G. Müller 31.

[3] Cf. also Vürtheim 53; R. D. Murray 96. Murray discusses (91 ff.) also other points of difference between *Supp.* and *P.V.*

[4] No one is likely to be convinced by the arguments of H. Jurenka, *Wien. Stud.* 23 (1901) 220 ff., who tried to prove that the *Pers.* must be earlier than the *Supp.* on the grounds that no actor in the *Pers.* wears the high-soled cothurnus, whereas Danaus does so in the *Supp.*

[5] See, for example, Wilamowitz, *Hermes* 21 (1886) 603 ff. (= *Kl. Schr.* I. 153 ff.); *Hermes* 32 (1897) 393; *Sitz. Ak. Wiss. Berlin* (1903. 1) 447; *Interpr.* 6 ff., 50 f., 117, 244 ff.; Dörpfeld–Reisch, *Das griechische Theater* (Athens 1896) 195 ff. (cf. 186) and 370 ff.; G. Müller 43 ff.; A. Frickenhaus, *Die altgriechische Bühne* (Strassburg 1917) 71 ff.; R. C. Flickinger, *The Greek theater and its drama* (3rd ed. Chicago 1926) 65 f. (cf. 346 f.) and 226 ff.; Vürtheim 88 f.; F. Focke, *Hermes* 65 (1930) 275 ff.; Pickard-Cambridge 10 and 32 ff.; Lesky, *Hermes* 72 (1937) 126 f.; *Trag. Dichtung* 64 and 68; *Greek tragedy* 64, 67, 72 f.; *A history of Greek literature* (Eng. tr.

it is thought, belongs to the earlier Aeschylean plays, written before the introduction of a background building as found in the *Oresteia*.[1] So far as the dating of the *Supplices* is concerned there is no difficulty in this view. The κοινοβωμία with its statues of the gods would be similar to the images upon which the Chorus throw themselves in the *Septem* (185: cf. 265).[2] Nothing makes it impossible that the background building was introduced at some time in the late 460's.[3] But it is not even certain that there was no such background in the *Supplices*, or indeed in the other earlier plays of Aeschylus. The view has recently been revived that a skene did exist from early times, both a raised stage and a background building.[4] Arnott argues that the κοινοβωμία was to be found on this raised stage.

The only possible conclusion is that the *Supplices* provides us with no reliable internal evidence, whether political or non-political, for the dating of the trilogy. At most it tends to support

London 1966) 250 f.; M. Bieber, *The history of the Greek and Roman theater* (2nd ed. Princeton 1961) 22 and 57: cf. also G. Murray, *Aeschylus the creator of tragedy* (Oxford 1940) 50 ff.

[1] Cf. Vitruvius 7 *praef.* 11 'primum Agatharchus Athenis Aeschylo docente tragoediam scenam pinxit et de ea commentarium reliquit'); but cf. also Arist. *Poet.* 1449a 18. See Pickard-Cambridge 124. A. Rumpf, *J.H.S.* 67 (1947) 13, puts Agatharchus in the second half of the fifth century: cf. also T. B. L. Webster, *Greek theatre production* (London 1956) 13 f.

[2] D. van Nes, *Die maritime Bildersprache des Aischylos* (Groningen 1963) 87 ff., suggests that the metaphor at *Supp.* 345 (πρύμναν πόλεος) is a conscious reference to the ship-of-state motif used earlier in the *Sept.*

[3] Dörpfeld–Reisch (200) put the innovation *c.* 465 (also Flickinger 66 and 226 ff.; G. Müller 44 ff.; Frickenhaus, *loc. cit.*). Müller argued that a number of lost plays seem to demand a skene, and that there is hardly room between *Septem* and *Oresteia* to fit them in as well as the Danaid trilogy. But arguments from lost plays (see also Dörpfeld–Reisch 119 f.; Wilamowitz, *Interpr.* 244 ff.) are too hazardous to have such weight.

[4] P. Arnott, *Greek scenic conventions in the fifth century B.C.* (Oxford 1962) 4 ff., 22 ff., 46. For earlier statements of this view cf. esp. B. Todt, *Philol.* 48 (1889) 505 ff.; O. Navarre, *Dionysos. Étude sur l'organisation matérielle du théâtre Athénien* (Paris 1895) 87 ff. See further Pickard-Cambridge, who accepts (37) the possibility of a 'simple background representing a public building or palace' for *Pers.* and *Sept.*; Webster (8), who holds that 'the *Persae*, like all later plays, demands a stage-building with a practicable door unless we should think rather of Dareios appearing on the roof of his tomb' (cf. 165 f.). Murray (55 f.) envisages a palace-front for the *Persae*, and for the *Supplices* at the back of the orchestra the wall of the actor's dressing-room 'so treated as to look like a High Place': cf. also E. Bethe, *Prolegomena zur Geschichte des Theaters im Alterthum* (Leipzig 1896) 83 ff., and *Hermes* 59 (1924) 108 ff.

a date in the late 460's, the only relevant period in which we know for certain that there was a climate of opinion at Athens favourable to Argos. It is enough to be sure that it gives us no reason for rejecting the evidence of the papyrus fragment. Since then arguments from style and structure have been seen to be equally inconclusive, there is no longer any reason to refuse to accept what the papyrus tells us. It remains the only external and objective evidence for the dating of the trilogy, and its information must be accepted.

CHAPTER V

THE TRILOGY

I

That the *Supplices* belonged to a trilogy has been almost universally accepted, since the suggestion was first made by A. W. von Schlegel in 1811,[1] the other titles being the Αἰγύπτιοι (or Θαλαμοποιοί) and Δαναΐδες. Of the plots of these plays H. J. Rose says,[2] 'Since our text of the former play consists of one word (fgt. 5, simply the name of Zagreus) and for the latter we have but ten complete lines, I regard as waste of labour any attempt to make out how the matter was handled.' He might have added that even the attribution of fragment 5 is doubtful. From the Δαναΐδες we have two certain fragments, one of which is evidently corrupt, and capable of a variety of interpretations. The task of reconstructing the trilogy may seem, then, a thankless one, and yet very many scholars have undertaken it. The present chapter will seek to re-examine the evidence on which they base their conclusions, and to determine its reliability. Some of their arguments are affected by the new dating of the trilogy.

The details of the story are given by ps.-Apollodorus ii. 1. 4 f.; Hyginus, *Fab.* 168 and 170; Pausanias ii. 15. 5; 16. 1; 19. 3 ff.; 20. 7; 21. 1; 24. 2; 25. 4; 37. 1 and 2; 38. 2 and 4; iii. 12. 2; vii. 21. 13; x. 10. 5: by the scholiast at Homer, *Iliad* A 42 (quoting genuine Apollodorus) and Δ 171: by Euripides, *Orestes* 871–3, and frs. 228 and 846 N²; and the scholiast at Aeschylus, *P.V.* 853, Euripides, *Hecuba* 886, *Orestes*, 857, 871, and 932: by Pindar and the scholia at *Nemeans* x. 6 (10) and *Pythians* ix. 112 (195) ff.: by Ovid, *Heroides* xiv and Horace, *Odes* iii. 11: by the scholiast at Statius, *Theb.* ii. 222 and vi. 269: and by Servius on *Aeneid* x. 497. In addition there are scattered

[1] *Vorlesungen über dram. Kunst u. Lit.* (2nd ed. Heidelberg 1817) I. 158.

[2] *A commentary on the surviving plays of Aeschylus* (Amsterdam 1957) I. 5.

references in other authors. The story of Amymone, which Aeschylus treated in his satyr-play, is also known from many sources, and these are conveniently listed by Frazer in his edition of Apollodorus.[1]

The most remarkable feature of the above accounts is their lack of agreement on almost every detail of the story. If we ask what is essential, and what Aeschylus could not have failed to use, we find only four elements which are common to all the versions, or at least not contradicted by one or more of them. First the story concerns two brothers Danaus and Aegyptus, descendants of Io, the former with fifty daughters, the other with fifty sons. Secondly the brothers quarrel. Thirdly the fifty sons marry the fifty daughters, who are commanded by Danaus to murder their husbands on their wedding-night. And fourthly all obey, with a single exception, that of Hypermestra who spares her husband Lynceus.

In everything else there is disagreement, so that Pausanias' remark,[2] τὰ δὲ ἀπὸ τούτου καὶ οἱ πάντες ὁμοίως ἴσασι, is more than usually exasperating to anyone who seeks to reduce to order the chaos of the evidence. In most versions Danaus and Aegyptus are the sons of Belus, but in Σ *Hec.* 886 their mother is apparently Io herself.[3] Various grounds are given for the quarrel between the two brothers. Ps.-Apollodorus, Hyginus, Σ *Iliad* A 42, Σ *Hec.* 886, and Servius report that the quarrel concerned the kingship, and that the wedding was merely a stratagem in the general struggle; in Σ *Iliad* Δ 171 the wedding comes before the quarrel. Hyginus is alone in recording that Aegyptus wanted to kill not only Danaus but his daughters too. The usual scene of the quarrel is Egypt, but Σ *Hec.* 886 sets it in Argos. Σ *Iliad* A 42, followed by Libanius, *Narr.* 6 p. 36 (Foerster), puts the murder in Egypt, while it is normally held to have been committed at Argos. In Σ *Orestes* 857, 932 (cf. 1247, *Phoen.* 107), as well as in Ovid, the Argive king is Pelasgus, whereas elsewhere he is Gelanor (or Hellanor). Ps.-Apollodorus reports

[1] Loeb ed. (1921) i. 138 n. 2.

[2] ii. 16. 1.

[3] But Mr E. W. Whittle points out to me that this is not the only possible interpretation of Αἴγυπτος καὶ Δαναὸς ἀδελφοὶ ἦσαν ἀπὸ Ἰοῦς τῆς Ἰνάχου θυγατρός.

simply that on Danaus' arrival he surrenders the kingdom to him: Pausanias[1] tells how the claim of Danaus was heard by the people of Argos, who decided in his favour after a wolf had fought and overcome a bull, the leader of a herd that was pasturing in front of the city wall. In Hyginus, Σ *Hec.* 886, and Σ *Or.* 872 the initiative for the marriage evidently comes from Danaus himself, while for Apollodorus, Servius and Σ Statius, *Theb.* ii. 222 it is the sons of Aegyptus who demand it. An oracle element is introduced by several writers. In Σ *Iliad* A 42 Danaus arranges the murder in Egypt, since he has learnt from an oracle that one of the sons of Aegyptus will kill him.[2] Σ *P.V.* 853 attributes the flight from Egypt to the oracle. Σ *Or.* 872 records the oracle in Argos after the wedding has taken place. Two, or possibly three, reasons are given for Hypermestra's disobedience. In Σ *Hec.* 886, Σ *P.V.* 853 and Σ Pind. *Pyth.* ix. 112 (195) she falls in love with Lynceus; ps.-Apollodorus, Σ *Iliad* Δ 171, and Σ Pind. *Nem.* x. 6 (10) give as motive that he has spared her virginity. This may also be Ovid's explanation, unless the 'virgo' of line 55 is to be taken merely as a reference to her tender years. Otherwise Ovid mentions only Hypermestra's 'timor et pietas' (line 49).

There is as little unanimity on the consequences of the murder. In ps.-Apollodorus, and apparently Ovid, Danaus imprisons Hypermestra for disobeying his command, but in the former she is afterwards reunited with Lynceus. Pausanias says[3] that she was formally put on trial, and acquitted by the Argives, after which she dedicated an image to Aphrodite Nikephoros. Her sisters are purified in ps.-Apollodorus by Athena and Hermes at the command of Zeus. Σ *Hec.* 886 has them killed along with their father by an avenging Lynceus, while the well-known story of their punishment in the underworld is recorded by Hyginus, and by Servius in whose version Danaus alone is killed by Lynceus. In Ovid it appears that all are dead save Hypermestra and Lynceus. It is obvious that the oracle story presupposes the vengeance of Lynceus.[4] Danaus is

[1] ii. 19. 3–4.

[2] Cf. Σ Statius, *Theb.* ii. 222 and vi. 269.

[3] ii. 19. 6.

[4] Cf. G. A. Megas, *Hermes* 68 (1933) 422.

formally prosecuted by Aegyptus in *Orestes* 871–3 and one of the scholia there, Aegyptus having come from Egypt for this express purpose: in Euripides fr. 846 he came earlier in company with his sons. If the text of Ovid, *Her.* xiv. 24 is correct, Aegyptus is actually ensconced in the royal palace at Argos. Ps.-Apollodorus, Pind. *Pyth.* ix. 112 (195) ff. and scholia, and Pausanias[1] tell how Danaus marries off his daughters to the victors in an athletic contest. Hyginus mentions the second marriage, but makes it take place after the death of Danaus.

There are numerous less important discrepancies, or elements which appear in only one or two of the sources. Ps.-Apollodorus, Hyginus, and Σ *Iliad* A 42 record that it was Athena herself who advised Danaus and his daughters to flee from Egypt. In ps.-Apollodorus and Σ *Iliad* A 42 they call at Rhodes on their journey to Argos. The *Marmor Parium* adds that Danaus left five of his daughters there as priestesses, while Diodorus reports[2] that three of them died in Rhodes. Neither version can be reconciled with the story of the wedding and the murder. Ps.-Apollodorus and Hyginus give different lists of names for the Danaids and their husbands, and in Eustathius *ad* Dion. Per. 805 it is Bebryce who spares her husband Hippolytus. Pausanias alone describes[3] how after the murder Lynceus fled to the place called Lyrceia, and communicated with Hypermestra by means of torch-signals. Ps.-Apollodorus makes the Danaids bury the heads of their bridegrooms at Lerna, while Pausanias puts their bodies there,[4] their heads on Larisa.

Clearly such sources as these must be treated with extreme caution as a basis for the reconstruction of Aeschylus' trilogy. It would be helpful if we could say that any of them was entirely dependent upon Aeschylus, and it is indeed tempting to do this, choosing that account which best fits one's preconception of what Aeschylus must have written. Hermann wrote,[5] 'Aegyptus, wie Hygin, vermuthlich aus dem Aeschylus, erzählt, schickt seine söhne nach Argos, mit dem befehl den Danaus umzubringen oder ihm nicht wieder vor augen zu kommen'. And yet

[1] iii. 12. 2. [2] v. 58. [3] ii. 25. 4. [4] ii. 24. 2.

[5] Edition (Berlin 1852) I. 332. That is the version also of Σ Stat. *Theb.* ii. 222.

there is not the slightest hint of any such thing in the *Supplices* of Aeschylus. M. Croiset too supposed that Hyginus is probably close to Aeschylus' trilogy,[1] while Miss Cunningham points out[2] that only Hyginus agrees with Aeschylus in making the proposed marriage not the sequel to but the motive for Danaus' flight.

Other scholars have favoured ps.-Apollodorus as more truly reproducing the plots of tragedy.[3] Frazer says,[4] 'How closely Apollodorus followed his authorities may be seen by a comparison of his narratives with the extant originals from which he drew them, such as the *Oedipus Tyrannus* of Sophocles, the *Alcestis* and *Medea* of Euripides, the *Odyssey*, and above all the *Argonautica* of Apollonius Rhodius'. Unfortunately, however, though ps.-Apollodorus in ii. 1 names several authors, Aeschylus is not amongst them. Clearly the single satyr who in his account attacks Amymone does not come directly from the chorus of satyrs that Aeschylus must have used. As A. Nathansky pointed out,[5] ps.-Apollodorus tells the story before the arrival of the sons of Aegyptus, thus presupposing a version in which the murder has already taken place in Egypt. Thus his account is contaminated and not entirely dependent upon Aeschylus. And the same is true of Hyginus. As Rose says,[6] hardly a story is told without some discrepancy from the tragic plot as we know it. His learning is acquired from some mythological hand-book containing material derived from every possible poetic source, and dating apparently from the late Alexandrian period.[7]

With ps.-Apollodorus and Hyginus are probably to be classed the Homeric scholia. Schwarz pointed out[8] that even the subscription of genuine Apollodorus at Σ *Iliad* A 42, and elsewhere, is open to question, and in any case it is not expressly stated that the whole excerpt is in fact quoted from him. Schwarz's

[1] *Eschyle* (Paris 1928) 47.
[2] *Rh. Mus.* 96 (1953) 229.
[3] Cf. Welcker, *Aesch. Trilogie Prom.* (Darmstadt 1824) 395.
[4] P. xviii.
[5] *Wien. Stud.* 32 (1910) 25.
[6] *Hyginus* viii ff.; cf. Idem, *Modern methods* (St Andrews 1930) III. 37 ff.
[7] Cf. Bethe, *Quaestiones Diodoreae mythographae* (Diss. Gött. 1889); A. Werth, *Schedae philol. H. Usener obl.* (Bonn 1891) 109 ff. A similar work was written by Parthenius for Ovid.
[8] *R.-E.* i. B. 2875 ff.; cf. *Jahrb. f. Philol.* Suppl. 12 (1881) 457 f.

warning is well-founded: 'Denn es ist unbedingt festzuhalten, daß die mythographische Überlieferung günstigen Falles nur den Einfluß einer Tragödie auf die Sage wiederspiegelt, aber von der Tragödie selbst, von dem Gang des Stückes, all den Dingen, die für die Reconstruction in erster Linie wichtig sind, keine Vorstellung geben will und kann.' E. Howald, commenting on Aeschylus' surprising choice of the mere reception of the Suppliants at Argos as the theme of an entire play, also remarks[1] that the knowledge of the saga is useless in itself for the reconstruction of a drama: 'Die einfache Erzählung der für das Verständnis der Fabel wichtigen Einzelheiten in der richtigen Reihenfolge sagt nicht das geringste über die tatsächlichen Verhältnisse des Dramas aus. Dinge, die für den Fortgang der Handlung gänzlich unwesentlich sind, können ganze Szenen einnehmen; handlungsmäßig Wichtiges kann zurücktreten müssen.'

Many sources were available to the composer of a mythological hand-book. Apollodorus quotes Hesiod, Acusilaus, Pherecydes, and Asclepiades. To these we may add the lost poems of the Epic Cycle, and such prose writers as Hecataeus and Hellanicus, and later Dionysius Scytobrachion, Lysimachus, Satyrus,[2] Theopompus of Cnidos,[3] etc. Other dramatists who handled the story are Phrynichus, Timesitheus,[4] Theodectes,[5] Aristophanes,[6] and Diphilus.[7] Nicochares, the comedian, wrote an 'Αμυμώνη.[8]

The attempt was made by Th. Birt[9] to prove that Ovid's method was different, and that he did indeed draw straight from Aeschylus. His argument was complicated and found little acceptance.[10] It was based on Propertius ii. 34, where the poet

[1] *Gr. Tragödie* (Munich and Berlin 1930) 53.

[2] ὁ τοὺς ἀρχαίους μύθους συναγαγών Dion. Hal. *Ant.* i. 68.

[3] τῷ συναγαγόντι τοὺς μύθους Plut. *Caes.* 48.

[4] Cf. *Suda.*

[5] Nauck² p. 802.

[6] Frs. 245–65 K.

[7] Fr. 25 K.

[8] Kock I. p. 770.

[9] *Rh. Mus.* 32 (1877) 397 ff.: cf. H. Bornecque (Budé edition of *Heroides*, Paris 1928, p. x), who also claims Aeschylus as the source of *Her.* xiv.

[10] Cf. esp. J. M. Reinkens, *De Aesch. Danaidibus* (Düsseldorf 1886) and N. Wecklein, *Studien zu den Hiketiden des Aesch.* (*Sitz. bay. Ak. München* 1893 ii.) 414–16; Wilamowitz, *Aischylos. Interpretationen* (Berlin 1914) 20 n. 1: also K. Kruse, ed. *Supp.* (Stralsund 1861) 13; Nathansky 16.

accuses a certain Lynceus of trying to seduce Cynthia. Birt argued that this man, who is apparently an imitator of Aeschylus, must have handled the latter's Danaid trilogy, to give point to his nickname. Thus it follows that a version of Aeschylus' trilogy was available to Ovid. However, even if all this be true, it does not follow that Ovid used such a version. Birt pointed out that there are indeed certain similarities between Ovid and Aeschylus. In particular both give the name Pelasgus to the king of Argos.[1] Haupt indeed tried to remove Pelasgus from Ovid and from Aeschylus, and his reading of 'tyranni' instead of 'Pelasgi' at line 23[2] is supported by the authority of late manuscripts. But clearly Pelasgus is an integral part of the tradition, since he is found also at Σ *Orestes* 857 and 932. But since this is so, we cannot conclude that Ovid borrowed Pelasgus directly from Aeschylus. Ed. Meyer[3] remarked that those who, like Hesiod, put Pelasgus in Arcadia, obviously could not use him in Argos. This does not necessarily imply that Pelasgus is peculiar to Aeschylus' version or indeed that he was his invention. Moreover Ovid seems from lines 23–4 to be following an account that has Aegyptus already installed in the palace at Argos. It is difficult to reconcile this with Aeschylus' version so far as it is given in the *Supplices* at least; for there it is the Danaids who are entertained by Pelasgus.[4] Birt tried to evade the difficulty by reading 'nec' for 'et' at line 24, but the necessity for this hardly supports his theory, and, as Wecklein pointed out,[5] the emendation renders pointless the word 'armatas'.

The evidence then is not strong enough to allow us to use Ovid for the reconstruction of the trilogy of Aeschylus. Wilamo-

[1] This is true, as Canter's emendation of Πελασγός for Πελασγοῦ at *Supp.* 251 has been rightly accepted by all except Haupt and Paley. It is proved by the following lines, since it would be absurd to say that the people was called Pelasgian after their king, a Pelasgian, unless his name was in fact Pelasgus. Haupt was forced by his theory to emend 1010 by adding ὁ before Πελασγός.

[2] Ducimur Inachides magni sub tecta Pelasgi,
Et socer armatas accipit ipse nurus.

[3] *Forschungen zur alten Geschichte* (Halle 1892) I. 88.

[4] Hermann (*Opuscula* II. 323 f.) held that the 'socer' was Pelasgus, performing the function of father-in-law. Welcker, *Tril.* 405, preferred to read 'tyranni' at line 23.

[5] *Studien* 415.

witz says,[1] 'Ich hätte eine so schwere Gelehrsamkeit dem Ovid auch nimmermehr zugetraut'. Even Birt failed to accept the implications of his own argument; for where Ovid clearly states that Hypermestra's sisters are all dead, Birt was forced to understand this metaphorically to make it square with his conception of the version used by Aeschylus.

Perhaps even less helpful is Pausanias, since much of his information clearly came not so much from literary sources as from the explanations given him by his guides as he visited the curiosities and tourist-sites of Argos. Thus the story of the fight between the wolf and bull[2] explains the Temple of Apollo Lycius, said to have been dedicated by Danaus. The trial of Hypermestra accounts for the place-name Κριτήριον,[3] while the intercession of Aphrodite results in the dedication of the sanctuary and image of Ἀφροδίτη Πειθώ[4] and Νικηφόρος.[5] Pausanias also sees a stone image of Aphrodite by the sea,[6] and this is said to have been dedicated by the Danaids. Apparently no explanation is given him of this, or perhaps it conflicts with his account of Hypermestra's trial, so he chooses not to record it. Finally the annual torch-festival at Lyrceia is explained by Lynceus' flight there after the murder, when he used torch-signals to communicate with Hypermestra.[7] It would obviously be unwise to look for traces of Aeschylus in much of this.

A priori we might suppose that the scholia to Euripides offer evidence of a more reliable kind; for at least their authors were undeniably familiar with one of the tragedians, and may be presumed to have read the others too. But even they must be treated with caution. Σ *Hecuba* 886 makes Danaus the aggressor, who drives his brother out of Argos, so that Aeschylus is ruled out here as source. The information given by Euripides himself that Aegyptus came to Argos, and that this was the prevalent version,[8] is valuable for its proximity to Aeschylus' own period.

[1] *Interpr.* 20. On the other hand *Ox. Pap.* xxvii. 2457 shows that Ovid followed Euripides' *Aeolus* in *Her.* xi: cf. H. Lloyd-Jones, *Gnomon* 35 (1963) 443.

[2] ii. 19. 3.

[3] ii. 20. 7.

[4] ii. 21. 1 where Ἀφροδίτης is correctly read for Ἀρτέμιδος.

[5] ii. 19. 6.

[6] ii. 37. 1 and 2.

[7] ii. 25. 4.

[8] *Orestes* 871 and fr. 846.

Also of the fifth century is the dithyrambic poet Melanippides whose Δαναΐδες (fr. 1) tells of the masculine characteristics of the girls.

Generally, however, later writers offer little reliable evidence for the reconstruction of Aeschylus' trilogy. We are left with the four elements that are common to all or most of the versions, the relationship of Danaus and Aegyptus to Io, the quarrel, the marriage leading to the murder, and the disobedience of Hypermestra. It is disquieting then to find that of these apparent essentials Aeschylus uses only three. For nowhere in the *Supplices* is there any suggestion of a personal quarrel between the two brothers. The Danaids flee because they do not want to marry their cousins. The initiative is theirs, and the position of their father in this matter is, if not subordinate,[1] at least inseparable from his daughters'. For Wilamowitz this proved that Aeschylus was not master of his material.[2] Von Fritz is right to look for another reason. The most plausible interpretation of αὐτογενεῖ φυξανορίᾳ (line 8)[3] indicates that Aeschylus was concerned at the very beginning of the trilogy to emphasize this point, the independent nature of the girls' decision. This important difference between Aeschylus and the traditional account is confirmed by Σ *P.V.* 855: καὶ τὸ μὲν ἀληθὲς τῆς ἱστορίας οὕτως ἔχει (i.e. D. was afraid because of the oracle that he would be killed by the sons of Aegyptus)· ὁ δὲ παρὼν ποιητής φησι, διὰ τοῦτο ἐλεύσεται εἰς τὸ Ἄργος ἡ θηλύσπορος γέννα...διὰ τὸ μὴ θέλειν συνελθεῖν εἰς γάμον τοῖς ἐξαδέλφοις αὐτῶν. How many other divergencies may not be lurking in the lost plays of the trilogy?

The origin of the Danaid myth has received much attention,

[1] Cf. F. Focke, *NGG* (1922) 178; J. Coman, *L'idée de la Némésis chez Eschyle* (Paris 1931) 111; K. von Fritz, *Philol.* 91 (1936) 126 f. and 258 (= *Antike und moderne Tragödie* (Berlin 1962) 164 f. and 181 f.); W. Kraus, *Die Schutzsuchenden* (Frankfurt/Main 1948) 163. Croiset, *op. cit.* 49, says that Aegyptus sends his sons in pursuit of the Danaids since he is afraid that they may marry strangers and become powerful enemies. There is not a scrap of evidence in Aeschylus for this: it is the version of Servius.

[2] *Interpr.* 13: 'Es ist verkehrte Welt, wenn der Vater Annex seiner Töchter ist. Da ist also offenbar, daß der Dichter seines Stoffes nicht Herr geworden ist.' Cf. chap. III pp. 126 f. above.

[3] Cf. p. 222 below.

and, though it is not of direct relevance to Aeschylus' treatment of it, it is important to know what elements are original and fundamental, and to trace as far as possible the development of the myth by pre-Aeschylean writers. The story has both a Greek and an Egyptian setting,[1] the former apparently being localized at the Heraeum at Argos.[2] According to Nilsson[3] Egypt enters the story in the twelfth century, at the time of the raids by the Danuna among the Peoples of the Sea, and he suggests that a crowd of Danaan women may have been captured and made concubines of the Egyptians. A. B. Cook, who accepts the identification of the Danaoi with the Danuna, followed L. B. Holland in his theory that the Danaoi (represented in the legend by their eponymous hero Danaus) came to Argos from Egypt *c.* 1500 B.C., and that it was they who built the tholos-tombs.[4] He argued further that they built also tholoid wells or reservoirs, and that the origin of their name was Illyrian, meaning the 'River-folk' or 'Water-folk'. This, he held, would explain the traditional connection of Danaus and his daughters with the water-supply of Argos.[5] M. C. Astour argues[6] that the whole Danaan cycle is of West Semitic origin and that the Danaoi/Danunians were a West Semitic people who came to Argolis probably between 1550 and 1450 B.C. It is by no means certain however that the Danuna are to be equated with the Danaoi in the first place.[7] Other scholars refer the introduction of Egypt

[1] Cf. W. Kranz, *Stasimon* (Berlin 1933) 106.

[2] Cf. P. Friedländer, *Argolica* (Berlin 1905) 22 ff.; P. Mazon, *Eschyle* (6th ed. Budé Paris 1953) I. 4.

[3] *The Mycenaean origin of Greek mythology* (Cambridge 1932) 66 f.: cf. also J. Vürtheim, *Aischylos' Schutzflehende* (Amsterdam 1928) 9 and 121; H. Weir Smyth, *Aeschylean tragedy* (California 1924) 46.

[4] *Zeus* III. 1 (Cambridge 1940) 354 ff.; L. B. Holland, *Harv. Stud.* 39 (1928) 59 ff., esp. 73 ff. Holland suggested (76 n. 2) that the *Parian Marble*'s reference to Danaus' ship of πεντήκοντα κωπῶν may in its ultimate source have given rise to the idea that D. had come in a ship with ΠΕΝΤΕΚΟΝΤΑ ΚΟΡΟΝ, the Π being mistaken for a P.

[5] Cf. also J. Lindsay, *The Clashing Rocks* (London 1965) 82. For L. the sacred land of Egypt merely stands for 'the spiritworld conjured up by ritual' (95).

[6] *Hellenosemitica* (Leiden 1965) 1 ff. For other attempts at linking the myth of Danaus with Egyptian history see J. L. Myres, *Who were the Greeks?* (California 1930) 119 ff., 320 ff., 347; F. Schachermeyr, *Archiv Orientální* 17 (1949) ii. 331 ff. (esp. 345 ff.); J. Bérard, *Syria* 29 (1952) 1 ff.

[7] Cf. D. L. Page, *History and the Homeric Iliad* (California 1959) 22–3.

to the story to the period (seventh century) in which Psammetichus was opening the harbours of Egypt to the Greeks, and receiving the assistance of Greek soldiers from Asia in his struggles against his enemies;[1] and to the following century in which Amasis established Greek traders at Naucratis.[2]

It seems then that the final development of the myth may have been comparatively late. The older commentators tried to explain the story of the murder in terms of nature-symbolism, derived from the springs of the Argive plain; the Danaids being fountain-nymphs, and the sons of Aegyptus the streams which flood in winter, and, except for that at Lerna, dry up in summer.[3] But such nature-symbolism theories are less fashionable now, and this one was satisfactorily refuted by Friedländer, who pointed out the absurdity of supposing that streams could be murdered by springs.[4] C. Bonner added that the word κεφαλή is not normally used in Greek for the source of a river,[5] while Megas remarked that, as far as their names are concerned, most of the Danaids have no connection with springs.[6] Simpler is the view of Cook (368 f.) that 'the wholesale endogamic marriage of the Danaïdes with the Aigyptiadai was regarded as a most potent fertility-charm'.[7] Very dubious are theories that

[1] Cf. esp. H. D. Müller, *Mythologie der griechischen Stämme* (Göttingen 1857) I. 53 ff.; E. Maass, *De Aesch. Supp. commentatio* (Gryphiswaldiae 1890) xxxi; Meyer, *Forschungen* I. 77 ff., and *Geschichte des Altertums* III (3rd ed. Stuttgart 1939) 430 f.; Waser, *Arch. f. Rel.-Wiss.* (1899) 53; Wecklein, *Äschylos. Die Schutzflehenden* (Leipzig 1902) 8 f. (also *Studien* 410 f.); L. Deubner, *Philol.* 64 (1905) 488; Vürtheim 9 f. and 121; Mazon 4. According to Wecklein the story was transferred to Egypt through the connecting of the name Αἴγυπτος with the river Nile.

[2] It is said by many (e.g. Meyer, *Forschungen* I. 77 f.; Weir Smyth 46 f.) that the Greeks were quick to identify Io with Isis. Since both had sons with a bull shape this is plausible enough. But there is no certain evidence for the identification before Callimachus (*Epigr.* 57). Herodotus ii. 41 is usually quoted, but is contradicted by ii. 59 (Ἶσις δέ ἐστι κατὰ τὴν Ἑλλήνων γλῶσσαν Δημήτηρ); cf. esp. Friedländer 9 f.; Deubner 488 f.; Wilamowitz, *Interpr.* 18; Kranz 103.

[3] See, for example, Meyer, *Forschungen* I. 74 ff.; Waser in *R.-E.* iv. B. 2087 ff., and *Arch. f. Rel.-Wiss.* (1899) 54 f.; Bernhard in Roscher's *Lexicon* I. 950 f.; Wecklein, ed. 3 f., and *Studien* 397 ff.; Preller–Robert, *Griechische Mythologie* (4th ed. Berlin 1920) II. 1. 266 f.; I. Trencsényi-Waldapfel, *Acta Ant. Hung.* 12 (1964) 266 f.

[4] P. 24.

[5] *Harv. Stud.* 13 (1902) 144 ff.; also *TAPhA* 31 (1900) 28 ff.

[6] *Hermes* 68. 415; cf. also Vürtheim 17 and 29; Nilsson 64; Cook 357 f.

[7] For J. Harrison too, *Themis* (2nd ed. Cambridge 1927) 529 f., the Danaids 'are well-nymphs, but also projections of the ancient rain-making ceremonies, they carry water to make rain'; cf. also Trencsényi-Waldapfel 267 f. Lindsay (82 ff.)

connect the fifty Danaids with the fifty weeks of the year,[1] or with the fifty moons of the Olympic cycle,[2] or hold that the myth is virtually 'ein handelsepos'.[3] Megas aptly quotes Wilamowitz:[4] 'Lange haben wir verkannt, daß in weitem Umfang als Heroensage erscheint, was gar keinen geschichtlichen Inhalt hat, sondern als Märchen oder Novelle zu fassen ist. Das liegt daran, daß für diese reizvollen Wandergeschichten, die in den Märchen namenlos zu sein pflegen, die Griechen heroische Träger wählen...Da soll man sich durch die heroischen Namen und die späteren poetischen und geographischen Ausschmückungen nicht beirren lassen.'

Friedländer traced four stages in the development of the myth. The first two are, he said, associated with the Heraeum at Argos, and deal with the stories of Io and Hypermestra. These two became connected, and what he called version A develops, corresponding with the account of Σ *Hecuba* 886.[5] In version B Danaus is made to come from Egypt, and the scene is shifted from the Heraeum to the town of Argos and the district of Lerna. Important is Friedländer's view that the story of the punishment of the Danaids in the underworld was already part of version A, and that this becomes in B the story of how Danaus sends his daughters for water.

argues that the Danaid myth 'represents a distortion of fertility-ritual and initiation-ordeal. The later cult of races and the mating of the Argonauts and the Lemnian women (with races attached) represent the original happy side of the ritual-myth, which thus asserts itself in a doublet reversing the murder tales' (94). Cf. also Appendix pp. 234 f. below.

[1] Welcker, *Kl. Schr.* v. 50 n. 1; also Astour 78.

[2] Schwenck, *Rh. Mus.* 10 (1856) 377 f.

[3] Schwarz, *Jahrb. f. Philol.* 147 (1893) 95 ff.

[4] *Sitz. Ak. Wiss. Berlin* (1925) 59 (= *Kl. Schr.* v. 2. 80 f.).

[5] Waser, *R.-E.* iv. B. 2095, and *Arch. f. Rel.-Wiss.* (1899) 52, also thought that Σ *Hec.* 886 preserved a version closest to the original form of the story; also Friedländer 6 and Vürtheim 121. *Contra* Wilamowitz, *Interpr.* 23 n. 1, who argued that Aegyptus, who in this account plays a leading role, cannot have done so until the story was transferred to Egypt. Nilsson too (64 n. 71) accuses Friedländer of arbitrarily selecting this version: cf. also Deubner 489 n. 25; E. A. Wolff, *Aeschylus' Danaid trilogy: a study* (Diss. Columbia University 1957) 25. It is difficult however to see how it could have arisen at any later date in the development of the tale. Astour, who argues that this version is younger than Aeschylus because it already follows his representation of the Aigyptiads' invasion of Argos, ascribes it to Greek chauvinism, which 'refused to accept the un-Greek origin of such a famous dynasty as the ancient Argive one' (82): cf. also Megas 421.

Valuable work on the myth was done by Bonner and by Megas (who oddly nowhere refers to Bonner), in the application of the techniques of comparative mythology. Bonner found a group of strikingly similar folk-stories, from areas as varied as the Caucasus and Iceland, and including the English nursery-tale of Hop-o'-my-thumb. He wrote, 'The features of the legend that are common to most of the versions may be gathered from the following outline':

A band of brothers, wandering in a forest by night, lost their way and sought refuge in a hut or a cavern inhabited by an old woman and her daughters, the number of whom always corresponds to that of the brothers. Some versions say that the features of the women indicated their savage and monstrous nature. But at any rate they received the young men with the appearance of hospitality, and each of the sisters passed the night with one of the guests. The youngest brother, however, who was the shrewdest of all, suspected that some treachery was intended, and, in order to save himself and his brothers, resorted to a ruse. This takes different forms in the several versions of the story. Usually it consists in exchanging the night-caps of the girls for the hats worn by the young men, or else the hair of the girls is cut short after they have fallen asleep, or there is a shifting of positions. Later, the tale goes on, when all appeared to be asleep, the old woman came in with a huge knife to kill the young men, but on account of the darkness she failed to detect the trick, cut off the heads of her own daughters, and did not discover the mistake until day had dawned and the young men had fled.[1]

Bonner pointed out that these modern stories share with the Danaid myth the following features: the men and women are identical in number, and the sexual relation appears in both cases. The parent of the girls is the instigator of the crime, and the method adopted is that of decapitation. In an Icelandic story a girl held captive by the ogress and her daughters warns the brothers of their danger, and she is afterwards punished by being made to draw water constantly from one well and pour it into another. Finally, if Σ *Hec.* 886 is indeed the oldest version of the Danaid myth, it has its parallel in the death of the witch's daughters. The only important difference is that in the modern tales all the brothers escape, while the sisters are killed.[2]

[1] *Harv. Stud.* 13. 149.

[2] Cf. Cook 359.

From such comparisons Bonner concluded that it is only later tradition that invents for the Danaids a justification for the murder of their husbands and adds that the maidens were purified. The great variety to be found in the later versions, he claimed, supports his argument. 'The task of the Danaids is, indeed, a later addition to the myth in this sense, that a moralizing fable that makes the blood-stained sisterhood expiate their crime in Hades must be later than the rude folk-story which is the basis of the Danaid myth. In that, as we have seen, the wicked sisters were put to death by the sole survivor of the fifty brothers, and there was an end of the matter.'[1] The story of the murder is thus to be distinguished from that of Danaus, the eponymous ancestor of the Danaan race, and the story of Amymone is also to be set apart.[2]

Megas also compared the story with other tales, of which he found the common motif to be expulsion, flight, and pursuit. His conclusions differed slightly from those of Bonner, but he agreed that in the original form the surviving brother probably returned and killed his uncle and his cousins. His other important point of agreement with Bonner was his conclusion that Hypermestra is an integral part of the original story, against those who hold that she is a later addition designed to preserve the genealogy of the Argive kings.[3]

It is usually argued that the punishment of the Danaids in the underworld must be a late element, since the earliest literary evidence for it is the pseudo-Platonic *Axiochus*, while there is no certain evidence in art before the end of the Roman Republic.[4] Most scholars say that the punishment was transferred to the Danaids from the fate of the uninitiated in the Mysteries. The theory of Rohde has won much acceptance. According to the first version of this[5] those who died uninitiated in the Mysteries (ἀτελεῖς ἱερῶν) were condemned to ὑδρεῖαι ἀτελεῖς, at a later date the Danaids being substituted for the uninitiated, since

[1] P. 173.

[2] Preller–Robert 274.

[3] Haupt, ed. *Supp.* (Leipzig 1829) 75; H. D. Müller 61; Preller–Robert 271.

[4] Cf. esp. J. Carcopino, *La basilique pythagoricienne de la Porte Majeure* (Paris 1926) 288 ff.

[5] *Psyche* (1st ed. Freiburg and Leipzig 1894) 292 n. 1.

they were γάμων ἀτελεῖς. Rohde's argument rests on the supposed identification of marriage with a τέλος, a sacred rite. Later he revised his theory,[1] and postulated a primitive superstition that those who died unmarried were doomed to the eternal carrying of water to a bridal-bath. This superstition was later applied first by the mystic poets to the uninitiated, and then to the Danaids. The idea of a word-play on ἀτελεῖς was, however, denied by C. Robert[2] and by Bonner,[3] who pointed out that the vessels carried by the Danaids in works of art are not in fact λουτροφόροι, and that it is not a bath-tub that they are to fill. There is, moreover, no evidence in Greek folk-lore that the souls of the unmarried were made to carry water eternally in the underworld. It is just as likely that the punishment was transferred from specific persons to a general class as *vice versa*.[4] The peculiar nature of the task, argued Bonner, has no particular reference to either the Danaids or the ἄγαμοι. Probably, he said, it grew out of a proverb about the uselessness of attempting to fill a leaky vessel. Finally, the lateness of the evidence may be due purely to coincidence. Bonner's arguments are not all convincing, but they are at least strong enough to rule out any categorical statement that Aeschylus could not possibly have known the version of the story in which the Danaids were punished in the underworld.

Among Aeschylus' sources we might expect to find the poems of the Epic cycle. A little is known of their treatment of the Argive sagas. The Φορωνίς (fr. 4K) tells of

> Καλλιθόη κλειδοῦχος ὀλυμπιάδος βασιλείης
> Ἥρης Ἀργείης, ἣ στέμμασι καὶ θυσάνοισι
> πρώτη κόσμησεν πέρι κίονα μακρὸν ἀνάσσης,

apparently Io's double (cf. *Supp.* 291–2). The Ἠοῖαι (fr. 146 (163) Rz) deals with the family of Inachus. Eight fragments survive of the Αἰγίμιος of which 3 and 4 deal with Io, 5 and 6 with Argus. The interesting feature of this poem is that the

[1] *Psyche* (2nd ed. Freiburg 1898) I. 326 ff. (Eng. tr. of the 8th ed. Appx. III. 586–8). For a bibliography of the subject see Appendix pp. 234 f. below.

[2] *Die Nekyia des Polygnot* (Halle 1892) 52 n. 27.

[3] Pp. 164 ff.

[4] Cf. Hirzel, *Comm. in hon. Momms.* 14 n. 5.

birth of Epaphus took place in Euboea. If Severyns is right[1] the legend of Io cannot have been its main theme, since it must have dealt primarily with some aspect of the Heracles legend. In Hesiod's Κατάλογος the birth of Epaphus is located in Egypt, and the Io and Danaid stories seem to be now connected.[2] The most important of all these poems is the Δαναΐδες, a long epic poem of 6,500 lines,[3] which is held to have been responsible for uniting the Io, Danaid, and possibly Amymone stories in their final form; though according to Wilamowitz it must be earlier than the Αἰγίμιος, if the latter poem knows of Epaphus, since there is no independent trace of that hero in Greece.[4] Severyns suggests that the Αἰγίμιος may be a poem of transition from the Danaid to the Heraclean epics. The Δαναΐδες probably was composed in the sixth century, and Wilamowitz may well be right in saying that its origin was Cyrene.[5] Preller–Robert suggest[6] that the list of names given by ps.-Apollodorus for the Danaids and their cousins may go back to this epic stage, since they have an epic character and epic prosody, but there is no reason why this could not have been imitated at a later stage.

Of Aeschylus' debt to these sources all that we can say with certainty is that he was not wholly dependent upon any one of them. In Hesiod the father of Io is Peiren, and it is Zeus, not Hera (as at *Supp.* 299) who changes Io into a cow.[7] The setting of Euboea excludes the Αἰγίμιος as Aeschylus' source at least in this respect. Moreover it contradicts *Supp.* 305 by making Argus the son of Argus and Ismene.[8] Thus most scholars conclude that the Δαναΐδες must have been Aeschylus' source.[9] They ignore

[1] *Musée Belge* 30 (1926) 124 ff.

[2] Cf. Wecklein, ed. *Supp.* 8: Preller–Robert 265; Vürtheim (56 f.) recognizes that both were treated in the Κατάλογος, but questions whether they were joined.

[3] *I.G.* xiv. 1292. fr. II l. 10.

[4] *Interpr.* 18; cf. Vürtheim 55 f. and 58. Meyer held (*Forschungen* 93 n. 2) that the Αἰγίμιος was a fairly late epic.

[5] P. 19: for the Δαναΐδες cf. Meyer 82 (also 88 n. 1); Wecklein, *Studien* 410 f.; Vürtheim 121 f.; P. Mazon, *Eschyle* (Budé 6th ed. Paris 1953) I. 5. Astour (81 n. 8) puts it not after the seventh century.

[6] P. 267 n. 3.

[7] Fr. 187 Rz. (4 K). Cf. Wolff, *Columbia Diss.* 31.

[8] Cf. Meyer 69.

[9] E.g. Meyer 69; Wecklein (Ζωμαρίδης), *Aeschylus* II (Athens 1896) 308; Friedländer 12; Bernhard in Roscher's *Lexicon* I. 951; Wilamowitz 16 and 24; Weir Smyth 49; *GGL* I. 2. 194; Carcopino 281; Mazon 5; Wolff, *Columbia Diss.* 22; Astour 81 f. Focke (186) is more cautious: cf. also Bethe in *R.-E.* iv. B. 2092 for a sceptical view.

the fact that the one significant fragment of the Δαναΐδες that we have is inconsistent with the version of the *Supplices*. The fragment (fr. 1 K)[1] runs as follows:

> καὶ τότ' ἄρ' ὡπλίζοντο θοῶς Δαναοῖο θύγατρες
> πρόσθεν ἐϋρρεῖος ποταμοῦ Νείλοιο ἄνακτος.

This is clearly a reference to a battle fought by the Danaids in Egypt, and of such a battle there is in the *Supplices* not a trace.[2] Meyer indeed understood the fragment as a description of the Danaids' preparations for departure from Egypt (ὡπλίζοντο).[3] But such an interpretation is ruled out by the context in Clement, which clearly refers to war.[4] It is even possible that the Δαναΐδες followed the version in which the murder also took place in Egypt.[5]

It seems then that Aeschylus must have used more than one source, adapting them possibly to suit his own dramatic purpose. Prose writers too would provide him with material. Hecataeus, for example, also reports on the beer-drinking habits of the Egyptians,[6] but he differs from Aeschylus in his definition of the Pelasgoi.[7] He does not bring Aegyptus in person to Argos.[8] We are told that[9] Λυγκεὺς πολεμήσας τῷ Δαναῷ βασιλεῖ τοῦτον ἐφόνευσε καὶ ἔλαβε τὴν βασιλείαν καὶ τὴν θυγατέρα αὐτοῦ, καθὼς ὁ Ἀρχίλοχος ὁ σοφώτατος συνεγράψατο. Pindar, telling of the athletic-contest by which Danaus arranged the second marriage of his daughters, relates[10] that only forty-eight of them were disposed of in this way, so he presumably knows of the different fates of Hypermestra and Amymone. Hyper-

[1] We owe it to Clement of Alexandria, *Strom.* iv. 19.

[2] For the different view of Wilamowitz cf. p. 220 below. He envisaged a battle in which the Danaids were defeated. That the present fragment refers to a victory seems to be indicated by the context in Clement.

[3] P. 82 n. 3.

[4] Cf. Wecklein, ed. *Supp.* 2; Vürtheim 13.

[5] Cf. Bonner 132; Astour 81 n. 8. But Astour goes beyond the evidence in his statement that the version at Σ *Il.* Α 42 (cf. p. 164 above) apparently derives from this epic poem, and 'must therefore be considered older and more original than the genealogical catalogues which followed the epics'.

[6] Cf. *Supp.* 761 and 953 with Hecataeus, Jacoby, *F. Gr. Hist.* I. F. 323 (pp. 41–2): cf. Wecklein, ed. 10.

[7] Fr. 119; cf. Kranz 295.

[8] Σ *Or.* 872 (=*F. Gr. Hist.* I. F. 19).

[9] Malalas, *Chronogr.* iv. 68 (fr. 150). Bergk suggested that another name, perhaps Ἀρχέμαχος, lies hidden in Ἀρχίλοχος.

[10] *Pyth.* ix. 112 (195).

mestra's behaviour is indeed mentioned by him elsewhere.[1] Ps.-Apollodorus, who also records the athletic-contest, tells first of the purification of the Danaids by Athena and Hermes, and, though this element is not found in Pindar, it does not prove that he did not know of it, since he is quite capable of seeking to whitewash the Danaids by selecting only what suits his purpose.[2] Kraus says[3] that for his knowledge of the Amymone story Pindar must be dependent upon Aeschylus, as she and Hypermestra are unlikely to have been connected in epic. But since the Ninth *Pythian*, composed in 478 (or 474), is now known to be earlier than the Danaid trilogy of Aeschylus, this is clearly not so. There is no reason why Amymone and Hypermestra should not have been joined in Argive tradition before the composition of the Δαναΐδες. It is interesting that the Ninth *Pythian* was composed for a Cyrenian.[4] At any rate the suggestion of von Fritz[5] that Aeschylus may have invented the plot of the 'Αμυμώνη seems ruled out by the late dating of the play. Before Aeschylus Phrynichus had written a Δαναΐδες and an Αἰγύπτιοι, of which we know only that he brought Aegyptus in person to Argos with his sons.[6]

The only conclusion possible is that other authors, whether early or late, offer very slight evidence for the reconstruction of Aeschylus' trilogy. What then of Aeschylus' own treatment of the story in the *Prometheus* 853 ff.? There we are told of the flight of the Danaids from Egypt to Argos to avoid a marriage with their cousins, of the murder of forty-nine of the husbands, of the sparing of one by his wife,[7] and of the founding of the Argive royal line as a result of this marriage. This is clearly a more reliable source for the Danaid trilogy than any account of the story in another

[1] *Nem.* x. 6 (10).

[2] Cf. Pindar's treatment of the Tantalus story at *Ol.* i. 36 (56) ff. Cf. also von Fritz, *Philol.* 91. 131.

[3] P. 172; cf. von Fritz 131 n. 3. (the suggestion is omitted from *Antike und moderne Tragödie* 479 n. 8).

[4] Cf. Wilamowitz 24. See p. 178 above.

[5] P. 269.

[6] Σ *Or.* 872.

[7] Μίαν δὲ παίδων ἵμερος θέλξει τὸ μὴ
κτεῖναι σύνευνον, ἀλλ' ἀπαμβλυνθήσεται
γνώμην· δυοῖν δὲ θάτερον βουλήσεται,
κλύειν ἄναλκις μᾶλλον ἢ μιαιφόνος.

author. Yet even here we must admit that Aeschylus may have altered details to suit the different purposes of the two trilogies.[1] Thus the wanderings of Io are recounted in much greater detail in the *Prometheus* than in the *Supplices*. In the latter it is at Argos that Zeus commits adultery with Io, while in the *Prometheus* this does not take place until Io's wanderings have been completed in Egypt.[2] In the *Prometheus* the father of Io is given as Inachus (663 and 705), while in the *Supplices* Inachus appears only as a river, and Io, the priestess of Hera (291), apparently has no connection with the royal family. Nathansky points out[3] that Sophocles gave inconsistent portrayals of Odysseus' character in the *Ajax* and the *Philoctetes*, while the same is true of Menelaus' wife in Euripides' *Orestes* and his *Helen*, and of Creon in the *O.T.* and the *O.C.*

The *Supplices* itself contains hints of coming events, and where these are clear they are invaluable for the reconstruction of the lost plays.[4] Thus at the very end of the play the anxious note of foreboding with which the Chorus withdraws into the city has been taken by almost all critics as a hint that the Danaids will indeed be forced to marry their cousins,[5] while it seems from 1061 (τὰ θεῶν μηδὲν ἀγάζειν), that the Danaids are in danger of offending against the gods. From many passages[6] it is certain that the fate of the city of Argos will be of some concern in following plays, and in particular that, by offering refuge to the Suppliants, it must inevitably find itself involved in war. Pelasgus' words at 442 are perfectly clear: ἄνευ δὲ λύπης

[1] Cf. C. del Grande, *Hybris* (Naples 1947) 94.

[2] Cf. 608, 645 ff., 738–40, 834 f., 848–51, 898.

[3] *Wien. Stud.* 32. 16–17.

[4] Cf. esp. F. Stoessl, *Die Trilogie des Aischylos* (Baden bei Wien 1937) 84 f. and 108 f.; R. P. Winnington-Ingram, *J.H.S.* 81 (1961) 141.

[5] 1050–1 (μετὰ πολλῶν δὲ γάμων ἅδε τελευτὰ προτερᾶν πέλοι γυναικῶν) is better understood thus than with Haupt as a reference to the coming murder (he compares the murder of their husbands by the women of Lemnos). As Tucker says (*The 'Supplices' of Aeschylus* (London and New York 1889) *ad loc.*), it is unlikely that the Danaids have already contemplated the murder. If the lines are spoken by the handmaids Haupt's interpretation is out of the question.

[6] 342, 356–8, 377, 400–1, 439, *442*, 449, 454, 474 ff., 612, 740, 746–7, 934 ff., *950*, 1044. Winnington-Ingram suggests (145) that 955 f. look forward to a siege of Argos following the defeat by the sons of Aegyptus. He rightly stresses the importance of the fate of Argos for the trilogy.

οὐδαμοῦ καταστροφή. Stoessl finds significant the opposition between Egyptian and Argive gods at 921–2 and believes that this opposition must be reconciled at the end of the third play. But this depends upon his interpretation of the meaning of the trilogy, and does not follow necessarily from the passage in the *Supplices*. Wilamowitz[1] makes much of the fact that at 605 ff. Danaus and his daughters are awarded the status only of metics, not of full citizens, and Stoessl suggests that this may have been of importance in the third play. But it is doubtful if any significance can be attached to this. At least neither Danaus nor his daughters make any complaint about their new status. It is the same as that accorded to the Furies at the end of the *Eumenides* (1011 and 1018). At 957 ff. Pelasgus offers the Danaids a choice of dwelling: they can live either in the royal palace or in a state residence. It is curious that this detail, with the additional information that the rooms will be rent-free, should be repeated at 1009 ff. Perhaps P. Richter is right,[2] and the matter is no more than a device to bring Danaus back on the scene. Birt said[3] that in the second play Danaus and his daughters must get the town lodging, and the sons of Aegyptus Pelasgus' palace, as befitted the victors in the war: but there seems to be no reason why the subject should be introduced here at all. Aeschylus may be preparing the most suitable conditions for the murder,[4] but it is difficult to see how the choice of residence would make much difference, or again why it is so important as to be mentioned at all; unless Winnington-Ingram is right in his suggestion[5] that Zeus Xenios presides over the second play, as Zeus Hikesios does over the *Supplices*. If Danaus becomes king and the murder is committed in the royal apartments, then it is an offence against Zeus Xenios, resulting in pollution for Danaus and his daughters and for the city of Argos too. Other lines too have been selected by commentators as indications of coming events, and some of these will be noticed later. But usually they are too slight to offer anything approaching proof, and can be

[1] *Hermes* 22 (1887) 256 ff. (= *Kl. Schr.* v. 1. 339 ff.): cf. Focke 170.

[2] *Zur Dramaturgie des Aeschylus* (1892) 119–20: cf. Weir Smyth 59–60.

[3] *Rh. Mus.* 32. 425–6.

[4] Wilamowitz, *Interpr.* 21.

[5] P. 146. Cf. also p. 202 n. 2 below.

twisted to fit in with a multitude of preconceptions. The danger of the method can be well seen in the *Agamemnon*, where, if the other plays had been lost, we might conclude from 675 that Menelaus must return in the second or the third play, from 1410 that Clytaemestra is due to be banished, and from 1603 that the entire family of Agamemnon is to be wiped out.

The following sections will attempt to examine some of the principal theories that have been developed concerning the reconstruction of the trilogy. It should be clear from our discussion of the sources available to scholars that all such theories are highly speculative, and that while some are obviously more plausible than others, actual proof can never be attained. As Nathansky says,[1] 'Nur muß man sich hüten, ein Spiel mit Möglichkeiten für eine Ergründung von Tatsachen zu halten, einen selbständig auf Grund dürftiger Fingerzeige entworfenen Dramenplan für den Plan des Aischylos oder Sophokles zu erklären'. The discovery of the hypothesis of the *Septem* in 1848 showed how wrong the theories of scholars can be.[2]

II

Since we have only one complete trilogy from the whole of Greek tragedy, we should be suspicious of all theories which are based on the supposed principles or rules on which Aeschylus constructed his trilogies. Schlegel,[3] for example, saw in the three plays of the trilogy the thesis, antithesis, and synthesis of a tragic situation. O. F. Gruppe said[4] that the natural development of an Aeschylean trilogy is through the preparation and motive in the first play, the deed in the second, and the judgement and reconciliation in the third. J. H. T. Schmidt[5] was apparently so familiar with Aeschylus' practice as to be able to

[1] P. 9. For similar warnings cf. Wilamowitz, *Hermes* 22 (1887) 258 (= *Kl. Schr.* v. 1. 341); K. G. A. Alberti, *De Aesch. Choro Supp.* (Diss. Inaug. Berlin 1841) 19.

[2] Welcker, for example (*Tril.* 354 ff.), postulated a trilogy consisting of *Nemea Septem, Phoenissae*. In 1832 he substituted the *Eleusinioi* for the third play.

[3] *Vorlesungen* I. 139.

[4] *Ariadne* (Berlin 1834) 74.

[5] *De Aesch. Supp.* (Augustae Vindelicorum 1839) 5. G. Norwood, *Greek tragedy* (4th ed. London 1948) 108, asserts, 'The second play of a trilogy was usually more statuesque than the other two'.

write, 'Accedit, quod Aeschylus, qui in trilogiis ternas fabulas ita coniungere consueverat, ut alia ex alia nexa et omnes inter se aptae colligataeque essent, in extrema quavis antecedenti, quae in ea, quae proxime succederet, agerentur, certis quibusdam indiciis significavit'. Stoessl goes even further. Having reconstructed the second play of the Danaid trilogy on the principle that every scene and event in the *Supplices* must have its counterpart in the next play (the Herald scene, for example, in the former corresponds to an appearance in the latter of Aphrodite, foretelling the defeat of the Argives and advising the Danaids to marry their cousins), he concludes that, the mood of the first two plays being diametrically opposed at their beginning and end and identical in the middle, he has discovered a law of composition for the Aeschylean trilogy; one which, he says, is supported by the *Oresteia*. The first two plays are formally bound and symmetrical, the third freer. It has a twofold construction, in that it both reconciles the insoluble contradictions of the preceding plays, and soothes the excitement of the spectator. But the hypothetical reconstruction of a lost play and the existence of a single extant trilogy are hardly enough to support so elaborate a theory, particularly when the theory is itself derived from the principle.[1] It is indeed tempting to use the *Oresteia*, the only example of a trilogy available to us, as a model for the reconstruction of the Danaid trilogy. And the temptation is increased by the appearance in some of the later accounts of a trial of either Danaus or Hypermestra. Yet there is no intrinsic reason why, because Aeschylus ended one trilogy with a trial-scene, he should have done so in another, or why, if he did, he should have treated it in the same way on both occasions. Nor can it be assumed that all of Aeschylus' trilogies ended with a reconciliation, that they had a 'happy' ending.[2] Can we even take it for granted that the three plays were always as closely bound together as in the *Oresteia*? Is it not possible that the three

[1] Cf. A. Lesky, *Die tragische Dichtung der Hellenen* (2nd ed. Göttingen 1964) 69 n. 1; M. Untersteiner, *Origini della tragedia e del tragico* (1955) 375 n. 2.

[2] The Theban Trilogy did not. C. J. Herington argues, *TAPhA* 94 (1963) 113 ff., that it was towards the end of his life that Aeschylus swung from fear or resignation to hope.

plays of a trilogy might sometimes deal with three only loosely connected aspects of a story, in much the same way that the satyr-play is believed to have been often joined to the trilogy? It is certainly surprising that Aeschylus should have devoted a whole play to the arrival of the Danaids in Argos and their reception there.[1] We cannot therefore rule out entirely the possibility that Aeschylus may have assumed in his audience a background of knowledge of the story, and dealt in his trilogy only with certain aspects of it. For the purposes of discussion, however, it may be assumed that the major events were handled.

Schlegel believed that the *Supplices* was the second play of its trilogy, and his view was upheld by Conz, Haupt, C. O. Müller, Paley and at first by Welcker, though he later changed his mind.[2] According to Müller this order is established by the lack of dramatic interest in the *Supplices*, though we may question both the supposed lack and the conclusion that he drew from it. Nathansky used the same argument to prove that the play came first.[3] But the principal reason for putting the *Supplices* second is the need that these writers felt for some account of the fore-history in Egypt, and in particular of the quarrel between Danaus and Aegyptus. Most scholars have, however, accepted the convincing arguments put forward first by Gruppe[4] and A. Tittler.[5] These are twofold: first the *Supplices* does indeed provide adequate preparation for the trilogy. The situation is made abundantly clear in the Parodos and in the stichomythia between the King and the Danaids. It is true that nothing is said of any quarrel between Aegyptus and Danaus, but this would be all the more surprising if it had formed the plot of the

[1] Cf. p. 168 above: M. Croiset suggested that the theme was chosen as dealing with one of the great events of Argive national history. The central point of the drama, he said, is the establishment of Danaus at Argos. If this is true of the trilogy as a whole, it certainly does not emerge from the *Supplices*, in which the reception of Danaus plays a very minor part compared with that of his daughters.

[2] Schlegel, *Vorlesungen* I. 158; Conz, ed. Aesch. (Tübingen 1820) xi; Haupt, ed. *Supp.* (Leipzig 1829) 109 ff.; Müller, *Gesch. d. gr. Lit.* (Stuttgart 1882) I. 542 ff.; Paley, ed. Aesch. (4th ed. London 1879) 3; Welcker, *Tril.* 390 ff. (for his change of mind cf. *Kl. Schr.* IV. 100 ff.).

[3] Pp. 14–15.

[4] Pp. 72 ff.

[5] *Zeits. f. d. Altertumsw.* 118 (1838) 951 ff.: cf. also Croiset 48.

preceding play.[1] And secondly at the end of the *Supplices* we are still in the early stages of the action. It is impossible to see how the situation could be resolved in a single following play. Equally difficult and unnecessary is the suggestion of J. H. T. Schmidt[2] that the present trilogy was preceded by another embracing the events in Egypt, the last play of which was the Αἰγύπτιοι. If the audience was required to have certain background knowledge not given in the first play of the Danaid trilogy, there were other sources for it than a previous trilogy of Aeschylus. He did not invent the myth. The position of the *Supplices* as first play has now been so universally accepted that discussion would hardly have been necessary had the question not been recently raised by C. del Grande,[3] who wishes to put the Αἰγύπτιοι first. But he rests his argument solely on his conception of the ὕβρις of the sons of Aegyptus and of the Danaids, which, he says, must be exemplified in successive plays. But this is only speculation, and he does not attempt to answer the arguments that put the *Supplices* first. At one time Hermann thought[4] that the Δαναΐδες might follow the *Supplices* in a dilogy, but he later abandoned this idea himself. H. Hirt[5] was the first to see that the Ἀμυμώνη was a satyr-play, and its place in the Danaid trilogy has now been confirmed by *Ox. Pap.* 2256 no. 3.

The same papyrus fragment proves that the Δαναΐδες is either the name of the third play of the trilogy, or possibly a title for the trilogy as a whole. Some of the earlier commentators, on the strength of a passage in Strabo[6] quoting from the Ἱκετίδες ἢ Δαναΐδες, held that these two titles referred to the same play.[7] Wecklein, however, observed[8] that both titles appear separately

[1] Cf. p. 171 above.
[2] *Op. cit.*
[3] *Hybris* 90 ff.
[4] *Opusc.* II. 306 ff.
[5] In Böttiger's *Amalthea* II (Leipzig 1822) 280.
[6] V. 221.
[7] The theory is usually attributed to Stanley, but it was anticipated apparently by Casaubon in a MS note in the margin of Petrus Victorius' edition (1557), now in the Cambridge University Library. Cf. also Hartung, ed. Aesch. (Leipzig 1854) 54 ff. Pauw, ed. Aesch. (1745) 1097, took the title to be an error in the Catalogue for Δανάη, to which he ascribed frs. 125. 20–26 M (44 N²) and 126 M (45 N²), fr. 124 M (43 N²) being from a different Aeschylus; cf. p. 232 below.
[8] Wecklein, *Studien* 412.

in the Catalogue of Aeschylus' plays. Most probably Strabo is quoting from memory and is uncertain from which member of the trilogy he is quoting.[1] It is interesting that Erasmus suffers from a similar confusion, when he states that Aeschylus calls the Egyptians κυνοθρασεῖς in the Δαναΐδες, whereas he must be referring to *Supp.* 758.[2] We have still to determine whether the Δαναΐδες is the title of the third play or whether it is the name of the whole trilogy, or indeed whether it does duty for both. Birt[3] held that it was an alternative title for all three plays, which, he said, were the Ἱκετίδες, the Θαλαμοποιοί, and the Αἰγύπτιοι. Wilamowitz conjectured[4] that Aeschylus gave only a single name to the trilogy, and that the individual titles were added by later grammarians. This might account for the strangeness of calling one play the Ἱκετίδες and another the Δαναΐδες, when the Suppliants are in fact the Danaids. The main objection to this theory is that, so far as we can tell, all the titles that appear in the Catalogue are of separate plays so that there would be no place for the Δαναΐδες.[5] The title may indeed have been applied to the whole trilogy, but it must have been also the name of one of the individual plays. And that it was the third play seems to be now proved by the papyrus fragment. Thus Stoessl's attempt[6] to take it as the second play is shown to be a failure.

Much more difficult is the title of the second play. Hermann argued[7] that it was the Θαλαμοποιοί, named after the chorus which took over after the sons of Aegyptus had been murdered. Welcker held[8] that both titles referred to the same play, and that the sons of Aegyptus were themselves the Θαλαμοποιοί, or

[1] Cf. chap. 1 p. 14 above.
[2] Quoted by Stanley in a MS note to his edition of 1663.
[3] *Op. cit.*
[4] Ed. Aesch. (Berlin 1914) 379: cf. also M. Pohlenz, *Die gr. Tragödie* (2nd ed. Göttingen 1954) 51 and *Erläuterungen* 22; Mazon 10 n. 1. Schmid, *GGL* I. 2. 194 n. 5, cites fr. 126 M (45 N²) (καθαίρομαι γῆρας) which is quoted from the Δαναΐδες (cf. p. 232 below), and which, he argued, would fit the second play, where the suitors draw Pelasgus into battle. But this is far too doubtful to be adduced as evidence, and the parallels drawn from E. *Heracl.* 796 and 851 do not prove anything.
[5] Cf. Wecklein, *Studien* 412.
[6] *Op. cit.*
[7] Ed. Aesch. (Leipzig 1852) I. 329 ff. (also *Opusc.* VIII. 180 ff.).
[8] *Kl. Schr.* IV. 128 ff.

rather that they directed the work. Wecklein agreed[1] that the play had two titles, but held that the Θαλαμοποιοί are the actual builders, and that when they depart to begin their work, their place is taken perhaps by the sons of Aegyptus. Kruse, Weil, and Oberdick,[2] in their editions, and Nathansky[3] take the chorus to be the Danaids themselves, as supervisors of the work. Hartung called the play Θαλαμηπόλοι, and assigned the chorus to the fifty maids of the *Supplices*.[4] Miss Wolff suggests[5] that the Θαλαμοποιοί was an alternative title, used with an ironical double meaning with reference to the Danaids.

What then of the Αἰγύπτιοι, which has been taken by most other scholars as the title of the second play? It is doubtful if it can be banished altogether. Hermann was forced to explain away the quotation from the Αἰγύπτιοι that appears in the *Etymologicum Gudianum* (p. 578. 10), and in slightly different form in *Cod. Baroc.* 50, Ἐκλογαὶ διαφορῶν λέξεων.[6] The former reads as follows: Ζαγρεύς· ὁ μεγάλως ἀγρεύων, ὡς 'πότνια Γῆ, Ζαγρεῦ τε θεῶν πανυπέρτατε πάντων' ὁ τὴν Ἀλκμαιονίδα γράψας ἔφη. τινὲς δὲ τὸν Ζαγρέα υἱὸν Ἅιδου φασίν, ὡς Αἰσχύλος ἐν Σισύφῳ 'Ζαγρεῖ τε νῦν μοι καὶ πολυξένῳ χαίρειν.' ἐν δὲ Αἰγυπτίοις οὕτως αὐτὸν τὸν Πλούτωνα καλεῖ 'τὸν ἀγραῖον, τὸν πολυξενώτατον, τὸν Δία τῶν κεκμηκότων.'[7] The similarity between this and *Supplices* 155 ff. is obvious, and it is natural to suppose that there is again a confusion between the two titles of a trilogy. If this is so, the Αἰγύπτιοι is most probably the second play.[8] Hermann, however, held that the *Et. Gud.* confused two entirely separate extracts, and wished to read: ἐν δὲ Αἰγυπτίοις οὕτως αὐτὸν τὸν Πλούτωνα καλεῖ· ἐν δὲ Ἱκετίσι τὸν Δία, τὸν γάϊον, τὸν πολυξενώτατον Ζῆνα τῶν κεκμηκότων.[9]

[1] Ed. 16 ff., and *Studien* 419 ff.

[2] J. Oberdick, *Die Schutzflehenden des Aeschylus* (Berlin 1869).

[3] P. 23.

[4] Ed. 55 ff.

[5] *Columbia Diss.* 39 ff.

[6] Quoted in Cramer's *Anecd. Oxon.* II (1835) 443.

[7] The text is that of E. A. de Stefani (Leipzig 1909). ἐν Σισύφῳ is the correction of Fiorillo for the ἐν σκύφῳ of dI. Αἰγυπτίοις is the reading of the Ἐκλογαί. dI in *Et. Gud.* has ἐν Αἰγύπτῳ, a title of which there is no trace elsewhere.

[8] Cf. Wilamowitz, *Interpr.* 19 and ed. 379; Pohlenz, *Erl.* 22. For Welcker (*Kl. Schr.* IV. 101) the Αἰγύπτιοι here is perhaps not a dramatic title but the name of the trilogy as a whole.

[9] Cf. also Wecklein (Ζωμαρίδης) II. 582.

Hermann pointed out, not unfairly, that if the Αἰγύπτιοι is a mistake for the Ἱκετίδες the name Ζαγρεύς must have stood in the text of the latter play. Thus at 156 F. W. Schneidewin read[1] τὸν ζάγριον for the τὸνταιον of M, while de Stefani suspects that ἀγραῖον in *Et. Gud.* may be a corruption of Ζαγρέα.[2] Certainly Schneidewin was justified in observing that γάϊος is always used with the meaning 'auf dem Lande', and that it is nowhere equivalent to κατάγεως, as χθόνιος is regularly to καταχθόνιος.[3] If then the *Et. Gud.* is really quoting from the *Supplices*, it would seem that τὸν γάϊον[4] can hardly be the correct reading there. The alternative is to accept Hermann's emendation of the *Et. Gud.* Birt held[5] that Aeschylus repeated virtually the same words in both plays, and Miss Wolff agrees[6] on the grounds that the differences do not look like mechanical errors in copying. But since the text of the *Supplices* is in any case corrupt, and the similarities are very much more striking than the differences, their arguments would prove convincing only if they could show parallels for such repetition in Aeschylus.

Hermann also objected to the Αἰγύπτιοι as title that if the sons of Aegyptus formed the Chorus, the play ought to be called the Αἰγυπτιάδαι.[7] To this Welcker rejoined[8] that the sons of Aegyptus were also Egyptian, while Kraus remarks[9] that Aeschylus seems to avoid the use of Αἴγυπτος for the country. He compares also the use of Δανααί instead of Δαναΐδες by Hesiod (fr. 24 Rz). The chief reason, however, for retaining the Αἰγύπτιοι as the second member of the Danaid trilogy is that its existence as a play is attested by the Catalogue of Aeschylus' plays as well as by the passage in the *Et. Gud.*, and that its

[1] *Rh. Mus.* 4 (1836) 230 f.; also *Philol.* 3 (1848) 369–71.

[2] In l. 2 d¹ omits the Z of Ζαγρεῦ, and it is supplied by d².

[3] Cf. Welcker, *Kl. Schr.* IV. 133; Tucker, ed. *Supp.* on 133 (156); also J. A. Schuursma, *De poetica vocabulorum abusione apud Aeschylum* (Amsterdam 1932) 72 f.

[4] The generally accepted emendation of Wellauer.

[5] P. 424 n. 4: cf. O. Hiltbrunner, *Wiederholungs- und Motivtechnik bei Aischylos* (Berne 1950) 33.

[6] *Eranos* 56 (1958) 123 f.; also *Columbia Diss.* 43 ff.

[7] Ed. I. 332 (also *Opusc.* VIII. 182 f.).

[8] *Kl. Schr.* IV. 111; cf. also Wecklein, ed. 17, and *Studien* 422; Wolff, *Columbia Diss.* 42. Hermann's point was made also by G. W. Nitzsch, *Sagenpoesie* (Brunswick 1852) 563, and by Birt 419.

[9] P. 167 n. 36.

appropriateness in connection with the *Supplices* is unquestioned. Welcker wrote,[1] 'Daß die Aegypter nicht zu den beiden andern Stücken gehört haben könnten, darf wenigstens Niemand aussprechen ohne einen andern Mythus anzuführen, worin Aegypter auf die Bühne gebracht werden konnten, die wir hier gelandet in Argos, in einem der berühmtesten Mythen, den auch Phrynichos schon aufgeführt hatte, vor uns haben'. Perhaps in the uncertainty of our knowledge Welcker exaggerates the responsibility of the critic to find another suitable place for the Αἰγύπτιοι, but it is certainly true that those who uphold the claims of the Θαλαμοποιοί must show very good reason why that title is in place only here.

Their case gains little support from its non-appearance in the Catalogue. If A. Dieterich was right,[2] this Catalogue originally had a fifth column, containing those plays which we know to be Aeschylean, but which do not appear in the list as it has come down to us; and in this fifth column Dieterich could find no place for the Θαλαμοποιοί. Consequently he agreed with Welcker that it must be the same play as the Αἰγύπτιοι. But is it necessary to trouble ourselves with it at all? It is cited only once, and that by Pollux (vii. 122), who, as Wilamowitz remarks,[3] very often makes mistakes with poet's names. Thus the very existence of an Aeschylean play with this title is dubious. And even if it does exist, is it at home in the Danaid trilogy? Hermann himself admitted that the Θαλαμοποιοί could be the first play of a Δανάη trilogy, or that it could be joined with the Ἰξίων and Περραιβίδες. What exactly was the function of the Θαλαμοποιοί? Pollux suggests, τάχα δὲ καὶ οἱ θαλαμοποιοὶ εἶδος τέχνης, which, as Wecklein pointed out,[4] does not support the theory that they were either the Danaids or

[1] *Kl. Schr.* IV. 101.

[2] *Rh. Mus.* 48 (1893) 141 ff. (= *Kl. Schr.* III ff.). Cf. earlier Th. Bergk, *Gr. Literaturgeschichte* III (Berlin 1884) 284 n. 34. Wilamowitz, ed. 8, and more recently W. Steffen, *Studia Aeschylea* (Archiwum Filologiczne 1. Wrocław 1958) 9 ff., raised pertinent objections to Dieterich's theory.

[3] *Interpr.* 19 n. 2.

[4] *Studien* 419. Nathansky, 23, seized on τάχα to prove that Pollux was himself in doubt, but it is on Pollux that the case itself rests for the Θαλαμοποιοί; cf. J. Lammers, *Die Doppel- und Halbchöre in der antiken Tragödie* (Paderborn 1931) 41 n. 3.

their cousins engaged in supervising the building of their marriage-chambers. Whoever the Θαλαμοποιοί were, they must presumably at some stage have disappeared to carry out their duties, and this means that we have to postulate a second chorus. Thus Hermann said that the Θαλαμοποιοί took over as Chorus after the murder, though why they should appear at all only after the demand for their services has expired it is difficult to understand. Wecklein[1] took it the other way round. It is the sons of Aegyptus who appear at the end, when the servants have departed to begin their work. We might object to this that the construction of fifty marriage-chambers is a major operation, and hardly to be completed in the short space of an Aeschylean exodos,[2] but perhaps we should not make too much of the so-called Unity of Time.[3] Much more serious is the objection that nowhere in the whole of extant Greek tragedy does one chorus disappear to be replaced by another.[4] At *Eumenides* 231 the Chorus leaves the scene so that it can move to Athens, at *Ajax* 814 it does so to make room for Ajax' monologue. Other instances are Euripides' *Alcestis* 746 and *Helen* 385. But nowhere is there any evidence to support such a theory as we have been discussing.

It is not impossible that the Θαλαμοποιοί was the satyr-play of another tetralogy.[5] Other Aeschylean titles which imply some sort of activity are the Τροφοί, Δικτυουλκοί, Ἱκετίδες, Προπομποί, Τοξότιδες, Χοηφόροι, Κήρυκες, Ὀστολόγοι, Σεμέλη ἢ Ὑδροφόροι, and Ψυχαγωγοί, and of these the first, second, fifth, perhaps the eighth, and the ninth seem to have been satyr-plays, while of the Προπομποί practically nothing is known.

The whole question of the chorus of the Αἰγύπτιοι is of considerable importance, since many scholars have taken remarkable liberties with it in their reconstructions of the play. *A priori* a play with this title would have one chorus, consisting

[1] Wecklein, *Studien* 420 ff., ed. 17; cf. also Nathansky 23.

[2] For this reason there is some point to Hartung's Θαλαμηπόλοι. Unfortunately it is Θαλαμοποιοί that is transmitted.

[3] Cf. the *Agamemnon* where the Herald arrives so soon after the Beacon-speech.

[4] Cf. *GGL* I. 2. 71 n. 4.

[5] Cf. H. J. Mette, *Die Fragmente der Tragödien des Aischylos* (Berlin 1959) 259.

presumably of the sons of Aegyptus. It is true that the Ἑπτὰ ἐπὶ Θήβας has a plural title that does not refer to the chorus,[1] but this is the only certain example in the list of Aeschylus' plays,[2] so that as a parallel it should probably not be pressed too far. Moreover the 'Seven' could never form a tragic chorus, since they are so firmly individualized that an expansion of their number, as with the Furies of the *Eumenides*, is out of the question. The sons of Aegyptus, on the other hand, have no individual existence, and could very well form a chorus in correspondence with that of the *Supplices*.[3] Many theories[4] have, however, involved the use of a subsidiary chorus, and the likelihood of this must be examined. The use of such an extra chorus is perfectly well documented. It occurs in the *Eumenides* when the Προπομποί join in the final song as the procession leaves the Orchestra, and possibly also in the *Septem* at 1054 ff. A certain case is the *Hippolytus* of Euripides, where the Chorus of Huntsmen enter with Hippolytus even before the Parodos of the main Chorus. And the scholiast at line 58 reports that there were subsidiary choruses in Euripides' *Alexandrus* and *Antiope*.[5] Lammers argues[6] that 'Der lyrische Doppelchordialog, auch in seinem Extrem, der gesungenen Chorstichomythie, ist auf Grund der Analyse des Hiketidenstückes mit Sicherheit als eine (ob: die?) Urform, besser als ein Urbestandteil der Tragödie zu bezeichnen'.[7] Much of his case is thus based on the *Supplices*, where the

[1] Cf. Tittler 123 (1838) 991; Hermann, *Opusc.* III. 136; Kruse 15; Cunningham 230: in *Rh. Mus.* 105 (1962) 190 Miss Cunningham cites also the *Choe.*, where Electra 'is the only choephoros in the literal sense'.

[2] Schmid (*GGL* I. 2. 89 n. 8) cites also the Ἡρακλεῖδαι, Ἐπίγονοι, and Φορκίδες.

[3] See, for example, Gruppe, Welcker, Wilamowitz, von Fritz; A. Elisei, *Studi ital.* n.s. 6 (1928) 217 n. 1; H. D. F. Kitto, *Greek tragedy* (3rd ed. London 1961) 17; M. Gigante, *Parola del Passato* 11 (1956) 454; H. Lloyd-Jones (Loeb 2nd ed. 1957) II. 572.

[4] Cf. for example Welcker, *Kl. Schr.* IV. 114 ff.; Alberti, *op. cit.*; Kraus 168; Pohlenz, *Gr. Trag.* 51; Lesky, *Tr. Dichtung* 70, and *A history of Greek literature* (Eng. tr. London 1966) 252 f.; Winnington-Ingram 146.

[5] For a subsidiary chorus in the Φαέθων of Euripides cf. Wilamowitz, *Hermes* 18 (1883) 409 f. (=*Kl. Schr.* I. 123 f.); W. S. Barrett, *Euripides. Hippolytos* (Oxford 1964) 169: cf. also the discussion of the Gyges fragment by D. L. Page, *A new chapter in the history of Greek tragedy* (Cambridge 1951) 30 ff.

[6] Pp. 17 ff. Lammers finds many other examples, but none of his hypotheses can be proved. Cf. also Alberti, *op. cit.* See chap. III pp. 111 ff. above.

[7] P. 169.

Herald's men are said to form a chorus at 835 ff.,[1] and the Handmaidens another at 1034 ff. Gilbert Murray went further and in the Δράματος Πρόσωπα of his edition he gives a Chorus of Danaids with ἐξάρχων Danaus, a chorus of Argives with ἐξάρχων King Pelasgus, and a Chorus of Egyptians with ἐξάρχων the Herald; almost as if it had been so set down in the manuscript M. Thus there are no actors at all, only three choruses with their respective directors.[2] Miss Wolff carries the question over into the Αἰγύπτιοι,[3] by arguing that since there are four choruses in the *Supplices* (she includes the chorus of Handmaids), there were probably four also in the other plays of the trilogy. But the theories of Lammers and Murray are based upon the idea that the *Supplices* is the earliest extant play, and, as we know now that it is not, we can happily discount all attempts to find in it or to invent for the Αἰγύπτιοι a primitive treatment of the Chorus.

If then Aeschylus uses extra choruses in the *Supplices*, we have no reason to expect that they will be significantly different from those in the *Eumenides* and the *Hippolytus*, or indeed from those in the *Frogs* and *Wasps* of Aristophanes. The most notable characteristic of these is that they play only a small and unimportant part, and are present only for it. Nowhere are they used as a foil for or in opposition to the main chorus.[4] The supposed Chorus of Egyptians would thus follow the normal practice. On the other hand W. Nestle[5] and A. Peretti[6] point out the weakness of the evidence for such a chorus of Egyptians. M is no help, since it gives no indication of speaker. The arrival of a threatening person, accompanied by persons who remain

[1] Cf. P. Maas, *Greek metre* (Eng. tr. H. Lloyd-Jones, Oxford 1962) 54; Wilamowitz, *Hermes* 64 (1929) 461; Kranz 16; A. W. Pickard-Cambridge, *The theatre of Dionysus in Athens* (Oxford 1946) 31; Pohlenz, *Erl.* 20; D. W. Lucas, *The Greek tragic poets* (2nd ed. London 1959) 255 n. 27; Untersteiner *ad loc.*; Barrett 368.

[2] *The complete plays of Aeschylus* (London 1952) 7 ff.: *contra* del Grande, ΤΡΑΓΩΙΔΙΑ 345 f.

[3] *Eranos* 56. 127, and *Columbia Diss.* 50 f.

[4] Cf. Reisch in *R.-E.* v. 357 f.; *GGL* I. 2. 71 n. 5; Cunningham, *Rh. Mus.* 96. 231.

[5] *Deutsche Literaturzeitung* 52 (1931) 2269 ff.

[6] *Epirrema e tragedia* (Florence 1939) 83 ff.: also H. Lloyd-Jones, *L'Ant. Classique* 33 (1964) 366 ff.

silent, is a common motif in Aeschylus (cf. *Supp.* 234, 911, *Sept.* 181, *Ag.* 1577). And if Aeschylus had wanted to oppose another chorus to the Danaids, why did he not bring on the sons of Aegyptus themselves? It is doubtful too what significance can be attached to the corruption of the lyric verses of the Herald. Certainly one cannot prove that there was no chorus of Egyptians, but neither can one prove that there was: consequently its existence cannot be used as an argument to prove one somewhere else.

The Chorus of Handmaids is in a different case. It is said to take part in the last song of the play, in direct opposition to the Chorus of Danaids, reminding them of the claims of Aphrodite, and warning them that the future may not turn out as they hope.[1] Thus this subsidiary chorus is of a different character from any other known to us. Yet it seems to be well authenticated. There is an undoubted altercation in the last song, which would naturally imply the participation of others than the Danaids themselves. At 977 the maids are summoned to range themselves at the side of their mistresses, while at 1023 the command is given by the Chorus, ὑποδέξασθε ⟨δ'⟩ ὀπαδοὶ μέλος. Thus the Chorus of Handmaids has been assumed as a fact by nearly every critic.[2] Yet there are difficulties even here. First, the word ὑποδέχομαι, not found elsewhere in Aeschylus, never means 'receive in succession', in the sense of taking up a song. The word for this is διαδέχομαι.[3] The nearest parallel for ὑποδέχομαι seems to be Galen vi. 421, τὴν εἰς τὸ στόμα φορὰν τῶν περιττωμάτων ὑποδέχεται στόμαχος, which is not very close, and in any case late. Van der Graaf says that the word really means 'écouter avec bienveillance, accepter, croire', and compares Hesiod, *Theog.* 419 (ᾧ πρόφρων γε θεὰ ὑποδέξεται

[1] G. Méautis, *Eschyle et la trilogie* (Paris 1936) 64–6, commenting that it is this Chorus that expresses the profound thought of the poet, compares the Watchman in the *Agamemnon* and the Nurse in the *Choephori*.

[2] The theory of A. Boeckh, *Graecae tragoediae principum* (Heidelberg 1808) 60 ff., and others (cf. Croiset 65 n. 2) that the Maids formed part of the main Chorus was refuted by Alberti, *op. cit.* and by B. Todt, *Philol.* 48 (1889) 48 ff. If the maids took part in the last song, they must have been silent until then.

[3] Cf. H. Freericks, *De Aesch. Supp. choro* (Duderstadt 1883) 73 ff.; Tucker *ad loc.*; C. van der Graaf, *Mnem.* 3rd ser. 10 (1942) 283. For διαδέχομαι cf. Plat. *Rep.* 576b and *Laws* 900c; Hdt. viii. 142. 1.

εὐχάς), Hdt. viii. 106, and Lysias xxv. 11.[1] A problem is presented by the word ὀπαδοί. Can we be certain that the reference is to the maids? Certainly they are addressed at 977, but at 985 the word ὀπαδούς means Danaus' bodyguard, while at 492 ὀπάονας has a similar meaning.[2] More difficult is the question of 954, where M reads:

> ὑμεῖς δὲ πᾶσαι ξὺν φίλοις ὀπάοσιν
> θράσος λαβοῦσαι στείχετ' εὐερκῆ πόλιν

and most editors accept Schütz's emendation of φίλαις for φίλοις, to make it refer to the maids. The emendation is an easy one, and there is no difficulty about the feminine use of ὀπάων (cf. ὀπαδόν *O.C.* 1092, ὀπάων Hom. *Hym. Dem.* 440): moreover φίλοις is an odd epithet to find with ὀπάοσιν meaning soldiers. Yet the very necessity for emendation must weaken the case for the Handmaids. The MS text as it stands gives more point to θράσος λαβοῦσαι, the reason for taking courage being the presence of the bodyguard.[3] And there may even be an echo of 492 ff., where, as van der Graaf points out, the words ὀπάονες, στείχω, and θράσος also occur. The Chorus of Handmaids is rejected by Hermann, Bamberger, Paley, Freericks, Richter, Preller–Robert,[4] Süsskand,[5] van der Graaf, E. T. Owen,[6] and Cantarella, though not all their arguments are convincing. The supposed impertinence of the maids, for example, need hardly be taken seriously. And it is not easy to see why, if they do not take an active part, they should be summoned at all, or why half of the Danaid Chorus should suddenly come to recognize the claims of Aphrodite. Probably the question must remain open. However, the doubt is great enough to make it very dangerous to assume subsidiary choruses for the Αἰγύπτιοι, especially if they are supposed to play in it any significant part.

[1] Cf. also M. L. West (ed. *Theogony*, Oxford 1966) *ad. loc.* ('ὑποδέξεται: not merely "receives" but "accepts"').

[2] For the relationship in general of ὀπάων to ὀπαδός cf. G. Björck, *Das Alpha impurum und die tragische Kunstsprache* (Uppsala 1950) 109 f.

[3] Cf. Freericks 74.

[4] II. I. 269 n. I.

[5] *Philol. Wochenschr.* 40 (1920) 767 f.

[6] *The harmony of Aesch.* (Toronto 1952) 17.

Not everyone has accepted the conclusion that the sons of Aegyptus must be the chorus of the second play. Apart from those who make it the θαλαμοποιοί, Tittler supposed[1] a chorus of Argive elders, Reinkens[2] Danaus' bodyguard of young Argives. Some believe[3] that the Danaids are the chorus of all three plays, Kraus on the grounds that the chorus is itself the dramatic heroine, so that it is unlikely to resign its place for an entire play. Stoessl gives also a simpler reason: the Chorus does not require to change its costume. Nathansky says, 'Es wäre ja auch in höchstem Grade sonderbar, wenn in derselben Trilogie der Chor, der in dem ersten Stücke der Träger der Handlung war, in den folgenden oder auch nur in deren einem in die Rolle eines wohlwollenden Zuschauers gedrängt wurde'. The only piece of evidence for Nathansky's rule, the *Oresteia*, is also apparently in the highest degree exceptional; or rather, since the case is different, there is no evidence at all.

The principal objections to the sons of Aegyptus as Chorus are twofold. First they are considered morally unsuited to be the chorus of a Greek tragedy.[4] To this we may reply that nowhere else in extant tragedy is the chorus also the protagonist.[5] In any case our knowledge of their character is derived only from the biased account of their cousins, and from the admittedly unprepossessing behaviour of their representative, the Herald. We cannot be certain that in the Αἰγύπτιοι Aeschylus did not present a very different side of the picture. Perhaps, if we had the play, we might be agreeably surprised by finding that Aegyptus' sons were not so bad after all. The second difficulty is caused by the plot itself. Obviously if the murder is committed in the course of the play, the Chorus cannot have been the victims. But it is simpler to conclude that the murder takes place between the second and the third plays, and this is accepted by

[1] 123 (1838) 991 ff.

[2] P. 12.

[3] For example, Nathansky 23; Croiset 69; Stoessl 107; Kraus 168; Winnington-Ingram 146 n. 31 ('This trilogy will have been extraordinarily closely knit, if it had unity of chorus as well as approximate unity of time and place').

[4] Cf. esp. Tittler 992; Schmidt 416; Kruse 14–15; Oberdick 2; Wecklein, *Studien* 422; Birt 419; Nathansky 22.

[5] Kraus's argument (167 f.) that the satyr-element is still present in so old a play is now no longer valid.

most scholars. It is argued further[1] that the preparation of the murder plot would be impossible in the presence of a chorus composed of the victims. It would perhaps be difficult, but not impossible if effective use were made of hints and double meanings, perfectly clear to the audience, but meaningless to the sons of Aegyptus. The tragic chorus can be notoriously slow to understand.[2]

There can be little doubt that the second play deals with the events leading up to the murder, if it does not include the murder itself. And this involves the question of how the Danaids came to marry their cousins after their apparently successful plea for protection in the preceding play. According to Wilamowitz[3] the marriage could be the result of a compromise between Pelasgus and the sons of Aegyptus. By this the Danaids are to marry their cousins, but it is to be a real marriage, not one in which the husbands are in the position of κεκτημένοι (cf. *Supp.* 337). But this theory raises more problems than it solves. Kitto is right in saying[4] that the Danaids very clearly object to any marriage with their cousins, so there must be some compulsion before they accept it. Moreover it is far from certain that the sons of Aegyptus have any lawful claim at all (cf. pp. 217 ff. below), so the conduct of Pelasgus must seem shabby to say the least.[5] Finally the real ground of the murder is removed if a compromise has been approved.[6] Much more plausible is the view that there was war between the Egyptians and the Argives, and that the latter were defeated or at least reduced to accepting their opponents' terms. Kitto rightly demands[7] that we find a justification for the stratagem of Danaus, a ground for the Argives to look for a compromise without losing their honour, and no easy victory for the Egyptians. And this demand is satisfied by a war. This view is strongly supported by the hints

1 Cf. for example Tittler, *loc. cit.*; Wecklein, *Studien* 418, ed. 16; Nathansky 22.

2 Cf. for example the Cassandra scene in the *Agamemnon*.

3 *Interpr.* 20–1. Weil also held that Pelasgus probably made peace with the Egyptians. Focke (181 n. 3) agrees with Wilamowitz, and von Fritz (128) says that his view is tempting.

4 P. 18.

5 Cf. Kraus 166.

6 Cf. B. Snell, *Aischylos und das Handeln im Drama* (=*Philol.* Suppl. 20. 1 (1928)) 57; von Fritz, *loc. cit.*

7 2nd ed. (1950) 18.

that we have already seen in the *Supplices*.[1] Wilamowitz argued that a war is improbable if the sons of Aegyptus form the chorus, but it is perfectly possible that the war is fought between the two plays, and that it is only narrated in the Αἰγύπτιοι.[2] It was noted above[3] that there are strong hints in the *Supplices* that the fate of the city of Argos must be of some concern in the following play. It is the sufferings of a war that Pelasgus fears for Argos, a war that is inevitable if the Danaids are to be protected.

Pohlenz says,[4] 'Es ist die Tragödie der Polis, die wir miterleben'. And Kitto remarks[5] that the Argives are the tragic victims of a situation. The *Supplices* indeed (and the trilogy as a whole) is first and foremost the tragedy of the Danaids and their cousins, but the fate of Argos is inextricably bound up with the fate of the Suppliants, so that it is unlikely to be ignored in the second play. There it seems that the Danaids' prayer (625 ff.) will remain unanswered. Argos is represented in the *Supplices* by its king, Pelasgus, and the latter's emphasis at 365 ff. on his constitutional position indicates that Aeschylus is interested not so much in the inner conflict of the individual Pelasgus as in the situation in which Argos itself will be placed by its reception or rejection of the Danaids' plea. Nevertheless it is through Pelasgus that the situation of Argos is made clear in the first play, so we may expect that his fate will be dealt with in the second. Hermann indeed believed[6] that Pelasgus remained king throughout the whole action, and he rightly says that it would be most inept merely to announce a change of throne in a prologue, as Welcker suggested.[7] Welcker explained it[8] by the different characters of Pelasgus and Danaus. 'Jener ist ganz der Mann ein Reich zu verlieren, dieser eins zu erwerben; jener, ein Sohn oder Enkel der alten Mutter Erde, die biedre und fromme Einfalt Pelasgischer thatenloser Vorzeit, dieser, ein Abkömmling

[1] P. 181 above.

[2] Cf. Oberdick, *loc. cit.*; Wecklein, *Studien* 417; von Fritz 128.

[3] P. 181.

[4] *Gr. Trag.* 51.

[5] 2nd ed. 19. For A. Lesky (*J.H.S.* 86 (1966) 79), on the other hand, with Pelasgus' decision at 468 ff. 'the theme of a final decision by the people of Argos has lost much of its weight'. But cf. chap IV p. 154.

[6] *Opusc.* II. 322 ff.

[7] *Tril.* 394.

[8] *Kl. Schr.* IV. 105.

des Olympischen Zeus, den unternehmenden Heldengeist des Danaervolks auszudrücken.' Similar were the views of Droysen, and of Tittler and Kruse, who introduce the omen of the wolf and the bull as related by Pausanias.[1] Oberdick made Pelasgus see his duty and retire willingly from Argos.[2] Weil put the abdication at the end of the trilogy, and based it on the order of Aphrodite. None of these theories provides adequate motivation for the retirement of Pelasgus from the scene. It is not enough to say with Harsh[3] that the establishment of Danaus' line at Argos is, in a way, the subject of the whole tetralogy. This is in itself pure speculation, and fails to give satisfactory dramatic grounds for the change of throne. Welcker's contrast between the characters of Danaus and Pelasgus was convincingly refuted by Weil[4] and Wecklein.[5] Pelasgus' indecision springs only from his anxiety to spare his city the horrors of war. Once he has made up his mind there is nothing cowardly or indecisive about him. Thus either Hermann is right, and Pelasgus does remain king throughout all three plays, or some other method must be found for disposing of him. Preller–Robert[6] and Focke[7] point out that since in the *Supplices* Io is not a member of the royal family, Danaus can make no claim to the throne as a family-right. It seems unlikely too that the omen of the wolf and the bull, mentioned only by Pausanias, comes from Aeschylus' play. Thus the death of Pelasgus in battle is the most plausible solution, and has been accepted as such by the majority of scholars. Hermann's view cannot be disproved, but it is difficult to reconcile it with the other sources that make Danaus become king at Argos, with Megas' theory[8] that this was an original element in the myth, and with the necessity for Danaus to be in a position to organize the murder. Welcker pointed out[9] that the granting of a bodyguard to Danaus is the traditional first step in the acquisition of a Greek tyranny.

[1] Cf. p. 165 above.

[2] Cf. also Meyer, *Forschungen* 85 f.

[3] P.W. Harsh, *Handbook of classical drama* (California 1944) 42; cf. *GGL* 199f. and 202.

[4] Ed. vi.

[5] Ed. 18.

[6] II. I. 269.

[7] P. 170.

[8] P. 427.

[9] *Kl. Schr.* IV. 109: cf. also Wecklein, ed. 18; Winnington-Ingram 142 n. 9.

It may be that some light has been thrown upon this whole question by the publication of *Oxyrhynchus Papyri* 2251,[1] which is believed by M. L. Cunningham[2] to be a fragment of the Αἰγύπτιοι. The fragment reads as follows:

1 χειρ. [
ἰδὲ γὰρ ὦ Ζ[εῦ] ξέ[νιε] ν [.] . [
τ]ὸν ξενοδόκον κατασκ̣[
ἐ]στιν χάρις ἐν θ[εο]ῖς
5] . [.]σι τοῖς δικαίοις.
τοιγὰρ κ[. . .]π̣ρισσ̣ο̣μ[
κόμας [ἀ]φειδεῖ χε.[
τόδ' ἄνα[υ]λον βρέγμαπ[. .] . [
δυρομ[έν]α σὸν πότμον γό[οισ
κτλ.

2. ν[ῦν δόμον Snell: ν[ῦν κείμενον Webster (ap. Cunningham).
3. κατασκ̣ [αφέντα Snell: κατασ⟨φ⟩[αγέντ' ἀναξίως Cunningham (ἀναξίως post Webster); κατασκαπτόμενον Mette.
4. εἶ γ' ἐ]στὶν Snell: ἆρ' ἐ]στιν Page: ποῦ ']στιν Webster: οὐκ ἐ]στὶν Mette.
5. ἀνδρά]σι reiecit Lobel: ἐπ]ι̣δ̣[οῦ]σι Snell.
6. κ[ατα]πρίσσομ[αι (vel -μένα) Lobel.
7. χερ̣[ι Snell.
8. ⟨φεῦ⟩ τόδ' ἄνα[υλον βρέγμαπ[αχές μέλος Cunningham: τόδ' ἄνα[υ]λον βρέγμα π[ατά]σ̣[σω Snell.

Miss Cunningham says,[3]

The context of the fragment is fairly certainly a scene where the death of a ξενοδόκος conspicuous for his righteousness has just been announced. [For] the first intelligible couplet, ll. 2–3, calls upon Zeus, the god of hospitality, to look upon a man of hospitality. The next couplet contains some reference to the favour shown by the gods towards the just. Then follow four lines of wild lamentation, almost certainly a dirge, sung by a female chorus or soloist (cf. δυρομένα l. 9). These four lines are linked to the preceding passage by τοιγάρ which seems always to carry with it a strong causal force (see Denniston *Greek particles*, p. 565, 'τοιγάρ bears a strong logical force "therefore", "in consequence", even "that is why", never sinking to the rank of a mere progressive particle').

From this she deduces not implausibly that the ξενοδόκος is dead. Clearly this fragment would fit very well into the context of the Αἰγύπτιοι. If we could be certain of the attribution the

[1] Lobel vol. XX (1952).
[2] *Rh. Mus.* 96 (1953) 223 ff.; also *Rh. Mus.* 105 (1962) 189 f.
[3] Pp. 224 and 228.

implications would be important. First, the fate of Pelasgus would be definitely established, and secondly, the sons of Aegyptus would (unless the fragment is sung by an extra chorus of Argive women) be ruled out as the chorus of the play. This would be composed either of the Danaids or of women of Argos. Miss Cunningham favours the Danaids as main Chorus, with the sons of Aegyptus making a spectacular entrance towards the end of the play.[1] Miss Wolff,[2] believing that there were four choruses in the play, examines their possible permutations and combinations. Certainly more than one chorus would be necessary, if, as she holds, fr. 121 M (5 N²) is spoken by the sons of Aegyptus. But neither this nor its place in the play can be considered certain. The whole question of extra choruses, as we have seen, is very doubtful, and if fr. 2251 is from the Αἰγύπτιοι, it would be safe to conclude only that the chorus is a female one, though a brief appearance of a single subsidiary chorus is not impossible.

How certain is the attribution of the fragment? It would fit in well with the important place that we have assigned to the Argos motif.[3] And it is evident from *Ox. Pap.* 2256. 3 that the Danaid trilogy was indeed read at Oxyrhynchus. It is interesting that fr. 2250 mentions a βασιλεύς, and that it also uses the word βαθύπλουτος, which occurs elsewhere in Aeschylus only in the *Supplices* (554).[4] There are however difficulties. Miss Cunningham's emendation, necessary for her conjecture κατασ⟨φ⟩[α-γέντ' is hardly justifiable, even though she can quote a parallel for the reverse corruption.[5] The whole fragment is too uncertain for this. It is true that Lobel writes 'κ̣[, or perhaps β; neither normal', and the letter in the facsimile does not really look like either. But it looks even less like φ. It is a pity too that, owing to the loss of the end of the second line, we cannot determine

[1] Cf. also Winnington-Ingram 146; Webster in Pickard-Cambridge, *Dithyramb, tragedy, and comedy* (2nd ed. Oxford 1962) 61.

[2] *Eranos* 56 (1958) 127–8; *Columbia Diss.* 50 f.

[3] Cf. Cunningham 231.

[4] Snell, *Gnomon* 25 (1953) 436, suggests the Ἰσθμιασταί for this fragment.

[5] A. *Sept.* 46. In *Rh. Mus.* 105 Miss Cunningham argues that the reading κατασκαφέντα is still consonant with the ascription of the fragment to the Αἰγύπτιοι, δόμον κατασκ. being used metaphorically (cf. *Choe.* 50).

whether ξενοδόκον is adjective or noun. Lloyd-Jones remarks[1] that 'for all we know many hospitable persons may have suffered destruction in lost plays of Aeschylus', yet, as Miss Cunningham says, such themes are not particularly common in Greek tragedy, while 'the Aeschylean Catalogue does not suggest any obvious alternatives'. However, tempting as it is to accept the fragment for the Αἰγύπτιοι, the evidence is just not strong enough, and we are not entitled to draw conclusions from it.[2]

It seems then that most of the important questions concerning the Αἰγύπτιοι depend for their solution on the answers to other questions equally uncertain. Thus definite conclusions are impossible. Concerning the detailed treatment of the play it is even more difficult to speculate. How, for example, were the negotiations carried out? Welcker and Tittler[3] introduce Lynceus as the intermediary, Wecklein denies[4] that this is Aeschylean. How large was the part played by Danaus in the decision to murder the bridegrooms? According to Miss Elisei[5] Danaus is the instigator in every decision to be made, so that the Danaids are only obeying their father's orders when they murder their husbands. Kraus, on the other hand, argues[6] that to make Danaus the principal author of the plan is contrary to the division of the dramatic functions in the *Supplices*. The murder, he holds, is the last consequence of the Danaids' own resistance when driven to extremes. But it is at least as plausible to suggest that Danaus' small part in the first play is compensated by a

[1] Loeb *Aesch.*[2] 571.

[2] Miss Wolff, Untersteiner (*Le Origini della tragedia e del tragico* 375 n. 2), and Winnington-Ingram (146 n. 28) incline to accept the fragment. Pohlenz (*Erl.* 21) and Lesky (*Tr. Dichtung* 69) are doubtful about Miss Cunningham's emendation. Lloyd-Jones says the evidence is wholly insufficient. Winnington-Ingram points out that ἰδέ (l. 1) is in harmony with the frequent use of ὁρᾶν and ἐφορᾶν of deities in the *Supp.* (cf. in general V. Citti, *Il linguaggio religioso e liturgico nelle tragedie di Eschilo* (Bologna 1962) 16 f.). For Zeus Xenios cf. p. 182 above; also *Supp.* 671 f. Snell suggests hesitantly (437) that the fragment may refer to a fate like that of Semele.

[3] Welcker, *Kl. Schr.* IV. 113; Tittler 123 (1838) 994: also Winnington-Ingram 146 f.

[4] *Studien* 418 f.

[5] P. 201: cf. also Weir Smyth 58; Winnington-Ingram 145 (but with caution). See further chap. III p. 129 above.

[6] P. 167; cf. also von Fritz 256 ff.

larger one in the second. According to Hartung[1] the murder plan is suggested by Aphrodite, while Tittler, on the basis of fr. 742 M (388 N²) which he ascribes to this play, makes Artemis the author of the plan.[2] When the Αἰγύπτιοι was believed to be the first play of the trilogy, there was some ground for assigning Athena a place in it as the adviser of Danaus and his daughters, in antithesis to the appearance of Aphrodite in the third play.[3] But with the Αἰγύπτιοι in second place there is no room for Athena.[4] What is the scene of the play? If the battle is already over when the play begins, the scene may well be Argos, perhaps in front of the palace.[5] Tittler gave a most detailed reconstruction of the play, beginning with the Argive elders sacrificing in front of the palace. A messenger enters to relate the battle of the wolf and the bull. But *Supp.* 450 ff. can certainly not be taken as evidence for anything in the second play, and it is highly improbable that Aeschylus used the bull/wolf motif at all. The detailed reconstruction of Tittler, like that of Stoessl,[6] is impossible to substantiate. Wecklein says[7] that ps.-Apollodorus' list of names may come from the betrothal-scene, and he quotes as parallel the messenger-scene in the *Septem*. But a list of fifty couples would be somewhat more tedious than that of seven. How does the play end? Gruppe suggested[8] that it ended with a ὑμέναιος κατακοιμητικός corresponding with a ὑμέναιος διεγερτικός at the beginning of the third play. Welcker said[9] that this would spoil the horrible impression of the exit. That the married couples leave the scene in procession together is accepted by Tittler, Wecklein, Nathansky, Croiset, Kraus, and Pohlenz. Obviously it is pure speculation. If Miss Wolff is right, and the fragment in the *Etymologicum Gudianum* is indeed from the

[1] P. 57.

[2] 121 (1838) 977, and 124. 1002: cf. C. Steinweg, *Aischylos* (Halle 1924) 14.

[3] Cf. Welcker, *Tril.* 392; R. H. Klausen, *Theologumena Aeschyli tragici* (Berlin 1829) 176.

[4] Artemis, not Athena, is referred to at *Supp.* 145; cf. chap. IV p. 157.

[5] Cf. Wecklein, *Studien* 418 f.: Croiset 69. Nathansky 32 cites fr. 343. 31–3 M (379 N²) saying that the altar must be in front of the palace, but there is no certainty that the fragment is from this play.

[6] Cf. p. 184 above.

[7] *Studien* 421.

[8] P. 78; cf. Wecklein, *Studien* 421, ed. 18.

[9] *Kl. Schr.* IV. 116; cf. Wecklein (Ζωμαρίδης) II. 330.

Αἰγύπτιοι, what is its context? Miss Wolff says that the rhythmic effects possibly convey the Egyptians' mood of fierce determination. The title Ζαγρεύς is connected with omophagic rites, and the Egyptians probably associate Dionysus with the hunt, and with the pursuit and slaying of their enemies. But it is doubtful whether all this can be extracted from the fragment. If Hermann is right, and only the word Ζαγρεύς belongs to the Αἰγύπτιοι, it could occur in practically any context.

III

The reconstruction of the Δαναΐδες is an even more difficult task than that of the Αἰγύπτιοι, since it involves the interpretation of the meaning of the trilogy, as well as of the *Supplices*, which is in itself by no means straightforward. It is easy to fall into the temptation of deducing the events of the third play from a theory of the inner meaning of the trilogy, which in itself depends upon a preconceived notion of the plot. Clearly, if the Αἰγύπτιοι led up to the Danaids' murder of their husbands, the third play must deal with the consequences of that murder. And we have seen already that those consequences are very variously related by the mythographers and other later sources. The most disputed question is whether the play dealt with the fate of Hypermestra or of the other sisters. The single substantial piece of evidence is fr. 125 M (44 N²), quoted by Athenaeus xiii. 600 b:[1]

καὶ ὁ σεμνότατος Αἰσχύλος ἐν ταῖς Δαναΐσιν αὐτὴν παράγει τὴν Ἀφροδίτην λέγουσαν·

ἐρᾷ μὲν ἁγνὸς οὐρανὸς τρῶσαι χθόνα,
ἔρως δὲ γαῖαν λαμβάνει γάμου τυχεῖν,
ὄμβρος δ' ἀπ' εὐνάεντος οὐρανοῦ πεσὼν
†ἔκυσε† γαῖαν, ἡ δὲ τίκτεται βροτοῖς
5 μήλων τε βοσκὰς καὶ βίον Δημήτριον,
δενδρῶτις ὥρα δ' ἐκ νοτίζοντος γάμου
τέλειός ἐστι· τῶν δ' ἐγὼ παραίτιος.

6 δένδρων τις corr. Hermann.

[1] Eustathius in error ascribes the lines (he omits lines 6–7) to Aeschylus of Alexandria, who is mentioned in Athen. 599 e. Only Pauw has ever taken Eustathius seriously. Cf. Loeb ed. p. 395.

It is interesting that the ends of lines 20 and 24 of *Ox. Pap.* 2255 fr. 14[1] coincide with the ends of the first and fifth lines of this fragment. Mette indeed prints the fragments together in his edition. But, as Lobel points out, if lines 21–3 had been lines 2–4 of fr. 44 their length would have been sufficient to make their ends visible. The question is in any case of no great importance, since the new fragment is not clear enough to be useful.

What must the context of fr. 44 have been? The meaning is clear: Aphrodite is praising the power and function of ἔρως in the constant renewal of the life of the earth. Obviously the fragment is not out of place in a trilogy that is concerned with a marriage and its consequences. Many scholars have favoured the idea that a trial was held in the Δαναΐδες and most of these have attributed Aphrodite's speech to this. Hermann indeed held[2] that there were two trials, of Hypermestra and of her sisters, but he was followed only by Schmidt.[3] Welcker[4] and Gruppe[5] pointed out the impossible clumsiness that this idea would entail, and argued that there was only one trial, that of Hypermestra. Their view has been accepted by a long line of scholars, some of whom seek to justify it by argument, but many of whom state it as if it were a proven fact.[6] Thus Ridgeway says,[7] 'We know for certain that Aphrodite herself came forward as advocate for Hypermnestra and triumphantly vindicated her action, on the ground that she was completely justified by love towards her young husband'. And Diamantopoulos more recently says,[8] with equal certainty, 'The "desire for children", the motive of Hypermnestra's disobedience to her family, is defended in court by Aphrodite, and rewarded by the Argive demos, which absolves her from guilt'. It is as well to remind ourselves that we are told by Athenaeus that Aphrodite is the speaker; this and nothing more. Yet it was only his conviction that the fragment proved the trial of Hypermestra that made Hermann conceive his theory of the double-trial. Ed. Meyer

[1] Vol. xx Lobel. [2] *Opusc.* II. 321. [3] P. 12 n. 12.
[4] *Tril.* 404. [5] P. 79.
[6] Cf. the remarks on the subject of D. S. Robertson, *C.R.* 38 (1924) 51.
[7] *The origin of tragedy* (Cambridge 1910) 203 (also in *Cambridge Praelections* (1906) 164); cf. also Weir Smyth 22 f. and 44. [8] *J.H.S.* 77 (1957) 222.

says,[1] 'Der Kern der Erzählung von dem Proceß oder vielmehr der Rettung der Hypermnestra vor dem Zorne ihres Vaters ist vielleicht älter, aber ihre Ausbildung ist gewiß das Werk des Aeschylos'. Murray[2] assures us that Aphrodite presided over the court, while Steinweg affirms[3] that Aphrodite defends, Danaus prosecutes, perhaps with the assistance of the Danaids and of Artemis, and that it is Hera who decides the case. Murray says that the trial was for perjury and unchastity, the Danaids having presumably sworn an oath to murder their husbands, while Welcker and Hermann emphasize the danger from Lynceus that Hypermestra's disobedience had left.[4]

That Aeschylus dealt with the fate of Hypermestra is probable, since she is one of the few elements common to all versions of the story, and, as we have seen,[5] is an original part of it; since also she appears in the account given by Aeschylus himself at *P.V.* 865. Yet there are serious objections to any reconstruction that involves her trial. First, the evidence for such a trial is slight, Pausanias alone being hardly a reliable guide for a plot of Aeschylus.[6] Secondly, it seems highly unlikely that when forty-nine women murder their husbands and one does not, Aeschylus should have considered that it was only the behaviour of the latter that needed to be explained and justified. This is the argument of D. S. Robertson,[7] who says that it is incredible that the author of the *Oresteia* can have assumed that the Danaids were obviously guiltless. Thus he substitutes for the trial of Hypermestra a trial of Danaus and the other forty-nine daughters, in which Aphrodite is the prosecutor. Her speech, he claims, would fit as well into this context as into the other.[8] Irrespective of the question of moral guilt, we might expect the survivor, Lynceus, to take some interest in the murder of his brothers. As C. O. Müller says,[9] the duty of avenging blood

[1] *Forschungen* 84: cf. *Geschichte des Altertums* IV. 1 (3rd ed. Stier) (Stuttgart 1939) 428.
[2] *Complete plays* 12. [3] P. 15.
[4] Hermann, *Opusc.* II. 332: Welcker, *Kl. Schr.* IV. 118, mentions the oracle of Σ *Or.* 857 and Σ *Iliad* A 42.
[5] Cf. p. 176 above. [6] Cf. p. 170 above. [7] *Loc. cit.*
[8] Robertson's view was anticipated by H. L. Ahrens, *Zeitschr. f. d. Alt. Wiss.* (1844) 4.
[9] *Gesch. der gr. Litt.* (Stuttgart 1882) I. 89 ff. Cf. Plato, *Laws* ix. 871.

formed at Athens the basis of a great portion of the penal code, and it was one which was implanted in the Greek mind since the days of Homer. It is significant that all later authors praise the conduct of Hypermestra, and consider her sisters' deed as monstrous.[1] Compare, for example, Statius, *Theb.* iv. 133 ff., Nonnus, *Dionysiaca* iii. 308 ff., and especially the famous lines of Horace (*Odes* iii. 11. 33 ff.):

> Una de multis face nuptiali
> digna periurum fuit in parentem
> splendide mendax et in omne virgo
> nobilis aevum.

Finally the trial of Hypermestra is an obstacle to those who believe that the trilogy must be a unity. Hermann says[2] that the title of the play and the subject-matter of the *Supplices* make it unlikely that the trial of Hypermestra is the only theme. The title is not very significant, as the Danaids may well have been the chorus,[3] but certainly there must be a considerable change of emphasis from the first to the third play if Hypermestra is to emerge as the heroine of the latter. The possibility of such a change of direction is well discussed and rejected by von Fritz.[4] It is denied too by Stoessl,[5] on the grounds that it would make impossible the solution of the problems raised in the *Supplices*. Some try to prepare for the change by introducing Lynceus already in the second play,[6] while Tittler brings on also Hypermestra.[7] But it is doubtful if anything is gained by adding further confusion to the Αἰγύπτιοι. And, as Nathansky points out,[8] a scene between Lynceus and Hypermestra is difficult to imagine in front of the chorus, however it was composed. There have been many proponents of a chorus of fifty Danaids for the last play.[9] None has ever explained who appeared to take the place

[1] Cf. Preller–Robert 271; Vürtheim 27 f.

[2] *Opusc.* II. 321; cf. Wolff, *Eranos* 56 (1958) 133.

[3] The *Choephori* is not principally concerned with the doings of the Libation-Bearers. Cf. also S. *Trach.* and E. *Phoen.*

[4] Pp. 252 ff.

[5] P. 100.

[6] Cf. p. 202 above.

[7] 122 (1838) 985 and 123. 994.

[8] P. 32.

[9] For the theory that the tragic chorus originally consisted of fifty see for example Wilamowitz, *Interpr.* 4, and *Einleitung in die griechische Tragödie* (reprinted Berlin 1921) 91; Tucker xvi and xxiii; R. C. Flickinger, *The Greek theater and its drama*

of Hypermestra. Or were we to imagine a chorus of forty-nine?[1] The difficulty is lessened with a representative chorus of twelve, but it would still be interesting to know, if other trilogies were extant, whether there was any parallel for the emergence of a single character from a chorus. The revised dating of the trilogy has now rendered perhaps invalid one of the traditional arguments against a trial of Hypermestra, namely the difficulty of staging it with only two actors.[2] We do not know when Sophocles introduced the third, but it could have been before 463. On the other hand only two actors are employed in the *Supplices*, so perhaps Aeschylus had not yet adopted the third.

Is it easier to reconstruct the Δαναΐδες with a trial of Danaus and his other daughters? The view of Ahrens and Robertson has been accepted by Paley[3] and by Stoessl.[4] Robertson suggests that Athena and Hermes may have been defending counsel. Stoessl imagines that equal voting by a jury of Egyptian and Argive nobles led to an acquittal, as in the *Eumenides*, though it is difficult to see why the one play should necessarily have been so exact a copy of the other. A trial of the Danaids raises its own

(3rd ed. Chicago 1926) 133; E. Kalinka, *Die Urform der griechischen Tragödie* (Innsbruck 1924) 43 f.; Lammers 20 f. and 149; Kranz, *Stasimon* 144; Murray, *Aeschylus the creator of tragedy* (Oxford 1940) 49 f.; Pohlenz 52 and 136; Untersteiner 255 n. 12; A. D. Fitton-Brown, *C.R.* n.s. 7 (1957) 1–4; R. Böhme, *Bühnenbearbeitung Äschyleischer Tragödien* (Basel/Stuttgart 1956 and 1959) I. 122 and II. 54 ff.; L. Aylen, in *Classical drama and its influence*, Essays presented to H. D. F. Kitto (London 1965) 92 f.; W. J. W. Koster, *Welke is de oudste bewaard gebleven Tragedie?* (*Med. ned. Akad.* N.R. 29 (1966)) 22. Now that the Danaid trilogy is seen to be late, there is no reason to doubt that its chorus consisted of twelve people. Indeed it is doubtful if the tragic chorus ever consisted of fifty. For the unreliability of the evidence of Pollux cf. H. Lloyd-Jones, *L'Ant. Class.* 33 (1964) 365 ff.: also Hermann, *Opusc.* II. 128 ff. and 139 ff.; *GGL* I. 2. 41 and 56; Peretti 85 ff.; Pickard-Cambridge, *Dithyramb, tragedy, and comedy* (1st ed. Oxford 1927) 87 ff., *The theatre of Dionysus in Athens* 31 f., and *The dramatic festivals of Athens* (Oxford 1953) 241; Lesky, *J.H.S.* 86 (1966) 79, and *Tr. Dichtung* 66 f.: *contra* Fitton-Brown, *loc. cit.*

[1] Kitto (22 n. 2) is inclined to favour this idea as an effect 'perhaps not too bold for Aeschylus'.

[2] Cf. Stoessl 101; Kraus 173; also Croiset 70; Winnington-Ingram 149 n. 45. Kruse and Oberdick require three actors for their reconstruction. Nathansky tried to surmount the difficulty (34) by making Danaus leave the stage after his prosecuting speech, to return later as Aphrodite. But this is pure evasion. Miss Wolff suggests (*Eranos* 56. 131) that the jury may have been a secondary chorus, with its leader acting as spokesman: cf. also *Columbia Diss.* 57.

[3] 4th ed. (London 1879) 3. But he also says (88) that probably A. treated of Hypermestra's trial in the Danaids.

[4] P. 105.

particular problems. The main objection has been that since in Aeschylus Aegyptus does not come in person to Argos, there is no one to conduct the prosecution.[1] We do not know for certain that Aegyptus does not appear. He does not indeed seem to be with his sons at *Supp.* 906 and 928, but there is no reason why he should not have arrived between the second and the third plays, or during the third between the announcement of the murder and the trial. Von Fritz says[2] that there is no time for this, as it is a long way from Egypt to Argos, but Aeschylus did not trouble with such questions in the *Agamemnon* when he let the king arrive so soon after the fall of Troy had been announced by the beacons. The presence of Aegyptus is assumed by Welcker, Gruppe, Hartung, Robertson, and Stoessl. Phrynichus, we are told by the second scholiast at E. *Or.* 871, brought Aegyptus to Argos along with his sons,[3] though this was not the usual tradition. The first scholiast at the same place says that Aegyptus arrived after the murder. Euripides, fr. 846 (from the *Archelaus*), says that the normal account did bring Aegyptus with his sons, and Euripides is of course closer than his scholiast to Aeschylus. Yet it seems that the latter can have introduced Aegyptus only after the murder. Thus, unless Euripides is writing loosely, he cannot have had Aeschylus in mind. This, however, does not prove that there was no trial of Danaus and the Danaids. Von Fritz suggests[4] that Aphrodite could have prosecuted. Lynceus too would doubtless have been glad to perform the function.

Does fr. 125M (44N²) fit into such a context? Robertson says that it would serve as well for the prosecution of the Danaids as for the defence of Hypermestra. To which von Fritz replies that Aphrodite would then be found to praise the sons of Aegyptus, and that since the Danaids did not love but hated their cousins the praise of ἔρως would be pointless.[5] Vürtheim too[6] says that the omnipotence of ἔρως would be no argument for the wrong-

[1] Cf. Kruse 15; Wilamowitz, *Interpr.* 23; Vürtheim 71 ff.; Kraus 170. Winnington-Ingram says (148) 'If any action was taken against Danaus and the Danaids, it must have been taken by the *polis*'.

[2] P. 130.

[3] Even if Aeschylus follows Phrynichus closely in the *Persae* (cf. Robertson 52), it does not follow that he does so also here.

[4] P. 131.

[5] P. 249.

[6] Pp. 72 f.

ness of the Danaids' deed, since they had no love for their husbands. It may be, however, that the kind of ἔρως that Aeschylus is describing has nothing to do with the mere feelings of women for their husbands, and that the Danaids are guilty of not submitting to a different kind of ἔρως.[1] Vürtheim rightly says that Aphrodite could only have accelerated the sentence of the Danaids, but he adds, 'Was der Dichter nicht gewollt hat, dem Zuschauer unangenehm gewesen wäre, und was die Sage gar verbot'; all of which statements are open to question. Stoessl objects that as only two actors are available, Aphrodite must be the sole prosecutor, and that, since the verdict must be an acquittal, this implies the defeat of Aphrodite.[2] Robertson too assumes an acquittal, and almost everyone agrees.[3] Probable as this assumption is, it cannot be regarded as absolutely certain. It would indeed be awkward to have the Chorus executed in the middle or at the end of the play,[4] but it is possible that the final Exodos takes them out to their death. Perhaps too the Danaids did not form the chorus. Gruppe postulated one of Argive elders. Miss Elisei points out that at least Amymone must stay alive to play her part in the satyr-play, but we do not know how close was the connection between satyr-play and trilogy.

Yet the objections are strong enough to make a trial of Danaids very doubtful. There seems in fact to be no necessity for a trial of any kind. Perhaps it would have been less readily assumed if so many scholars had not been anxious to find parallels with the *Eumenides*. If the Δαναΐδες is concerned with Hypermestra, it is much more natural that her disobedience should be dealt with inside the family, and that she should appear before Danaus and the Chorus, with Aphrodite appearing to decide the issue.[5] Perjury and treason are pure

[1] Cf. p. 226 below.

[2] This is the basis of Stoessl's argument that the Δαναΐδες must be the second play of the trilogy.

[3] Del Grande, *Hybris* 92, suggests that Lynceus may have killed Danaus and his daughters. F. Dümmler, *Delphika* (Basel 1894) 22, inclines to accept the punishment of the Danaids in the Underworld.

[4] Cf. Wilamowitz, *Interpr.* 23; A. Körte, *Philol. Wochenschr.* 49 (1929) 372; Elisei 218 f.; Stoessl 101.

[5] Cf. Pohlenz, *Erl.* 21; Kraus 173 f.; Lesky, *Tr. Dichtung* 71 and *History of Greek literature* 253.

figments of the imagination of scholars, and it is difficult to see how a charge of unchastity can be brought when a marriage has been properly carried out. The Danaids too can be the centre of interest without being tried before the audience in a formal court. Winnington-Ingram puts forward the hypothesis[1] that at an Argive assembly held off stage, as in the *Supplices*, Danaus asked the people to condemn Hypermestra, and was instead himself condemned along with the other Danaids. He finds hints of this coming theme at 480 ff., 492 ff., 985 ff. Ps.-Apollodorus tells the story of the Danaids' purification by Athena and Hermes at the command of Zeus. This account is accepted as Aeschylean by for example Kruse and Vürtheim, who combine it with the trial of Hypermestra, and by Robertson, who makes the purification follow the Danaids' acquittal. Von Fritz accepts it independently of any trial. Winnington-Ingram considers the possibility (150 n. 50) that either Hermes (cf. 220, 920) or Apollo (cf. 214–16) might have played the role. Kraus points out[2] that such a purification for blood does not necessarily imply any moral or legal justification, which for him is irrelevant. A. Maddalena says[3] that the purification of the Danaids is unacceptable, but he does not tell us why.

The whole question would be so much more easily solved if we knew how we were meant to regard the character of the Danaids. But this is unfortunately far from clear from the one surviving play. It is the whole interpretation of the trilogy that is in doubt. Schmid took the convenient view[4] that, 'In dem uns erhaltenen Nachlaß des Aischylos ist die Danaidentrilogie das einzige Drama, in dem nicht ein theologisch-weltanschauliches Problem in Vordergrund steht. Es handelt sich hier nur um die dramatische Entwicklung zu einem schicksalhaft (d.h. in der Sagenüberlieferung) gegebenen Ziel hin.' This simple faith has not been shared by others, whose manifold interpretations of the theme of the play have been well summarized by R. D. Murray:[5] '(1) the struggle of the Danaids against

[1] Pp. 148 f. Cf. also chap. IV p. 153 n. 6 above.
[2] P. 169.
[3] *Interpretazioni Eschilee* (Turin 1953) 100 n. 23.
[4] *GGL* I. 2. 202.
[5] *The motif of Io in Aeschylus' Suppliants* (Princeton 1958) 3–4.

marriage; (2) the formal establishment of the institution of matrimony and the concomitant change in the status of women; (3) the emancipation of women; (4) the question of the right of women to refuse forced marriage, and the establishment of the Thesmophoria; (5) the sanctity of marriage; (6) the question of exogamy versus endogamy; (7) the rights of the suppliant; (8) the conflict between divine custom and state law; (9) the conflict between human rights and the divine ordinance which is not yet fully expressed in human laws, customs and needs; (10) the will of Zeus, which brings harmony out of chaos'.[1] He might have added the theory of Gilbert Murray[2] that the theme is 'the need to combine the sacredness of virginity with the acceptance of marriage': it is by the fact of love, he says, that γάμος is justified, and violation transformed into a sacrament.

Most of these theories have fortunately no great importance for our purpose, since for us the question is relatively simple: were the Danaids right or wrong to reject and then to murder their husbands, or rather were they so obviously right that the question was not even worth discussing in the third play? Many have answered this question in the affirmative. Only Hypermestra sins, we are told,[3] the others rightly obey their father. Wilamowitz remarks,[4] 'Der mord eines verhaßten gatten ist an sich kein exemplarisches verbrechen', while for Schwarz,[5] 'seeräubern gegenüber ist eben alles erlaubt gewesen'. J. J. Bachofen says,[6] 'In allen Versionen der Sage ist die Gewalt, die

[1] (1) Wilamowitz, *Interpr.* (2) Thomson, *Aeschylus and Athens.* (3) A. Süsskand, *Philol. Wochenschr.* 40 (1920) 738–44 and 761–8. (4) D. S. Robertson, *op. cit.* (5) Mazon 3–11. (6) W. Ridgeway 193. (7) Vürtheim, ed. (8) H. Bogner, *Der tragische Gegensatz* (Heidelberg 1947) 104–39. (9) Von Fritz, *op. cit.* (10) J. T. Sheppard, *C.Q.* 5 (1911) 220–9.

[2] *Complete plays* 25. For Aylen (92 ff.) the trilogy presents the view that 'it is no good running away from the world; the world is as it is, and will not be otherwise'. 'Aeschylus takes the virgin's fear of sex as an image of man's fear of the power that governs the world.' For A. Diamantopoulos, *J.H.S.* 57 (1957) 225 f., the conflict is between the laws and customs of the aristocratic order (represented by the Danaids) and the spirit and principles of the age of Cleisthenes (represented by the rulers of Argos): cf. also Lindsay, *The Clashing Rocks* 92 f.

[3] Wecklein (Ζωμαρίδης) II. 321 f., and Wecklein, ed. 16; Carcopino 282.

[4] On E. *Her.* 1016 (2nd ed. Berlin 1895 II. 221).

[5] *N. Jahrb. f. Philol.* 147 (1893) 104.

[6] *Mutterrecht* (Stuttgart 1861) 94.

freche gottverhaßte Gewalt auf Seite des Aegyptos, das Recht auf Seite der Danaiden' (which is patently untrue). For Gruppe the deed is obviously justified because the sons of Aegyptus are strange and foreign.[1] According to many scholars[2] there is a simple opposition between the ὕβρις of the Egyptians and the δίκη and the αἰδώς of the Danaids. But can anyone who has read the *Supplices* believe that the murder is quite unrelated to the character of the Danaids, that it is nothing more than an act of simple obedience to the girls' father? One may question too whether the Athenians would consider the murder of forty-nine husbands, no matter how hated, any more straightforward and normal a deed than would a twentieth-century audience. The Danaids may very well have been right to reject the marriage with their cousins (and here an antithesis between ὕβρις and αἰδώς is legitimate), but does this necessarily give them a perfect right to commit murder? It is this distinction between the rejection and the murder that so many critics have ignored. Coman indeed poses the question,[3] Are the Danaids not guilty of ὕβρις in killing their husbands? But he answers, No; for they are in a position of legitimate defence.

Many scholars have held that the matter is not so straightforward. Even Kraus, who denies the need for moral or legal justification, admits the necessity for purification for the shedding of blood. It was argued above[4] that the second play must deal in some way with the position of the city of Argos. We may expect this to be of some concern here too, where the killing of forty-nine husbands must give rise to a pollution just as great as that feared by Pelasgus in the *Supplices* when the Danaids threaten to commit suicide (455 ff.).[5] Throughout the whole trilogy the fortunes of the Suppliants must be intimately connected with those of the state that gives them refuge. But

[1] Pp. 79 f.: cf. Süsskand 740 ff. For H. N. Couch, *TAPhA* 63 (1932) liv f., the Danaids symbolize 'the persistence of Greek tradition in a barbarian environment' (Egypt).

[2] For example, *GGL* I. 2. 202; H. G. Robertson, *C.R.* 50 (1936) 105; Snell 52 ff.; Coman 101 ff.; D. Kaufmann-Bühler, *Begriff und Funktion der Dike in den Trag. des Aisch.* (Heidelberg 1951) 47 ff.

[3] P. 110.

[4] P. 198.

[5] Cf. Winnington-Ingram 146 and p. 182 above.

there is much to support those who go further and say that there is something at fault in the Danaids' character, and that their deed must be seen in relation to this. It is unnecessary to accept the extreme view of Schmidt, according to which the Danaids and their cousins represent the two faults of an oriental religion, which Aeschylus wishes to contrast with the superior Greek religion.[1] More credible is del Grande's antithesis[2] between the ὕβρις of the sons of Aegyptus and that of the Danaids. 'Probably there is something excessive about the loathing of the Danaids for marriage with their cousins', says Lucas.[3] The end of the *Supplices* seems to imply that the Danaids are offending against Aphrodite herself: whether it is that some of their own number dimly realize this, or that the maids are introduced, like Danaus and Pelasgus, to represent the norm from which the Danaids have departed.[4] And we are not justified in taking this as some kind of universal element in the female character; the Danaids are not suffragettes. Only at 749 is there any general statement about the lot of women as such.[5] An interesting analysis of the methods which the Danaids use to gain their ends is given by Méautis.[6] Just as Achilles, through Thetis, brought pressure to bear upon Zeus to secure the defeat of the Greeks at Troy, so, he says, the Danaids seek to constrain both Zeus and Pelasgus (cf. their half-magical refrains), finally by the threat of suicide and all the pollution that that would entail. They obtain their

[1] *Op. cit.* The sons of Aegyptus represent sensual indulgence, and at the other extreme the Danaids have fallen victims to the idle contemplation of the divine that leads to a life removed from duty.

[2] P. 90: cf. Maddalena 97.

[3] 1st ed. 83 (cf. 2nd ed. 81 f.): see also G. Perrotta, *I tragici greci* (Messina–Florence [1931]) 20f.; Kitto 17f. and 20 ('The Danaids, like Hippolytus in Euripides' play, give all their devotion to Artemis and none to Aphrodite as, presumably, the Egyptians give all theirs to Aphrodite and none to Artemis. But goddesses are parts of a whole, and the Whole is Zeus'); G. F. Else, *The origin and early form of Greek tragedy* (Harvard 1965) 98; Winnington-Ingram 141 f.; Citti 3, 30, 129; Aylen (95 f.; also *Greek tragedy and the modern world* 54) points out that it is unnatural for women to pray to have mastery (κράτος) over their men, as the Danaids do at 1068.

[4] Cf. W. Nestle, *Menschliche Existenz und politische Erziehung in der Tragödie des Aischylos* (*Tüb. Beitr.* 23 Stuttgart–Berlin 1934) 18f.; Vürtheim 118; Focke 180ff.; Kitto 16; Mazon 8; Lesky, *Tr. Dichtung* 70: see p. 194 above.

[5] Cf. Snell 56.

[6] Pp. 47 ff.; cf. also J. T. Sheppard, *C.Q.* 5. 224 ff.; Perrotta 61; Citti 20.

desires, but they do so by force, not by right, as they wrongly imagine. This is their tragedy, that they force their will upon Zeus, and then imagine it to be his.

The crucial question is obviously this: why are the Danaids so reluctant to marry their cousins? It has been hotly disputed by scholars. The simplest answers can be ruled out almost at once. Miss Elisei says[1] that the Danaids refuse the marriage and hate their cousins just because their father does. The family enmity is common to all versions of the myth. But it is clear that Aeschylus must have deliberately sought to avoid this interpretation. A quarrel between the fathers is nowhere mentioned,[2] and it would have been simple enough for Aeschylus to do this if he had wished. However, Miss Elisei herself disposes successfully of the theory[3] that the Danaids are devotees of Artemis, and thus are consecrated to perpetual virginity. According to this view the girls see the attempt of their cousins to marry them as a form of sacrilege, and the murder is a sacrifice owed to Artemis. But it is impossible to support such a view by merely two invocations of the goddess (145 and 1030), invocations which are naturally explained by the nature of the Danaids' desire. And it is hard to see the point of Danaus' advice at 980 ff. if he knows that his daughters are in fact vowed to chastity. Equally unsuccessful is the attempt to take out of context Pelasgus' reference to the Amazon-like appearance of the Danaids (287).[4] As Miss Elisei says,[5] this is only the last of a series of paradigms, and in no way implies that the resemblance was more than skin-deep. One might as well suggest that because Pelasgus is reminded also of the Cypriot likeness, the girls are devotees of Aphrodite. In any case, unlike the Danaids, the Amazons are warlike by nature, and while they claim lordship over men they by no means reject sexual union with them.[6]

[1] P. 211.

[2] Cf. p. 171 above.

[3] Cf. Tittler 124 (1838) 999 ff.; P. F. Stuhr, *Die Religionssysteme der Hellenen* (Berlin 1838) 352; Schmidt 20 ff.; *GGL* I. 2. 196 ff.; N. Terzaghi, *Atene e Roma* 22 (1919) 187 ff.

[4] Cf. Bachofen 94 f.; Megas 422; and esp. Focke 172 ff., for whom the Amazon element in the Danaids is of central importance.

[5] Pp. 199 f.

[6] Cf. von Fritz 259 f. Weir Smyth (58) also rejects the comparison with the Amazons.

Untersteiner dismisses Miss Elisei's judgement[1] as 'del tutto banale'. His view is that the Amazons are a general reminiscence of a pre-Hellenic social and religious state, contemporary with the period in which the cult of the Dea Magna developed.[2] But even if this were true for the myth, it would have nothing to do with Aeschylus, except perhaps in suggesting the source of his simile.

Some of the early critics[3] said that the Danaids were quite right to flee from a marriage that was incestuous, though it was early remarked by Stanley[4] that the Greeks had no scruples about marriage between first cousins, while in Egyptian ruling circles it was normal for brother to marry sister. Moreover, had there been any such question of incest it would have been impossible for Lynceus and Hypermestra to have their marriage confirmed at the end of the trilogy.[5] Certainly the scholiast did not thus interpret the θέμις at line 37, where he comments: ὧν τὸ δίκαιον ἡμᾶς εἴργει, διὰ τὸ μὴ θανατωθῆναι τὸν πατέρα,[6] or at line 336, where his note is ᾤετο γὰρ αὐτὰς ἐκδεδόσθαι ἤδη ἄλλοις ἀνδράσιν. If then the question of incest comes in at all, it is not as simple as this. Nägelsbach argued[7] that, while the Danaids were technically ἐπίκληροι so that their cousins had a legal right to marry them, yet such a marriage seemed to the girls incestuous by the law of nature. Jurenka said[8] that, though the law was not interested in marriage between first cousins, humane men like Aeschylus doubtless felt the same as we do. The approach of E. Benveniste is rather different.[9] For him the Danaids represent a normal society governed by exogamy, so that their reaction is a normal one to a demand which violates the fundamental law of exogamy. More developed are the

[1] P. 149 n. 36.

[2] P. 143.

[3] E.g. Butler, Schütz, Hermann, Paley, and Schmidt.

[4] *Ad* 233; cf. also Weil, ed. vi; Haupt, ed. 84; Tittler 119 (1838) 959 ff.; Weir Smyth 55 f.

[5] Cf. Nathansky 36.

[6] Professor Lloyd-Jones points out to me that the use of θανατωθῆναι rather than τεθνηκέναι is curious, and might suggest that the sons of Aegyptus had tried to kill Danaus.

[7] *De religionibus Orestiam Aesch. continentibus* (Erlangae 1843) 34.

[8] *Wien. Stud.* 22 (1900) 191 f.

[9] *Rev. de l'Histoire des Religions* 136 (1949) 129 ff.

theories of Ridgeway[1] and Thomson,[2] according to which it is not the Danaids but the sons of Aegyptus who represent the normal views of Athenian society, where the next-of-kin has the right not only to marry an orphaned girl, but to force her to divorce her husband if she is already married. Ridgeway held that the Danaids' claim of incest would excite nothing but contempt in the audience. At one time, however, he argued, there was a stage when all property descended through the female, and in such a state of society exogamy was the normal rule. And in both the *Supplices* and the *Eumenides* he finds clear traces of a transition to a succession through the male. Thomson rejects the last part of Ridgeway's argument, finding no trace in the *Supplices* of a conflict between matrilineal and patrilineal inheritance. But in the question of the Aegyptians' right over the Danaids as ἐπίκληροι he is in full agreement. If a father dies leaving only daughters, they are obliged to marry their next-of-kin.

And there was nothing to prevent the father from bestowing his presumptive heiresses in this way before he died. Consequently, the match proposed by the sons of Aigyptos is already permissible and proper, and, as soon as Danaos dies, it will become a legal claim. In fleeing from Egypt to Argos, the daughters of Danaos are plainly seeking to evade their obligations. That is the light in which the dispute would inevitably have been regarded by a contemporary audience.[3]

For Thomson the whole question is the conflict between the sexes which, he says, is an essential feature of the transition from barbarism to civilization. 'To Aeschylus, living in the heyday of ancient democracy, the subjection of women was not only just, but preferable to the liberty which they had formerly enjoyed.'[4] The chief objection to Thomson's view is perhaps that, while he rightly rejects Ridgeway's theory that the transition from a matrilineal to a patrilineal inheritance could still be a burning

[1] *Origin of tragedy* (Cambridge 1910) 187 ff. (also in *Cambridge Praelections* (1906) 141 ff.).

[2] *Oresteia* (1st ed. Cambridge 1938) II. 341 ff., and *Aeschylus and Athens* (3rd ed. London 1966) 289 ff. The theory was anticipated to some extent by F. Dümmler, *Delphika* (Basel 1894) 21. Cf. also Trencsényi-Waldapfel, 268 f.

[3] *Aesch. and Athens* 289.

[4] P. 293.

issue in fifth-century Athens, Thomson himself fails to give a dramatically satisfactory explanation of the Danaids' passionate belief that a supposedly normal state of society is sinful. As Lucas says,[1] Thomson has no right to assume that the Athenians were still conscious of the facts and implications of a change which had taken place a long time before. Thomson's theory is in fact supported neither by the *Supplices* nor by Athenian law. For first, references to any question of incest are almost non-existent in the play. At line 8 most editors accept Bamberger's reading ἀλλ' αὐτογενεῖ φυξανορίᾳ, so that the passage reads:

οὔτιν' ἐφ' αἵματι δημηλασίαν
ψήφῳ πόλεως γνωσθεῖσαι,
ἀλλ' αὐτογενεῖ φυξανορίᾳ,
γάμον Αἰγύπτου παίδων ἀσεβῆ τ'
ὀνοταζόμεναι ⟨διάνοιαν⟩.
⟨διάνοιαν⟩ Weil.

This passage has been used to prove the most conflicting theories, and, as the text is so uncertain, it is doubtful if it should be used to support any argument at all. But it does seem fairly certain that Thomson's reading and interpretation are impossible. He read: ἀλλ' αὐτογενῆ φυξανορίᾳ γάμον...ἀσεβῆ τ', which words, he argues, mean that the Danaids are rejecting marriage with their cousins as incestuous and impious.[2] Yet it has been pointed out by many that αὐτογενής, a ἅπαξ λεγόμενον, on the analogy of other compound αὐτο- words, does not mean τοῦ αὐτοῦ γένους.[3] Thus it is not equivalent to συγγενῆ in *P.V.* 855, which, in any case, is probably just a descriptive epithet amplifying ἀνεψιῶν. It is true that at 226 Danaus says, ὄρνιθος ὄρνις πῶς ἂν ἁγνεύοι φαγών; but he follows it with πῶς δ' ἂν γαμῶν ἄκουσαν ἄκοντος πάρα ἁγνὸς γένοιτ' ἄν;. The marri-

[1] 1st ed. 237 n. 35; cf. 2nd ed. 256 n. 30.

[2] For this interpretation see also Headlam, *C.R.* 14 (1900) 111; O. Könnecke, *Woch. f. Klass. Philol.* 33 (1916) 387 f.; K. Kunst, *Die Frauengestalten im attischen Drama* (Vienna and Leipzig 1922) 3 n. 1; Elisei ('per fuggire uomini della medesima stirpe'); Schadewaldt, *Gnomon* 8 (1932) 10 f. Wecklein accepts Bamberger's emendation but interprets 'in der Absicht naheverwandten Männern zu entgehen'.

[3] Cf. Tittler 119 (1838) 961; Jurenka 182; Hiltbrunner 8 n. 10; Pohlenz, *Erl.* 18 f.; Wolff, *Eranos* 57. 23; and esp. von Fritz 122 n. 1: cf. also Lesky, *Tr. Dichtung* 70.

age is wrong because Danaus and his daughters do not wish it (cf. 36 ff.), and the significance of the reference to kinship is that the violence is aggravated since it is being applied by those who are their own relations, and therefore ought to behave better.[1]

As far as the law is concerned it is of vital importance that Danaus is still alive.[2] The question has been thoroughly examined by G. H. Macurdy,[3] who shows that though the next-of-kin can force an ἐπίκληρος to divorce her husband at her father's death, yet the property will remain with the children of the first husband.[4] This explains the Aegyptians' unseemly haste. If the Danaids bear children to other husbands, the cousins will have no claim to Danaus' estate. It is not even certain that the next-of-kin could in all cases compel the divorce.[5] Important for Thomson's argument is the passage at 335 ff., where the king is trying to discover from the Danaids the reason for their rejection of their cousins.

πότερα κατ' ἔχθραν, ἢ τὸ μὴ θέμις λέγεις;

he says, and the Chorus replies:

τίς δ' ἂν φίλους ὠνοῖτο τοὺς κεκτημένους;

This for Thomson and many others[6] means 'Who would care to buy relations for their lords and masters?' And this does seem to fit well with the following lines, where the king apparently says that houses prosper when the property is kept within the family, and the Chorus replies, 'Yes, and when things go wrong divorce is easy' (for if the woman had been married to an outsider her family would have protected her).[7] But it is very

[1] Cf. Hiltbrunner 11; Wolff, *Columbia Diss.* 114; also Weir Smyth 58; Winnington-Ingram 143 f.

[2] Cf. esp. Wilamowitz, *Interpr.* 13; Vürtheim 21 ff. and 93 f.; Weir Smyth 57; von Fritz 124; Lucas (2nd ed.) 81; Wolff, *Eranos* 57. 27; Kraus 136 n. 20. Meyer, with no evidence, said (83 f.) that in the original saga Danaus was already dead.

[3] *Cl. Phil.* 39 (1944) 95 ff.

[4] Cf. Isaeus viii. 31; [Dem.] xlvi. 20.

[5] Cf. W. Wyse, *The speeches of Isaeus* (Cambridge 1904) on iii. 64 (cf. also 42 and 68).

[6] E.g. Paley (who prints, however, ὄνοιτο), Tucker, Ridgeway, and Lucas.

[7] Cf. Plut. *Mor.* 289e (ἢ πολλῶν βοηθῶν τὰς γυναῖκας ὁρῶντες δι' ἀσθένειαν δεομένας, οὐκ ἐβούλοντο (i.e. the Romans) τὰς ἐγγὺς γένους συνοικίζειν, ὅπως, ἂν οἱ ἄνδρες ἀδικῶσιν αὐτάς, οἱ συγγενεῖς βοηθῶσιν;). I owe this reference to Mr E. W. Whittle.

doubtful if this is after all the meaning of the passage. φίλους in line 337 must be in answer to κατ' ἔχθραν in the previous line, so that it means 'friends' rather than 'relations'. Thus Wecklein's interpretation is more plausible than the other, 'Mit der Mitgift würde ich mir nur einen Herrn erkaufen; wie soll da von Liebe die Rede sein?' The reading ὄνοιτο is attractive, since M Σ have the accent ὤνοιτο.[1] Line 338 can mean 'Marriage may be advantageous in strengthening power, even if it is not based on love',[2] to which the Chorus replies bitterly, 'Yes, and when people are in trouble it is easy to desert them'.[3] As Miss Wolff points out, ἀπαλλαγή can hardly mean divorce here, as divorce would be the very thing that the Danaids would presumably want.

Yet there are passages in the play which indicate that the sons of Aegyptus may have a right of some kind over their cousins. At 387 ff. Pelasgus suspects the existence of such a right, and it is interesting that the Danaids evade his questions on this point. At 918 the Herald claims the girls as his own property, though at this stage it does not matter whether any right exists or not; for Pelasgus has received the Danaids as Suppliants, so cannot hand them over. Wilamowitz tried to solve the question by assuming[4] that the Danaids had been defeated in a battle in Egypt, and were thus the legitimate war-booty of their cousins. But if this were so why does Aeschylus not trouble to make it clear, especially in the parodos, where there was every opportunity for him to do so? There are one or two passages in the play (e.g. 742 and 950) which have been taken to prove a war in Egypt, but such ambiguous hints as these are hardly evidence enough.[5] Recognizing this Wilamowitz says there must be a lacuna after 336, and after 337, in which the whole question

[1] Robortello is followed by Boissonade, Paley, Campbell, Sidgwick, Headlam, Wilamowitz, Focke, and Kraus. Markscheffel's φιλοῦσ' is accepted with ὄνοιτο by Vürtheim, Pohlenz, and Murray. Oberdick reads φιλοῦσ' ὠνοῖτο. Hermann's φιλῶν ὠνοῖτο is unnecessary and pointless. Casaubon and Stanley suggested οἴοιτο.

[2] Cf. Wolff, *Columbia Diss.* 116.

[3] Cf. Hartung and Paley.

[4] *Interpr.* 15. A war in Egypt is accepted by Megas (422), Kunst (8 n. 2), and Elisei (211). Kruse had earlier made a similar suggestion.

[5] Cf. esp. Focke 172 f.; Snell 52 f.; H. G. Robertson n. 3. on 108; Kraus 163 n. 29: also p. 179 above.

of ἀγχιστεία is explained. But since this lacuna would destroy the obvious antithesis between κατ' ἔχθραν in 336 and φίλους in 337, Wilamowitz has found few followers here.[1] Others have suggested[2] that the whole question of right is reserved by Aeschylus for discussion in the third play. Though we are not justified in assuming this, it does seem that the question cannot be decided from the evidence of the first play alone. One may well ask whether Aeschylus meant the question to be asked at all. R. Lattimore remarks[3] that the fact that the girls are fleeing is more important than the reason why. If the fact were enough for the audience, perhaps it should be enough for us.

We must look then for the Danaids' motivation purely in their own character, and not in any simple obedience to a supposed moral or social principle. Do the Danaids reject their cousins alone, or are they averse to marriage with men in general? This is possibly the most keenly debated question of all. Many passages in the *Supplices* indicate that their hostility is confined to the sons of Aegyptus (e.g. 30, 80, 104, 223 ff., 335, 741, 750, 817, and 1063).[4] Kunst points out[5] the significance of 1031 f. where γάμος is qualified by ὑπ' ἀνάγκας, and of 1053 where its epithet is Αἰγυπτογενῆ. But an equal number of passages lead to the conclusion that the Danaids are rejecting men in general (e.g. 144 ff., 392, 426, 528 ff., 643, 790, 798–9, 804–7, 818, and 1017). Line 8 has often been adduced to prove this indiscriminate aversion, Wilamowitz having translated αὐτογενεῖ φυξανορίᾳ by 'aus angeborener Männerfeindschaft', 'inborn hatred of men'.[6] It is however doubtful if this is the

[1] Cf. Focke, *loc. cit.* and 174 n. 1; Snell, *loc. cit.*; Elisei 213; von Fritz 122; Kaufmann-Bühler, *loc. cit.* Nestle accepts the lacuna, and Winnington-Ingram is inclined to favour the hypothesis (143 n. 15).

[2] E.g. Wecklein (Ζωμαρίδης) II. 332; Nathansky 35.

[3] *The poetry of Greek tragedy* (Johns Hopkins 1958) 17. For similar views cf. Headlam, *C.R.* 14. 111 f.; Croiset 59 n. 1; Howald 53 f.; Coman 105; Pohlenz, *Erl.* 20; Winnington-Ingram 143 f.

[4] Cf. Weil v–vi; Nestle 11 n. 2; H. G. Robertson 107 n. 3; Süsskand 741; Elisei, *loc. cit.*; Wolff, *Columbia Diss.* 35.

[5] P. 4 n. 1.

[6] *Interpr.* 15. This has been accepted by Vürtheim 17 ff., and n. *ad loc.*; Körte, *Philol. Wochenschr.* 49 (1929) 372; *GGL* I. 2. 196; Kraus 164 n. 31; Maddalena 84 and 99 n. 3; Lucas 81; Méautis, *Eschyle* 49 (cf. *L'authenticité et la date du Prométhée Enchaîné d'Eschyle* (Neuchâtel 1960) 38.

meaning of the passage, where the antithesis seems rather to be between the forced banishment described in lines 6–7, and the voluntary flight from marriage that has been conceived by the Danaids themselves (not forced upon them by either the state or their father). Thus von Fritz translates, 'sondern aus einem allein der eigenen Brust entsprungenen Entschluß zur Flucht vor diesen Männern'.[1] However, though this passage cannot be used to prove a general aversion, it is difficult to explain away the many others which do indicate such a thing. Miss Elisei has tried to do so, by finding a specific reference in all the apparently general expressions. 'È caratteristico alla natura umana, nei momenti di forte tensione psichica, di preferire l'espressione generica alla particolare.'[2] And Gilbert Murray argues similarly that 'A girl pressed to marry an unwelcome suitor usually says that she does not wish to marry at all'.[3] But the references are too many and too clear to make such explanations plausible.[4] Yet an innate aversion to men cannot be the only answer, otherwise Danaus' advice at 980 ff. would be superfluous and pointless. According to Wilamowitz[5] we must just accept the contradictory nature of the Danaids' character. Von Fritz attempts[6] to explain it in terms of the inner tragic meaning of the trilogy. According to his view a general φυξανορία is not in the character of the Danaids, but their aversion to their cousins has led them to a general aversion to every marriage: or, as Miss Wolff puts it, their pathological aversion to the very thought of marriage is brought about by the normal reaction of women to attack by force.[7] Kaufmann-Bühler objects that the references to the general and specific aversions are not so distinct in the play as to make such a development probable, and he says that a psychological development is in any case unlikely in an early play of Aeschylus. The revised dating takes away the

[1] P. 123; cf. Paley *ad loc.*; Jurenka 182; Kaufmann-Bühler 49. Lesky, *Tr. Dichtung* 70; Wolff, *Eranos* 57 (1959) 23; Pohlenz, *Erl.* 18, accepts the antithesis but objects to von Fritz that he has reversed the ratio of motives. Pohlenz says that it is not the act of flight, but the peculiarity of character that is denoted.

[2] P. 207.

[3] *Complete plays* 17.

[4] Cf. Hiltbrunner 8 n. 10.

[5] *Interpr.* 11 f.

[6] Pp. 260 ff.; cf. also Winnington-Ingram 144; Lesky, *Tr. Dichtung* 70.

[7] *Eranos* 57. 34: cf. also Kunst 3–4.

force of the latter argument, and, while it is true that the references to the two kinds of aversion are equally distributed throughout the play, there seems to be no reason why the development should be represented in a straight line. The Danaids' hatred may have become pathological even before the play begins. In any case a linear development is not entirely invisible. At 78 ff. the Danaids are still able to conceive of a marriage that is in harmony with justice.[1]

Hiltbrunner,[2] taking αὐτογενεῖ φυξανορίᾳ as equivalent to ἐξ αὐτοῦ τοῦ γένους, holds that the flight of the Danaids is explained and justified by the miraculous birth of their ancestor Epaphus. Union by means of natural γάμος is for Epaphus' descendants a sin. 'Die Ueberzeugung, daß ihr ganzes Geschlecht durch den bei seiner Erschaffung wirkenden göttlichen Willen zur Agamie bestimmt ist, ist der zentrale Antrieb ihres Handelns.'[3] Since Aeschylus omits to tell us this, Hiltbrunner has to assume that it is explained in his supposed lacuna at line 336.[4] His theory is hardly supported by his belief that the trilogy ends in the recognition of the natural law of γάμος, or by the fact that every generation between Epaphus and the Danaids themselves has been produced in the normal manner.[5]

Perhaps only one thing emerges from the whole discussion as proved beyond reasonable doubt. The character of the Danaids, the motivation of their flight, the reason for and justification of the murder of their husbands, are of intense interest, and cannot possibly have been passed over in the third play as not even worthy of discussion. The argument of Thomson, though in general unacceptable, is valuable in that it dispels the illusion that the Danaids are mere representatives of a Hellenic culture against a barbarian one;[6] for they reject a marriage that is in itself perfectly legitimate and conventional. The reason then is to be sought within their own character, and the sympathy of

[1] Cf. Wolff, *Columbia Diss.* 100.
[2] Pp. 8 ff.
[3] P. 12.
[4] Hiltbrunner (19 ff.) also rearranges the order of the lines.
[5] Cf. Hiltbrunner 33 f.
[6] For this view see for example Weir Smyth 43.

the audience depends upon Aeschylus' dramatic portrayal of that, not upon the acceptance of any sociological, religious, or political ideas. Does this conclusion help with the reconstruction of the Δαναΐδες? R. D. Murray, in his interesting study of the imagery of the *Supplices*, concludes that this play did after all deal with the trial of Hypermestra. He finds the key to the understanding of the trilogy in the motif of Io. 'The Danaids' atavistic obsession that they are, in some sense, a reincarnation of Io, is a determining and dominant element of their character. Yet their perception of similarity between themselves and Io is woefully limited and superficial.'[1] For they ignore the fact that the Epaphus whom they invoke was himself the issue of the enforced union of Io and Zeus; that Zeus, who released Io from her sufferings, was himself responsible for them; that such a release implied submission to the male and motherhood. Thus 'ultimately it is Hypermestra, the new Io, who resolves the problems posed in the trilogy, although she must be assisted by the divine wisdom and guidance'.[2] Yet even if we accept the whole of Murray's argument,[3] it is doubtful if it will really support his conclusions about the reconstruction of the last play. For Aeschylus could use Hypermestra to resolve the problems of the trilogy without finding it necessary to put her on trial. In fact there seems no reason why to perform this function she need even appear at all.[4] If the Danaids were right Hypermestra was wrong, but if, according to Murray's more probable view, Hypermestra chose the better part, the Danaids obviously chose the worse. Whether Aeschylus treated the vindication of Hypermestra in relation to the fate of the

[1] P. 69. Cf. also Aylen (93 ff.; also *Greek tragedy and the modern world* 52 ff.) who argues in similar terms from the parallelism with Io that the Danaids are mistaken and their flight wrong-headed. Cf. further Thomson, *Aeschylus and Athens* 287 f.; Trencsényi-Waldapfel 263; Winnington-Ingram 151 (but for him the Danaids are right to flee from a violent marriage. What they fail to realize is that the story of Io ended with an act of gentleness).

[2] Cf. also Winnington-Ingram 151.

[3] The imagery of contrast of male and female (27 ff.) is so obvious in the context that it is doubtful if any significance can be attached to it. And why is there 'every reason to suppose that the use of the four images was not interrupted by the end of the *Suppliants*, but that they continued to serve the poet well in the remaining plays of the trilogy'? (43). This is to beg the question.

[4] Cf. Kraus 175.

Danaids or *vice versa* it is impossible to say.[1] Neither can have been ignored.

How must the trilogy have ended? If we discount the likelihood of an unhappy ending, we may expect the natural order to have been in some way restored, presumably by the intervention of Aphrodite, praising the function of ἔρως, and the acceptance of this by the Danaids. In harmony with this would be Hypermestra's sparing of her husband, perhaps through her desire for children. But her motive is not necessarily the same as at *P.V.* 865, a line which is in any case itself ambiguous, since παίδων can be taken either with ἵμερος or with μίαν.[2] E. Harrison said[3] that the caesura does not decide for the latter, while the former is more consonant with the tragic poets' use of παῖς. But the rhythm of the words does not support his conclusion,[4] since it is μίαν and ἵμερος rather than παίδων that are stressed. Winnington-Ingram argues persuasively[5] that ἵμερος θέλξει in the *P.V.* must be understood in the light of the references to sexual desire in the *Supplices* (1003–5, 1039 f.), and that in the Danaid trilogy first Hypermestra and then her sisters will become 'susceptible to the charm of sexual desire'. Some of the older scholars[6] followed ps.-Apollodorus, etc., in saying that Lynceus was saved because he spared his wife's virginity. Birt[7] gives *pietas* as the motive, thus bringing Aeschylus into line not only with Ovid but with nineteenth-century ideas concerning the proprieties: 'Et quidem necesse erat pro nobilitate cothurni Aeschylei eam quae alias (*P.V.* 865) amans fuisse dicitur, ubi primas in tragoedia partes actura est, iam non cupiditati suae

[1] Cf. Wolff, *Eranos* 56. 133; Stoessl 112.

[2] 'Desire for children' is accepted by Sheppard, *C.Q.* 5. 221 f., and *Greek tragedy* (Cambridge 1920) 30; Perrotta 21 and 49; Méautis, *Eschyle* 69 f., and *Prométhée* 36; H. J. Rose, *ad loc.*; Mazon 8; Diamantopoulos 222; R. D. Murray 60; Kitto 16; E. K. Borthwick, *A.J.Ph.* 84 (1963) 240 n. 59; Lesky, *Greek tragedy* (Eng. tr. London 1965) 71.

[3] *Proc. Camb. Philol. Soc.* 160–2 (1935) 8 (wrongly reported by R. D. Murray 60 n. 6).

[4] Cf. Thomson, *Aeschylus and Athens* (2nd ed. 1946) 451 n. 22; Wolff, *Columbia Diss.* 62.

[5] P. 147. He points to the use of πεντηκοντάπαις at 853. For love as the motive cf. also Welcker, *Kl. Schr.* IV. 119; Hermann, *Opusc.* II. 331 and 334; Wecklein, ed. 15; Nathansky 10; Preller–Robert 271; Weir Smyth 43; Trencsényi-Waldapfel 264.

[6] E.g. Weil xi–xii.

[7] P. 426.

inservire sed sententiae morali. Amari fortasse se dicere puellae licebat, se amare non licebat.' It seems at least certain from fr. 125 M (44 N^2) that ἔρως for Aeschylus did not denote the passion of a Phaedra, and some confirmation of this is to be found in the passage, unreliable perhaps in itself, in *Frogs* 1043 ff. where Aeschylus boasts

> ἀλλ' οὐ μὰ Δί' οὐ Φαίδρας ἐποίουν πόρνας οὐδὲ Σθενεβοίας,
> οὐδ' οἶδ' οὐδεὶς ἥντιν' ἐρῶσαν πώποτ' ἐποίησα γυναῖκα.

and Euripides replies:

> μὰ Δί' οὐ γὰρ ἐπῆν τῆς 'Αφροδίτης οὐδέν σοι.

It is possible that the play ends with preparations for the second marriage of the Danaids, perhaps by means of the athletic-contest described by Pindar.[1] Some have seen this as a punishment or humiliation for the Danaids.[2] Miss Wolff argues that it should be considered rather as an honour.[3] It is simpler to understand it with most scholars merely as the reconciliation of the Danaids to marriage: their φυξανορία is conquered and the natural order of things restored. The second marriage would naturally be ordained by Aphrodite, and some have thought that the antithesis between her and Artemis was made explicit in the last play, with the triumph of Aphrodite.[4] Pohlenz objects to a second marriage[5] that it is awkward on the same day as the murder, and that so many suitors can hardly be collected in so short a time. But at the end of the play the race and remarriage could merely be proclaimed. It is possible that the anger of Hera against the family of Io is finally appeased,[6] though, as Welcker pointed out,[7] no trace of her anger seems to remain in the trilogy. She is hardly, as Kraus says, the great enemy in the *Supplices*, though perhaps her very absence is significant, since

[1] For a recent statement of this view cf. Aylen (94 and 97), who argues on the basis of the imagery of the play. Winnington-Ingram (144) suggests a supplementary chorus of bridegrooms.

[2] E.g. A. Schöll, *Beiträge zur Kenntnis der trag. Poesie* (Berlin 1839) 22; Wilamowitz, *Interpr.* 23; M. Delcourt, *Eschyle* 45; Perrotta 21; Mazon 9; Kitto 19 f.

[3] *Eranos* 56. 134 f., and *Columbia Diss.* 60 f.

[4] E.g. *GGL* I. 2. 200; Tittler 121 (1838) 975 ff.

[5] *Erl.* 21.

[6] Cf. Kruse 22; Nathansky 35 and 37; Kraus 180.

[7] *Kl. Schr.* IV. 125.

the Danaids might be expected to invoke the principal goddess of Argos.[1] Many have taken *P.V.* 869 ff. to prove that Aeschylus made much of the founding of the royal line at Argos through the issue of Hypermestra and Lynceus. For Welcker[2] the crowning of Danaus and the founding of the Danai is a 'Hauptzug' of the trilogy as a whole, while according to Schmid[3] the excitement of the trilogy arises from the opposition between the Danaids' aversion to marriage and the fated goal of their marriage, which is the founding of the Argive royal family. But all this is pure speculation. Clearly Hypermestra's descendants are important in the *Prometheus*, as one of them is destined to rescue Prometheus. There is no reason why Aeschylus should necessarily have laid the same emphasis on them in the Δαναΐδες. Kruse suggests[4] that an offering may have been made to Aphrodite at the end of the play (cf. Paus. ii. 19 and 21). It seems probable that some promise was made of blessings to Argos, so that the Danaids' prayer at *Supp.* 625 ff., the prayer that they themselves had rendered fruitless by the pollution that they brought upon the city by murdering their husbands, might at last be fulfilled.[5] According to Herodotus (ii. 171) it was the Danaids who introduced the Thesmophoria from Egypt and taught the rites to the Pelasgian women. Some have held that Aeschylus ended his trilogy with the institution of this festival,[6] as a 'religious institution safeguarding the dignity of women' (Robertson), or as a means of conciliation for the defeated sex (Thomson). Vürtheim points out[7] the difficulties in the way of this theory. The rite of the Thesmophoria provides no evidence that Demeter Thesmophoros was thought of as the protectress of the

[1] Cf. Hiltbrunner 17 n. 30; Méautis, *Eschyle* 65–6.

[2] *Kl. Schr.* IV. 104.

[3] *GGL* I. 2. 197 (cf. 199 f.); cf. also Weil xiii; Kruse 12; Nathansky 37.

[4] P. 21. Meyer, *Forschungen* 84 (cf. Weir Smyth 45), says that there were dedications to Aphrodite and to Artemis.

[5] Cf. Owen 14–15 and 17; Cunningham 231. Cf. pp. 182 and 214 above. Note esp. the reference to Zeus Xenios at 671 f.

[6] Tittler 121 (1838) 975; Stuhr 347 ff.; D. S. Robertson 53; Thomson, *Oresteia* 343 and *Aeschylus and Athens* 294 f.; Wolff, *Eranos* 56. 137; Winnington-Ingram 151 n. 52 (but with reservations); Trencsényi-Waldapfel 265.

[7] Pp. 74 ff. Vürtheim cites Nilsson, *Gr. Feste* 323 ff. and Farnell, *Cults of the Greek States* III. 81.

marriage-right of women, and θεσμοφόρος itself probably does not mean 'nuptiarum legifera'. There is indeed no particular reason why Aeschylus should have ended all his trilogies with an αἴτιον at all.

Also from the Δαναΐδες is the fragment quoted by the scholiast at Pindar *Pyth.* iii. 19 (fr. 124 M, 43 N²): τὸ 'ὑποκουρίζεσθαι ἀοιδαῖς' εἶπε διὰ τὸ τοὺς ὑμνοῦντας ἐπευφημιζομένους λέγειν 'σὺν κόροις τε καὶ κόραις'. Αἰσχύλος Δαναΐσι·

> κἄπειτα δ' εἶσι λαμπρὸν ἡλίου φάος
> ἕως ἐγείρω πρευμενεῖς τοὺς νυμφίους
> νόμοισι θέντων σὺν κόροις τε καὶ κόραις.

The fragment is so obviously corrupt that one sympathizes with Weil's remark,[1] 'hoc unum affirmaverim, eos corruptos esse neque intellegi posse'. Hermann tried to translate the manuscript reading: 'Tum vero it lumen solis usque dum excito (dicens) "favere iubento sponsos, ut mos est, cum pueris ac puellis".' But κἄπειτα δ', the necessity for supplying a verb of saying, the lack of object for ἐγείρω, and the strange use of both εἶσι and νόμοισι are all serious difficulties.[2] There has been a host of emendations, most of them dangerous in so short a fragment, particularly when we do not know whether it forms a sentence complete in itself. The best sense is provided by Wilamowitz:

> κἄπειτα δ' εὖτε λαμπρὸν ἡλίου φάος
> ἕως ἐγείρῃ, πρευμενεῖς τοὺς νυμφίους
> νόμοισι θέντων σὺν κόροις τε καὶ κόραις.

The fragment appears to be part of a description of a ὑμέναιος διεγερτικός, such as is mentioned elsewhere only by Theocritus xviii. 54 ff. and Σ (cf. Gow's commentary). The evening epithalamium was sung by the friends of the bride,[3] and they, it seems, returned the following morning to sing a waking-song. It is not clear whether σὺν κόροις τε καὶ κόραις is a wish that the marriage may prove fruitful,[4] or a reference to the boys and

[1] P. xii.

[2] Cf. esp. Birt 421; Kraus 176 n. 44; Weir Smyth (Loeb ed. II. 394).

[3] Cf. Pind. *Pyth.* iii. 17 and Σ; Theocr. xviii. 7–8; Catullus lxi. 36.

[4] As the scholiast takes it; cf. Hesych. *s.v.* κουριζόμενοι: Hermann, *Opusc.* II. 327; Welcker, *Tril.* 396 n. 669.

girls who are to join in the song. Gruppe wrongly concluded[1] that the play begins with the ὑμέναιος διεγερτικός. Clearly the fragment is merely from a description of it. What is the most suitable context for such a description? The most popular view has been that the fragment comes from a prologue to the play, in which either Danaus ironically, or a servant in earnest,[2] announces the preparations for the morning hymn immediately before the discovery of the murder. It was objected[3] that since the earliest known prologue is that of the *Phoenissae* of Phrynichus, there could not have been one in an early play of Aeschylus, but the revised dating disposes of this argument (cf. also chap. III pp. 121 f. above). Miss Wolff says,[4] '*The Suppliants* has no prologue, and we would expect all the plays of the tetralogy to be uniform in this matter'. But there is no reason why we should expect any such thing.[5] Birt's attempt[6] to refer the fragment to the evening hymenaeal led necessarily to his conclusion that the Δαναΐδες is not the third play. He said that the fragment belongs to the second play, where the *Thalamorum curatores* illustrate in song the fate of the marriage. Others, taking εἶσι (or ἄνεισι) as historic present,[7] ascribe the fragment to a speech of Danaus in his prosecution of Hypermestra, the speech in which he described the murder and the events leading up to it.[8] More recently attempts have been made to give the fragment a future reference. According to Focke[9] its context is after the acquittal of Hypermestra, and it forms part of the announcement of a festival involving Hypermestra and Lynceus. But Focke fails to explain why the acquittal should be followed by

[1] P. 78.

[2] Cf. e.g. Tittler 124 (1838) 1002–3; Wecklein, ed. 18 f.; Kruse 19; Vürtheim 70 f.: cf. also Wilamowitz, *Interpr.* 21–2. Conz thought that the speaker was Aegyptus, Butler Aphrodite.

[3] Cf. von Fritz 135 and 267 (omitted from *Antike und moderne Tragödie* 172 and 190): cf. also Focke 180; Kraus 176.

[4] *Eranos* 56. 130, and *Columbia Diss.* 55.

[5] Cf. Winnington-Ingram 145 n. 24.

[6] Pp. 421 f. and 424.

[7] εἶμι as a historic present is very dubious. With even a genuine present sense it is rare outside Homer. There is one probable example in Aesch. at *Eum.* 242 and a possible one at *Sept.* 373: cf. Kühner–Gerth, *Gr. Grammatik* I. 139 f.: also Ed. Fraenkel, *Sitz. bay. ak. München* (1957) iii. 5 f.

[8] Cf. Welcker, *Kl. Schr.* IV. 118; Hermann, *Opusc.* II. 325 ff.; Nathansky 26 and 34. Weir Smyth, Loeb ed. 394, ascribes it to a speech of Danaus at his own trial.

[9] Pp. 180 f.

such a festival, and why it should involve a waking-song that is appropriate only on the morning after the wedding.[1] Others refer the fragment to the second marriage and suggest that the third play ends with the preparations for this. Pohlenz says,[2] 'Den Abschluß der ganzen Trilogie bildete die Anordnung, daß künftig, wenn nach der Hochzeitsnacht Eos das strahlende Licht der Sonne weckt, Chöre von Knaben und Mädchen die Neuvermählten zur Einsegnung ihres Liebesbundes mit einem Liede begrüßen sollten'. The trilogy thus ended with an αἴτιον.[3] Attractive as this theory is it is not easy to see why Aeschylus should have introduced the details of a waking-song for a marriage that is to take place only after the trilogy is completed. The interpretation of Kraus is rather different.[4] He points out that the use of πρευμενεῖς is interesting, being especially peculiar to the cult of the dead.[5] He concludes from this that νυμφίους refers to the dead sons of Aegyptus, whose vengeance might be feared and whose souls must be satisfied and appeased before the second marriage can take place. Here Kraus finds the explanation of a Greek marriage-custom. There is, however, no evidence for any such custom, and we may again wonder what is the relevance of the waking-song. Moreover it is doubtful if in the context of a second marriage the word νυμφίους could refer to the dead husbands of the first. In the corrupt state of the text it seems that no conclusions are possible.

Several other fragments are quoted from unspecified plays of Aeschylus, and have been attributed to one or other play of the trilogy. Hermann thought that fr. 601 M (301 N²), ἀπάτης δικαίας οὐκ ἀποστατεῖ θεός, would fit the Danaids' defence,[6] Oberdick that fr. 726 M (373 N²), δεινοὶ πλέκειν τοι μηχανὰς Αἰγύπτιοι, suited a context in which Danaus was conceiving his

[1] Cf. von Fritz 134 f.

[2] *Gr. Trag.* 50, and *Erl.* 22; cf. von Fritz 267 f.; *GGL* I. 2. 200 n. 2; Wolff, *Eranos* 56. 130 and *Columbia Diss.* 62 f.

[3] Cf. Hyginus, who says (*Fab.* 273) that Danaus was the first to introduce the Hymenaeus.

[4] Pp. 175 ff.; cf. also Harsh 44.

[5] P. 177 n. 45.

[6] *Opusc.* II. 329. Welcker, Hartung, Oberdick, Wecklein, and Nathansky also assigned it to this trilogy.

plan with the agreement of the assembly.[1] The line seems however to have passed into a kind of proverb,[2] in which it is the Egyptian race that is characterized as deceitful, and it is doubtful if this would have happened if it had referred in the first instance merely to the sons of Aegyptus.[3] Other suggestions are fr. 601 f(a) M (302 N²), ψευδῶν δὲ καιρὸν ἔσθ' ὅπου τιμᾷ θεός, fr. 628 M (317 N²), οἴκοι μένειν χρὴ τὸν καλῶς εὐδαίμονα κτλ., and fr. 343. 31–3 M (379 N²)

> ὑμεῖς δὲ βωμὸν τόνδε καὶ πυρὸς σέλας
> κύκλῳ περίστητ' ἐν λόχῳ τ' ἀπείρονι
> εὔξασθε,

which Burges wished to restore after line 212 of the *Supplices*.[4] Mette restores it in *Ox. Pap.* 2245 fr. 1, which is attributed to the *Prometheus Pyrphoros* or *Pyrkaeus*. Frs. 608 M (452 N²), 744 M (463 N²) and 633 M (318 N²)[5] have also been assigned to the trilogy. Herodotus tells us (ii. 156. 6) that Aeschylus made Artemis the daughter of Demeter (cf. also Paus. viii. 37. 6), and that he took this over from the Egyptians (fr. 653 M, 333 N²). He may have done this somewhere in the Danaid trilogy.[6] Tittler also wished to ascribe fr. 742 M (388 N²) to the second play. All these fragments are possible citations from the trilogy, but every one would fit equally well elsewhere, and certainly none should be used as evidence for the reconstruction of the trilogy. Tittler, for example, had no right to see in fr. 742 confirmation of his view that Artemis instructed the Danaids to murder their husbands.[7]

There is more evidence for fr. 126 M (45 N²), καθαίρομαι

[1] Cf. also Welcker, Hermann, Wecklein, and Nathansky (for N. Danaus is persuading his daughters to his plan).

[2] Cf. Σ Theocr. xv. 48–50; Σ Ar. *Clouds* 1130; Steph. Byz. *s.v.* Αἴγυπτος; and other references in Nauck and Mette.

[3] Αἴγυπτος (or -ιος) is not used in the *Supplices* of Egypt. Mr E. W. Whittle points out to me however that *Supp.* 761 gave rise to a proverb with an altered meaning: cf. Zenob. ii. 73; *Suda* s.v. βύβλον.

[4] Fr. 601 f(a) Hermann and Wecklein; fr. 628 Hermann; fr. 343. 31–3 Hermann, Wecklein, Nathansky.

[5] Fr. 608 Hermann and Welcker; fr. 744 Hartung; fr. 633 Wecklein. Burges wished to restore it at *Supp.* 953. Hartung put it in the *Eleusinioi*, Droysen in the Κήρυκες.

[6] Cf. Tittler, Welcker, Nathansky, and *GGL* 200 n. 3.

[7] 124 (1838) 999 ff.

γῆρας, since it is quoted by Hesychius from the 'δαίσι', and most scholars have accepted Musurus' emendation Δαναΐσι. Hesychius explains καθαίρομαι by ἐκδύομαι. Wecklein[1] and Kraus[2] hold that the fragment is spoken by Danaus on learning of the success of the murder, Welcker ascribed it to his speech before the judges.[3] Hermann, thinking that the sentiment is unworthy of a grave and dignified man, suggested[4] that Hesychius has altered the quotation and that Aeschylus originally wrote something like

καθαίρεται δὲ γῆρας ἀνθρώπων φύσις,

the speaker being Aphrodite. His suggestion apparently commended itself to no one. Schmid thought that the fragment must come from the second play.[5] But it is not quite certain that Δαναΐσι is the correct reading for δαίσι. Stanley originally suggested Δανάῃ, and Cantarella remarks[6] that this title may have fallen out of the Catalogue if it had originally stood beside Δαναΐδες. He thinks it may belong with the Φορκίδες, Πολυδέκτης, and Δικτυουλκοί.

Recently a papyrus fragment was published,[7] which could be from the Δαναΐδες.[8] The interesting lines are the following:

4	]κọṿθ' ἅλα[
13	].ον εὐ̣σεβ̣εῖν ἀεί[
14	].ọι με παρθένος[
15	]..τεταγμένην ἀ[-
16	]γὰ̣ρ ọὖν πορεύε̣ται[
17	]. ὑ̣βρίζοντας̣...μ̣[-
18	]. μ̣ι̣αι μετέρχεται[

Gigante restores them as follows:

4	πεντή]κονθ' ἅλα
13	τὴν Θέμιν οὐρανοῦχ]ον εὖ σέβειν ἀεί.
14	οὐ κτείν]ει με παρθένος
15	τεταγμένην ἄ[την
16	θηλύσπορος στόλος]γὰρ οὖν πορεύεται
18	πληγῆι[μιᾶι μετέρχεται.

[1] Ed. 19. [2] P. 174. [3] *Kl. Schr.* IV. 118.
[4] *Opusc.* II. 335–6. [5] Cf. p. 187 n. 4 above.
[6] *I nuovi frammenti Eschilei di Ossirinco* (Naples 1948) 67 ff.
[7] *Literarische griechische Texte der Heidelberger Papyrussammlung* (Heidelberg 1956) 186.
[8] Cf. M. Gigante, *Parola del Passato* 11 (1956) 449 ff.

The fragment, says Gigante, must come from the beginning of the Δαναΐδες, and Lynceus is the speaker. The whole thing is however so fragmentary as to render Gigante's restoration hardly even probable. πεντήκοντα, a by no means certain supplement,[1] is a common enough figure in Greek mythology, and there is hardly a tragedy in which the words εὐσεβεῖν and ὑβρίζοντας would not fit.

The plot of the Ἀμυμώνη presents no particular problems, though it is impossible to reconstruct it in any detail. Three fragments are quoted from it, but they tell us little. They may all have been spoken by Poseidon. It has been remarked[2] that the play seems to mirror the whole course of the trilogy. Amymone resists the satyr's attempt to violate her, but succumbs to the persuasion of Poseidon. And out of their union is born Nauplius, the founder of a distinguished line. Von Fritz suggested that Aeschylus may even have invented the plot for this purpose. But Pindar seems to have known the story,[3] so its appropriateness can have been only coincidence. We are not entitled to deduce from it any detail of the reconstruction of the trilogy itself.

Our entire discussion has dealt with uncertainties and possibilities, and at hardly any stage have definite conclusions been possible. Many theories have been developed, some more plausible than others, but none which could not be demolished by a single fortunate papyrus find. At the end we are left with the one certain fact with which we began. Somewhere in the Δαναΐδες Aphrodite appears and makes a speech praising the power of ἔρως.

[1] Prof. D. L. Page suggests to me as possibilities]κόν θ' ἅλα or ἥ]κονθ' ἅλα.

[2] Von Fritz 268 f.: cf. also Winnington-Ingram 147 and 151 ('In either case [i.e. Hypermestra and Amymone] a woman who has rejected sexual desire under the mode of βία, of force and violence, comes to accept it under the mode of πειθώ, of persuasion and enchantment. She who would not be forced is successfully wooed'); Wolff, *Columbia Diss.* 65; Aylen 97 f.; Trencsényi-Waldapfel 269 f.

[3] Cf. p. 180 above.

APPENDIX

THE PUNISHMENT OF THE DANAIDS IN THE UNDERWORLD

The following hold that the punishment of the Danaids in the Underworld is a late addition to the legend, and that it was transferred to them from the fate of the uninitiated in the Mysteries:

K. G. Haupt. Ed. *Supplices* (Leipzig 1829) 76.
U. von Wilamowitz-Moellendorff. *Homerische Untersuchungen* (Berlin 1884) 202.
A. Dieterich. *Nekyia* (Leipzig 1893) 70 n. 1.
O. Waser. *Arch. f. Rel.-Wiss.* 2 (1899) 47 ff., esp. 56 ff.
Preller–Robert. *Griechische Mythologie* II. 1 (4th ed. Berlin 1920) 227.
J. Carcopino. *La basilique Pythagoricienne de la Porte Majeure* (Paris 1926) 280 ff.
J. Coman. *L'idée de la Némésis chez Eschyle* (Paris 1931) 112 n. 3.
M. P. Nilsson. *The Mycenaean origin of Greek mythology* (Cambridge 1932; reprinted 1963) 64 n. 71.
P. Mazon. *Eschyle* (Budé 6th ed. Paris 1953) I. 9 n. 4.
M. C. Astour. *Hellenosemitica* (Leiden 1965) 73.

The following say that the story is late, but do not refer to the Mysteries:

H. D. Müller. *Mythologie der griechischen Stämme* (Göttingen 1857) I. 62 f.
C. Kruse. Ed. *Supplices* (Stralsund 1861) 19.
K. von Fritz. *Philol.* 91 (1936) 129 (= *Antike und moderne Tragödie* (Berlin 1962) 167).
W. Kraus. Ed. *Supplices* (Frankfurt/Main 1948) 169.
H. D. F. Kitto. *Greek tragedy* (3rd ed. London 1961) 19.
A. Lesky. *A history of Greek literature* (Eng. tr. Willis and de Heer, London 1966) 253.

Rohde's equation of the ἄγαμοι with the ἀτελεῖς is accepted by Dieterich, Waser, and Carcopino; and also by:

E. Kuhnert. *Jahrb. Arch. Inst.* 8 (1893) 110 ff.
U. von Wilamowitz-Moellendorff. *Euripides Herakles* (2nd ed. Berlin 1895) II. 321.

P. Friedländer. *Argolica* (Berlin 1905) 19 f.
A. Dieterich. *Arch. f. Rel.-Wiss.* 8 (1905) 48.
G. A. Megas. *Hermes* 68 (1933) 425 n. 3.

Cf. also C. A. Lobeck, *Aglaophamus* (Regimontii Prussorum 1829) 646 ff.; J. Lindsay, *The Clashing Rocks* (London 1965) 82. Megas held that the fate of the ἄγαμοι was transferred to the Danaids and to the ἀμύητοι independently. Jane Harrison, *Prolegomena to the study of Greek religion* (Cambridge 1903) 614 ff., esp. 621 f., found it impossible to say whether the story was transferred from the uninitiated to the Danaids or *vice versa*. 'Each form arose separately, and the point is their ultimate *contaminatio*' (623 n. 3).

Rohde's equation is questioned by:

C. Robert. *Die Nekyia des Polygnot* (Halle 1892) 52 n. 27.
A. Milchhöfer. *Philol.* 53 (1894) 397 n. 14.
C. Bonner. *Harv. Stud.* 13 (1902) 164 ff.

Cf. also J. Vürtheim, Ed. *Supplices* (Amsterdam 1928) 25 ff. A. B. Cook, who discusses the evidence very fully in *Zeus* III. 1 (Cambridge 1940) 37 ff., finds Rohde's theory unsatisfactory in that the Danaids were in fact married to the sons of Aegyptus. For him the Danaids were punished in an appropriate way for frustrating a fertility-charm, their marriage. He compares the ritual water-carrying of the priests of Osiris at Acanthus in Egypt (338 f., 354). Cf. also J. Harrison and Trencsényi-Waldapfel (see p. 173 n. 7 above) for whom the Danaids 'carry water to make rain'.

Gilbert Murray, *The complete plays of Aeschylus* (London 1952) 12, suggested that the story might be a misinterpretation of a work of art, and this is accepted by E. A. Wolff, *Eranos* 56 (1958) 139. P. F. Stuhr, *Die Religionssysteme der Hellenen* (Berlin 1838) 347 ff., thought that the water-carrying was to be considered as a symbol of house-work, and that the Danaids' punishment was the pointless, hopeless life of one who had not fulfilled herself as a housewife. W. Schmid, *GGL* I. 2. 196 n. 2, said that the punishment is derived from the labour of endless water-carrying of the women of δίψιον Ἄργος.

N. Wecklein, *Studien zu den Hiketiden des Aeschylos*, *Sitz. bay. Ak. München* (1893) ii. 404, thought that the story may be as old as Aeschylus; it is only the ethical interpretation that is late. Cf. also Ed. Meyer, *Forschungen zur alten Geschichte* (Halle 1892; reprinted 1966) I. 76 n. 1; Bonner, *op. cit.*; G. Thomson, *Aeschylus and Athens* (3rd ed. London 1966) 294.

BIBLIOGRAPHY

I

The following editions of the *Supplices* are referred to most frequently:

Hartung, J. A. *Aeschylos' Werke: griechisch mit metrischer Uebersetzung und prüfenden und erklärenden Anmerkungen* (Leipzig 1852–5).

Haupt, C. G. *Aeschylearum quaestionum specimen primum (–quartum)* (Leipzig 1826–30).

Hermann, G. *Aeschyli Tragoediae* (Berlin 1852).

Kraus, W. *Die Schutzsuchenden: Griechisch und deutsch mit einer erläuternden Abhandlung* (Frankfurt/Main 1948).

Kruse, C. *Aeschylos: Griechisch und deutsch mit Lesarten, Versmaaßen und Commentar* (Stralsund 1861).

Mazon, P. *Eschyle* (Budé, 6th ed. Paris 1953).

Murray, G. *Aeschyli septem quae supersunt tragoediae* (2nd ed. Oxford 1955).

Oberdick, J. *Die Schutzflehenden des Aeschylus* (Berlin 1869).

Paley, F. A. *Aeschyli Tragoediae* (4th ed. London 1879).

Rose, H. J. *A commentary on the surviving plays of Aeschylus* (Amsterdam 1957).

Tucker, T. G. *The 'Supplices' of Aeschylus: a revised text with introduction, critical notes, commentary and translation* (London and New York 1889).

Vürtheim, J. *Aischylos' Schutzflehende: mit ausführlicher Einleitung / Text Kommentar / Exkursen und Sachregister* (Amsterdam 1928).

Wecklein, N. *Äschylos. Die Schutzflehenden: mit Einleitung und Anmerkungen* (Leipzig 1902).

Wecklein–Ζωμαριδης. Αἰσχυλου δραματα σῳζομενα και ἀπολωλοτων ἀποσπασματα. Μετα ἐξηγητικων και κριτικων σημειωσεων [Ἑλληνικος Φιλολογικος Συλλογος. Ζωγραφειος Ἑλληνικη Βιβλιοθηκη] (Leipzig 1891–1910).

Weil, H. *Aeschyli quae supersunt tragoediae* (Giessae 1861–7).

Wilamowitz-Moellendorff, U. von. *Aeschyli Tragoediae* (Berlin 1914: reprinted 1958).

II

Achelis, Th. O. H. 'De Aristophanis Byzantii argumentis fabularum', *Philol.* 72 (1913) 414–41 and 518–45; 73 (1914) 122–53.

Alberti, K. G. A. *De Aeschyli choro Supplicum* (Diss. Inaug. Berlin 1841).

Aly, W. *De Aeschyli copia verborum* (Berlin 1906).
Andrewes, A. 'Athens and Aegina, 510–480 B.C.', *BSA* 37 (1936–7) 1–7.
—— 'Ephoros Book I and the kings of Argos', *C.Q.* n.s. I (1951) 39–45.
Arnott, P. *Greek scenic conventions in the fifth century B.C.* (Oxford 1962).
Astour, M. C. *Hellenosemitica: an ethnic and cultural study in West Semitic impact on Mycenaean Greece* (Leiden 1965).
Aylen, L. *Greek tragedy and the modern world* (London 1964).
—— 'The vulgarity of tragedy', in *Classical drama and its influence.* Essays presented to H. D. F. Kitto (London 1965) 85–100.
Bachofen, J. J. *Mutterrecht* (Stuttgart 1861).
Barrett, W. S. *Euripides. Hippolytos* (Oxford 1964).
Beloch, K. J. *Griechische Geschichte* II. 1 (2nd ed. Strassburg 1914) II. 2 (2nd ed. Strassburg 1916).
Benveniste, E. 'La légende des Danaïdes', *Rev. de l'Hist. des Religions* 136 (1949) 129–38.
Bergk, Th. *Griechische Literaturgeschichte* III (Berlin 1884).
Bergson, L. *L'épithète ornementale dans Eschyle, Sophocle, et Euripide* (Lund 1956).
Bernhard, in Roscher's *Lexicon* I. 949–52 *s.v.* Danaiden.
Bethe, E. *Prolegomena zur Geschichte des Theaters im Alterthum* (Leipzig 1896).
—— 'Die griechische Tragödie und die Musik', *N.Jbb.* 19 (1907) 81–95.
—— 'Der Spielplatz des Aischylos', *Hermes* 59 (1924) 108–17.
Bickel, E. 'Geistererscheinungen bei Aischylos', *Rh. Mus.* 91 (1942) 123–64.
Bieber, M. *The history of the Greek and Roman theater* (2nd ed. Princeton 1961).
Birklein, F. *Entwicklungsgeschichte des substantivierten Infinitivs* (Schanz: *Beiträge zur historischen Syntax der griechischen Sprache* III. 1: Würzburg 1888).
Birt, Th. 'Animadversiones ad Ovidi heroidum epistulas', *Rh. Mus.* 32 (1877) 386–432.
Björck, G. *Das Alpha impurum und die tragische Kunstsprache. Attische Wort- und Stilstudien* (Acta Societatis Litterarum Humaniorum Regiae Upsaliensis 39. Uppsala 1950).
Blumenthal, A. von, in *R.-E.* vi. A. 1. 62–4 *s.v.* Thespis.
—— in *R.-E.* xx. 1. 911–17 *s.v.* Phrynichos.
Bock, M. 'Aischylos und Akragas', *Gymnasium* 65 (1958) 402–50.
Boeckh, A. *Graecae tragoediae principum* (Heidelberg 1808).
Böhme, R. *Bühnenbearbeitung Äschyleischer Tragödien* (Basel/Stuttgart 1956 und 1959) 2 vols.

Bonner, C. 'The Danaid-myth', *TAPhA* 31 (1900) 27–36.
—— 'A study of the Danaid myth', *Harv. Stud.* 13 (1902) 129–73.
Borthwick, E. K. 'The Oxyrhynchus musical monody and some ancient fertility superstitions', *A.J.Ph.* 84 (1963) 225–43.
Bowra, C. M. *Primitive song* (London 1962).
Bradač, F. 'Der Gebrauch von ἄρχω und ἄρχομαι bei Homer', *Philol. Wochenschr.* 50 (1930) 248–9.
Broadhead, H. D. *The Persae of Aeschylus* (Cambridge 1960).
Brommer, F. 'Amymone', *Mitt. Arch. Inst.* 63/4 (1938/9) 171–6.
—— *Satyrspiele. Bilder griechischen Vasen* (Berlin 1944).
Bücheler, F. 'Aeschylus und der Parthenon', *Rh. Mus.* 40 (1885) 627–9.
Burn, A. R. *Persia and the Greeks* (London 1962).
Bury, J. B. 'The Epicene Oracle concerning Argos and Miletus', *Beiträge zur alten Geschichte* (*Klio*) 2 (1902) 14–25.
Busolt, G. *Griechische Geschichte* II (2nd ed. Gotha 1895) III. 1 (Gotha 1897).
Bywater, I. *Aristotle on the art of poetry* (Oxford 1909).
Capps, E. 'The catalogues of victors at the Dionysia and Lenaea, CIA. II 977', *A.J.Ph.* 20 (1899) 388–405.
—— 'Epigraphical problems in the history of Attic comedy', *A.J.Ph.* 28 (1907) 179–99 (esp. 191).
Carcopino, J. *La basilique pythagoricienne de la Porte Majeure* (Paris 1926).
Cary, M. 'When was Themistocles ostracised?', *C.R.* 36 (1922) 161–2.
—— in *The Cambridge Ancient History* IV (Cambridge 1926).
Cataudella, Q. 'Eschilo in Sicilia', *Dioniso* 37 (1963) 5–24.
Cavaignac, E. 'Eschyle et Thémistocle', *Rev. de Philol.* 45 (1921) 102–6.
—— 'A propos d'un document nouveau: La fin de Thémistocle', *La Nouvelle Clio* 7–9 (1955–7) 123–5.
Ceadel, E. B. 'Resolved feet in the trimeters of Euripides and the chronology of the plays', *C.Q.* 35 (1941) 66–89.
Citti, V. *Il linguaggio religioso e liturgico nelle tragedie di Eschilo.* Università degli Studi di Bologna. Facoltà di Lettere e Filosofia. Studi pubblicati dall'Istituto di Filologia Classica x (Bologna 1962).
Clay, D. M. *A formal analysis of the vocabularies of Aeschylus, Sophocles and Euripides* part I (Minneapolis 1960), part II (Athens 1958).
Cohn, L. in *R.-E.* ii A. 994–1005 *s.v.* Aristophanes (14).
Coman, J. *L'idée de la Némésis chez Eschyle* (Paris 1931).
Comparetti, D. 'Les dithyrambes de Bacchylide', in *Mélanges H. Weil* (Paris 1898) 25–38.

Conomis, N. C. 'The dochmiacs of Greek drama', *Hermes* 92 (1964) 23–50.

Cook, A. B. *Zeus: A study in ancient religion* III. 1 (Cambridge 1940).

Corno, D. del, 'P. Ox. 2256, 3 e le rappresentazioni postume di Eschilo', *Dioniso* 19 (1956) 277–91.

Costa, C. D. N. 'Plots and politics in Aeschylus', *G. & R.* 2nd ser. 9 (1962) 22–34.

Couch, H. N. 'The loathing of the Danaids', *TAPhA* 63 (1932) liv–lv.

Croiset, M. *Eschyle. Études sur l'invention dramatique dans son théâtre* (Paris 1928).

Crusius, O., in *R.-E.* ii. A. 836–41 *s.v.* Arion.

—— in *R.-E.* v. A. 1203–30 *s.v.* Dithyrambos.

—— 'Aus den Dichtungen des Bakchylides', *Philol.* 57 (1898) 150–83.

Cunningham, M. L. 'A fragment of Aeschylus' Aigyptioi?', *Rh. Mus.* 96 (1953) 223–31.

—— 'Second thoughts on Oxyrhynchus Papyri, xx, 2251', *Rh. Mus.* 105 (1962) 189–90.

Dale, A. M. *The lyric metres of Greek drama* (2nd ed. Cambridge 1968).

—— 'The chorus in the action of Greek tragedy', in *Classical drama and its influence*, Essays presented to H. D. F. Kitto (London 1965) 15–27.

Davison, J. A. 'The date of the *Prometheia*', *TAPhA* 80 (1949) 66–93.

—— 'Ox. Pap. 2256, Fr. 3', *C.R.* n.s. 3 (1953) 144.

Dawe, R. D. 'Inconsistency of plot and character in Aeschylus', *Proc. Camb. Philol. Soc.* n.s. 9 (1963) 21–62.

Deichgräber, K. 'Die Perser des Aischylos', *NGG*, Phil.-hist. Kl. N.F. I. 4 (1941) 155–202.

Denniston, J. D. 'Lyric iambics in Greek drama', in *Greek poetry and life* (Essays presented to G. Murray, Oxford 1936) 121–44.

—— 'Pauses in the tragic senarius', *C.Q.* 30 (1936) 73–9 (also 192).

—— *The Greek particles* (2nd ed. Oxford 1954).

Denniston–Page, *Aeschylus. Agamemnon* (Oxford 1957).

Descroix, J. *Le trimètre iambique* (Mâcon 1931).

Deubner, L. 'Zur Iosage', *Philol.* 64 (1905) 481–92.

Diamantopoulos, A. 'The Danaid trilogy of Aeschylus', *J.H.S* 77 (1957) 220–9.

Diels, H. 'Seneca und Lucan', *Abh. Berl. Akad.* (1885) ii.

—— 'Ein Phrynichoscitat', *Rh. Mus.* 56 (1901) 29–36.

Dieterich, A., in *R.-E.* i. A. 1065–84 *s.v.* Aischylos.

—— 'Die Entstehung der Tragödie', *Arch. f. Rel.-Wiss.* 11 (1908) 163–96 (=*Kl. Schr.*, Leipzig and Berlin 1911, 414–39).

Dodds, E. R. 'Notes on the Oresteia', *C.Q.* n.s. 3 (1953) 11–21.

Dodds, E. R. 'Morals and politics in the "Oresteia"', *Proc. Camb. Philol. Soc.* n.s. 6 (1960) 19–31.
Dörpfeld, W. 'Die Zeit des älteren Parthenon', *Mitt. Arch. Inst.* 27 (1902) 379–416.
Dörpfeld–Reisch, *Das griechische Theater* (Athens 1896).
Dover, K. J. 'The political aspect of Aeschylus's *Eumenides*', *J.H.S.* 77 (1957) 230–7.
Dümmler, F. *Delphika* (Basel 1894).
Dumortier, J. *Les images dans la poésie d'Eschyle* (Paris 1935).
—— *Le vocabulaire médical d'Eschyle et les écrits hippocratiques* (Paris 1935).
Earp, F. R. *The style of Aeschylus* (Cambridge 1948).
—— 'The date of the *Supplices* of Aeschylus', *G. & R.* 22 (1953) 118–23.
Egermann, F. 'Menschliche Haltung und tragisches Geschick bei Aischylos', *Gymnasium* 68 (1961) 502–19.
Ehrenberg, V. 'Origins of democracy', *Historia* 1 (1950) 515–47, esp. 517–24.
—— *Sophocles and Pericles* (Oxford 1954).
Eitrem, S. in *R.-E.* ix. 2. 1732–43 *s.v.* Io.
Elisei, A. 'Le Danaidi nelle "Supplici" di Eschilo', *Studi ital.* n.s. 6 (1928) 197–219.
Else, G. F. 'Aristotle and satyr-play I', *TAPh* 70 (1939) 139–57.
—— 'The case of the third actor', *TAPhA* 76 (1945) 1–10.
—— 'The origin of ΤΡΑΓΩΙΔΙΑ', *Hermes* 85 (1957) 17–46.
—— *Aristotle's Poetics: the argument* (Harvard 1957).
—— 'ΥΠΟΚΡΙΤΗΣ', *Wien Stud.* 72 (1959) 75–107.
—— *The origin and early form of Greek tragedy* (Martin Classical Lectures 20, Harvard 1965).
Engelmann, R., in Roscher's *Lexicon* II. A. 263–80 *s.v.* Io.
—— 'Die Io-Sage', *Jahrb. Arch. Inst.* 18 (1903) 37–58.
Farnell, L. R. *The cults of the Greek states* V (Oxford 1909).
Flickinger, R. C. 'Tragedy and the satyric drama', *Cl. Phil.* 8 (1913) 261–83.
—— *The Greek theater and its drama* (all references are to the 3rd ed. Chicago 1926).
Focke, F. 'Aeschylus' Hiketiden', *NGG* (1922) 165–88.
—— 'Aischylos' Prometheus', *Hermes* 65 (1930) 259–304.
Forrest, W. G. 'Themistokles and Argos', *C.Q.* n.s. 10 (1960) 221–41.
Fowler, B. H. 'The imagery of the "Prometheus Bound"', *A.J.Ph.* 78 (1957) 173–84.
Fraenkel, Ed. 'Der Zeushymnus im Agamemnon des Aischylos', *Philol.* 86 (1931) 1–17.
—— *Aeschylus. Agamemnon* (Oxford 1950).

Franklin, S. B. *Traces of epic influence in the tragedies of Aeschylus* (Baltimore 1895).
Freericks, H. *De Aeschyli Supplicum choro* (Duderstadt 1883).
Freymuth, G. *Tautologie und Abundanz bei Aeschylus* (Diss. Berlin 1939).
—— 'Zur ΜΙΛΗΤΟΥ ΑΛΩΣΙΣ des Phrynichos', *Philol.* 99 (1955) 51–69.
Frickenhaus, A. 'Zum Ursprung von Satyrspiel und Tragödie', *Jahrb. Arch. Inst.* 32 (1917) 1–15.
—— *Die altgriechische Bühne* (Schriften der Wissenschaftlichen Gesellschaft in Strassburg 31. Heft) (Strassburg 1917).
Friedländer, P. *Argolica* (Berlin 1905).
Fritz, K. von, 'Die Danaidentrilogie des Aeschylus', *Philol.* 91 (1936) 121–36 and 249–69 (=*Antike und moderne Tragödie* 160–92).
—— *Antike und moderne Tragödie* (Berlin 1962).
Geffcken, J. *Griechische Literaturgeschichte* (Bibliothek der klassischen Altertumswissenschaften IV. 1 Heidelberg 1926).
Gigante, M. 'Eschilo in un papiro di Heidelberg?', *Parola del Passato* 11 (1956) 449–56.
Gigli, M. 'Dell'imitazione Omerica di Eschilo', *Riv. indo-greca ital.* 12 (1928) i. 43–59, ii. 33–50.
Gilbert, G. *Handbuch der griechischen Staatsalterthümer* II (Leipzig 1885).
Gomme, A. W. 'Athenian notes', *A.J.Ph.* 65 (1944) 321–39 (esp. 321–31).
—— *A historical commentary on Thucydides* I (Oxford 1945).
Graaf, C. van der, 'Le chœur final des Suppliants d'Éschyle', *Mnem.* 3rd ser. 10 (1941–2) 280–5.
Grande, C. del, *Hybris. Colpa e castigo nell'espressione poetica e letteraria degli scrittori della Grecia antica da Omero a Cleante* (Naples 1947).
—— ΤΡΑΓΩΙΔΙΑ. *Essenza e genesi della tragedia* (2nd ed. Milan–Naples 1962).
Grene and Lattimore, *The complete Greek tragedies. Oresteia* (Chicago 1953).
Gross, A. *Die Stichomythie in der griechischen Tragödie und Komödie* (Berlin 1905).
Gruppe, O. F. *Ariadne* (Berlin 1834).
Gudeman, A. *Aristoteles* Περὶ Ποιητικῆς (Berlin and Leipzig 1934).
Haigh, A. E. *The tragic drama of the Greeks* (Oxford 1896).
Hammond, N. G. L. 'Studies in Greek chronology of the sixth and fifth centuries B.C.', *Historia* 4 (1955) 371–411.
—— 'The great earthquake in Lacedaemon; a reply', *Historia* 8 (1959) 490.

Harrison, E. 'Verse-weight', *C.Q.* 8 (1914) 206–11.

—— 'Αἰσχύλος Σοφοκλεΐζων', *Proc. Camb. Philol. Soc.* 118–20 (1921) 14–15.

Harrison, J. *Themis. A study in the social origins of Greek religion* (2nd ed. Cambridge 1927: reprinted 1963).

Harsh, P. W. *A handbook of classical drama* (California 1944).

Headlam, W. 'Aeschylea', *C.R.* 12 (1898) 189–93.

—— 'Upon Aeschylus I', *C.R.* 14 (1900) 106–19 (esp. 111–12).

—— 'Metaphor, with a note on transference of epithets', *C.R.* 16 (1902) 434–42.

Herington, C. J. 'The influence of old comedy on Aeschylus' later trilogies', *TAPhA* 94 (1963) 113–25.

—— 'A unique technical feature of the *Prometheus Bound*', *C.R.* n.s. 13 (1963) 5–7.

Hermann, G. 'De choro Eumenidum Aeschyli dissertatio prima', *Opuscula* II (Leipzig 1827) 124–38.

—— 'De compositione tetralogiarum tragicarum', *Opusc.* II 306–18.

—— 'De Aeschyli Danaidibus', *Opusc.* II. 319–36.

—— 'Ueber einige Trilogien des Aeschylus', *Opusc.* VIII (Leipzig 1877) 173–84.

Hiltbrunner, O. *Wiederholungs- und Motivtechnik bei Aischylos* (Gött. Diss. Berne 1950).

Hoffmann, O. 'Das dorische ᾱ im Trimeter und Tetrameter der attischen Tragödie', *Rh. Mus.* 69 (1914) 244–52.

Hölzle, R. *Zum Aufbau der lyrischen Partien des Aischylos* (Diss. Freiburg i. Br. 1934).

Hoppin, J. C. 'Argos, Io, and the *Prometheia* of Aeschylus', *Harv. Stud.* 12 (1901) 335–45.

Horneffer, M. *De strophica sententiarum in canticis tragicorum Graecorum responsione* (Jen. Diss. 1914).

How and Wells, *A Commentary on Herodotus V–IX* (2nd ed. Oxford 1928).

Howald, E. *Die griechische Tragödie* (Munich and Berlin 1930).

Jacoby, F. *Die Fragmente der griechischen Historiker* (Berlin 1923–) [*F. Gr. Hist.*]

Jaeger, W. *Paideia: the ideals of Greek culture* I (Eng. tr. of 2nd ed. Highet, Oxford 1939).

Jebb, R. C. *Bacchylides* (Cambridge 1905).

Jens, W. *Die Stichomythie in der frühen griechischen Tragödie* (*Zetemata*, Monographien zur klass. Altertums. Heft 11– Munich 1955).

Johansen, H. F. 'Sentence-structure in Aeschylus' Suppliants', *Class. et Med.* 15 (1954) 1–59.

Jones, H. J. F. *On Aristotle and Greek tragedy* (London 1962).

Jurenka, H. 'Ad Supplices Aeschyleam Adversaria I', *Wien. Stud.* 22 (1900) 181–93.

Kakridis, J. Th. 'Οἱ Ἱκέτιδες τοῦ Αἰσχύλου', *Hellenika* 13 (1954) 165–70.

Kalinka, E. *Die Urform der griechischen Tragödie* (Comment. Aenipontanae x Innsbruck 1924).

Kaufmann-Bühler, D. *Begriff und Funktion der Dike in den Tragödien des Aischylos* (Heidelberg 1951).

Kenyon, F. G. *The poems of Bacchylides* (London 1897).

Kitto, H. D. F. *Form and meaning in drama* (London 1956).

—— *Greek tragedy* (2nd ed. London 1950; 3rd ed. 1961).

Klaffenbach, G. 'Das Jahr der Kapitulation von Ithome und der Ansiedlung der Messenier', *Historia* 1 (1950) 231–5.

Kolbe, W. 'Diodors Wert für die Geschichte der Pentekontaetie', *Hermes* 72 (1937) 241–69.

Koller, H. *Die Mimesis in der Antike* (Diss. Bernenses 1. 5 1954).

—— 'Hypokrisis und Hypokrites', *Mus. Helv.* 14 (1957) 100–7.

—— 'Dithyrambos und Tragödie', *Glotta* 40 (1962) 183–95.

Könnecke, O., review of Helmreich, *Der Chor im Drama des Äschylus*, *Woch. f. Klass. Philol.* 33 (1916) 385–92.

Körte, A. 'Die Entstehungszeit der Hiketiden des Aischylos', in *Mélanges Nicole* (Geneva 1905) 289–300.

—— review of Nestle, *Die Struktur des Eingangs*. *Philol. Wochenschr.* 48 (1928) 1297–1302.

—— review of Vürtheim, *Philol. Wochenschr.* 49 (1929) 369–75.

Koster, W. J. W. 'Welke is de oudste bewaard gebleven Tragedie?', *Med. d. Ned. Akad. v. Wetenschappen*, Afd. Letterkunde N.R. 29 (1966) nr. 4.

Kranz, W. 'Zwei Lieder des "Agamemnon"', *Hermes* 54 (1919) 301–20.

—— 'Die Urform der attischen Tragödie und Komödie', *N. Jbb.* 43 (1919) 145–68.

—— *Stasimon* (Berlin 1933).

Kumaniecki, C. F. *De elocutionis Aeschyleae natura* (= *Archivum Filologiczne* nr. 12, Krakow 1935).

Kunst, K. *Die Frauengestalten im attischen Drama* (Vienna and Leipzig 1922).

Lammers, J. *Die Doppel- und Halbchöre in der antiken Tragödie* (Paderborn 1931).

Lasserre, F. 'Zur verstümmelten Didaskalie P Oxy 2256 Fr. 3', *Hermes* 83 (1955) 128.

Lavagnini, B. 'Per la cronologia delle "Supplici" di Eschilo', *Riv. di Fil. e di Istr. Class.* n.s. 10 (1932) 370.

Lechner, M. *De Aeschyli studio Homerico* (Erlangen 1862).

Lees, J. T. 'The metaphor in Aeschylus', in *Studies in honor of B. L. Gildersleeve* (Baltimore 1902) 483–96.

Lenschau, T. 'Bericht über griechische Geschichte (1907–1914)', in *Bursian's Jahresbericht* 180 (1919) 109–261.

Leo, F. 'Der Monolog im Drama. Ein Beitrag zur griechisch-römischen Poetik', *Abh. Ges. Wiss. Gött.*, Phil.-hist. Kl. N.F. 10 (1908) Nr. 5.

—— *Plautinische Forschungen* (2nd ed. Berlin 1912).

Lesky, A. 'Zur Entwicklung des Sprechverses in der Tragödie', *Wien. Stud.* 47 (1929) 3–13 (=*Gesammelte Schriften* (Berne and Munich 1966) 83–91).

—— 'Die Orestie des Aischylos', *Hermes* 66 (1931) 190–214 (=*Gesammelte Schriften* 92–110).

—— 'Der Kommos der Choephoren', *Sitz. Wien. Akad.*, Phil.-hist. Kl. 221. 3 (1943).

—— 'Die Datierung der Hiketiden und der Tragiker Mesatos', *Hermes* 82 (1954) 1–13 (=*Gesammelte Schriften* 220–32).

—— 'Hypokrites', in *Studi in onore di U. E. Paoli* (Florence 1955) 471–6 (=*Gesammelte Schriften* 239–46).

—— 'Eteokles in den *Sieben gegen Theben*', *Wien. Stud.* 74 (1961) 5–17 (=*Gesammelte Schriften* 269–74).

—— *Die tragische Dichtung der Hellenen* (2nd ed. Göttingen 1964).

—— *Greek tragedy* (Eng. tr. H. A. Frankfort 1965).

—— *A history of Greek literature* (Eng. tr. of 2nd ed. Willis and de Heer, London 1966).

—— 'Decision and responsibility in the tragedy of Aeschylus', *J.H.S.* 86 (1966) 78–85.

Lewis, D. M. 'Ithome again', *Historia* 2 (1953–4) 412–18.

Lindsay, J. *The Clashing Rocks: a study of early Greek religion and culture and the origins of drama* (London 1965).

Livingstone, R. W. 'The problem of the Eumenides of Aeschylus', *J.H.S.* 45 (1925) 120–31.

Lloyd-Jones, H. Loeb *Aeschylus* (2nd ed. 1957).

—— 'The end of the *Seven Against Thebes*', *C.Q.* n.s. 9 (1959) 80–115.

—— review of von Fritz, *Antike und moderne Tragödie*, *Gnomon* 34 (1962) 737–47.

—— 'The "Supplices" of Aeschylus: the new date and old problems', *L'Antiquité Classique* 33 (1964) 356–74.

Lobel, E., in Lobel, Wegener, and Roberts, *The Oxyrhynchus Papyri* part xx (London Egypt Exploration Society 1952).

Lucas, D. W. *The Greek tragic poets* (1st ed. 1950, 2nd ed. London 1959)

Maas, P. *Greek metre* (tr. H. Lloyd-Jones, Oxford 1962).

Macan, R. W. *Herodotus IV–VI* (London 1895) I.

Macurdy, G. H. 'Has the Danaid trilogy a social problem?', *Cl. Phil.* 39 (1944) 95–100.
Maddalena, A. *Interpretazioni Eschilee* (Turin 1953).
Marx, F. 'Der Tragiker Phrynichus', *Rh. Mus.* 77 (1928) 337–60.
Méautis, G. *Eschyle et la trilogie* (Paris 1936).
—— *L'authenticité et la date du Prométhée Enchaîné d'Eschyle.* (Université de Neuchâtel. Recueil de travaux publiés par la Faculté des Lettres 29 Fasc.) (Neuchâtel 1960) [*Prométhée*].
Megas, G. A. 'Die Sage von Danaos und den Danaiden', *Hermes* 68 (1933) 415–28.
Meritt, Wade-Gery, and McGregor, *Athenian tribute lists* III (Princeton 1950) [*ATL*].
Mette, H. J. 'Literaturbericht über Aischylos für die Jahre 1950 bis 1954', *Gymnasium* 62 (1955) 393–407, esp. 397–8.
—— *Die Fragmente der Tragödien des Aischylos* (Deutsche Akad. d. Wiss. zu Berlin. Schr. d. Sek. f. Altertums. 15 Berlin 1959).
—— *Der verlorene Aischylos* (Deutsche Akad. d. Wiss. zu Berlin. Schr. d. Sek. f. Altertums. 35 Berlin 1963).
Meyer, Ed. *Geschichte des Altertums* IV. I (3rd ed. Stier, Stuttgart 1939: reprinted 1954).
—— *Forschungen zur alten Geschichte* (Halle 1892: reprinted 1966).
Mielke, H. *Die Bildersprache des Aischylos* (Diss. Breslau 1934).
Müller, C. O. *Dissertations on the Eumenides of Aeschylus* (Eng. tr. Cambridge 1835).
Müller, G. *De Aeschyli Supplicum tempore atque indole* (Halis Saxonum 1908).
Munro, J. A. R. 'Some observations on the Persian wars', *J.H.S.* 19 (1899) 185–97; *J.H.S.* 22 (1902) 294–332.
—— in *The Cambridge Ancient History* IV (Cambridge 1926).
Münscher, K. 'Der Bau der Lieder des Aischylos', *Hermes* 59 (1924) 204–31.
Murray, G., in J. Harrison, *Themis* 341–63.
—— *Aeschylus the creator of tragedy* (Oxford 1940).
—— *The complete plays of Aeschylus* (London 1952).
Murray, R. D. *The motif of Io in Aeschylus' Suppliants* (Princeton 1958).
Myres, J. L. 'The structure of stichomythia in Attic tragedy', *Proc. Brit. Acad.* 36 (1948) 199–231.
—— *Herodotus father of history* (Oxford 1953).
Nathansky, A. 'Des Aischylos Danais', *Wien. Stud.* 32 (1910) 7–37.
Nes, D. van, *Die maritime Bildersprache des Aischylos* (Groningen 1963).
Nestle, W. 'Die Weltanschauung des Aischylos II', *N.Jbb.* 19 (1907) 305–33.
—— *Die Struktur des Eingangs in der attischen Tragödie* (*Tüb. Beiträge zur Altertumsw.* 10 Stuttgart 1930).

Nestle, W. *Menschliche Existenz und politische Erziehung in der Tragödie des Aischylos* (*Tüb. Beiträge zur Altertumsw.* 23 Stuttgart 1934).
—— review of Kranz, *Stasimon*, *Gnomon* 10 (1934) 404–15.
Neustadt, E. 'Wort und Geschehen in Aischylos Agamemnon', *Hermes* 64 (1929) 243–65.
Nilsson, M. P. 'Der Ursprung der Tragödie', *N. Jbb.* 27 (1911) 609–42 and 673–96 (= *Opuscula Selecta* I (Skrifter Utgivna av Svenska Institutet i Athen: Acta Instituti Atheniensis Regni Sueciae 8° Series II: Lund 1951) 61–145).
—— *The Mycenaean origin of Greek mythology* (Sather Classical Lectures 8 Cambridge 1932: reprinted 1963).
Norwood, G. *Greek tragedy* (4th ed. London 1948).
Orgels, P. 'Une révolution dans la chronologie d'Eschyle. A propos de *P. Oxy.* 2256, fr. 3', *Bull. de L'Acad. Roy. de Belgique* 5th ser. 41 (1955) 528–36.
Otterlo, W. A. A. van, *Beschouwingen over het archaïsche Element in den Stijl van Aeschylus* (Utrecht 1937).
Owen, E. T. *The harmony of Aeschylus* (Toronto 1952).
Page, D. L. *Euripides. Medea* (Oxford 1938).
—— *A new chapter in the history of Greek tragedy* (Cambridge 1951).
—— 'ὑποκριτής', *C.R.* n.s. 6 (1956) 191–2.
Patzer, H. 'Die dramatische Handlung der *Sieben gegen Theben*', *Harv. Stud.* 63 (1958) 97–119.
—— *Die Anfänge der griechischen Tragödie* (Schriften der wissenschaftlichen Gesellschaft in der Johann Wolfgang Goethe-Universität Frankfurt/Main Geisteswissenschaftliche Reihe Nr. 3 Wiesbaden 1962).
Pauly–Wissowa, *Real-Encyclopädie der classischen Altertumswissenschaft* (Stuttgart 1894–) [*R.-E.*].
Pearson, A. C. *The fragments of Sophocles* (Cambridge 1917).
Peradotto, J. J. 'Some patterns of nature imagery in the *Oresteia*', *A.J.Ph.* 85 (1964) 378–93.
Peretti, A. 'Osservazioni sulla lingua del "Prometeo" Eschileo', *Studi ital.* n.s. 5 (1927) 165–231.
—— review of Hölzle, *Riv. di Fil. e di Istr. Class.* n.s. 15 (1937) 56–61.
—— *Epirrema e tragedia* (Pubblicazioni della R. Università degli Studi di Firenze. Facoltà di Lettere e Filosofia, ser. 3 vol. 9) (Florence 1939).
Perrotta, G. *I tragici greci* (Messina–Florence [1931]).
Petersen, E. *Die attische Tragödie als Bild und Bühnenkunst* (Bonn 1915).
Pickard-Cambridge, A. W. *Dithyramb, tragedy, and comedy* (1st ed. Oxford 1927; 2nd ed. revised by T. B. L. Webster, Oxford 1962).
—— *The theatre of Dionysus in Athens* (Oxford 1946: reprinted 1956).
—— *The dramatic festivals of Athens* (Oxford 1953).

Pieraccioni, D. 'Il volume xx dei Papiri di Ossirinco', *Maia* 5 (1952) 288–95 (esp. 289–90).
Podlecki, A. J. 'The character of Eteocles in Aeschylus' *Septem*', *TAPhA* 95 (1964) 283–99.
—— *The political background of Aeschylean tragedy* (Ann Arbor 1966).
Pohlenz, M. 'Die Anfänge der griechischen Poetik', *NGG* (1920) ii. 142–78 (=*Kl. Schr.* (Hildesheim 1965) II. 436–72).
—— 'Das Satyrspiel und Pratinas von Phleius', *NGG* (1926) ii. 298–321 (=*Kl. Schr.* II. 473–96).
—— *Die griechische Tragödie* (1st ed. 1930, 2nd ed. Göttingen 1954); *Die gr. Tragödie. Erläuterungen* [*Erl.*].
Porzig, W. *Aischylos* (Staat und Geist. Arbeiten im Dienste der Besinnung und des Aufbaus. Band III) (Leipzig 1926).
Post, L. A. 'The Seven against Thebes as propaganda for Pericles', *Class. Weekly* 44 (1950–1) 49–52.
—— *From Homer to Menander* (Sather Classical Lectures 23 California 1951).
Preller–Robert, *Griechische Mythologie* II. 1 (4th ed. Berlin 1920).
Privitera, G. A. 'Archiloco e il ditirambo letterario pre-Simonideo', *Maia* 9 (1957) 95–110.
Quincey, J. H. 'Orestes and the Argive alliance', *C.Q.* n.s. 14 (1964) 190–206.
Raddatz, in *R.-E.* ix. 1. 414–24 *s.v.* Hypotheseis.
Regenbogen, O. 'Bemerkungen zu den Sieben des Aischylos', *Hermes* 68 (1933) 51–69 (=*Kl. Schr.* (Munich 1961) 36–56).
Reinhardt, K. *Aischylos als Regisseur und Theologe* (Berne 1949).
Reinkens, J. M. *De Aeschyli Danaidibus* (Düsseldorf 1886).
Reisch, E., in *R.-E.* v. A. 394–401 *s.v.* Didaskaliai.
—— 'Zur Vorgeschichte der attischen Tragödie', in *Festschrift Theodor Gomperz* (Vienna 1902) 451–73.
Richardson, L. J. D. 'Further remarks on an epic idiom in Aeschylus', *Eranos* 55 (1957) 1–6.
Ridgeway, W., in *Cambridge Praelections* (1906) 141–64.
—— *The origin of tragedy with special reference to the Greek tragedians* (Cambridge 1910).
Robert, C. 'Theseus und Meleagros bei Bakchylides', *Hermes* 33 (1898), 130–59.
Robertson, D. S. 'The end of the *Supplices* trilogy of Aeschylus', *C.R.* 38 (1924) 51–3.
—— *Proc. Camb. Philol. Soc.* 169–71 (1938) 9–10.
Robertson, H. G. 'Δίκη and Ὕβρις in Aeschylus' Suppliants', *C.R.* 50 (1936) 104–9.
—— 'Legal expressions in Aeschylus', *Cl. Phil.* 34 (1939) 209–19.

Rohde, E. *Psyche* (1st ed. Freiburg and Leipzig 1894; 2nd ed. Freiburg 1898) (Eng. tr. of 8th ed. Hillis, London 1925).

Roos, E. *Die tragische Orchestik im Zerrbild der altattischen Komödie* (Lund 1951).

Rooy, C. A. van, 'Ithome: a note', *Historia* 3 (1954–5) 407–12.

Roscher, W. H. *Ausführliches Lexicon der griechischen und römischen Mythologie* (Leipzig 1884–1937).

Rose, H. J. 'On an epic idiom in Aeschylus', *Eranos* 45 (1947) 88–99; and 'Further epic idioms in Aeschylus', *Eranos* 46 (1948) 72.

Rossbach and Westphal, *Theorie der musischen Künste der Hellenen* (3rd ed. Leipzig 1889).

Roussel, P. 'Remarques sur les *Suppliantes* et le *Prométhée* d'Eschyle', *Rev. de Philol.* 44 (1920) 241–7.

Rudberg, G. 'Thespis und die Tragödie', *Eranos* 45 (1947) 13–21.

Schadewaldt, W. *Monolog und Selbstgespräch. Untersuchungen zur Formgeschichte der griechischen Tragödie* (*Neue Philol. Untersuch.* 2 (Berlin 1926)).

—— 'Der Kommos in Aischylos' Choephoren', *Hermes* 67 (1932) 312–54 (= *Hellas und Hesperien* (Zürich and Stuttgart 1960) 106–41).

Scharf, J. 'Noch einmal Ithome', *Historia* 3 (1954–5) 153–62.

Schlegel, A. W. von, *Vorlesungen über dramatische Kunst und Litteratur* (2nd ed. Heidelberg 1817).

Schmid, W. *Untersuchungen zum Gefesselten Prometheus* (*Tüb. Beiträge zur Altertumsw.* 9 Stuttgart 1929).

Schmid–Stählin, *Geschichte der griechischen Literatur* I. 2 (Munich 1934: reprinted 1959) (Müller's *Handbuch der Altertumswissenschaft* VII. 1. 2) [*GGL*].

Schmidt, J. H. T. *De Aeschyli Supplicibus* (Augustae Vindelicorum 1839).

Schuursma, J. A. *De poetica vocabulorum abusione apud Aeschylum* (Amsterdam 1932).

Schwarz, W. 'Die Danaidensage', *Neue Jahrb. f. Philol.* 147 (1893) 95–112.

Sealey, R. 'The great earthquake in Lacedaemon', *Historia* 6 (1957) 368–71.

Seewald, J. *Untersuchungen zu Stil und Komposition der aischyleischen Tragödie* (Greifswalder Beitr. zur Lit.- und Stilforsch. XIV) (Greifswald 1936).

Severyns, A. *Bacchylide* (Bibliothèque de la Faculté de Philosophie de l'Université de Liége: Liége and Paris 1933).

Seymour, P. A. 'The "Servile Interregnum" at Argos', *J.H.S.* 42 (1922) 24–30.

Sheppard, J. T. 'The first scene of the Suppliants of Aeschylus', *C.Q.* 5 (1911) 220–9.

Smertenko, C. M. 'The political sympathies of Aeschylus', *J.H.S.* 52 (1932) 233–5.

Smyth, H. Weir, *Aeschylean tragedy* (Sather Classical Lectures 2 California 1924).

—— Loeb *Aeschylus* (2nd ed. Lloyd-Jones, London and Harvard 1957).

Snell, B. 'Aischylos und das Handeln im Drama', *Philol. Suppl.* 20 (1928) 1–164.

—— *The discovery of the mind* (Eng. tr. of 2nd ed. Rosenmeyer Oxford 1953).

—— review of *Ox. Pap. xx*, *Gnomon* 25 (1953) 433–40.

Solmsen, F. 'The Erinys in Aischylos' Septem', *TAPhA* 68 (1937) 197–211.

Spring E. 'A study of exposition in Greek tragedy', *Harv. Stud.* 28 (1917) 135–224.

Stahl, J. M. 'Arion und Thespis', *Rh. Mus.* 69 (1914) 587–96.

Stanford, W. B. *Greek metaphor* (Oxford 1936).

—— 'Traces of Sicilian influence in Aeschylus', *Proc. of Royal Irish Acad.* 44 Sec. c (1937–8) 229–40.

—— *Aeschylus in his style* (Dublin 1942).

Steinweg, C. *Aischylos. Sein Werk und die von ihm ausgehende Entwicklung* (Halle 1924).

Stevens, P. T. 'Colloquial expressions in Aeschylus and Sophocles', *C.Q.* 39 (1945) 95–105.

Stoessl, F. *Die Trilogie des Aischylos. Formgesetze und Wege der Rekonstruktion* (Baden b. Wien 1937).

—— 'Die Phoinissen des Phrynichos und die Perser des Aischylos', *Mus. Helv.* 2 (1945) 148–65.

—— 'Aeschylus as a political thinker', *A.J.Ph.* 73 (1952) 113–39.

—— in *R.-E.* xxiii. 1. 632–41, and *R.-E.* xxiii. 2. 2312–2440 (esp. 2312–2319) *s.v.* Prologos.

Stuhr, P. F. *Die Religionssysteme der Hellenen in ihrer geschichtlichen Entwicklung* (Berlin 1838).

Süsskand, A. 'Einführung in die Hiketiden des Aischylos', *Philol. Wochenschr.* 40 (1920) 738–44 and 761–8.

Terzaghi, N. 'Il "No" delle Danaidi', *Atene e Roma* 22 (1919) 187–97 (= *Prometeo. Scritti di Archeologia e Filologia* (Turin 1966) 129–44).

Thomson, G. *The Oresteia of Aeschylus* (1st ed. Cambridge 1938; 2nd ed. Amsterdam and Prague 1966).

—— *Aeschylus and Athens* (3rd ed. London 1966).

Tièche, E. *Thespis* (Leipzig and Berlin 1933).

Tittler, A. 'De Danaidum fabulae Aeschyli compositione dramatica', *Zeits. f. d. Altertums.* 118 (1838) 951–8; 119. 959–66; 120. 967–9; 121. 975–9; 122. 983–6; 123. 991–4; 124. 999–1003.

Trencsényi-Waldapfel, I. 'Les Suppliantes d'Eschyle', *Acta Antiqua Hung.* 12 (1964) 259–76.

Turner, E. G. 'Roman Oxyrhynchus', *The Journal of Egyptian Archaeology* 38 (1952) 78–93 (esp. 91 ff.).

—— review of *Ox. Pap. xx*, *C.R.* n.s. 4 (1954) 20–4.

Untersteiner, M. *Le Origini della tragedia e del tragico. Dalla preistoria a Eschilo* (Turin 1955).

Wackernagel, J. *Studien zum griechischen Perfektum* (Göttingen 1904) (=*Kl. Schr.* II (Göttingen [1953]) 1000–21).

Wade-Gery, H. T. *Essays in Greek history* (Oxford 1958) (also *BSA* 37 (1936–7) 263–70.

Walker, E. M., in *The Cambridge Ancient History* IV (Cambridge 1926).

Waser, O. in *R.-E.* iv. B. 2094–8 *s.v.* Danaos.

—— 'Danaos und die Danaiden', *Arch. f. Rel.-Wiss.* 2 (1899) 47–63.

Weber, P. *Entwicklungsgeschichte der Absichtssätze* (Schanz: *Beiträge zur historischen Syntax der griechischen Sprache* II. 1 Würzburg 1884).

Webster, T. B. L. 'The architecture of sentences', in *Studies in French language and mediaeval literature presented to Professor M. K. Pope* (Manchester 1939) 381–92.

—— 'A study of Greek sentence construction', *A.J.Ph.* 62 (1941) 385–415.

——'Recent scholarship on Greek tragedy', *Diogenes* 5 (1954) 85–100 (esp. 86–8).

—— *Greek theatre production* (London 1956).

—— *see* Pickard-Cambridge, *Dithyramb, tragedy, and comedy.*

Wecklein, N. 'Ueber eine Trilogie des Aeschylos und über die Trilogie überhaupt', *Sitz. bay. Ak. München* (1891) 327–85.

—— 'Studien zu den Hiketiden des Aeschylos', *Sitz. bay. Ak. München* (1893) ii. 393–450 [*Studien*].

—— 'Über den Bau Äschyleischer Chorgesänge', *Philol.* 82 (1927) 467–71.

Weil, H. 'Des traces de remaniement dans les drames d'Eschyle', *Revue des études grecques* 1 (1888) 7–26.

Welcker, F. G. *Die Aeschyleische Trilogie Prometheus* (Darmstadt 1824).

—— 'Des Aeschylus Schutzflehende, Aegypter, und Danaiden', *Kl. Schr.* IV (Bonn 1861) 100–27.

—— 'Zu des Aeschylus Schutzflehenden', *Kl. Schr.* IV. 128–35.

Wells, J. *Studies in Herodotus* (Oxford 1923).

Wilamowitz-Moellendorff, T. von, *Die dramatische Technik des Sophokles* (*Philol. Unters.* 22, Berlin 1917).

Wilamowitz-Moellendorff, U. von, 'Die Bühne des Aischylos', *Hermes* 21 (1886) 597–622 (=*Kl. Schr.* I (Berlin 1935) 148–72).

—— 'Demotika der Metoeken', *Hermes* 22 (1887) Excurs 2. 256–9 (=*Kl. Schr.* V. 1 (Berlin 1937) 339–42).

—— *Aristoteles und Athen* (Berlin 1893).
—— *Euripides. Herakles* (2nd ed. Berlin 1895).
—— 'Die Perser des Aischylos', *Hermes* 32 (1897) 382–98.
—— review of Kenyon in *GGA* (1898) 125–60.
—— *Timotheos. Die Perser* (Leipzig 1903).
—— 'Der Schluß der Sieben des Aischylos', *Sitz. Ak. Wiss. Berlin* (1903. 1) 436–50.
—— 'Die Spürhunde des Sophokles', *N.Jbb.* 29 (1912) 449–76 (= *Kl. Schr.* I. 347–83).
—— *Aischylos. Interpretationen* (Berlin 1914: reprinted 1966) [*Interpr.*].
—— *Sappho und Simonides* (Berlin 1913).
—— *Einleitung in die griechische Tragödie* (3rd ed. Berlin 1921).
—— *Griechische Verskunst* (Berlin 1921).
Wilhelm, A. *Urkunden dramatischer Aufführungen in Athen* (Vienna 1906).
Willetts, R. F. 'The servile interregnum at Argos', *Hermes* 87 (1959) 495–506.
Winnington-Ingram, R. P. 'The Danaid trilogy of Aeschylus', *J.H.S.* 61 (1961) 141–52.
Winterstein, A. *Der Ursprung der Tragödie. Ein Psychoanalytischer Beitrag zur Geschichte des gr. Theaters* (Leipzig/Vienna/Zürich 1925).
Wölfell, R. *Gleich- und Anklänge bei Äschylus* (Progr. Bamberg 1906).
Wolff, E. 'Die Entscheidung des Eteocles in den *Sieben gegen Theben*', *Harv. Stud.* 63 (1958) 89–95.
Wolff, E. A. *Aeschylus' Danaid trilogy: a study* (Diss. Columbia Univ. 1957). Résumé in *Dissertation Abstracts* xvii (1957) 1757–8. Ann Arbor, Mich., Univ. Microfilms 1957.
—— 'The date of Aeschylus' Danaid tetralogy', *Eranos* 56 (1958) 119–39, and 57 (1959) 6–34.
Yorke, E. C. 'Trisyllabic feet in the dialogue of Aeschylus', *C.Q.* 30 (1936) 116–19.
—— 'The date of the *Prometheus Vinctus*', *C.Q.* 30 (1936) 153–4.
—— 'Mesatus tragicus', *C.Q.* n.s. 4 (1954) 183–4.
—— 'The date of the *Supplices* of Aeschylus', *C.R.* n.s. 4 (1954) 10–11.
Yule, G. U. *The statistical study of literary vocabulary* (Cambridge 1944).
Ziegler, K., in *R.-E.* vi. A. 2 *s.v.* Tragoedia (1899–2075).
Zuntz, G. *The political plays of Euripides* (Manchester 1955).

INDEX OF PASSAGES CITED

A. AESCHYLUS

B. OTHER WORKS

INDEX OF PASSAGES CITED

INDEX OF PASSAGES CITED

SUBJECT INDEX

PA 3825 .S7 G3 1969
Garvie, A. F.
Aeschylus' Supplices